D1602353

Struggling with Development

Struggling with Development

The Politics of Hunger and Gender in the Philippines

Lynn M. Kwiatkowski

Westview Press
A Member of Perseus Books, L.L.C.

Copyright © 1998 by Westview Press, A Member of Perseus Books, L.L.C.

Published in 1998 in the United States of America by Westview Press, 5500 Central Avenue, Boulder, Colorado 80301-2877, and in the United Kingdom by Westview Press, 12 Hid's Copse Road, Cumnor Hill, Oxford OX2 9JJ

A CIP catalog record for this book is available from the Library of Congress.
ISBN 0-8133-3408-X

The paper used in this publication meets the requirements of the American National Standard for Permanence of Paper for Printed Library Materials Z39.48-1984.

10   9   8   7   6   5   4   3   2   1

To my mother and father,
Lorraine and Theodore Kwiatkowski,
who taught me the importance of trying to
understand the perspectives of all people

Contents

List of Tables and Photographs		ix
Acknowledgments		xi
1	**Introduction**	1
2	**Developing Hunger in the Philippines**	33
3	**Gendered Experiences in Ifugao**	61
4	**Violence and Uncertainty**	103
5	**Spirituality and Hunger**	145
6	**Interpreting Hunger Biomedically**	181
7	**Maintaining Inequality**	231
8	**Power and Contradiction: Unlikely Alliances**	263
9	**Conclusion**	291
Glossary		305
List of Acronyms		309
Bibliography		311
Index		341

Tables and Photographs

Tables

6.1   Most Commonly Eaten Food in Ifugao   227
6.2   Other Available Food in Ifugao, Eaten Less Often by the Poor   228
6.3   Food Supplements Offered by Government
        and Private Organizations   229

Photographs

1.1   "Native" and "modern" houses dot the terraced mountainsides
        of Ifugao Province.   4
1.2   "Native" one room houses.   5
1.3   Market and some tourist establishments in a *poblacion* of an Ifugao
        municipality.   6

2.1   A severely malnourished Ifugao girl.   42
2.2   Men carrying a patient in a "native ambulance" in Ifugao.   52

3.1   Elderly Ifugao woman working during a rice harvest.   63
3.2   Ifugao men building a stone wall that lines a paved mountain road.   97

4.1   The NPA ransacked and partially set afire this government
        office in 1986.   119
4.2   A health NGO displayed this poster in its office outside Ifugao.   137

5.1   *Mumbaki* ("native priests") praying over sacrificial offerings during
        a *dinupdup baki* healing ritual to cure an ill man.   149
5.2   An internationally-sponsored Christian health clinic in Ifugao.   166

6.1   An Ifugao child being weighed during a government-sponsored,
        weight-monitoring program for children under six years of age.   187
6.2   An Ifugao woman who has goiter.   192

6.3   A young Ifugao boy caring for his younger sibling while
      his parents work.   210
6.4   A preschool girl fends for herself at lunchtime, while her
      grandparent guardians work in their rice fields.   213

7.1   A UNICEF/Philippine government-sponsored Nutrition Day
      seminar, teaching Ifugao women how to cook nutritious meals.   247

8.1   Ifugao people sharing food during a house-blessing *baki* ritual.   277

9.1   Malnourished twins and their sister and mother.   294

Acknowledgments

My most profound gratitude is extended to the numerous Ifugao people who befriended me, assisted me in countless ways in my effort to understand their lives, and took me into their homes and work sites with the utmost openness, generosity, and hospitality. I cannot name all of the Ifugao people who did so much for me during the four years that I lived in Ifugao Province, in order to maintain their confidentiality. I only hope that they each know that my appreciation for them is immense, and that they will always be warmly remembered.

I would like to extend special thanks to my dissertation committee and former professors, who guided and supported me during the writing of my dissertation, from which this ethnography stems. I am especially grateful to Nancy Scheper-Hughes for teaching me to critically deconstruct accepted ways of knowing and thinking, and for her warm support and encouragement. I am also thankful for Jim Anderson's guidance and support during my study of Philippine cultures and society. I will always appreciate Judith Justice for leading me toward a critical view of international development practices, and for her assistance and support throughout my research project. I am grateful to Michael Watts for teaching me ways to understand peasants, and for his insightful guidance during my research and the writing of my dissertation. I would also like to thank Fred Dunn, who helped me to understand how culture and biology intersect, and Gerald Berreman, for furthering my study and understanding of social inequality.

I am very grateful for the insightful discussions I had with scholars of Philippine studies while I was living in the Philippines, particularly with Susan D. Russell, June Brett, Michael Tan, Catherine Q. Castaneda, Kiko Datar, Romana de los Reyes, Jeanne Illo, and Lydia Casambre, each of whom I would like to thank for sharing their ideas with me. I am also grateful to the many kind and helpful staff members of the numerous Philippine government, non-government, and international development agencies I met in Ifugao, Baguio City, Manila, and Quezon City, who each extended their assistance, graciousness, and patience to me while conducting my research at their institutions. They assisted me in learning about and understanding their organizations' goals, practices, and research, and Philippine society.

I am also deeply indebted to the colleagues and friends who offered insightful suggestions to drafts of my dissertation and book, with special thanks to Sheila Tully, Donna Goldstein, Jiemin Bao, Lanfranco Blanchetti, and Lawrence Cohen for their cogent comments, support, and friendship. Cynthia Keppley Mahmood offered thoughtful and helpful comments and generous support of this project. Mark Moberg and David Gartman provided me with much appreciated guidance and encouragement during the final years of writing my ethnography.

Karl Yambert of Westview Press made the publication of this ethnography possible with his strong support and guidance throughout the process of writing the final manuscript. Jennifer Chen, also of Westview Press, was always patient and helpful in aiding me with the development of the text. Martin L. Lasater provided a keen reading of the original manuscript and excellent editorial assistance.

To my parents Lorraine and Theodore Kwiatkowski, to whom this book is dedicated, brother John, sister Jane, and relatives, I extend my deepest gratitude for their constant encouragement. I thank Pia Ferrer and her family for the tremendous hospitality and generosity they offered to me during my visits to Manila. I am grateful to Ellen Gunty, Nadine Fernandez, Liz London, Brian Doucette, Jane Margold, Rip and Alison Anzalone, and Dale Buscher for their friendship, strength, and encouragement while I wrote my dissertation. I would also like to thank the many other friends, both in the Philippines and in the United States, who were so generous to me, and who made my research in the Philippines and the writing of this ethnography both possible and enjoyable. I offer my fullest appreciation to all of them.

I am especially grateful to Neill Matheson for his insightful advice, intellectual inspiration, and unending encouragement which provided me with the support I needed to accomplish the publication of this ethnography.

My initial field research visit in 1990, and my later follow-up field research visit in 1993, were both supported by the Jacob K. Javits Fellows Program and two grants from the University of California at Berkeley, Office of the Dean of the Graduate Division. The majority of my research, conducted in 1992, was made possible by a Fulbright-Hays Fellowship, administered by the Philippine-American Educational Foundation, to which I am grateful for funding and facilitating my research in the Philippines. I was affiliated with the Institute of Philippine Culture, at Ateneo de Manila University, during my 1992 research, where I enjoyed the assistance and support of the Institute staff. Upon returning to the University of California, the writing of my dissertation was funded by the Jacob K. Javits Fellows Program. The University of South Alabama provided me with financial and administrative support during the final phase of writing and publishing my ethnography. I am truly grateful for the financial and administrative support that I received from each of these organizations, without which this ethnography would not have been possible.

All personal and place names have not been used in this ethnography, in order to protect the identity of persons with whom I worked in Ifugao.

Lynn M. Kwiatkowski

Struggling with Development

1

Introduction

Malnutrition and unequal access to food remain as severe problems in most non-industrialized countries, despite development intervention in these countries for almost a century.[1] In this book, I will analyze the problem of malnutrition primarily in relation to gender and development ideology and practices in upland Ifugao communities, located on Northern Luzon island of the Philippines. My aim, based upon research conducted primarily in the early 1990s, is to show how western derived and oriented biomedical and international development programs, as historically specific cultural forces, have not substantially alleviated malnutrition in the Philippines.[2] Instead, the programs have more often ignored and perpetuated or extended social structures of inequality (particularly socioeconomic, gender, and ethnic inequality) that are the fundamental causes of malnutrition. While structures of inequality operated on the local level within Ifugao, each was influenced by those operating at national and international levels (such as social class, international economic relationships, etc.).

Gender inequality was not ignored in Ifugao, but rather focused on by some development organizations through their programs during the early 1990s. Some of the development programs resulted in adverse effects for women, even when they expressly tried to improve women's position in society. Simultaneous attempts by Philippine national biomedical and international development programs to raise women's social status and to alleviate malnutrition in Ifugao had not been highly successful since they largely ignored the social relations of power influencing these problems.[3] I will explore these propositions by analyzing biomedical and international development discourse and practices in Ifugao society in relation to gender, political violence, religion, and women's experience of malnutrition within their families and communities. I argue against the recent drive for the inclusion of women in international development programs, in light of their ineffectiveness and, in some cases, adverse effects on peoples they intended to benefit.

To understand the complexity of the social relations that influence malnutrition, I assess how diverse unequal power relations—including gender, economic, religious, government, biomedical, political, and international (i.e., colonial, neocolonial, and development)—interrelated, supported, or contradicted each other as they operated within and outside of Ifugao. I also address how they influenced the nutritional status of Ifugao people. Development personnel often ignored the complexity of unequal social relations operating within local communities. The personnel tended to focus on instituting projects that were usually politically and culturally decontextualized. Development agents at the planning level often advocated quick, technological fixes for social problems, usually serving the political and economic interests of donor governments.

Malnutrition is broadly defined here to be "the deterioration of health status and or social and productive performance of individuals arising from an intake of food either too low in quantity, or of the wrong kind, or both" (Jonsson 1981:2). Malnutrition is the biomedical understanding of hunger, which specifies and differentiates among the various nutrients needed for a well sustained mind and body. Biomedicine delineates different forms of hunger. In the biomedical construction, malnutrition is commonly a condition derived from poverty, as well as basic food and nutrient deprivation, or a result of illness causing malnutrition (such as loss of nutrients with continuous diarrheal episodes). But rarely does the biomedical construction of malnutrition include an analysis of malnutrition as one tragic and continuing outcome of processes of power and exploitation operating on international, national, and local community levels.

Related to this, I address the power of state supported and directed biomedicine, as well as other private biomedical organizations in Ifugao, to exert a dominant role in Ifugao people's attempts to alleviate malnutrition. This analysis includes an examination of the dialectical relationship between the Philippine state and biomedicine in the Philippines. In addition, the Philippine government's western derived, biomedical health care program joined with international development and aid organizations in an attempt to alleviate malnutrition. In looking at this relationship, I address how biomedicine is a part of the global system of power relations (Doyal and Pennell 1981; Baer, Singer and Johnsen 1986). Biomedicine ideally operates through ideologies of individualism and the superiority of technological and scientific knowledge and progress. Biomedicine is a reflection of the social ideological model of the larger society. Through biomedical ideology and practice, the individual body is the focus of (mainly physical) treatment, rather than the rectification of social relations producing ill health (Scheper-Hughes and Lock 1987; Baer, Singer and Johnsen 1986).

Biomedicine's influence on malnutrition and the institutionalization of biomedicine in Ifugao society must be understood in the context of the economic, political, and social conditions within Ifugao. Malnutrition is generated and reproduced through conflicts and tensions among different social groups and classes, which can appear in all arenas of society, including medical, gendered, state, political, religious, etc. (Navarro 1986). The perpetuation of malnutrition, despite biomedical and international development practices, is due in large part to their maintenance of an unequal sociopolitical order. It involves the view that social problems are best resolved by a social evolutionary "progress" of societies toward industrialization, macro-level economic growth, development, technologization, and westernization. In this paradigm, western industrialized countries were models to be aspired to and arrived at through modern technological, scientific, and "democratic" development practices in the Philippines. Instead of resolving social problems through international development, however, development institutions and practices often maintain social inequality, effected in large measure through the power of western states to plan and manage the lives of non-western peoples through development, aid (Escobar 1995, 1988), and biomedical ideology and practices, for economic and political gain.

Changes brought about through development programs, appearing on the surface to be positive or progressive, often reinforce some of the existing problems or create new problems for the people on whom changes were imposed. The hegemony of the western development paradigm in Ifugao, viewed by development agents and many Ifugao people as an inevitable and beneficial process of social change, was a function of the power invested in dominant forms of knowledge (Escobar 1995; Foucault 1990) imposed upon the Filipino people through centuries of colonialism and neocolonialism.[4] The view of development as being progressive became widely accepted in the Philippines, though not without resistance or reinterpretation (Cordillera Peoples Alliance 1993; Kerkvliet 1990; Drucker 1988; Ileto 1988).

Ifugao Society

I entered Ifugao for the first time in 1984 as a Peace Corps Volunteer. I was struck by their poverty and the remoteness of the villages, set deep in the Cordillera mountains of central Northern Luzon island. I was also impressed by the generosity and warmth of Ifugao people, despite their economic insecurity. At the time, I had hoped to contribute to the "development" of their community. Only later did I realize that international development was one of many powerful forces impinging on their lives and maintaining a state of poverty for the majority.

For Ifugao people, the word "Ifugao" designated the name of their ethno-linguistic group, province, and language. Ifugao was most commonly known for its remarkable rice terraced mountainsides, involving extensive irrigation systems running throughout the mountains. Largely an agricultural society, Ifugao had been integrated into the Philippine state market economy since at least the turn of the century. This integration generated widespread social changes in every area of Ifugao life, including economic, political, gendered, religious, and educational.

Certain Ifugao cultural norms and traits persisted, however, with some alteration over time. These traits included the strength of the Ifugao bilateral kinship system, bilateral inheritance, values and practices associated with the local Ifugao cosmology, some cultural constructs of gender roles, the use of prayer to cure illness, and livelihood activities. These cultural traits were supplemented with, and in some

PHOTO 1.1 "Native" and "modern" houses dot the terraced mountainsides of Ifugao Province.

cases overriden by, modern technologies, beliefs, and social structures, such as those found in biomedicine, Christianity, and state political structure. The majority of contemporary Ifugao people had been exposed to national and international processes and events through government, radio, development agents, travel, and—for some—newspapers, television, video, outmigration, and discussions with international tourists.

Agricultural production and small animal husbandry remained the primary sources of livelihood for the majority of Ifugao residents. Agricultural work was conducted largely through traditional practices, although some areas made use of water buffalo and plows. In most areas, plowing was accomplished using a spade. However, many business and salaried positions also were occupied by Ifugao people, and the development of some areas of Ifugao as popular tourist spots for tourists generated a modest tourist industry of hotels and restaurants, as well as craft production and trade. Wood carving of decorative objects and weaving of textiles and baskets were crafts practiced in Ifugao. Most wood carvings were intended for export to foreign countries. Some municipalities had small but thriving market centers, but most had none. All municipalities had a few small shops from which canned and dry goods could be purchased (commonly called *sari-sari* stores), and there were weekly fresh market days in some municipal centers.

PHOTO 1.2 "Native" one room houses historically have been built in close proximity to each other.

The Ifugao residential pattern outside of municipality centers consisted of small clusters of houses (some traditional and some modern) scattered throughout the mountains. Residence was usually ambilocal, although increasing rates of outmigration due to population growth and limited employment opportunities recently had altered this pattern of residence. Ifugao local religion consisted of a highly developed mixture of polytheism, mythology, and belief in ancestral and other spirits (Barton 1919:3). Despite the tremendous impact of modernization, religion and ritual—whether local or Christian—were still integral aspects of everyday life for most Ifugao people, as they were important components of agriculture, healing, marriage, death, birth, and other life cycle events.

Ifugao people had contact with a number of outsiders who generated differing degrees of cultural change. Trade had transpired in Ifugao for many centuries, including early trade with nearby villagers, members of lowland ethnic groups, and Chinese and Japanese traders. By the mid-nineteenth century the Ifugao area was infiltrated by the Spanish. Foreign missionaries had visited Ifugao since Spain's colonization of the Philippines. The American colonizers occupied Ifugao for about forty-five years. Contemporary Ifugao people had contact with other Filipino peoples, as well as people from many parts of the world.

PHOTO 1.3 Markets and some tourist establishments have emerged during the twentieth century in the central barrios, or *poblacions*, of Ifugao municipalities.

Although the Spanish colonizers tried to administer the Ifugao people, Ifugao was incorporated formally into a state system during the American occupation. Becoming a national province in 1966, Ifugao in the early 1990s was a province of the Cordillera Administrative Region of the national government. It was composed of ten municipalities. It had to abide by national laws, as well as regional, provincial, and municipal. Ifugao was represented by one Congressman in the national Congress. Its local provincial government system was composed of a governor, vice governor, provincial board (*Sangguniang Panlalawigan*), and provincial government agencies. Governing at the local municipal level were mayors, vice mayors, municipal councils (*Sangguniang Bayan*), other municipal government agencies, and barrio (barrios, or villages, are a subdivision of a municipality) captains. In 1992 and 1993, security in Ifugao Province included both the local police and the national military, which had stationed a battalion in Ifugao to fight Filipino Communist rebels, known as the New People's Army (NPA). Thus, Ifugao was well incorporated into the Philippine state and its modern political system.

During the last ninety years, economic and cultural development activities have increased in Ifugao. An educational system was established by the American occupiers in the early part of this century, requiring all Ifugao children to attend formal schools, although this requirement was not always enforced. In recent years government and private biomedical services have been available in all Ifugao municipalities, though their services, technology, and medical supplies were limited at the time of my research.

Ifugao municipalities were somewhat modernized in their centers; but outside the centers, infrastructure and services in the barrios were limited. Most homes had no running water, electricity, or toilets. Food generally was cooked over firewood, although a small percentage of Ifugao people used gas stoves. There were very few roads in Ifugao, so most travel was accomplished on foot. Health conditions were poor; and malnutrition was prevalent, especially among children and women.

The average family size was about six to eight members. There were few employment opportunities, so although parents and elder siblings strived to send their children and siblings to college, many Ifugao college graduates had difficulty finding employment either inside or outside of Ifugao. When college graduates returned to Ifugao, most did not want to work in the farms since they considered such labor to be below their new educational status. In modern Ifugao society, with increasing prices of commodities and services, agricultural families have had to develop numerous work strategies to earn enough cash to survive. Nonetheless, most Ifugao families continued to live below the poverty line in the early 1990s.

Ifugao people had experienced conditions of war for decades, including tribal wars and headhunting expeditions. The region witnessed Spanish and American colonization, World War II, and the contemporary low intensity conflict (LIC) fought between the Philippine government and Communist New Peoples Army revolutionaries.

Hunger in the Philippines and Ifugao

Using biomedical constructions of hunger and malnutrition, it was estimated that in 1991 70 percent of Filipino people experienced some form of malnutrition, and 72 percent of Philippine households were unable to afford food that would meet minimum recommended dietary requirements (IBON Databank 1991:16; Tan 1991:15).[5] The percentage of malnourished Filipino people had been slowly rising: in 1982, 67 percent of the people were malnourished in the Philippines, and in

1987, 69.2 percent of the people were malnourished (UNICEF 1990b:32). While figures cited for child malnutrition vary, some scholars estimate that by the early 1990s as many as 70 to 80 percent of Filipino children under six years old exhibited varying degrees of malnutrition (Chant and McIlwaine 1995). Fifty percent of pregnant Filipino women were cited as having anemia during the same period (Chant and McIlwaine 1995). In 1991 almost half of all Filipino people lived below the poverty level defined by the Philippine government, and the Philippines ranked seventh among countries having the highest poverty rates in the world (HAIN 1992:356).[6] In 1987 vitamin and other nutritional deficiencies were ranked as the ninth leading cause of mortality in the Philippines and as a frequent contributor to the eight preceding leading causes of mortality (UNICEF 1990b:31).[7]

Ifugao has been considered one of the poorest provinces in the Philippines. It was designated by the United Nations Children's Fund (UNICEF) as one of seven "worst-off" provinces in the Philippines, based on a number of social indicators such as malnutrition rate, infant mortality rate, educational enrollment rate, and family income (UNICEF 1990b:70). Although the standards UNICEF used in defining Ifugao as a "worst-off" province were derived from western standards, many lower class Ifugao people perceived themselves to be lacking in food, income, employment, and basic social services. It should be noted here that I am not using the term "social class" in a strict Marxian sense, that is, in terms of individuals' relationship to the means of production. There are studies critiquing the appropriateness of the use of "class" to analyze Southeast Asian social groups (Kerkvliet 1990; Pertierra 1988; Turner 1980; Evers 1973b). For the purpose of my analysis, the term is being used more loosely in reference to socioeconomic and status levels. Social class groups as defined by Ifugao people will be discussed in greater detail in Chapter 3.

In 1991, 33.4 percent of Ifugao children under six years old were found to be moderately and severely malnourished by the Ifugao government Provincial Nutrition Committee.[8] The rates of reported malnutrition in Ifugao varied among organizations, however, and were not entirely reliable. UNICEF reported 14.06 percent of Ifugao children under six years old moderately and severely malnourished in 1990, as compared to 21 percent in 1989 (UNICEF 1992a; UNICEF 1990a:1). Also, these rates did not include first degree malnourished children in this age group, who comprised the largest number of malnourished children in Ifugao. The inclusion of first degree malnourished children could make the rate of malnourished children under six years old to be 50 percent or higher. Nor did the reports include nutritional deficiencies of the Ifugao population at large, especially in terms of iron, iodine, and vitamin A, B, and C deficiencies. Chronic protein energy malnutrition was the most prevalent form of malnutrition among pre-school and school children in Ifugao, while women had high rates of iodine and iron deficiencies.

In 1989 the life expectancy rate among Ifugao people was 57.9 years, compared with a 1989 national average of 64.3 (UNICEF 1990b:66, 71). The 1990 infant mortality rate in Ifugao per 1000 live births was 76.6 (UNICEF 1992a:2), compared with a 1989 national average of forty-four infant deaths per 1000 live births and a 1989 Singapore national average of eight infant deaths per 1000 live births (Tan 1991:198).

To combat these nutritional trends, as well as other health and social problems, numerous government, international development, non-government (NGOs), and religious organizations had been actively operating in Ifugao since at least the late 1980s. These agencies included a joint UNICEF/Philippine government develop-ment program (the Ifugao Area Based Child Survival Development [ABCSD] Programme, also called the Ifugao Child Survival and Women Development program, first implemented in 1988); a European Community (EC) development program (the Central Cordillera Agricultural Programme, or CECAP, also first implemented in 1988); two NGO health programs also first implemented in the late 1980s; other NGO organizations; and numerous NGO Christian aid programs, some of which provided food supplementation programs.[9]

The first three programs had the enhancement of women's health and social position as either a major or minor component of their mission. The joint UNICEF/Philippine government program had been "geared towards the enhance-ment of the total development of Ifugao children and women." It had designated three Program Plans of Action (PPAs): "PPA I - Health and Nutrition; PPA 2 - Children and Women Development; and PPA 3 - Program Support." (UNICEF 1993:2).

Anthropological Approaches to Hunger

The study of food, food production related to social organization, and hunger has been undertaken by anthropologists since the early part of this century, beginning with Malinowski's functional analysis of a human hierarchy of needs in the 1930s.[10] Anthropologists have long recognized that nutrition is situated within the context of a social, biological, cultural, and political reality. Although nutritional anthropologists have made calls for the joining of both cultural and biological aspects of nutrition and nutritional problems, the larger, macro-level political and economic processes which influence nutritional status often have not been included in their analyses (Oculi 1987:5). Much of the recent anthropological literature on malnutrition reports on cultural practices and beliefs surrounding food and diet, nutrition education, sanitation, nutrient deficiencies, and the role of infectious diseases in influencing malnutrition.[11] Some theorists, for example, argue that community nutrition programs integrated into primary health care can effectively reduce malnutrition among young children without economic growth, even for the poor (Melville 1985:229). Others argue that "ignorance" (especially of women) and cultural beliefs and practices (which are deemed by some western scholars as "inappropriate") are the main causes of malnutrition.[12]

Some scholars who view poverty and the lack of adequate food as the main causes of malnutrition find the solution to the problem in technological fixes such as high yielding crop varieties, the production of cash crops, or income generating programs. Other anthropologists and scholars argue, on the other hand, that it is the intersection of a poor socioeconomic situation, power relations, domination, and exploitation that fundamentally causes malnutrition and inhibits the rearing of healthy, well nourished children.[13]

In this analysis, I assess the role of the state and other power relations (particularly international, social class, gender, and religious) in influencing the nutritional status of social collectivities. Using a critical-interpretive theoretical orientation, I assess the position of the Philippines within the global economy (Lock and Scheper-Hughes 1990). My analysis involves an investigation of how outside forces have articulated with the internal social structural and cultural processes of the Philippine nation generally, and Ifugao society specifically, to produce and maintain widespread malnutrition both historically and during the early 1990s. I also explore how these processes impact on the personal experiences of Ifugao individuals, especially Ifugao women, many of whom are themselves malnourished and parent malnourished children. I also investigate cultural meanings Ifugao people give to conceptions of their bodies, food, health, illness, and hunger.

I also draw on a political economic theoretical orientation in medical anthropology, which concentrates on the structural relationship among economic processes, political power, and ideologies, and their consequences for the health of individuals in local settings. This perspective regards culturally informed interactions between social actors and political economic processes as dialectically related, thus the importance of ethnographic as well as social structural analysis (Morsy 1990; Frankenberg 1980).[14] Political economic studies of malnutrition have analyzed the impact of historical and current political and economic processes on the nutritional status of individuals and groups in both developed and underdeveloped countries. Baer, Singer, and Johnsen (1986) stress the importance of analyzing the power differentials which shape social processes, particularly in health care systems (Baer and Singer 1995; Baer, Singer, and Johnsen 1986). Taking a broader macro-level perspective, many medical anthropologists have tried to understand the social mechanisms by which local power relations and global forces impinge on the body (Morsy 1990:31).

In studies of malnutrition, therefore, an assessment must be made of the processes of power differentiation within a society which control an individual's access to food, health care, employment opportunities, land, and housing. But it is not adequate to assess this situation only in terms of social class conflicts. Power involved in gender, political, medical, and religious relations must also be considered.[15]

The problems of malnutrition and hunger are not only caused by lack of an adequate food supply to feed the world's population (Lappe and Collins 1986), or simply by overpopulation (Population Reference Bureau 1984). Nor are they fundamentally problems of uncontrollable natural disasters that devastate agricultural production (Jackson and Ugalde 1985), or a lack of adequate technology in underdeveloped countries (Lappe and Collins 1986).[16] Although each of these can be viewed as factors which contribute to and exacerbate malnutrition and hunger, they are rooted more fundamentally in complex systems of historical and contemporary social and cultural relations.

Numerous recent studies of malnutrition by anthropologists and other scholars have focused primarily on phenomena related to malnutrition at community and individual levels.[17] Other significant research on hunger or malnutrition has focused primarily on macro-level processes, assessing political and economic phenomena related to malnutrition and hunger.[18] Fewer studies have addressed international, national, and local phenomena influencing hunger, malnutrition, and famine.[19]

Much of the past research addressing malnutrition in the Philippines has focused on processes which occur on the individual, household, and community levels.[20] While these studies contribute important understandings of practices and experiences of malnutrition on the local level, they lack an indepth consideration of the socioeconomic and sociopolitical context of the Philippine communities under study, a context which significantly contributes to the problem of malnutrition.[21]

Gender and Hunger

Recent anthropological studies of malnutrition have examined relationships between gender and malnutrition, famine and hunger, or women and hunger.[22] Anthropological and other research focusing on women and malnutrition or hunger have analyzed gender specific social and cultural problems associated with these conditions. These have included the cultural construction of the vulnerability of women to malnutrition;[23] the effect of culture and historical social and economic conditions on women's responses to hunger and child death;[24] the intersection of social class, gender, and hunger;[25] the breastfeeding versus bottlefeeding debate;[26] culturally prescribed sex-differential nutrition;[27] the significance of mother's education on the nutritional status of her children;[28] and women's emic perceptions of malnutrition and hunger.[29]

Women often carry more responsibilities than men in peasant societies, since women often work both as farmers and as the primary childcare providers and domestic laborers within their households.[30] As women often are also the primary family and community members concerned with nutrition, the heavy workload of lower class women—and, in some societies such as Ifugao, middle and upper class women—can influence the nutritional status of their children.

An important example clearly pointing to the significance of investigating malnutrition with regard to gendered power and social class relations is Schoepf's study of the effects of socioeconomic changes on the matrilineal Lemba society. Among the Lemba living in Zaire, the social value of women is emphasized. Although not fully equal to men, Schoepf argues that Lemba women maintain a high social position in relation to men, and that they are not dependent on men. Schoepf also argues that the high position of Lemba women is correlated with greater nutritional equality among Lemba females and males than found between women and men of other social groups with patrilineal forms of organization and a lower position of women in relation to men. However, greater social class differentiation due to increasing insertion into commodity production in recent years has been causing the devaluation of Lemba women's position, and it may result in the lowering of their nutritional status. Schoepf suggests that in less class stratified societies, and where gender ideology is not discriminatory, the nutritional status of both sexes is less differentiated (Schoepf 1987). As will be shown later, this argument has strongly influenced the goals and structuring of recently implemented health and development programs in Ifugao, and elsewhere, in attempts to alleviate malnutrition.

Relatedly, my analysis of the relationship between women and their children's nutritional status and differential pay rates for men and women in Ifugao is supported by a recent study which focused on the relationship between the value of women's time and wages and malnutrition. This study was conducted by Senauer and other researchers in both Philippine and Sri Lankan communities (Senauer 1990). The study found that as women's value of time (estimated in terms of wage rates, even for non-paid labor) in households rose, both their and their children's intrahousehold allocation of calories increased. As the value of women's time increased, based on calculated increases in their wages, their position within the household was also enhanced, as well as their own and their children's nutrient shares among all household members. Interestingly, Senauer also found that as the husband's wages rose, both he and his wife did relatively better in terms of calorie intake, but their relative intrahousehold allocation of calories to their children declined. This study demonstrated the importance of the value of women's time, high wage rates for women, and women's social position in the household (in part based on women's economic contribution to the household in terms of cash) in relation to women and their children's nutritional well-being. However, increased family income may not guarantee increased nutritional well-being. When families do acquire higher wages it is equally important to investigate who has control over wages, how the increased wages are spent by men and women, and, as this study assessed, how increased wages of men or women influence their respective nutritional status—and their children's—within the household and community.

Schrijvers also argued for the importance of the link between gender relations and undernourishment, asserting that poverty and undernourishment are directly connected to the relations of production between men and women. She found in Sri Lanka, as I also found in Ifugao, that outside of agriculture there are few employment opportunities for women, and that women's pay as agricultural day-laborers is only one-half to two-thirds that of males. She found the western-exported ideology of development programs of women as primarily domestic laborers and mothers, and of males as household "breadwinners," to be culturally inappropriate in many non-western societies, where most women engage in full time labor outside of the home (Schrijvers 1988).

The importance of considering gender relations as well as class status in relation to malnutrition was also exemplified through a study by Schoepf and Schoepf, which assessed an agricultural policy of the Zaire government. The policy was instituted to benefit the poor, but it resulted in increased agricultural opportunities and financial benefits for men, as newly designated owners of land and as legal heads of households, but none for women as producers of food. This case indicated that a woman's position in the community and family is crucial to her ability to benefit from increased production efforts through government or development programs (Schoepf and Schoepf 1987).

Sex-differential nutrition practices and statuses have been well documented by researchers for many societies, wherein girls and women in particular societies, such as India, have been found to have lower nutritional statuses than boys and men in the same societies.[31] To some degree, this has been found to be the case in the Philippines between women and men, and between boys and girls zero to six years old, and in Ifugao specifically for boys and girls zero to six years old.[32] One argument explains this difference through the Malthusian, functionalist view that female nutrition deprivation can be a culturally adaptive means of population control when food scarcity exists, and that limiting women's intake of food may have positive survival value for the group (Rosenberg 1980). However, this functionalist view ignores the social and political construction of ideas of "food scarcity," lacking an analysis which would differentiate among social groups experiencing food scarcity and those which are not. It also ignores both dynamism and social change in societies, and the strategies women use to overcome problems of hunger and malnutrition. For instance, Brown found that in the Dominican Republic women take on a series of different mates in order to retain their independence, mobility, and control over their economic resources, and to alleviate malnutrition in their families. Through this strategy, they are able to take care of themselves and their children more efficiently. Single mothers in the Dominican Republic also rely on their own mothers to assist in child care and on sharing children with other families (Brown 1975).

Research on gender and malnutrition has also disproved the myth that men need more food than women because of their greater physical size, or that "If the men do not have sufficient energy to do the work required to produce food or earn a living, everyone in the group may starve" (Rosenberg 1980). This ideology does not consider the great nutritional needs of many women who expend high numbers of calories while engaging in daily strenuous physical labor (which may be increasing due to changes in patterns of labor activities for both women and men), and who have increased nutritional needs during pregnancy and lactation.[33] The myths also reduce women's role in societies to one of total dependence on males, ignoring the tremendous contribution of women to food production and income generation in many societies.[34]

It has been further argued that since a woman's role is crucial in the household, including the preparation of food, the nutritional status of the population is likely to be strongly influenced by the various elements and forces that act upon and influence women's behavior (Eide and Steady 1980). This has led to the inappropriate social construction of women in all societies primarily in the role of "mother" and provider of child care, regardless of their own culturally defined social roles. It has also influenced the emergence of the focus on women in development programs to improve their children's poor nutritional status. For example, intense debate has transpired on the extent to which "mother's" education influences malnutrition among families within the same social class. Some researchers have found that in rural areas the education of the mother is a strong determinant of child nutritional status, while others have found that the effect of mother's education could be modified by considering the sex of the children (Bhuiya et al. 1989).[35] On the other hand, one scholar found mother's education to be unrelated to nutrition (Thomas 1981). Other studies deem poor women to be ignorant of nutrition knowledge and argue that their ignorance is a main cause of malnutrition (Oyeneye 1991; Huston 1979).

Each of these studies' focus on women, their stress on women's lack of education, and their defining women as ignorant, indirectly places the majority of responsibility for the nutritional health of family members on women. This stress on women also subtly blames them whenever their children are poorly nourished. Although a few studies have included men's educational status related to child malnutrition as well as women's (Senauer 1990; Strauss 1987), more often researchers, and development agents, rarely investigate the role "fathers" play in the nutritional well-being of their children, or the greater role they could play to reduce some of the responsibility women bear for child and nutritional care. I will examine how this view was reproduced in national and international health and development programs in Ifugao.[36]

Some studies have noted men's negative influence on their children's nutritional status, particularly in patriarchal societies where men have control over women's bodies. In many societies, including the west African nation of Mali, and in Ifugao society to some extent, poor women have little power to contest their husbands' demands that they bear many children or engage in intercourse often, without the use of contraception, despite the (often repressed) objections of their wives (Dettwyler 1994). Women's continuous pregnancies, lack of spacing between pregnancies, and large family size have all influenced their children's poor nutritional statuses and high rates of child death, and women's own poor nutritional statuses (Dettwyler 1994; Scheper-Hughes 1987). Many women themselves resist contraceptive use (including Ifugao women), for complicated reasons. Still, both men's resistance to contraception when women desire to use it, and many women's perceived lack of power to object to their husbands' demands, have influenced the nutritional status of women and children.

Other anthropologists have looked at emic perceptions of hunger and malnutrition. Scheper-Hughes found that the poor of northeast Brazil understand their hunger through the idiom of *nervos*, a polysemic folk concept, the symptoms of which include trembling, nervousness, fainting, seizures, and paralysis of limbs. For the poor, *nervos* was originally a critical reflection on the exploitative social conditions under which they lived and worked. But the biomedical profession in northeastern Brazil appropriated the folk concept of *nervos* to identify it as an individual illness, rather than a social illness, and to hide the hunger from which it often stems (Scheper-Hughes 1992).

Ultimately, the transformation of unequal social structures through a restructuring of the class system and the redistribution of resources would not alone solve the problem of malnutrition, since gendered power relations have been found to be significant in the social production of malnutrition.[37] Although the redistribution of resources, including land, capital, and food resources, should be an integral aspect of any solution to widespread malnutrition in a society, it must be accompanied by a reassessment of women's and men's gender social roles and positions, and the influence of these on children's nutritional and overall well-being.

Each of these issues will be discussed in regard to Ifugao women and their children's nutritional status. Many of the theoretical propositions cited in the above studies were held by practitioners of international development programs in Ifugao. The idea that as women's social position within their societies generally, and within their households specifically, increased, their own and their children's nutritional status might also increase, was significant in shaping a number of the programs. As a result, a major component of the development programs was the enhancement of women's social position in order to increase their own and their children's nutritional statuses. Gender, social class, malnutrition, and poverty are each socially generated, and each is influenced by historically specific political and economic processes. I will discuss how the development programs' failure to address the historical institutionalization of unequal gender and class relations within Ifugao society undermined the programs' goal of raising Ifugao women's social position and nutritional status. Although I analyze gender relations, I primarily emphasize women's lives because of my focus on women in development programs in relation to malnutrition.

A contemporary study of malnutrition in the Philippines would be incomplete without an assessment of the international development organizations' practices, paradigms, and discourse revolving around and influencing the problem of malnutrition. International development organizations are pervasive forces of power currently operating in local Philippine communities. While they are rarely viewed as forces of power, particularly by people within the societies in which they operate, the following section will demonstrate that international health and development programs do exert a powerful, hegemonic political and cultural force in non-western, non-industrialized societies. They significantly alter important aspects of the lives of poor peoples in these societies, and they often set women up as the scapegoat for hunger and the failures of existing unequal political and economic systems.

Perspectives on Development

International development is viewed here as an historically specific cultural construction that originated in the West as a mode of planned social and economic change (Hobart 1993). Development is the representation of the power of western nations to order the world according to their conception of knowledge (that is, scientific knowledge) and the best means of "developing" other societies, usually to the West's own advantage. International development is a set of discourse and practices, and it is a strategy in the social management of underdevelopment (Escobar 1988:430). Development discourse and practices have enabled industrialized, usually western, countries to arrange significant aspects of social and economic life in poor countries to become the object of calculation by experts in sciences developed for that purpose (Escobar 1988). This has included the management of health, illness, and malnutrition.

Recently, anthropologists and other scholars have critically analyzed development from a Foucaultian perspective, viewing development as a system of knowledge and power. Some scholars have deconstructed the development paradigm in an effort to understand its hegemonic effects on people throughout the world.[38] Anthropologists have sought to expose the devastating problems created by development for cultural indigenous groups around the globe (Bodley 1988). Other anthropologists have offered critiques of development, focusing on the assumptions integral to development, the roots of international development in colonialism and national development planning, and the cultural problems arising from development practices and the attendant bureaucratic decision making processes.[39] Scholars of Southeast Asia, including anthropologists, have critically examined the processes, adverse effects, and assumptions underlying development practices in the region, including the Philippines.[40] Anthropologists and other scholars have looked at the history of anthropologists' participatory role in development, some supporting that involvement (Hoben 1982) and others critiquing their role in development.[41]

Before moving on to literature regarding gender and development, I would like to discuss some theoretical propositions in the development literature that are relevant to this analysis. To begin, Escobar proposes that development discourse and practices extend modern western self-knowledge, and that they have sought to recontain and control, in the terrain of representation, the former colonies, now conceived of as the "Third World" (Escobar 1991:661). He argues that the segmentation of the world into First, Second, and Third Worlds is an historically produced, culturally constructed phenomenon, often accepted uncritically by anthropologists and development agents.

Stavrianos positions the emergence of the Third World with the rise of a dynamic capitalist society, which expanded and established a worldwide hegemony by the nineteenth century. The term "Third World" was constructed only in the postwar years, first used in a political context but now more commonly used in an economic context. Initially after the Second World War, Third World countries were those which remained non-aligned with the First World western capitalist countries or with the Second World socialist countries. The phrase lost its political rationale with a relaxing of the Cold War, however, and the category "Third World" began to take on economic connotations following the delineation of the categories "developed" and "underdeveloped" societies. According to the development paradigm, the contemporary Third World's underdeveloped societies include countries in Latin America, Africa (excluding South Africa), and Asia (excluding Japan and possibly Singapore, Hong Kong, Taiwan, South Korea, and China).

This history depicts how the construction and creation of the Third World was historically specific and politically and economically motivated (Stavrianos 1981:33-34). The representation of these societies as a conglomerate of less than developed societies through development discourse perpetuates the notion of western supremacy, ideas of social evolutionism, and ethnocentrism on the part of western peoples.

The linear thinking involved in viewing as natural the process of changing non-western societies to achieve a social and material status similar to that of western countries, categorized as the process of "development," rings of social evolutionism. This ideology, perpetuated through discourses of contemporary development agents, conjures up notions of late eighteenth century classical social evolutionary syntheses, which explained each world society as exhibiting a particular stage in a process of social evolution. In this model, societies follow natural laws of social evolution, proceeding through stages of social development from primitive, to savage, to barbaric, to horticultural, to agricultural, and, finally, to western style civilization. Proponents of this model view European societies as the highest form of civilization, beginning with the classical Greek and Roman societies. Unlike the earlier social evolutionary view that societies naturally pass through designated evolutionary social stages, the contemporary model of development emphasizes that direct and massive intervention, or penetration (Hobart 1993), by "developed" or First World societies into "underdeveloped" societies can lead them toward "modernization," sometimes still called civilization, as exhibited in western societies.

Western "development" of non-western countries began during the 1940s (Hobart 1993; Escobar 1991:658), but the mission and notion of developing other societies to conform to standards of western civilization began centuries before, with the spread of Christian religious ideologies throughout the globe beginning in the sixteenth century (Comaroff and Comaroff 1991). This mission was intertwined with the conquering, westernizing, and developing of other territories, natural resources, and bodies, mainly to the benefit of the elite of the colonizing nations.

Theories of eugenics (Francis Galton) and bioengineering were prominent during the first half of the twentieth century, extending ideas of planning and development to the nature of human beings themselves. Social engineering paradigms were developed during this period, such as Frederick Taylor's "scientific management," stressing efficiency in production and techniques of comprehensive planning and cost-benefit analysis in businesses.

The contemporary development model also coincided with modernist notions of social Darwinian evolution, which presupposed the inevitable survival of the fittest societies. Those societies lowest on the social evolutionary ladder, through conflict or intervention, would inevitably be destroyed or culturally and socially transformed by more advanced societies so that their traditional form would disappear. This theory justified colonial, and later neocolonial, intervention by non-western societies.

National development planning during this century has been defined by Robertson as an institution which serves as one of the principle means by which modern states have brought political power to bear on the organization of national resources to achieve more rapid growth by the pursuit of industrialization (Robertson 1984:2). International development planning is an extension of the concept and practices of national development planning. Although planning, both on an individual and community level, has always occurred in societies, development planning on a national and international scale is a more recent phenomenon. While state intervention in national economies has also existed for centuries, national and international development planning on a global scale was instituted during the twentieth century. National and international planning have been made possible by the development of industrial processes and the formation of nation states with political centers of power (Robertson 1984:2).

The postwar foreign policy of the United States oversaw a period of great expansion of U.S. development aid to foreign countries, based on the implicit assumption that all societies should conform to the U.S. model, that is, as modern, democratic, capitalist, and industrial societies. But developing countries would not necessarily be equal to the United States, as industrialized, western nations have tried to retain their economic and political dominance over non-western countries and to continue their exploitation of these countries' resources and labor.

The decades of the 1940s and 1950s were noted for their ideas of "modernization" and "stages of economic growth" and the rise of development planning in colonial countries. During World War II, much of the interest in the development of colonies stemmed from the need to incorporate them into the war effort. After the war, the devastated European countries were viewed as needing planned development, as did the colonies, resulting in the American Marshall Plan for Europe (1948–1952). Colonial planning and decolonization became more pressing during this time, due to pressure from groups within the colonizing states and social unrest in the colonies (Robertson 1984).

Both multilateral and bilateral aid greatly increased during and following the war.[42] American aid increased during this period, motivated by anti-communist ideology and the desire to expand and consolidate American capitalist interests abroad, including in the Philippines. The same can be said for aid given to former colonies after they acquired independence—again, such as the Philippines. In 1945 the International Bank for Reconstruction and Development (currently named the World Bank) was established.[43] In 1949 U.S. President Harry Truman pledged to extend American scientific and technical expertise to underdeveloped countries for humanitarian reasons and to enhance American economic and security interests. Other national and international—mainly western and eastern bloc—planning and development organizations proliferated during this period (Robertson 1984).

W.W. Rostow's modernization theory of stages of economic growth, reminiscent of nineteenth century social evolutionary theory, has also lent support to the contemporary development model. Modern, industrial, capitalist, western societies were viewed by Rostow as the highest form of social structure and organization, toward which all societies would inevitably develop. Planners were viewed as being apolitical and scientifically objective, working on problems of an economic and technical nature. Rostow's five stages of growth, as part of his "Non-Communist Manifesto," included: the traditional society, the preconditions for takeoff to industrial growth, the take-off point, the drive to maturity toward an industrial society, and, lastly, the age of high mass consumption (Rostow 1960). In this model, during the 1960s Britain and the United States represented the highest social form. World Bank policies actually were set along the lines of Rostow's ideas of growth and modernization during the 1940s and 1950s, and the model's assumptions continue to inform Bank policies today.

There are many problems with this model, including: the assumption of the inevitability of progress and growth through modernization techniques; the lack of consideration of political factors which influence growth; the unfounded assumption of unlimited growth and resources; the lack of consideration of power relations invested in development planning and techniques; and the disregard of class, ethnic, and gender differentiation which influence the distribution of the assumed benefits of modernization. Moreover, the modernization model is positivistic and entails an ethnocentric interpretation of the emergence of capitalism and the industrial revolution in western Europe. This model requires a fundamental transformation of societies from "traditional" forms, which are thought to inhibit economic growth, to "modern" forms, believed to promote economic growth. Modernization usually entails the rapid transformation of traditional values, institutions, cultures, and practices, to be replaced by more, so-called, rational, scientific, and efficient ideologies and practices, as essential aspects of economic development (Hoben 1982:352).

Some economists and development planners think that an effective capitalist development model depends on a strong, authoritative, but democratic state structure.[44] Modernization advocates strive for homogeneity, control, comprehensiveness, and integration in development planning. However, although order, progress, and welfare for all people are goals of planning and development in development discourse, the rapid and continuous changes entailed in modernization involve processes of disorganization and dislocation and the emergence of grave, new social problems for many people.

In the postwar period, development activities have been intertwined with western industrial nations' capitalist expansion throughout the world. In 1997 U.S. President William Clinton said that, "since the fall of communism, [U.S.] Peace Corps units have begun work in a large number of newly democratic nations from Eastern Europe to Central Asia, helping to nurture and strengthen free markets by teaching new entrepreneurs how to get their businesses running" (*Mobile Register* 1998:8A). This expansion created situations of dependency both through exploitation of resources and labor (Frank 1969) and provision of monetary assistance in the form of high interest loans. These practices also affected western nations themselves. Although these processes can be seen in numerous societies throughout the world, it is important to analyze how each society responded to, interpreted, and refashioned capitalist expansion in culturally mediated ways (Morgan 1987).

In the contemporary post-colonial period, the reasons offered by officials of western nations for the continuation of international development have not changed fundamentally; the rationale for development remains the enhancement of the material interests of donor countries. For example, J. Brian Atwood, appointed director of the U.S. Agency for International Development (USAID), stated in October 1993 that the primary significance of U.S. foreign aid for the development of Third World countries was to create markets for U.S. produced goods to benefit U.S. citizens. He said, "We have achieved a lot of growth in the developing world in the last ten years. . . . [With continued growth there will be more] opportunities to send [U.S.] commodities to the Third World. [The] U.S. market share has [already] grown from 35 percent to 45 percent in Third World [countries]." He emphasized that he and other U.S. government personnel, "Have to convince people in the U.S. that *it is in their interests* to support development" (Atwood 1993, my emphasis). It can be seen through this statement that the interests of peoples of other countries, which are to be developed and managed by the U.S. government, are not of primary importance. What is important is their consumptive and purchasing capabilities, to be organized and expanded through the U.S. capitalist driven and managed development paradigm.

However, spending for development is also justified in the United States today through the terminology of "environmentally sustainable development," which is argued to be necessary for the sustainability of human life. Sustainable development continues to be a hegemonic force of a monolithic cultural paradigm ("development") which is touted to be necessary for all societies. This ideology not only has been advocated by international development organizations but also accepted by many community based non-governmental institutions throughout the world. While the new "development" may be more sustainable, it continues to be a western paradigm of development geared toward the demands of the world market (Esteva 1992:16).

Most poor countries have become dependent to some degree on western nations, in part as a result of former colonial practices; contemporary neocolonial economic practices; foreign lending policies of the International Monetary Fund (IMF), the World Bank, and other lending institutions; the accumulation of massive debt by non-industrialized countries with high interest rates; the transnationalization of labor; transnational corporate investment practices; and increasing global militarization. But the management of poor nations is not attempted purely through economic means. The global hegemony of western cultural and social forms can be observed in many countries, effected in part through development practices, although these forms are usually reinterpreted, refashioned, and reappropriated through the cultural lenses of non-western peoples. Among others, these forms include political systems (often some semblance of democracy), medical systems (usually a form of biomedicine), formal educational systems, western popular culture (music, dance, performance, fashion), and language (usually English). One result of the hegemony of western cultural and social forms is the reliance on western products to meet new culturally prescribed needs. For example, exported western biomedicine creates dependency by non-western countries on western pharmaceutical companies to purchase drugs and other medical technologies introduced to their countries.

To reiterate, this analysis follows the emerging view of the development model as an historically specific form of knowledge, a form of power that constructs a particular reality of the world, imposed on peoples of non-western countries through a variety of strategies, technologies, and discourses. Development is a view of the world that seeks to erode non-western knowledge, practices, and cultures. It is a force perpetuated by western, industrialized countries seeking to manage and gain from the human and material resources of non-industrialized countries (Escobar 1995, 1988). For example, western biomedicine's focus on individual, technical, and bodily aspects of illness and healing diverts attention away from social causes of illness and problems such as hunger, malnutrition, and poverty. Biomedicine also allows for the penetration of the state into local communities through medical surveillance and monitoring, such as the weighing surveillance programs of governments, usually viewed as objective, non-politicized technology (Foucault 1994).

In considering development as it impinges on the problem of malnutrition, a closer analysis of gender and development must be undertaken, since the alleviation of malnutrition has been strongly associated by development agents and scholars with women's lives and gendered position, as has occurred in Ifugao.

Gender and Development

Discourse which called for the integration of women in development programs became prominent in the early 1970s. The rise of interest in women in development is usually associated with the publication of Esther Boserup's book, *Women's Role in Economic Development.*[45] Boserup argued that economic assistance should be provided for rural women as well as men. In 1973 the U.S. Congress institutionalized the strategy of incorporating women in development programs by mandating that USAID promote this practice. Congressional objectives were to promote the social position of women, as well as their general development, in non-industrialized societies. Later the United States designated 1975 as the International Women's Year, followed by the United Nations' similar designation of the decade 1976–1985 as the Decade for Women (St. Hilaire 1992:4).

St. Hilaire argues that this was the beginning of the objectification of women in the development process. Women, as "women in development" (WID), became subjects to be worked on, improved, labeled, altered, and westernized (St. Hilaire 1992:3). In Ifugao, for example, women were made to feel inadequate for having malnourished children and for not having met the mothering standards imposed on them from outsiders. In health care, development discourse often portrays women as individually responsible for the poor health of their families and their communities. The were subjected to questions about their mothering, their level of formal western-style education, their practices of sanitation, their sexual practices and reproductive choices, and their "primitive" and "backward" cultural practices. Women had to be integrated into the new market economy of the expanding capitalist world system and the state social structure. In Ifugao, issues such as the subjectivity of individual women, the sense of self each woman held, and the reasons why women were making certain choices were virtually nonexistent in development literature circulating there.

Like Escobar, St. Hilaire argues that development serves primarily as a mechanism for the management of underdevelopment. Both apply Foucault's concept of *dispotif* to development, a collection of theories, institutions, practices, and procedures through which individuals and collectivities are constituted as objects upon which to act, and simultaneously as subjects eventually capable of managing themselves in accordance with the terms of development (St. Hilaire 1992:2). Extending this view to women, St. Hilaire argues that the integration of women in development (referring here to large, western international development discourse and practices) reinscribes women in a new and more direct way in the relations of power and resistance in this *dispotif*, and that development is a new arena within which the social management of women occurs (St. Hilaire 1992:2-3).

Since the 1970s there has been a proliferation of literature on women and development.[46] Much of the scholarship has been critical of development policies which either fully exclude women or result in adverse effects for women, while benefitting men.[47] Still, many of these scholars tend to accept the western development model and to advocate women's involvement in development programs. Other studies analyzing women and development issues also critique development for similar reasons, but further critique the basic assumptions held by advocates of development and attempt a cultural deconstruction of development ideology and practices.[48] The latter position is advocated here, given the volumes of critical work produced on the ineffectiveness and unjustness of western development practices (Sachs 1992).

Warren and Bourque (1991) categorized four major approaches of scholars focusing their research on women and technology. The first category is the integrationist approach, characterized as being a liberal, reformist analysis, focused primarily on the professional and technical classes. Proponents of this perspective advocate a top-down approach to enhancing gender equality, particularly through the integration of women into formal decision making positions in government, business, and the professions. Change must occur in the political culture of education and the workplace. Integral to this process is discerning how institutions shape meaning and value, and how individuals can internalize and confront social norms.

The second category identified by Warren and Bourque is the appropriate technology approach, which advocates increasing local productivity through scientific rationality and technical efficiency, without reinforcing dependency on industrial nations. This also is viewed as a top-down approach, regarding decision making in developing appropriate technology. The goal is to increase women's productivity to allow them more time for other activities, including development.

The third category is the feminization of technology approach. This approach posits a radical feminist critique and strategy for social change. It seeks to redirect technology away from masculinist values toward new feminist values. This perspective does not advocate women's uncritical participation in western development programs.

The fourth category is the global economy approach. Analysts using this neo-Marxist approach focus on development as part of the process of the penetration of capitalism into the world economic system. Concern is given to the exploitation of lower classes by expansionist capitalist classes in the process of accumulating resources and wealth. According to Warren and Bourque, it asserts "the importance of an international perspective that sees various forms of inequality as interactive and central to explanations of current patterns of development" (Warren and Bourque 1991:289). The approach focuses on how national governments and international markets influence national planning, policy development, and the allocation of resources (Afshar 1987, in Warren and Bourque 1991:289; Warren and Bourque 1991:280-290). My analysis is most closely aligned with the global economy approach, as I attempt to place hunger, malnutrition, and development programs focusing on women and children in Ifugao in the context of the larger world economic system of which they are a part. I will analyze each of these issues in relation to the international, national, and local power relations and forms of inequality from which they stem and in which they are embedded.

Finally, there is far less literature on women and malnutrition which also analyzes development practices. Studies on gender and malnutrition have usually categorized women primarily as "mothers," losing sight of women being political and economic actors within social polities larger than the family and the local community. Women, as mothers, are often viewed as requiring education, development, and integration into the market economy. Yet, little inquiry has been made into how women perceived their own lives, their and their communities' malnourished children, their political positions, and their gendered positions.[49]

Conducting Anthropological Research in Ifugao

This ethnography is based on sixteen months of fieldwork in three communities in Ifugao Province, conducted at various times between 1990 and 1993, including a continuous twelve-month period. My research was influenced by my previous experience in Ifugao, from December 1984 until January 1987, as a Peace Corps volunteer. While in the Peace Corps, I was a Community Health Volunteer affiliated with the Philippine government Rural Health Unit (RHU) in an Ifugao municipality. For six months I lived in the center of the municipality, and for the remainder of my stay I lived in a barrio set deep in the mountains on a river, located approximately twenty-one kilometers from the municipal center. During that time, I engaged in primary health care activities and assisted in establishing a municipal library and building an irrigation system. My experiences taught me the difficulties and complexities involved in effecting substantial improvements in the lives of people through international development efforts.

My Peace Corps experience in Ifugao facilitated my later research in numerous ways. I conducted part of my research in a village in the municipality in which I had lived as a volunteer, and the remainder of my research in another nearby Ifugao municipality. For my fieldwork research, I arrived in Ifugao in 1990 with an already partially developed understanding of Ifugao culture and daily life. I did not experience the cultural differences from my own culture as intensely as I might have, since I already was familiar and comfortable with Ifugao culture and lifestyle. I was able to rekindle many friendships. I also understood much of the Ifugao language of the municipality in which I lived as a Peace Corps Volunteer. The language in the second municipality was quite different, necessitating my learning another Ifugao dialect. My friendships and familiarity with Ifugao thus hastened the progress of my research. Much of the initial processes of fieldwork for the researcher who enters a community for the first time had already been accomplished during my previous stay.

My Peace Corps experience in Ifugao deeply influenced my research, analysis, and writing, and contributed to the formulation of my present inquiry. Twenty-seven months working as a "development" agent in Ifugao caused me to question the appropriateness of western-based international development for people of non-western societies. I was particularly influenced by my observations of the contradictory and inconsistent policies of the U.S. government toward the Philippines and the Filipino people, including its foreign policy and development programs, which more often resulted in adverse rather than beneficial effects for the majority of the Filipino people. My work experience as a development agent also added a valuable, if admittedly limited, insider view of development processes.

For the first three months of my research in Ifugao in 1991 and 1992, I lived with two women (one in her fifties and her mother, who was in her eighties) in their modern, two story wooden house. For the remainder of my stay in Ifugao, I lived in a modern, two room, galvanized iron house in one of the barrios in which I conducted research.

Most of my research consisted of observing and participating in the daily lives of people living in Ifugao communities. Through this anthropological method of research, I was able partially to understand the ways in which Ifugao people conceived of and dealt with malnutrition during their daily lives: their work, rituals, celebrations, politics, gender relations, kinship relations, domestic relations, institutions, and play. I spent some time working with peasant women in their rice fields, planting and harvesting rice; I sat in stores while people managed their businesses or produced crafts; I attended numerous religious rituals and services, some specifically for curing illnesses and for agricultural production; I witnessed the birth of a child in a remote barrio; I visited health clinics and hospitals; I attended municipal events, including fiestas and national nutrition day festivities; and I attended funerals, weddings, graduation and birthday parties, election rallies, and a community house building feast.

In addition, I attended many government, international development organization, and NGO sponsored community meetings or events. In joining these meetings, I attempted to gain an understanding of these organizations' ideologies, their personnel's interaction with community members, and their approaches to development, health care, and the alleviation of malnutrition.

Also, I conducted numerous informal and formal, open-ended interviews with a variety of groups of people, inside and outside of Ifugao. These interviews included discussions with Ifugao men and women from a variety of social classes, professions, religious affiliations, and ages; government personnel and development agents; religious practitioners of a number of different religions; NGO workers; politicians; government soldiers; and Filipino university scholars.

During the first three months of 1992, I chose three barrios in which to conduct my research. One was located at a great distance from the center of a municipality and hosted a government RHU. Another had organized a NGO health clinic, as I was interested in learning about health NGOs as well as government and international health organizations. As it turned out, all of these types of health organizations operated in this barrio simultaneously. The third was the central barrio of one municipality, which made it different from the other two barrios since its people were residing in closer proximity to health and other government services, to a market, to public transportation, and to other services. The central barrio also had the greatest concentration of upper class families.

In the initial period of my research, I chose a representative sample of sixty-three households from the three barrios.[50] One family dropped out of the study due to the principle adults' unexpectedly increased workload. I conducted three sets of formal interviews with adults in each of the remaining households. The first set of questions were answered by either the principle man, woman, or both of the household. The second and third interviews were conducted only with the principle woman of the household, with the exceptions of the household whose principle adult was a single man and a small number of interviews that were conducted with the principle man also present.

I collected anthropometric measures of all members of each household in my research sample (as well as some Ifugao people who were not included in my sample but who wished to be measured) as one means of learning about their nutritional status. I collected three different measures from the same people at three month intervals to learn about seasonal variation in nutritional status.

I visited numerous government agencies, non-government agencies, and libraries at nearby universities, collecting locally printed materials and data from the media. The information I collected included historical information about Ifugao; local conditions and statistics on Ifugao Province; recent studies about Ifugao people related to gender, development, agriculture, and nutrition; political and economic information about the Philippines; and other topics.

For most of my research I was assisted by a full time Ifugao research assistant, who contributed to my research in innumerable ways. I also hired three part-time Ifugao research assistants to collect food recall lists for the members of the households in my research sample. The assistants and countless other Ifugao people contributed to this ethnography by offering their cultural insights and understanding.

Other than those interviews originally conducted in English, quotes included in this ethnography were translated by myself or a research assistant. Some grammatical changes in quotes derived from English language discussions were made to facilitate readability. Occasionally, discussions were paraphrased after a conversation where immediate notetaking was not feasible. I have tried to relate as much and as clearly as possible the intended meanings of the people with whom I spoke.

This ethnography and the following ideas are primarily my interpretations, observations, and study of malnutrition, gender, and development in Ifugao Province. They reflect my understanding of these issues when I left Ifugao in 1993. Being a European American woman from a western, industrialized country surely influenced my interpretations of gender relations in Ifugao society. This study, then, must represent only a "partial" truth (Clifford 1986:7) and only one view of the problem of malnutrition, gender, and development in Ifugao, of which there are certainly many more.

Struggling with Development

While I have provided in this chapter a brief portrayal of contemporary Ifugao society, in Chapter 2 I specify international and national processes and forces which have influenced both Ifugao society generally and malnutrition specifically. I assess historical, cultural, social, economic, political, and gendered processes in the Philippine nation in relation to malnutrition. I further discuss the Philippines' position in relation to other countries. I address how historical interactions (such as colonialism, trade, neocolonialism, the international division of labor, development, structural adjustment, etc.), in conjunction with national processes, have generated social inequality and influenced widespread malnutrition in the Philippines. Yet, these processes often were neglected by development organizations in their attempts to improve the economic and nutritional status of Ifugao people.

In Chapter 3 I present a glimpse of how Ifugao women experienced their daily lives, and how Ifugao gender roles and statuses were created and recreated by Ifugao people. I try to show how Ifugao women's gendered position was higher or lower than men's in different areas of their lives. This chapter provides a closer look at gender relations in Ifugao to better understand national health and international development programs' goals of improving Ifugao women's social position, as one aspect of their programs to alleviate malnutrition and other health problems among Ifugao people.

Chapter 4 contextualizes Ifugao people's lives within the violence and LIC with which they lived. Violence, colonization, and war have contributed in a variety of ways to problems of access to food for Ifugao people, thereby influencing their nutritional status. The current revolutionary war began, in part, as a strategy by lower class Filipinos to overcome extreme social inequality in the Philippines and unequal access to food and other resources (particularly land), each greatly influencing Ifugao people's nutritional status. Additionally, Philippine state policies of total war and low intensity conflict have had an impact on development programs, health care, and health care workers in Ifugao. In Ifugao, as elsewhere in the Philippines, both state military personnel and revolutionary soldiers attempted to use development and health care as a strategy of low intensity conflict. For example, the state military tried to repress health care workers who did not follow government sanctioned biomedical health care ideology.

Chapter 5 presents local and religious understandings of thinness, which are compared to the biomedical conception of malnutrition in the following chapter. Ifugao people used and created multiple forms and practices of healing and understandings of causes of illness. Christianity has penetrated Ifugao society and has introduced new forms of healing and ideas of illness causation, sometimes in line with biomedical theories. I discuss how the ill and hungry body has been used at times by both foreign and Ifugao Christians as a site of religious conversion or reinforcement of Christian ideologies.

In Chapter 6 I focus on biomedical constructions of malnutrition, women's understandings of and responses to the concept of malnutrition, and programs geared toward alleviating malnutrition. I also assess some of the micro-level family and community practices which operated in conjunction with larger macro-level processes to influence malnutrition. I discuss how women often found themselves at odds with biomedical programs, and the programs' definitions of and approaches to resolving malnutrition among children.

In Chapter 7 I address the cultural influence of development institutions on Ifugao women's social roles and value, comparing development and state agencies' discourse with their practices. I point out how attempts by development organizations in Ifugao to raise women's social position to enhance women and their children's nutritional and health status often resulted in reinforcement of women's lower status than men in some areas.

In spite of the limited benefits of development programs, the destructive impact of the western development paradigm on local cultures cannot be overestimated. In Ifugao this process occurred indirectly in conjunction with the Christianization of Ifugao people. As will be seen in Chapter 8, as well as in Chapter 5, western funded and oriented development practices and Christianity in Ifugao have slowly eroded and denigrated local ethnic ways of thinking and knowing, as well as local social and cultural organization and practices. This has included an erosion of local practices, such as ritual food sharing, that aided the Ifugao people (the poor especially) in maintaining a good nutritional status. But in Ifugao there has not been a total hegemony of western or Christian ideology. In the early 1990s there were often struggles and contradictions among different groups (i.e., government, international development, Christian, NGO, local Ifugao religion, and women) operating in Ifugao in response to the problem of malnutrition, making the development process more complex than development agents may have anticipated or understood it to be.

Notes

1. By "development" I am referring specifically to western based international (multilateral and bilateral) development programs. Development has involved the social construction of some countries as "developed" and others as "underdeveloped" societies to become economically, politically, and culturally similar to the "developed" countries. This involves the hegemony of ideologies of social evolution, scientific progress, the superiority of scientific technology, the need to become industrialized, etc. (Esteva 1992). In my use of

the terms "development" or "development programs," I am not referring to international emergency, disaster, or refugee relief aid.

2. Biomedical is used here to refer to the ethnomedical view and practices which use a concept of "Disease (which) refers to abnormalities in the structure and/or function of organs, pathological states whether or not they are culturally recognized" (Young 1982). It refers also to ethnomedical practices that participate in a cultural separation of the mind and body, nature and culture, and spirit and matter (Rhodes 1990:164; Scheper-Hughes and Lock 1987:8).

3. Power is understood here as a force that influences individuals or groups in particular directions.

4. Hegemony is a term that has been widely contested among social scientists, in part because Gramsci did not present a precise definition of the term in *The Prison Notebooks* (1971) (McKenna 1996; Comaroff and Comaroff 1991; and Anderson 1976). My use of "hegemony" follows the interpretation of anthropologists Jean and John Comaroff (1991), who stated that hegemony "refer[s] to that order of signs and practice, relations and distinctions, images and epistemologies—drawn from a historically situated cultural field—that come to be taken-for-granted as the natural and received shape of the world and everything that inhabits it. [Yet] hegemony is never total. . . . It is always threatened by the vitality that remains in the forms of life it thwarts. It follows, then, that the hegemonic is constantly being made—and, by the same token, may be unmade" (Comaroff and Comaroff 1991).

5. These figures include first, second, and third degree malnutrition, as well as nutrient deficiencies.

6. In October 1992 the nationally identified poverty level for a family of six in Ifugao was set at an annual income of 27,396 pesos (National Statistics Office, Republic of the Philippines 1992a).

7. The ten leading causes of mortality in the Philippines during the period 1985–1987 were (in rank order): pneumonia; diseases of the heart; tuberculosis, all forms; diseases of the vascular system; malignant neoplasms; diarrheal diseases; accidents; measles; avitaminoses and other nutritional deficiencies; and nephritis, nephrotic syndrome and nephrosis (UNICEF 1990b:31).

8. The Ifugao Provincial Nutrition Committee, 1991, Masterlist of High Risk and At Risk Families, Province of Ifugao. Unpublished report of the Ifugao Provincial Health Office, Lagawe, Ifugao.

9. I am not providing the names of these organizations due to the sensitive nature of the political situation surrounding these programs.

10. See De Castro 1952; Holmberg 1950; Richards 1948 [1932], 1939; Dubois 1944, 1941; Mead 1943; Evans-Pritchard 1940; and Malinowski 1939.

11. See Dettwyler 1994; Coreil and Mull 1988; Fishman, Evans, and Jenks 1988; Raphael 1988, 1985; Cassidy 1987, 1982; Laderman 1987, 1983; Lepowsky 1987; Pelto 1987; and Chen and Scrimshaw 1983.

12. See Dettwyler 1994; Oyeneye 1991; and Huston 1979.

13. See Scheper-Hughes 1992, 1984; Zaidi 1988; Brown, N. 1987; Cohen et al. 1985; Driver and Driver 1983; Luthra 1983; and Brown, S. 1975.

14. See also Ugalde 1985 and Marchione 1980.

15. For examples of studies analyzing hunger or malnutrition and gender, see St. Hilaire 1992; Morsy 1990; Browner 1989; Schoepf 1987; and Vaughan 1987.

16. See also Navarro 1985; Feder 1981; and Hartmann and Boyce 1979.

17. See Fishman, Evans, and Jenks 1988; Jelliffe and Jelliffe 1988; Laderman 1987, 1983; Lepowsky 1987; Pelto 1987; Ayers 1985; Raphael 1985; Black, Brown, and Becker 1983; Chen, Huq, and D'Souza 1980; and Solon 1979.

18. See Brun and Elling 1987; Lappe and Collins 1986; Cerqueira et al. 1985; Campbell 1984; Chossudovsky 1983; Bello, Kinley, and Elinson 1982; Bader 1981; Feder 1981; DeJanvry 1977; and George 1977.

19. For examples, see Scheper-Hughes 1992, 1987; Florencio 1989; Vaughan 1987; Watts 1983; Hartmann and Boyce 1979; and Taussig 1978.

20. These include topics such as intrahousehold allocation of resources in the Philippines based on birth order (Horton 1988); the influence of family income and family size on dietary intake (finding that reducing family size can be more effective than increasing household real income in preventing protein calorie malnutrition) (Magallanes 1984); cultural values and practices related to nutrition, such as breastfeeding (Tallo et al. 1979); and local practices such as the feeding of sugar to crying children, poor sanitary practices, carrying of babies most of the time, and little verbal stimulation (arguing that these influence both malnutrition and, relatedly, behavioral and mental development in Filipino children) (Guthrie et al. 1976).

21. There have been many studies of malnutrition, hunger, and health services in the Philippines that have contributed important findings to our understanding of malnutrition, including Dineros-Pineda 1992; Castaneda 1990; Florencio 1989; Brun and Elling 1987; Omawale 1984; Bello et al. 1982; Solon 1979; Balderrama et al. 1976; Bautista et al. 1974; and Bailey 1966.

22. See Scheper-Hughes 1992; Vaughan 1987; Bairagi 1986; Eide and Steady 1980; Rosenberg 1980; and George 1977.

23. Such as De Garine 1984.

24. Scheper-Hughes 1992.

25. See Fiag-oy 1988; Schoepf 1987; Schoepf and Schoepf 1987; Bairagi 1986; Eide and Steady 1980; Rosenberg 1980; and George 1977.

26. See Schramm Honculada 1988; Harris 1985; Raphael 1985; Campbell 1984; and Bader 1981.

27. See Bhuiya et al. 1989; Batliwala 1987; Miller 1987; Harris 1985; Chen et al. 1981; Rosenberg 1980; and Lindenbaum 1977.

28. See Bhuiya et al. 1989; Blau 1986; Caldwell 1986; Harris 1985; and Thomas 1981.

29. See Scheper-Hughes 1992, 1987; and De Garine 1984.

30. Peasants, while a highly contested concept, is used here to refer to families in which the characteristic unit of production is the peasant family household, and the predominant production engaged in is agriculture, either on their own small holding of land, communally owned land, or tenanted land. Peasants live in economies located within a territorial state, which extracts surplus from peasants, and while part of a larger economic system, are only partially engaged in market economies (Ellis 1988:12; Thorner 1987:66; Wolf 1966).

31. See Ghosh 1991; Bhuiya et al. 1989; Batliwala 1987; Miller 1987; Chen et al. 1981; and Rosenberg 1980.

32. See Tan 1991:67 and Senauer 1990:158.

33. See Batliwala 1987; Vaughan 1987; and Eide and Steady 1980.

34. For examples, see Vaughan 1987; Eide and Steady 1980; George 1977; Draper 1975; and Rubbo 1975.

35. See Lamperis 1991; Blau 1986; and Caldwell 1986.

36. One study which did look at the role of men on the nutritional status of their children is a study of the organization of home life in the Ciskei region of Africa. Disorganized homes (a "disorganized" home was one in which the father was absent due to migrant labor) in this region were found to have more severely malnourished children than those with present fathers of the same social class (Thomas 1981). Admittedly, women left to care for their children in their household without their spouses have a difficult and burdensome workload, again leaving primary responsibility for the daily nutritional welfare of their children to women. This study analyzed men's role in terms of men's absence, rather than in men's presence with their children.

37. Schoepf 1987; Vaughan 1987; and Eide and Steady 1980.

38. See Hobart 1993; Escobar 1992, 1991, 1988, 1987; Sachs 1992; St. Hilaire 1992; and Ileto 1988.

39. See Rubenstein and Lane 1990; Hill 1986; Justice 1986; Robertson 1984; Colson 1982; and Hoben 1980.

40. See Ghee 1988; Ileto 1988; Ong 1987; Scott 1985; Bello et al. 1982; Agpalo 1973; Evers 1973a; and Jocano 1973.

41. See Escobar 1991 and Taussig 1978.

42. Multilateral aid refers to aid donated by two or more states to another state (such as aid donated through the World Bank). Bilateral aid refers to aid donated from one state to another state.

43. The World Bank is composed of the International Bank for Reconstruction and Development (IBRD) and its affiliate the International Development Association (IDA). During the early 1990s, the Bank had 159 member countries; but it was dominated by the United States, which held the largest block of shares of the member countries. It was also dominated more comprehensively by the industrialized countries as a bloc.

44. Although historically it can be seen that the political interests of western states, particularly the United States, often led to the support of non-democratic state structures (e.g., U.S. support of Marcos in the Philippines and U.S. support of Samoza in Nicaragua).

45. Esther Boserup, *Women's Role in Economic Development* (New York: St. Martin's Press, 1970).

46. For example, see Moser 1992; Ostergaard 1992a, 1992b; Whitehead 1991; Tinker 1990a, 1990b; AID 1989; Agarwal 1988; Schrijvers 1988; Beneria and Sen 1982; and Young et al. 1981. Gender and development literature generally has covered issues such as work; intrahousehold allocation of food and other resources; health and nutrition; the household and its relation to wider economic and political structures; women's status; violence; religion; social class; housing; access to credit, technology, and other resources for income activities; differential wages; work in transnational factories; societal and household patriarchy; and the persistence of gender inequality.

47. See Ostergaard 1992a, 1992b; Whitehead and Bloom 1992; Young 1992; and Schrijvers 1988.

48. See St. Hilaire 1992; Mohanty 1991a, 1991b; Bourque and Warren 1990; Tinker 1990a, 1990b; Shiva 1988; Justice 1986; and Mueller 1986.

49. For an excellent example of this, see Scheper-Hughes 1992.

50. The factors I considered in choosing these households were their economic status; marital status; presence of children; age of the principle adults of the household; history of children's nutritional status in the household (obtained from local government health clinic

records); and location of the home. I used a wealth ranking procedure from Barbara E. Grandin's book, *Wealth Ranking in Smallholder Communities: A Field Manual* (Rugby: Intermediate Technology Publications, 1988), to locate the households' economic statuses. This procedure involved the participation of residents in defining local concepts of economic status and then ranking the households within their communities (approximately limited to 100 or less households). I attempted to choose the number of households from each of three social classes to be proportional to that of Ifugao Province as a whole.

2

Developing Hunger in the Philippines

Hunger and the high rate of malnutrition within the Filipino population has been the embodiment of historically developed international and national social power imbalances and inequality. This chapter draws a brief picture of the historical, social production of malnutrition in the Philippines generally, thereby situating the problem of hunger and malnutrition among Ifugao people within the larger, political economic world of which they are a part. I analyze the historical relationship between economic and power dynamics, both within and outside of the Philippine body politic, and the nutritional status of people inhabiting the Philippine islands to the early 1990s.

A central premise of this study is that widespread malnutrition in the Philippines in the early 1990s was due primarily to historically developed political and economic relations that created extreme social class inequality and unequal access to basic food resources, land, employment, and health services. Hunger in the Philippines cannot be understood apart from the dynamic historical processes of colonization, neocolonization, and international development practices, as well as internal power and economic relations, all of which resulted in widespread social inequality, poverty, and malnutrition.

These historical processes also led to an institutionalization of unbalanced relationships between the Philippine state and other nations. Reliance on wealthier, industrialized states was furthered through Philippine indebtedness to international credit institutions (such as the IMF and the World Bank) and through continued intervention of these organizations by means of structural adjustment programs (Montes 1992a, 1992b; Broad 1988; Bello et al. 1982). This imbalance inhibited attempts by the Philippine government to industrialize its society through foreign loans and assistance and to raise the living standard of the majority of Filipino people.

Equally important have been the dynamic processes of socioeconomic inequality internal to the Philippines, perpetuated by elites and an elite-ruled democratic Philippine government, in conjunction with other powerful states such as the United States, Europe, and Japan. Social inequality perpetuated by Filipino elites has included starkly unequal landownership patterns, reinforced by the government's neglect to implement a genuine agrarian reform program to benefit the majority of small landowning and landless peasants (Putzel 1992; Hayami et al. 1990).[1]

During the early 1990s, the Philippine government, a relatively small number of Filipino elites, and foreign businesspersons owned or controlled a disproportionately large share of Philippine resources. At the same time, almost half—at least 44.5 percent—of the Filipino people lived below the poverty level.[2] During 1991 the richest 20 percent of the Philippine population's share of national income was 54.6 percent, while the poorest 40 percent of the population's share was 13 percent. The bottom 20 percent of the population's share was only 4.7 percent (Tan 1995:7).[3] This situation has translated into differential access to basic resources among members of the Philippine social classes, including access to food and agricultural land. Unequal access to food had a significant impact on the nutritional status of the poor, who constituted a high percentage of the population.

Philippine Political Economy
and the Historical Development of Hunger

Widespread malnutrition in the Philippines was primarily the result of historical policies of international and national economic development and political and economic exploitation. Prior to Spanish colonization, which began in 1565, there had been no overall state organization linking all of the ethnic groups residing on the islands now comprising the Philippine nation, although some cohesiveness did exist among these groups through a well-developed system of trade and loose political compacts (Schirmer and Shalom 1987:1). There were, however, small incipient Muslim states, mainly in the southern islands of the Philippines. Muslims were expanding to the northern islands as well. Muslims had approached the islands by sea and had begun the process of conversion of indigenous people just prior to the Spanish arrival. At the time of the Spanish arrival, social and economic relations among most groups were based primarily on kinship and systems of social rank. The primary subsistence activities of the various groups included agricultural production, particularly the growing of dry rice and root crops, foraging, hunting, fishing, and local and foreign trade. Some land was owned by kin groups; other land was owned communally by members of local groups. Food was often shared among kin groups and among community members during ritual ceremonies. The method of agricultural food production used most widely was swidden (forest slash and burn) agriculture. The gathering of coastal zone and forest foods, as well as root crops, provided some insurance against hunger if harvests were not bountiful. A few groups relied primarily on hunting and gathering for their food supply. Small and large scale warfare was practiced within and between the ethnic groups.

Health practices among most groups were based historically on animistic and naturalistic beliefs, whereby illness was understood to be caused by displeased gods, spirits, ancestors, and powerful humans, or by organic causes. The propitiation of spirits or ancestors with offerings of food and prayers, and the use of natural herbal medicines and physically based curative techniques (such as massage or bone setting), were common methods of curing illness. Although undocumented, occasional hunger during the precolonial period probably was associated with crisis periods of local famine due to natural catastrophes (e.g., typhoons, volcanic eruptions, pest infestations such as locusts, and earthquakes), warfare, and diseases which attacked humans and draft animals (Owen 1987:108).

Spanish colonizers altered most ethnic groups' institutional, cultural, and social relations, many of which had provided some insurance against hunger. The Spanish gradually began to centralize control over the ethnic groups after establishing a central base in the lowland areas. New power relations, created through Spanish military force and by Catholic priests, influenced food accumulation, production, and access. The usurpation of food surplus by the colonizers was a significant factor in maintaining colonial rule. The Catholic mission system and Spanish administration imposed friar estate and hacienda systems of land control, concentrating populations under their control into towns and estates.

New ways of owning property were introduced by the Spanish, setting the stage for feudal landownership. Included were new forms of land tenure and new forms of political control. Historically, in addition to charisma, spiritual qualities, bravery, and oratorical and mediation skills, power for indigenous leaders was based on control of people rather than control of land. This was due to a small population relative to an abundance of land, shifting cultivation practices, and dispersed village settlements. Indigenous sovereignty over land and resources and the power of local leaders was reduced dramatically under the Spanish. Tributes were collected and the labor of indigenous people was forced and taxed, so that families had less control over and access to food resources and livelihood activities.

These colonizing techniques began a process of impoverishing indigenous people and eroding their agricultural subsistence base. Cash cropping was instituted during the Spanish colonial period, particularly of sugar and tobacco, and the Spanish extrapolated Philippine resources on a large scale. It is likely that the nutritional status of some indigenous people declined during the colonial period, due to the combined loss of their sovereignty over land and resources, and the colonial system's general stabilization of real income at a level just high enough to permit survival, reproduction, and labor (Owen 1987:15).

The Spanish used warfare and Catholic indoctrination and conversion to pacify indigenous people. Spanish atrocities included killing, imprisonment, usurpation of land and resources, and sexual abuse of women. Resistance to Spanish colonization was constant throughout the colonial period, and it was also directed against emerging indigenous elites who had been coopted by Spanish colonizers. In the Cordillera region of Northern Luzon, including Ifugao, resistance to the Spanish had been particularly strong and was successful for almost three hundred years. However, parts of these areas also fell under Spanish control by the mid to late nineteenth century (Jenista 1987). Indigenous resistance to the Spanish included popular uprisings among colonized peasants throughout the islands and aggressive attacks by some groups, including the Ifugao, to prevent occupation by the Spanish.

Spanish colonialism influenced the development of an indigenous elite in the Philippines and dynastic families. Spanish officials created a system of colonial administration whereby indigenous leaders were accorded formal power over villages and larger administrative units. The Spanish also expedited indigenous people's incorporation into the world economy. Agriculture was more fully commercialized by the nineteenth century, a time coinciding with the emergence of a national political elite (McCoy 1993:438). Chinese mestizos, benefitting from the emerging cash economy, began to accumulate land and other resources and were significant in the historical development of elite landed and entrepreneurial families and powerful political leaders in the Philippines (Sidel 1993:110).

Local resistance led by Jose Rizal, Andres Bonifacio, and, later, Emilio Aguinaldo coalesced into the national Philippine Revolution of 1896 against the Spanish (Schirmer and Shalom 1987:1). With the aid of the U.S. Army, the Filipino people finally defeated the Spanish in 1898. Soon after the victory over the Spanish, the Filipino people were once again colonized, this time by the United States, a process beginning in 1898 and ending in 1946. The victory over the Spanish in the Philippines had been concurrent with the U.S. triumph over the Spanish in Cuba, military successes finalized with the signing of the Treaty of Paris which removed Spain's control over its colonies (Schirmer and Shalom 1987:1). Following the joint victory over the Spanish colonizers, the U.S. government reneged on its promise of independence to the Filipino people. The United States achieved colonization in 1901 by force, following three years of war against vigorous Filipino resistance, though fighting continued for at least another year.

There were a number of reasons for the U.S. colonization of the Philippines. At the turn of the century, the U.S. government was seeking to expand its foreign markets and trade for its manufactured goods. It was also attempting to establish greater global military and political power by creating colonial bases throughout the world, including the Philippines (Schirmer and Shalom 1987:6). The U.S. government was also seeking sources of raw materials for U.S. industry and to secure a position from which to exploit Chinese markets. Other reasons given by the U.S. government were racist ideologies of the imperative to civilize and Christianize Filipino people (Schirmer and Shalom 1987:7). These aims were sought both forcibly through militarization and subtly through development efforts, religious instruction, and the establishment of western-style political and educational systems.

In part, the United States altered the social organization of the Philippines through a new system of land titling—the Torrens system—whereby provincial Filipino elites expanded their private property. As a result of this system, tenancy became more widespread during the U.S. colonial period, coming at the expense of small landowning peasants (Hayami et al. 1990:37-8). Throughout this period, political and economic relationships created between Filipino elite landowners and the U.S. government and businesses resulted in the transition of a larger portion of agricultural lands from subsistence production to commodity production. Also, initially, the only persons allowed to vote and hold office under the American political system were men literate in Spanish or English, who owned enough land to pay substantial property taxes, and who formerly held office under Spanish colonial rule (Fegan 1993:53).

With the Payne-Aldrich Act of 1909, the United States established an economic system whereby U.S. citizens enjoyed full rights to all Philippine resources. The Payne-Aldrich Act also allowed for free trade between the United States and the Philippines, which primarily benefitted U.S. business and wealthy Filipino landowners, whose wealth increased with the sale of cash crops in tariff-free U.S. markets (Schirmer and Shalom 1987:36). In the drive by landowners to increase profits on export oriented cash crops, the free-trade policy also reinforced unequal landownership patterns and systems of exploitation against tenants. Poor living conditions of tenant farmers working on plantations and exploitative employment practices led to peasant unrest and periodic uprisings, as well as labor strikes in the 1920s and 1930s (Schirmer and Shalom 1987:37).

While the commoditization of agriculture benefitted elite Filipino landowners and U.S. agribusiness, it simultaneously impoverished many small farmers, primarily in the lowland areas. Much land previously cultivated to produce subsistence food for a rapidly growing population was instead used to generate profit by Filipino elite landowners or American agribusiness. Many of the tenant farmers gradually became heavily reliant on cash to purchase highly priced food, were often indebted, and had little choice but to work for plantation landlords since all or much of their land had been taken from them or their families. Agribusiness, however, did not penetrate into all areas of the country, and many farmers still owned small tracts of land, particularly in upland areas such as Ifugao.

The Philippines was increasingly integrated into the world market economy through U.S. business and trade, although historically people indigenous to the Philippines had traded with other Asian and European nations for centuries. In order to create Philippine dependence on the United States, colonial policy at the turn of the century encouraged the positioning of the United States as a market for Philippine export goods and a source of manufactured goods and investment capital (Schirmer 1987).

The majority of Filipino people gained little from their national resources. Under U.S. rule, the cash crop economy became more heavily reliant on the U.S. market. Not only were small farmers losing their right to own land, through usurpation by Filipino elites or U.S. agribusiness, but the Philippines as a whole was losing its agricultural subsistence base. Poverty and hunger increased and became more widespread, generating peasant and worker resistance activities and movements, some of which were led by the socialist and communist parties formed in 1929 and 1930 respectively (Schirmer and Shalom 1987:62). These movements were particularly strong in Central Luzon, an area having some of the highest tenancy rates in the country.

Under the presidency of Franklin Delano Roosevelt, the Tydings-McDuffie Act was passed in 1934, granting the Philippines independence after a ten-year transition period of Commonwealth status (Schirmer and Shalom 1987:37). In part, independence was formalized due to pressure from American interests—including sugar interests, the dairy industry, and the labor sector—which felt threatened by competition with Philippine imports. In addition to this pressure, the creation of the Philippines as a neocolony had been a U.S. government objective since the early 1900s (Tanada 1987). While the Philippines became a politically sovereign nation in 1946, following the joint U.S.-Philippine armies' defeat of the Japanese on the islands during World War II, the nation remained heavily economically dependent on the United States, particularly on U.S. investments, loans, manufactured goods, and the U.S. market.[4]

Economic development of the nation slowed, due in part to the continued expropriation of resources from the country by U.S. business. The U.S. government had ensured the continuation of American access to Philippine resources, labor, and industry after independence by implementing the Bell Trade Act and the Parity Amendment to the Philippine Constitution. The Bell Trade Act allowed American goods to enter the Philippines without quotas for eight years, then gradually increasing in tariff until 1973 when the full duty would be paid. On the other hand, Philippine export products would be subjected to quota upon entering the United States (Schirmer and Shalom 1987:88; Aspillera 1986:35). The Bell Trade Act also forbade Filipino businesspersons to export their major products (sugar, copra, timber, abaca, etc.) to countries other than the United States, despite offers of higher buying prices (Diokno 1987). The Bell Trade Act led to an upsurge in the number of U.S. multinationals established in the Philippines after 1946 (Aspillera 1986:36).

The acceptance of the Bell Trade Act in 1946 by the Philippine government was due in part to the U.S. government's tying of full development or rehabilitation aid for the Philippine government to the acceptance of the parity provision of the Act (Schirmer and Shalom 1987:90). This case provides one example of how development aid and economic advantage were used as strategies to achieve political and economic ends for U.S. government and business interests, to the detriment of the social welfare of the majority of the Filipino people, including, ultimately, their nutritional well-being. One interpretation of this Act was that it resulted in export cash crop expansion during this period, which contributed to the growing inability of the Philippines to become self-sufficient in staple foods and thus to greater hunger.

Nine years later, in 1955, the Laurel-Langley Agreement between the Philippine and U.S. governments reduced some of the imbalances established by the Bell Trade Act. It simultaneously extended, however, U.S. economic benefits by guaranteeing U.S. investors equal treatment with Filipinos in all areas of the economy, no longer limited to natural resources and public utilities (Schirmer and Shalom 1987:95). The U.S. naval and air bases in the Philippines were also to be retained until 1992, when they were finally removed by the Philippine Congress.

A peasant movement began during the 1920s in resistance to a continued unequal landownership system and repression under the colonial U.S. government, which generated widespread poverty and hunger. The movement involved small uprisings and incidents of peasant resistance and anger (Kerkvliet 1977). The *Hukbo ng Bayan Laban sa Hapon* (or simply *Huk*), or the Army of Resistance Against Japan movement, stemming from the earlier peasant movement, blossomed during World War II. The *Huks* fought against the Japanese invasion and occupation of the Philippines. The *Huks* were formally organized in 1942 in the Central Plain of Northern Luzon by various guerrilla bands, including the merged Communist Party and Socialist Party. Some *Huk* peasant soldiers had learned guerrilla warfare techniques through books from Chinese communist groups prior to the war. The formal organization of the *Huks* followed a victory over a Japanese military group by communist guerrillas (Lachica 1971). They cooperated with the United States Armed Forces in the Far East in the resistance against Japan.

By the end of the Second World War, the American colonial government and the Filipino elite feared any mass movement among the peasantry that may threaten their control over the nation's resources or that may have communist leanings. In spite of the *Huks'* assistance to the Philippine and U.S. governments during World War II, both governments betrayed the *Huks* after the war. The Philippine army, under Secretary of National Defense Ramon Magsaysay, and with the support of the U.S. Military Advisory Group and the Central Intelligence Agency (CIA), waged a military campaign against the *Huks* (Rosaldo 1980:164).

After the Philippines gained independence from the United States in 1946, the *Huks*, under communist leadership and socialist influence, attempted to seize national power as the renamed *Hukbong Magpapalaya ng Bayan*, or People's Liberation Army. In 1948 the *Huks* led a mass peasant rebellion against the Philippine government. Social injustice, increasing inequity of landownership, disparity between the small upper class and the larger lower classes, poverty, and chronic hunger, as well as the Philippine and U.S. governments' military campaign against them, all served as catalysts for the 1948 rebellion (Bello et al. 1982: 8).

The newly proclaimed Philippine Republic was experiencing monetary crisis, graft in high office, and mounting peasant unrest (Lachica 1971). The new postcolonial Philippine state had emerged as a "weak state" with elite political families exerting increased economic and political power in the provinces (McCoy 1993). During the 1948–1953 revolt, the *Huks* demanded land reform. The *Huk* rebellion was one of the largest instances of agrarian unrest in modern Philippine society (Kerkvliet 1977). The power of the *Huk* movement dissipated by the mid-1950s, having been defeated militarily by the Philippine and U.S. governments and politically undermined by increased state social development in the 1950s.

Still, the peasant movement remained intact and committed to the struggle for social reform. The *Huk* movement inspired members to pursue new forms of resistance, including the New Peoples Army (NPA), beginning in 1969.

By the 1960s, World Bank and IMF activity in the Philippines greatly expanded, as it had in other poor countries at that time. The IMF was able to promote its model of export-led growth through conditions attached to its loans (Broad 1988:30). These conditions usually required trading terms which were favorable to industrialized lending countries' business and political interests. The Philippines' previous economic strategy of import substitution had been failing as a path to industrialization, due to the limited domestic market influenced by the unequal class structure. U.S. economic intervention during this period was even greater, particularly through multilateral institutions such as the World Bank and IMF. There was also greater intervention of other foreign countries in the Philippines.

Poverty increased in the Philippines from the 1950s to the early 1970s, and poor families experienced increasing difficulty in meeting their nutritional requirements. Agricultural production was in crisis and the industrial sector stagnated during this period. Over two decades, the national income share of the lowest 20 percent of families had declined significantly in the rural areas, from 7 percent in 1956 to 4.4 percent in 1971. At the same time, the share of the top 20 percent of rural families increased from its already high level of 46.1 percent in 1956 to 51 percent in 1971 (International Labour Office 1974).

Ferdinand Marcos was elected president in 1965. Marcos welcomed IMF and World Bank loans and aid during his presidency. Marcos and his elite cronies accumulated exorbitant wealth from the Philippine government, mainly through corrupt and violent practices.[5] The Marcos regime was powerful, generating widespread resistance among the exploited and poverty stricken masses, and among some middle and upper class members whose interests were not being served by the Marcos regime and whose power Marcos was trying to restrain.

Marcos declared martial law in 1972, through which he was able to control opposition from a number of sources, including a growing resistance movement led by the National Democratic Front (NDF, a national umbrella organization that included the Communist Party of the Philippines [CPP] and the armed NPA), nationalist business elites angered by the elimination of their congressional representation, and the labor sector disaffected by the outlawing of union organizations.[6] Each of these groups were detrimentally affected by and opposed to increased IMF and World Bank policies. Martial law thus enabled the opening up of the Philippine economy to greater inflow of foreign capital and commodities (Bello et al. 1982:23).

The World Bank hailed Marcos' repression of political freedoms through martial law as providing "a positive climate for foreign investment" (Hildebrand 1991:9). The martial law ruling was followed by greatly increased World Bank and IMF lending in 1972–1974.[7] Also following the implementation of martial law, Marcos agreed to a commercial treaty with Japan, which the nationalist Philippine Congress had long opposed. The Asian Development Bank, along with various European and other countries, were also investing in and lending to the Philippines during this period.

The overall plan of the World Bank in the Philippines during the 1970s included lending for rural development to increase agricultural production, industrialization emphasizing labor intensive export manufacturing (with the strong participation of foreign capital), continued opening up of the economy, and lending for energy and infrastructure development (Bello et al. 1982:24). The World Bank had fostered a top-down development approach in many areas of Filipino economic life during that period, often oriented away from domestic needs or the needs of small farmers (Bello et al. 1982:xi).

Marcos supported the retention of the U.S. bases, which gave the United States additional leverage in economic and political policymaking in the Philippines. The United States supplied military aid, advice, and trainers to the Armed Forces of the Philippines under Marcos, assisting him in the state's campaign against the resistance movement and Marcos' opponents, despite numerous reports of human rights abuses committed by the police and military.

The IMF, World Bank, and other international credit institutions' interventions led to the further enrichment of Marcos and his cronies. In 1970, an estimated 5 percent of the population controlled 25 percent of the national income. Benefits of the program did not trickle down to the majority of Filipinos.

Agrarian Reform, Social Inequality, and Hunger

Agrarian reform had been given lip-service by the Philippine government for decades, but it was never successfully implemented. Philippine government land reform programs had their beginnings with the American colonial administration, which attempted to redress the Spanish colonial feudal land system and to alleviate peasant unrest stemming from the unequal landownership pattern. President Manuel L. Quezon, the first Philippine president during the Commonwealth period (1935–1939), was strongly influenced by U.S. land reform policies. President Quezon's agrarian reform program was initiated in response to rural unrest, due to social class confrontations in the rural sector. Historically, agrarian reform in the Philippines has been promoted during periods of political crisis when the powerful elite needed the support of the peasant sector (Hayami et al. 1990:4).

Agrarian reform programs in the Philippines historically have been limited to redistribution of tenanted lands and regulations on tenancy contracts, which severely limited the extent of agrarian reform (Hayami et al. 1990:6). Further agrarian reform programs were implemented following independence and prior to the Presidency of Ferdinand Marcos (1965–1986), one of which was prompted by the U.S. government, following a peasant uprising and U.S. involvement in the Cold War. None of these attempts at agrarian reform had a substantial impact on agricultural landownership patterns.

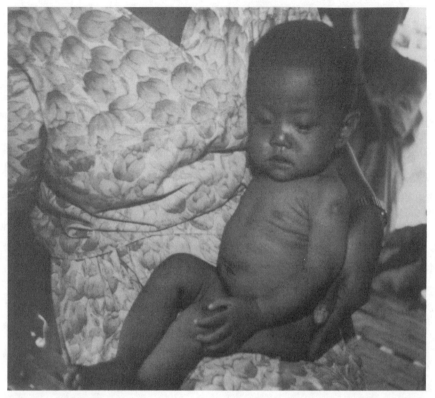

PHOTO 2.1 This Ifugao girl is severely malnourished. She had recently received a vaccination on her arm.

By the beginning of the 1970s the Philippines had one of the highest land tenancy rates in Southeast Asia (Bello et al. 1982: 69). Tenant sharecroppers were exploited by landowners, and often victimized by usurers, with irrigation fees usually controlled by the landed rural elites. Many peasant farmers thus were faced with inequitable control over land, credit, and irrigation facilities.

Marcos' land reform program under Proclamation 27, which began soon after martial law was declared in 1972, was never structured to fully redistribute the land. For instance, it only applied to 13.7 percent of the country's farm land, exempting many categories of land (McAfee 1985). Also, peasants who were illiterate, or who did not speak English or the national Filipino language, were at a great disadvantage when confronting government land reform legislation and program policies. Marcos' land reform program under martial law actually was aimed primarily at legitimizing the new political order ("The New Society"), as well as destroying the power held by the traditional landed elite, thereby centralizing power under Marcos' control (Hayami et al. 1990:81). Neither Marcos nor the IMF and World Bank were committed to the redistribution of land to the poor. At the end of implementation of the Marcos land reform program, only about 1,700 tenants received ownership of small tracts of land (Bello et al. 1982). James Putzel conservatively estimates that by 1985 approximately 56 percent of 3.9 million households dependent on agricultural income still had little or no land.[8] By the last year of his presidency, Marcos' land reform program had failed, with no real increases in food consumption for poor landless families. By the mid-1980s, government surveys reported that 69 percent of all Filipino children were underweight for their age, and that the average Filipino diet provided insufficient amounts of all nutrients except niacin (McAfee 1985).

An agrarian reform program that would redistribute land to genuinely benefit the poor still had not been implemented by the early 1990s. Following President Aquino's election into office in 1986, after the exile of President Marcos, the new 1987 Constitution guaranteed the implementation of an agrarian reform program by the Philippine government. President Aquino passed two executive orders (EO131 and EO229), reinforcing her commitment to agrarian reform and outlining a conservative approach to the implementation of agrarian reform. She did not actually launch the program, however, turning that task over to the newly constituted Congress. In 1988 the "pro-landlord" Philippine Congress passed Republic Act (RA) 6657, the Comprehensive Agrarian Reform Law (CARL), which determined the phasing of the program, priority areas, land retention limits, and land exemptions (Nieva 1993b:1; Putzel 1992:247; Hayami et al. 1990:71).

By 1993, the 1988 agrarian reform program was viewed by Philippine peasant groups as being inadequate to achieve genuine agrarian reform. Twelve farmer federations joined to form a national coalition, the Congress for a People's Agrarian Reform (CPAR). CPAR formulated an alternative agrarian reform proposal, the People's Agrarian Reform Code, which specified the problem areas of RA 6657 (Hayami et al. 1990:71). Some peasant groups implemented this proposal, or a form similar to it, at the community level; and peasant groups continued to lobby for amendments to RA 6657, advocating far greater redistributive measures (Hayami et al. 1990:53, 77).

After five years of RA 6657 implementation, landlessness still was pervasive in the Philippines. The average size of land owned by small peasant landowners was only about 1.5 hectares per family. In some areas, such as Ifugao, the size of owned irrigated rice fields averaged only about one quarter of a hectare. Even in areas where there was no agribusiness in the Philippines, landlessness was common. RA 6657 did not actually provide for a comprehensive redistribution of agricultural lands for many reasons. Putzel argued that by 1992 the basic structures of property relations and agricultural production had not been altered by RA 6657 (Putzel 1992:362).[9]

Development, International Loans,
and Structural Adjustment

The World Bank in the early 1970s promoted a technocratic model of rural development, blaming small farmholders' backward technology and low productivity for the crisis in agricultural production in the Philippines. Between 1960 and 1972, rice imports, the staple crop of the Filipino people, rose from $2 million to $34 million, as the agricultural sector was unable to meet the population's basic food needs (Bello et al. 1982:68).

In 1974 World Bank programs emphasized increasing the productivity of the poor, thereby providing for an equitable sharing in the benefits of growth, rather than emphasizing the redistribution of income, land, and resources (Bello et al. 1982:70). The problem of poverty was to be solved by increasing the production of small and large landowners through technological fixes, rather than by increasing small landowners or landless farmers' access to land and other resources.

A joint international-national rural development program to increase food productivity, establish greater social equity, and reduce hunger on a national scale was Masagana 99 (M99). M99 was instituted during the 1970s by the Marcos government and the World Bank as part of the worldwide "Green Revolution."[10] The World Bank's technological answer to low agricultural productivity, M99 was essentially a credit program for small farmers to enable them to purchase highly technical agricultural inputs, especially for rice production, to increase productivity.

M99 failed because of several factors, including the fact that the poorest small holders were never included in the program. At the height of the program in 1974, only 36 percent of all small rice farmers were participating in the program. The cost of the rice technology was extremely high, and yields for small farmers would not generate enough income to repay the loans. Indebtedness to rural banks was widespread. Also, the use of high yielding rice varieties resulted in the loss of soil fertility through the required application of petroleum based fertilizers (Bello et al. 1982:70).

The effects of M99 and other rural credit programs drove thousands of peasants into financial bankruptcy and ruin the fertility of their soil. The program likely had a negative effect on the nutritional status of poor families who participated in the program. Through the M99 program, the former dependency on rice imports had been changed to national dependence on Green Revolution agricultural inputs (seeds, fertilizers, etc.), mainly sold by western businesses.

Large agribusiness and large landowners, who had no difficulty obtaining financial capital, did benefit from the program. They produced greater quantities of rice than was previously possible, and the Philippines did export rice from 1977 through 1983. But by the mid-1980s the Philippines again was importing rice. In

1991 the Philippines exported rice, but the following year it imported rice due to drought and the late planting of the crop (*Philippine Daily Inquirer* 1992i:15).

By 1980 over 45 percent of the country's 10 million hectares of cultivatable land was planted in export crops such as pineapples, sugar, coconut, bananas, and rubber and palm oil trees (Bello et al. 1982). While Philippine agribusiness was exporting cash crops, the country was importing foods that could have been grown within the Philippines. This trade practice was also related to import liberalization policies imposed by the World Bank and IMF, benefitting U.S. and Filipino agribusiness. These policies had an adverse impact on the nutritional status of many poor families, since the increase in the land devoted to cash crop production resulted in less land available for food crops to feed the growing population. Also, employment opportunities were becoming scarce for the rapidly growing population. With only minimal wages paid for agricultural labor, a very small industrial sector concentrated in urban areas and export processing zones, and increasing inflation, unemployment, and food prices, poor Filipino people experienced great difficulty meeting their full nutritional needs.

By the late 1970s the World Bank began to change its development strategies. It moved from a practice of specific development projects lending (such as M99, or loans for dams or irrigation systems) toward broader sectoral or multisectoral economy wide lending, which was accompanied by macroeconomic conditions imposed on the recipient country (Broad 1988:xx). This approach, related to debt negotiating, had been usually implemented by the IMF until that time.

More recent World Bank structural adjustment loans and apex loans were geared toward solving the external debt crisis of poor countries and achieving "adjustment with growth."[11] Structural adjustment loans were designed to accelerate industrial growth, invigorate the agricultural sector, increase employment, and expand rapid growth of nontraditional exports (Gladwin 1993:88; Broad 1988:81). Structural adjustment was a response to the new international division of labor, wherein poor countries were moving toward industrialization, and to the global recession in the early 1980s (Gladwin 1993:88). The practice of attaching conditions to loans allowed the World Bank to designate national policy adjustments to recipient countries, as the IMF previously had done. The World Bank only awarded its multimillion dollar loans after the adjustments were initiated (Broad 1988:51).

By the late 1970s, the Philippines, like many other poor countries, had accumulated enormous debts acquired from private banks, and bilateral and multilateral sources. The large external debts of poor countries accorded the IMF greater power to intervene in their national policymaking since, in order for debt ridden countries to obtain additional loans from private banks, it had become almost a requirement to obtain an IMF "certificate of good standing" (Broad 1988:54).

As noted earlier, the Marcos period ended in 1986, following the 1983 assassination of exiled political leader Benigno Aquino, the election of his wife, Corazon Aquino, to presidential office, and the *Epifanio de los Santos* Avenue

(EDSA) People's Power "Revolution." Marcos left the Philippine nation economically devastated, and few improvements in the nutritional status of the population
as a whole could be observed. Corazon Aquino remained in office until 1992.
During her administration, the economic situation of the country and Filipino
people did not improve significantly, although there were some positive changes
in the political sphere.

President Fidel Ramos was elected into office in May 1992. President Ramos
had been Chief of the Philippine Constabulary and later a four-star general during
the Marcos era. Ramos was serving as Marcos' Chief of Staff when he and Defense
Minister Juan Ponce Enrile abandoned Marcos on February 22, 1986, to join forces
with the Philippine people's power "revolution" and the newly elected President
Corazon Aquino. Marcos had refused to accept Aquino's victory and had declared
that he was actually the winner of the 1986 presidential election. During the
Aquino administration, Ramos served as the head of the Department of National
Defense. He ran as a member of the *Partido Lakas Tao* (People Power Party),
which he founded during the 1992 presidential election as a conservative political
party.

The Aquino government accepted new IMF-World Bank loan packages and
other foreign loans and aid, allowing foreign lenders to continue to influence
planning and managing the Philippine economy through conditions attached to the
loans. Over a six-year period (1986–1991), the Aquino government accepted $4.4
billion in official development assistance (IBON 1992b:3). The Ramos government later continued to negotiate for further World Bank and IMF loans. Following
a March 1992 meeting of thirty-three foreign governments and international
financial institutions reviewing Philippine economic progress, an explicit message
was delivered to the Philippines: continued inflows of foreign loans and grants into
the Philippines are tied to a more liberalized economy (Chipongian 1992b:18).

Although borrowing slowed from 1987 to 1992, by June 1993 the Philippine
external debt reached U.S.$31.95 billion, up from U.S.$26 billion at the end of
1985 (*Philippine Daily Inquirer* 1992c:12; Esplanada 1993c:9). In 1992, 37 percent
of the annual Philippine government budget financed the external debt (IBON
1992c:3). In July 1992 President Ramos approved a U.S.$4.8 billion debt relief
package, previously negotiated by the Aquino administration with foreign banks.
The package was designed to reduce foreign debts by about U.S.$1.2 billion over
a six-year period and to allow a longer repayment period for about U.S.$3 billion
of commercial debts, with lower interest (Capco 1992a:1). The Freedom from Debt
Coalition filed a court suit to stop the Ramos administration from signing the debt
relief package, arguing that it would not effectively resolve the debt problem, but
to no avail (Capco 1992c:1).

Much of the debt payments had been paid for by remittances of overseas
contract workers, which totaled U.S.$5.8 billion from 1986 to 1991 (IBON
1992b:3). Many of the overseas workers who were funding external debt payments
were women, working as nurses and low-paid domestic servants, factory workers,

janitors, entertainers, and prostitutes. They joined the ranks of overseas workers due to high unemployment and underemployment and low wages earned in the Philippines. Most continue to send money to their families remaining at home.

By 1993 President Ramos was attempting to bring the Philippines to the status of a Newly Industrialized Country (NIC) by the year 2000, in part through programs such as foreign exchange reforms, changes in the banking system, tariff reductions, privatization, and infrastructure improvements (*Philippine Daily Inquirer* 1993e:1).

Food Production in the Philippines

As shown earlier, cash cropping increasingly replaced basic food crops grown in the Philippines, thereby reducing people's access to basic foods. Other factors related to food production and supply impeded the provision of an adequate supply of nutritious food for Filipinos and further weakened the Philippine economy. In compliance with World Bank and IMF mandates in the late 1980s, President Aquino continued import liberalization policies, including food imports. Food allowed free entry into the Philippines included rice, wheat, fish, sugarcane vinegar, chicken, and hundreds of other food items, many of which were produced in the Philippines (Constantino and Constantino 1988:33).

Cheaper imports can cause depression in prices of locally produced and harvested food products. Also, the increased role of transnational corporations (TNC) in food industry resulted in profits being exported out of the country, with smaller Filipino food industry entrepreneurs losing competitive ground to the TNCs. While Filipino people were experiencing widespread protein deficiency, fish and meat were being exported out of the country through foreign and locally owned businesses (Constantino and Constantino 1988:36).

Still, there had been an overall adequate food supply in the Philippines as of the late 1980s. Villavieja and others found that the Philippine food supply in 1989 was equivalent to 102.9 percent adequacy of calorie intake and 114.7 percent for protein requirements (Lumanta 1991:235, citing Villavieja et al. 1989). Malnutrition in the early 1990s was not primarily a supply problem, but rather a problem of unequal distribution of and access to available food (Lumanta 1991:236).

The National Health Care Program

Since the 1920s the Philippine government's health system has been based on a western style biomedical model of health care. From the 1960s to the present, primary health care has been stressed, particularly in rural areas. Primary health care in the Philippines includes the work of resident health volunteers and the practice of preventive as well as curative programs. Although this approach was promoted under the Marcos regime, the actual distribution of health services and resources within the country were highly skewed. Multimillion dollar hospital facilities were made available for the wealthy in urban areas, while shortages of health facilities, personnel, medicines, and materials as basic as bandages persisted in the rural areas. By 1993, it was still difficult to find highly trained health personnel to work and reside in the rural areas of the Philippines. The Philippines had the highest outmigration rate of nurses in the world, and outmigration of doctors was also very high. During that year, there was only one doctor for every 8,120 Filipinos, less than one-third of the average in other lower-middle-income economies (World Bank 1993, cited in Chant and McIlwaine 1995).

During the 1960s the first attempts to directly address nutritional problems and to coordinate nutrition activities among government agencies were made through the National Coordinating Council on Food and Nutrition (NCCFN), organized by the Food and Nutrition Research Institute (FNRI). By 1974, due to the rising prevalence of national malnutrition rates (78 percent of preschool age children were underweight for their age in 1974), President Marcos established the National Nutrition Council of the Philippines, or the Philippine Nutrition Program, and declared the problem of malnutrition a national priority to be coordinated by the National Nutrition Council (Lumanta 1991:238). The National Nutrition Council was an interdepartmental agency, funded primarily by the Philippine government and USAID during the 1970s and 1980s.

To address immediately the malnutrition problem, the Nutrition Intervention Program (NIP) of the National Nutrition Council included four government interventions: food assistance, or supplementary feeding of preschool and school children, and pregnant and lactating women; nutrition education; nutrition and nutrition related health services, including immunization of children and control of related communicable diseases; and promotion of and assistance for family food production activities (Lumanta 1991:241-242). The program was not highly successful for a number of reasons, one of which was the NIP's neglect to integrate the intervention with a comprehensive program of other socioeconomic development projects and the redistribution of national resources throughout the country. It failed to provide a linkage between malnutrition and the larger political economy of the Philippines. Nevertheless, although other approaches and methodologies were tried, the NIP approach was practiced until 1987 (Lumanta 1991:239).

Also in 1974, Imelda Marcos, Ferdinand Marcos' wife, established a private sector nutrition agency called the Nutrition Center of the Philippines (NCP). It reportedly was established by Imelda Marcos to collaborate with the National Nutrition Council and to encourage private sector involvement in national nutrition programs.

During the Marcos period, multinational companies aggressively marketed and sold vitamins and supplemental foods to Filipino parents for their malnourished children. The western multinational bottle-feeding industry profited from the sale of bottled milk products. As is well recognized, infant formula products are expensive and can cause or exacerbate malnutrition through misuse of the product, especially if there are inadequate facilities to properly use bottled milk products or a lack of knowledge of how to do so.

By 1989, national surveys on breastfeeding trends in the Philippines were showing a decline in the initiation and duration of breastfeeding, mostly in the urban areas. Causes for this decline in the urban areas had been the marketing campaigns of infant formula manufacturers which pressured women and health personnel into believing bottlefeeding was the best method of feeding children, and the increase in women entering the labor force without proper support systems to allow them to continue breastfeeding (BUNSO 1989). Breastfeeding in the rural areas, on the other hand, continued to be the norm due to cultural ideologies surrounding breastfeeding, even by 1993. Increased education regarding the benefits of breastfeeding by government and NGO health personnel during the early 1990s and the lack of money to purchase expensive bottled milk products also contributed to the high incidence of breast feeding in rural areas, including Ifugao. However, many poor rural women, including those in Ifugao, were purchasing less expensive, sugar laden condensed milk products to supplement their breastmilk, thinking that the nutritional content was similar to nutritionally rich, prepared infant solutions. Water was frequently added to the condensed milk to make it palatable, thereby reducing the nutritional content further and increasing risk of introducing bacteria and other pathogens into the children's digestive system. The multinational bottle feeding companies and milk distributors represent the power differential between large foreign and national businesses and poor women throughout the world, and the strong influence business and marketing has on nutrition ideology.

The Philippine government health structure remained free for Filipino citizens through the early 1990s, although expensive medicines had to be paid for, making treatment prohibitive for some patients at times. The programs had little effect on child malnutrition, in large part because of the limitations of resources and personnel for programs geared toward child malnutrition. While health personnel focused their care on the individual level, they could not compete with the effects of the larger political economic relations generating poverty and malnutrition.

In 1988 the National Nutrition Council adopted a new nutrition strategy, in addition to the previous NIP approach. The new Nutrition in Development (NID) approach aimed to integrate nutrition considerations in the government's overall development programs on agricultural and rural development. This was a multisectoral approach involving the policies and programs of the agriculture, labor, health, trade and industry, education and welfare sectors. The NID proposed that development planning at all levels should be reoriented so as to give priority to satisfying nutritional objectives, such as through the integration of nutrition objectives in the Medium Term Philippine Development Plan, 1988–1992 (Lumanta 1991:239).

The Philippine government's Department of Health (DOH) received a substantial share of its funding from official development assistance loans. During the first six months of 1992, the DOH received $57.96 million in official development assistance loans (Quimpo-Espino 1992c:17), while it received only 3.6 percent of the 1992 Philippine national budget. At the same time, the government continued to slash its spending for national agencies, including the DOH, as the 1993 budget proposal included a reduction of the aggregate budget for all national agencies from 1992 levels (Go 1992:17). National budget reductions had been prompted by budget deficit commitments under IMF economic stabilization programs.

Each municipality had a government funded RHU, consisting of a public health nurse, midwives (who were trained to be primary health care workers), and a sanitary engineer. But not all municipalities provided a government hospital; and medical equipment, materials, medicines, and other resources were scarce in many areas. McCoy has argued that the weakness of the postcolonial Philippine state and the interests of the powerful oligarchic families contributed to the Filipino people having to rely on their families for social services— including health care—usually provided by the state in many developing nations. The Philippine state asserted the importance of the family, including mutual aid among its members; and the Filipino family usually provided for the sick in areas where the government lacked adequate health care services (McCoy 1993:7). NGOs and international development organizations supplemented government and family health care services as well.

In December 1991 the Local Government Code (LGC) was implemented, which decentralized government functions and control. Local governments (regional, provincial, municipal, and barrio levels) were made responsible for the planning, funding, and budgeting of their local government agencies, including health services, using locally generated revenues. Under the new devolution of government programs and funds, the government district hospitals were placed under the jurisdiction of the provincial government and the RHUs were under the jurisdiction of the municipal government.

By 1992 the LGC was just beginning to be imple-mented, and many government employees found it quite confusing. Some criticized it as politicizing government funds, as they foresaw local government leaders and representative community members acquiring increased power to allocate government funds for all local government agencies.

Unfortunately, by 1993 the LGC had not proven to be as beneficial to communities as had been hoped by government officials. Government health workers, including members of the Philippine Public Health Association and the DOH, anticipated that the reorganization of the health system under the LGC might create numerous problems in health delivery. They protested the new law even before its implementation on December 13, 1991, in a nationwide mass action, but to no avail (HAIN 1991:359).

By mid-1993, health providers and patients alike had complained about a reduction in funding for local health units and services. Since local governments were relying mainly on their own local tax bases to fund their programs, funding of government services under the LGC was particularly difficult for provinces and municipalities having few resources, businesses, or industries, as was the case for Ifugao Province.

Fortunately, no health workers were forced to vacate their positions, although some workers experienced delays in obtaining their salaries. RHU midwives found there was a reduction in their supplies of medicines, which were to be distributed freely to indigent patients, aggravating an already limited supply. Indigent patients in many district hospitals could no longer receive even limited medicines and medical supplies free of charge, since the budgets of some hospitals had been reduced. Other hospitals experienced delays in the delivery of medicines and supplies due to new acquisition procedures.

By the early 1990s, the government nutrition program still included the NIP and involved nutrition education, immunization programs, sanitation, maternal care, Oral Rehydration Therapy (ORT), breastfeeding promotion, backyard gardening promotion, agricultural technical and financial assistance, and the establishment of income generating projects. Local community volunteers were trained as *Barangay* (barrio) Health Workers (BHW) and *Barangay* Nutrition Scholars (BNS) to assist other members of their community in nutrition education and to conduct the nutrition surveillance campaign, which included monthly weighing of preschool and school children.

Although the Philippine government, through the FNRI national surveys, reported that in 1989–1990, 14 percent of one to six year olds were moderately and severely underweight, as well as 5.5 percent of seven to ten year olds, the problem can be viewed as being more extensive. Tan noted in 1991 that if mild underweight cases were included (usually referred to as first degree malnutrition), national surveys show that approximately 70 percent of preschoolers would be considered undernourished. He also noted that the Philippine government used growth standards that were lower than those agreed upon by international bodies such as the World Health Organization (Tan 1991:24). Newer growth standards released to local government hospitals and RHUs in 1992 had growth standards that were even lower than those referred to by Tan in 1991.

Although government nutrition programs were useful and in great need, they needed to be implemented in conjunction with other social changes, such as agrarian reform, increased wages, limits on external debt payments, and limits on IMF-World Bank and other lending organizations' economic interventions. Although democratization was being promoted, substantial changes in providing equal access to resources and the means of production had not yet transpired by 1993. As will be depicted in later chapters, maximization of community participation and social mobilization could not realistically be accomplished in an atmosphere of "total war" (Aquino's and Ramos' internal war policy), wherein members of community organizations were accused of being communists by military personnel.[12]

PHOTO 2.2 Problems faced by Ifugao people choosing to use biomedical services included the lack of adequate biomedical facilities in distant barrios and difficulty transporting patients on narrow and steep mountain paths. Men sometimes carried patients in a "native ambulance" for more than six hours on mountain paths, as depicted above.

In spite of this, some NGO health work was effective in promoting positive social changes directly related to nutrition. For example, NGOs stimulated the enactment of legislation to regulate the promotion of breastmilk substitutes in the Philippines, namely the Philippine Milk Code, and to promote breastfeeding. NGOs had monitored the bottlefeeding industries' advertising campaigns and found a long record of violations. More work was being done to rectify this situation, and a strong push for promoting breastfeeding was being made by NGOs as well as the Philippine government (HAIN 1989a; BUNSO 1989). The pressures exerted by foreign multinational companies had not fully penetrated Filipino ideology.

Structural Adjustment, Gender, and Health Care

Gender inequality in the Philippines is evidenced in part through the ways in which women and men have been differentially affected by the political, cultural, and economic conditions historically produced in the Philippines. Structural adjustment policies have historically affected men and women in different ways, often to women's disadvantage, largely due to culturally derived western and Filipino gender biases.

As stated above, IMF and World Bank structural adjustment loan conditions in the Philippines, especially those accepted by presidents Aquino and Ramos, involved restrictions on government spending, including health care expenditures.[13] Private health services were very expensive and usually out of reach for the poor. This had substantial impact on Filipino women, particularly since women have special health needs. Further, cuts in government health expenditures had a negative impact on women's biomedical health work.

The Philippines has experienced a "brain drain" of nurses and doctors.[14] Budget reductions also placed greater responsibility on those government health workers, again predominantly women, who were already working under limited conditions in government hospitals and clinics, since less staff was hired during government hiring freezes. This situation placed a greater burden on locally trained, unpaid health volunteers to provide needed health services to poor people.[15] The majority of these volunteers were women, mainly due to the contemporary cultural notion that biomedical community health is women's work. This included women, and proportionally fewer men, recruited to volunteer as BNSs to monitor the nutritional status of children under six years old in their communities.

The promotion of volunteer health care providers was increased under the President Ramos government, through former Health Secretary Juan Flavier, in the face of more limited free government health services and expensive private health services. As one Ifugao government social worker said, "We have to utilize BNSs because we [the local social work office and the local health unit] are under-manned. We have only two [social workers] in our office." Government health volunteers were offered only a few gratuities for their work. In 1992 a BNS was paid only 55 pesos per month for her or his labor. The BNSs also were allowed free medicines for themselves and their family members at government hospitals and insurance for burial upon death of the BNS. BNS labor involved weighing all of the children under six years old in their barrio, educating parents about "good nutrition," picking up and delivering food supplements to recipient families, and other tasks. These activities usually were carried out over a minimum period of three or four days per month. The 55 pesos given to BNSs for one month's part-time work did not even reach the national daily wage, which in the Ifugao area was about 85 pesos at the time. The BNSs were not paid each month but only every six months.

One female Ifugao BNS, who is a grandmother and a farmer, said, "We are paid a 55 peso per month stipend. That is why we are always complaining. They [the government] should add at least 5 pesos, but they will not. That is why I am always sacrificing." This BNS said that she works about three days per month to fulfill her duties as a BNS, including hiking to children's homes to weigh them, carrying a scale on her way, distributing government issued food supplements for second and third degree malnourished children and pregnant women, and providing nutrition education to parents of malnourished children. She also worked during the evening hours to compile the weight records she collected for the DOH. She said, "That is why some of the BNSs are now out, because they do not like the 55 pesos. But for me, [I continue my work] because I love the children, and because some of my grandchildren, my nephews and nieces [are participants in the program]."

Some Ifugao government health professionals were aware of the low pay and suggested at a 1992 Municipal Nutrition Council Conference held in Ifugao that BNS salaries should be increased. One government health worker suggested the BNSs be paid a daily rate, dependent on the number of days it takes to weigh the children in their communities. There was no change implemented at that time, however.

Female health volunteers took on added health care responsibilities in the face of restricted government spending. This was sometimes carried out to the detriment of their own and their family's needs, since the majority of health volunteers were poor women.[16] At times their community work created conflict between themselves and their husbands, who asked them to spend more time working for their own families.

Although the 1987 Philippine Constitution mandated that women and men be treated equally in all respects, including paid equally for performing the same work, in reality Filipino women's wages were often lower than that of men (Center for Women's Resources Data Bank 1993:2). In 1993 monthly take-home pay was higher for males in the Philippines, even for the same positions, work experience, and educational level. In managerial and supervisory positions, women earned only 70 percent of what their male counterparts earned. In all labor areas, it was estimated that women earned only 35 percent of what males earned (Center for Women's Resources Data Bank 1993:2). With already extremely low daily wages, IMF-World Bank prescriptions to restrict wage increases affected women more severely than men, particularly single women heading households. This, in turn, could have affected the nutritional status of members of those households who fully relied on purchased foods, or who relied on them to supplement food production.

Many women are employed in TNCs in export processing zones in Southeast Asia. Women are perceived by many employers to be more passive, less likely to unionize, and as having greater patience for tedious, monotonous assembly line work (Gladwin 1993:97; Ong 1987). The women often receive low wages, and exploitative employment practices are frequent (Gladwin 1993:97; Ong 1987).[17] Pressure from the IMF-World Bank to maintain low worker wages severely curtailed the rights of female workers to obtain adequate wages and fair employment practices in TNCs, as well as in Philippine business establishments. This affected Ifugao women, since they were increasingly joining the transnational labor force in factories within and outside of the Philippines.

Rising unemployment and underemployment rates under structural adjustment also had detrimental effects on women, again particularly single women heads of households, since there were more cash earning employment opportunities for men than for women in the rural areas. In 1990 there were more females than males living in the urban areas, especially Metro Manila, seeking work or wishing to pursue their education (Center for Women's Resources Data Bank 1993:I). While it must be noted that many women were students in Metro Manila, only 46 percent of females were part of the formal labor force as compared to 72 percent of men in Metro Manila (Center for Women's Resources Data Bank 1993:II). Many women participated in the informal labor sector in Metro Manila; and a number of women from, or who had migrated to, cities seeking employment resorted to work in the sex industry in the face of high underemployment and unemployment rates.

Resistance and Revolution

The Philippine government had been waging an LIC against the revolutionary NPA since 1969. Resistance to increasing inequality, poverty, hunger, state and military repression of the body politic, and political and economic intervention in Philippine society by the United States, World Bank, and IMF, led to the revolutionary conflict. The resistance began in 1968 with the reestablishment of the CPP and the forming of the NPA, the armed wing of the CPP, the following year (Bello et al. 1982; Lachica 1971). The year 1969 marked the fourth year of the Ferdinand Marcos presidency.[18]

The contemporary war had its roots in the earlier peasant resistance movement against the U.S. colonial, and later Philippine, governments and elites. Members of the communist and socialist influenced *Huk* movement became important figures in the CPP and NPA.

The NDF resisted Marcos' oppression and U.S. political and economic intervention in the Philippines through social and military strategies. Included in the revolutionary NPA agenda was its armed struggle for greater social equality, genuine democracy, national freedom, an end to U.S. imperialism in the Philippines, the implementation of a genuine land reform program, respect for Filipino citizens' human rights, the right to employment, an increase in the Filipino people's living standards, an expansion of social services, and a communist-led government (Davis 1989).

During her six years in office, President Aquino struggled to institutionalize a democratic and legitimate government. Though she had overwhelming popular support, loyalty from members of Aquino's government and military was less certain. She survived at least six coup attempts instigated by political rivals and young military officers from the Reform the Armed Forces Movement (RAM). And she grappled with continued warfare against the NPA. The Aquino administration attempted to resolve the war through peace talks with the NPA. The peace talks included the Muslim Moro National Liberation Front (MNLF), which had been fighting for autonomy in the south of the Philippines. The peace talks proved to be ineffective. While Aquino did establish a more legitimate government in the Philippines, she did not essentially change the continuing problems of social class inequality, widespread poverty, government violations of human rights, government indebtedness to foreign lenders, neocolonialism, and corruption. She may have been limited in her capacity to enact substantial change because of the fragility of her government, as evidenced by the coup attempts against her government and the ongoing war, or because of her position as a member of the landowning class (Steinberg 1994).

The strength of the NPA/NDF declined after Aquino assumed the presidency. This occurred in part because the NPA/NDF was weakened when they made the tactical mistake of boycotting the snap election called by Marcos (Druckman and Green 1995). Since many Filipinos, including those aligned with the NPA/NDF, hoped that the Aquino administration would bring true democracy and equality to the Philippines, they ignored the directive for a boycott from the NPA/NDF and instead supported the Aquino government. Fidel Ramos, elected as President of the Philippines in 1992, also attempted peace talks with the NPA, but these were unsuccessful through 1993. At the same time, from 1991 to 1993 the Philippine government (under President Aquino and President Ramos) waged a stepped-up LIC strategy against the NPA. In 1992 and 1993, the military strategy was "total war" against the NPA.

During the same period, the CPP, NPA, and NDF were experiencing internal conflicts, debates, and ideological splits. These stemmed from earlier debates among members of these organizations, particularly during the 1980s, regarding the direction and strategies of the left movement.[19] The 1986 internal dissension over the decision to boycott the Marcos-Aquino snap election is an example of the conflicts which occurred during this period. During the early 1990s, splits occurred in the armed movement, the CPP, and the numerous overt leftist organizations. A group identified as the "Reaffirm" group emerged, comprising those who supported the directives of the CPP central leadership led by Jose Maria Sison. The positions of other groups that had split from the CPP-NPA (e.g., "Rejectionist," "Third Force," "Fourth Force") were less clearly defined. The splintered groups rejected the authority of the CPP central leadership, perceiving it to be authoritarian, but differed in their positions on other issues, such as whether there should be a military takeover of the government or whether a shift in power to the left should be achieved through legal political strategies.

There were a number of issues which continued to be debated among the CPP, NPA, and NDF factions in the early 1990s. The first was disagreement over tactics, strategies, and objectives of leftist politics, especially those involving the armed wing of the movement. The second was a debate over the relative importance of rural versus urban areas as sites of potential support for the left movement and locations to attack government forces. The third issue was disagreement over the structure of governance and decision making within the CPP and NPA (Kerkvliet 1996). The fourth was debate over the nature of socialism and the interpretation of the collapse of socialist regimes in Eastern Europe and the Soviet Union (Rocamora 1992). Other issues discussed included tactics for the peace talks, internal democracy, and the nature of the NDF program (Weekley 1996).

The problem of widespread hunger was woven into this historical context, as hunger still had not been adequately resolved by the Philippine state; instead, it had been exacerbated by national and international policies. The low intensity conflict pursued by the Philippine government against the NPA was an attempt to prohibit the implementation of NDF and NPA goals and to maintain the existing political structure.[20]

The power differential between the United States and the Philippines historically had a significant detrimental impact on the nutritional status of the Filipino population. Due in part to a long-term policy of liberal foreign investment and export-oriented agriculture and industry, the Philippines was not always entirely self-sufficient in staple food production. Large-scale cash crop agriculture removed many farmers from the subsistence farming sector and reduced the land area devoted to staple foods. In the early 1990s, these power differentials were reflected in the facts that at least 44.5 percent of the Filipino population had incomes below the poverty level and that many Filipino people had great difficulty in meeting their full nutritional needs.

The Philippine government and international aid agencies attempted to solve these problems by instituting technological fixes (such as the agricultural programs described above); the management of the Philippine economy through structural adjustment programs; medical strategies; or strategies integrating medical, agricultural, and social service elements. However, policies were not implemented which addressed the social structures within which these "fixes" and "strategies" were operating. State policies and international aid agency programs such as the IMF and World Bank often generated unequal social power relations and maintained these through the implementation of social programs focusing primarily on the individual, the family, and the local community.

Power is distributed in many ways in the Philippines. At the time of writing, health care was held primarily in the hands of biomedical experts, though traditional healers and local nonprofessional health workers still practiced health care. Diet and agriculture, once viewed as personal aspects of life, were viewed by some as belonging to the domain of professionals and experts and were becoming controlled by these experts. Through the created "need" for outside expert assistance, both from within and outside the country, ideology and belief systems were being transformed by political and economic systems. Often the needs and the desires of the people affected were ignored, as exemplified by the development projects described above.

On the surface, World Bank rural agricultural development programs in the Philippines can be viewed as having the aim of increasing large-scale agricultural production and the productivity of small farmers. In reality, a more important goal of the World Bank was to use rural development as a reform strategy to dissolve disaffection among Filipino peasants, and thus reduce their potential for revolt, in order to create a more stable social and political climate (Bello et al. 1982:25). While international rural development projects continued to be implemented in the countryside in cooperation with poor individuals and families, the income and nutritional status of the majority of these families had not significantly risen, and in fact had worsened over the decades with the intervention of the World Bank, IMF, and other foreign lending agencies (Tan 1995:34). In the past two decades, people of the Cordillera region have, in some cases, observed a direct link between counterinsurgency militarization in the region and rural development programs (Cordillera Peoples Alliance 1993:14-16). Reformist international development projects often served to suppress expressions of resistance to inequitable and unjust internationally influenced national economic, military, and social policies.

Economic assistance, both bilateral and multilateral, also served the political and economic interests of donor countries. While the IMF, World Bank, and donor countries required poor countries to liberalize trade, donor countries often restricted access to their own markets. A 1992 United Nations (UN) report stated that restricted access to the world's markets cost developing countries an annual $500 billion and helped to widen the income gap between rich and poor countries, a gap which doubled over thirty years (Mikkelsen 1992:2). By 1990 the richest 20 percent of the world's population had incomes sixty times greater than the incomes of the poorest 20 percent. Other reasons for this disparity given by the UN report were inadequate and misallocated foreign aid, the debt burden, and failure of the World Bank and IMF to ease it (*Philippine Daily Inquirer* 1992d:1, 6). Due to these and other problems, poor small farmers, wage laborers, and landless tenants have had, and likely will continue to have, difficulty attaining the necessary nutrients to sustain themselves and their families. Poor women are affected more severely in some cases, nutritionally and in other ways, as will be seen in the following chapters.

The health sector of the Philippine government did not ignore the nutritional problems of the Filipino people, and it attempted a number of programs to alleviate the situation. Many Philippine citizens responded to these difficult problems in numerous ways, including community organization, worker and farmer strikes, and armed resistance, among others. Large numbers of people pushed for extensive land reform and a shift from continued U.S. intervention in the Philippines, as exemplified by the national call for the removal of U.S. military bases in 1992. To better understand the lives of Ifugao women and their families, the next chapter looks at the daily experiences of Ifugao women and their gendered relationship to Ifugao men.

Notes

1. By "agrarian reform" I am referring to the reform of agrarian institutions, including credit and marketing institutions, and to the redistribution of property rights on land (Hayami et al. 1990:5).

2. This is a conservative 1991 estimate (original source was the Technical Working Group on Poverty Determination, NSCB). Other sources cite higher percentages of persons living at or below the poverty level in 1991, such as 70 percent cited by IBON (1992b:4).

3. Original source was the Technical Working Group on Poverty Determination, NSCB.

4. The Philippines was especially dependent on the U.S. market to sell sugar, one of its prime cash crops.

5. Marcos' cronies were Filipino elite men, and some women, who had acquired wealth and power through favors and protection from Marcos rather than through their own initiatives or abilities.

6. The NDF was a national umbrella organization of cause-oriented groups, established in 1973, to resist the repressive Marcos dictatorship. Among other groups it included the NPA, the Cordillera Peoples Alliance (CPA), Cordillera People's Democratic Front (CPDF), the *Makabayang Samahang Pangkalusugan* (MSP, or Patriotic Health Association), labor unions, and women's, church, teachers', and peasant groups (Rocamora 1992).

7. World Bank lending in FY1974 reached $165.1 million, compared to an average of $30 million per year for the previous five years (Bello et al. 1982:24).

8. The Philippine Department of Agrarian Reform suggested that 85 percent of Filipino peasants had no secure title to agricultural land by 1985 (Putzel 1992:25).

9. See James Putzel (1992) for an extensive analysis of the land reform process in the Philippines.

10. The Green Revolution was a technology package approach to farming in poor countries that attempted to increase yields without increasing cultivated crop areas (George 1977:87). Beginning in the 1940s, the plan basically failed for a variety of reasons.

11. Structural adjustment loans were geared to one or more specific sectors of the economy, such as industry, energy, or agriculture. The apex loans were specific to the financial sector, for example, Philippine industrial financing (Broad 1988:129).

12. The total war policy of the Aquino and Ramos administrations incorporated the LIC doctrine of counterinsurgency in the military campaign against the NPA-NDF in the late 1980s. The total war policy entailed a military approach together with political, economic, and psychological measures to destroy the armed NPA and its larger support network. Total war included techniques such as forced evacuations of civilians from their homes and communities, the formation of vigilante groups, food blockades, and abductions, as well as strategic development activities. Proponents of the strategy acknowledged that the main problems in the society were economic and political rather than military and advocated genuine land reform. Yet, in practice, the government did not follow through on all of its declarations (Mariano 1992:6, 7).

13. By 1991 only 25 percent of all Philippine health expenditures were shouldered by the government, leaving 75 percent to the private sector.

14. The main reasons for this phenomenon included: high unemployment rates; low salaries offered to government nurses and doctors, levels reinforced by IMF-World Bank austerity programs; less government funding provided for maintaining and upgrading the less than optimum conditions within hospitals and clinics in rural areas, again related to IMF-World Bank austerity programs; and difficult living conditions in rural areas where most hospitals and clinics were located.

15. Health volunteers included Philippine government sponsored BHWs and BNSs, and NGO sponsored Community Health Workers.

16. Upper class women did not tend to volunteer for health work, instead usually volunteering for charity organizations.

17. Linda Y. C. Lim has contested the idea that the majority of female factory workers in Third World countries are regularly underpaid and exploited (Lim 1990).

18. The CPP drafted a new party constitution to supplant the earlier 1938 charter of the merged CPP and Socialist Party of the Philippines (Davis 1989:43).

19. Some place the internal conflict earlier, beginning in the 1970s (Kerkvliet 1996).

20. See Chapter 4 for further discussion of the contemporary war.

3

Gendered Experiences in Ifugao

Gender categories in Ifugao (woman or *bfwabfwa-ee,* and man or *lala-ee*), as culturally and historically constructed artifacts (Errington 1990; Foucault 1990), have specific meanings attributed to them by Ifugao people. These meanings are related to the historical, cultural, political, and economic processes experienced and created daily by Ifugao subjects. They are categories that are dynamic and constantly in flux (Ong 1990:387), and variably experienced by Ifugao women and men of differing social groups. This chapter provides a context for understanding women's connection to the problem of malnutrition by considering gender relations, and for understanding the recent goals and programs of international and national development organizations that focusing on "women in development."

Women and Everyday Life

I found that women's lives in Ifugao were highly variable, since Ifugao women did not comprise one collective group of gendered persons with identical activities, interests, and positions. Ifugao women came from varying social classes, occupations, and religions, and had different educational attainments, among other variations. And each woman could occupy a variety of changing positions, in relation to each other and to men, depending upon specific contexts.

Ifugao women played a number of social roles. These roles were viewed mainly by Ifugao people as being performed in relation to other family members; rarely were they perceived as activities performed independently of their kin. These roles included, among others, that of worker, health care provider, child care provider, religious leader or member, landowner, craft producer, domestic laborer, mother, wife, sister, daughter, aunt, cousin, and, for a more limited number, community leader.

Of approximately 147,000 inhabitants of Ifugao in the early 1990s, 75 percent of Ifugao adults were peasant farmers, almost equally male and female. With their integration into a market economy, however, most peasants also regularly participated in other types of labor, such as short-term manual wage labor on government projects, craft production, small business, waged domestic labor, and short- or long-term migrant labor. Ifugao people also engaged in reciprocal labor for a variety of activities (such as agricultural, house building, child care, etc.). Some Ifugao people worked as professionals, mainly in government positions, while others worked in full-time wage labor or nonskilled positions, or in business. Most people engaged in multiple work activities.

Although 74 percent of all professionals in Ifugao were female, most of these women worked as low salaried teachers and nurses. Women dominated the health care arena, community volunteer service, and labor in their homes. Public health work, however, was defined largely by the government, although some health NGOs attempted to construct their own forms of health care. Women also dominated the business sector, where the majority were small business owners. However, in positions of authority and power, such as officials of the government, executives, managers, managing proprietors, and supervisors, 77 percent were male and only 23 percent were female (National Statistics Office, Republic of the Philippines 1992b). For example, in one barrio in which I conducted research, the barrio captain was male (the case in most barrios), and five men and two women comprised the barrio council. More women were elected as officers of the Parents-Teachers Association (PTA) in this barrio, however, with six women and four men elected as officers.

Virtually all Ifugao women were engaged in work outside of their homes, with the majority of Ifugao women being peasants. Women's agricultural labor was physically strenuous and demanding. A song sung by young girls, and sometimes by adult women, described planting rice:

> Planting rice is never fun
> Bend some more 'til the set of sun
> Cannot stand and cannot sit
> Cannot rest for a little bit
> La la la.[1]

Most of Ifugao women and men's labor was unpaid, particularly for peasants working on their own rice fields, swidden agricultural fields, gardens, and in their homes. Peasant women often worked cooperatively, particularly during rice planting and harvesting periods. They were often engaged in multiple forms of cash paying work, such as paid agricultural labor, craft production, and small business activities.

Other women worked as professionals in government offices, as teachers, service providers, businesswomen, cooks, day care custodians, maids, bankers, craftswomen, or in other employed labor. Many of these women, however, engaged in some agricultural labor as well, such as raising vegetables in their gardens or laboring in their own or others' rice fields.

PHOTO 3.1 Women's gendered labor included harvesting rice. Most Ifugao women continued to engage in agricultural labor during their later years, as is this elderly woman.

Women, particularly lower class women, were also often engaged in long term, unpaid or underpaid volunteer work, more so than men. This included volunteer health work, child care, and work on some local development projects. Volunteer work among lower class women usually was viewed as work which would improve their own lives and the lives of the people in their community who lacked basic social services.

Some Ifugao women, especially single women (both those who did and did not have children), engaged in short- or long-term migrant labor within the Philippines or overseas. The majority of Ifugao women working overseas worked either as nurses or domestic helpers; others worked in factories, as janitors, or in other non-skilled labor positions. Many of the women laboring as domestic helpers in foreign countries held professional degrees (particularly in teaching or nursing), but they earned more money working overseas than they could working in their own country. These women usually sent a large portion of their earnings to their family members remaining in Ifugao.

While many women reported positive experiences working overseas, others reported abusive treatment from their employers. One single Ifugao woman, approximately twenty-two years old, worked as a domestic helper in a Middle Eastern country for one year (1991–1992). She described having been locked in the home of her employers every day and ordered never to leave the house without her employers' accompanying her. When she was allowed to go out of the house with her employers, they instructed her to not speak to anyone, including other Filipino laborers. This made her feel very isolated and lonely. She worked without a day off for one year. Her female employer once slapped her in the face and accused her of having an affair with the employer's husband. Despite the abuse, limited mobility, silencing, and loneliness, she endured working because she liked her overseas job: "at least I could earn some money to help my younger sisters and brothers. . . . Here [in the Philippines], even though you work hard, you only make enough to eat." She viewed her work primarily in relation to her large family, which had been headed by her single mother since her father died. She said that she would like to work overseas again so she could earn more money for her family, which faced poverty, increased prices of commodities and services, and difficulty surviving as a female-headed household.

For the majority of women who remained in Ifugao, women's work inside the home included: child care; cooking, usually over a wood fire; washing clothing by hand in rivers, at open springs, at home, or at faucets located on a road; pounding rice to remove rice husks, using a large cement or wooden mortar and a wooden pestle; carrying water from an open spring or pipe to their homes, sometimes over great distance; cleaning their homes; cooking for and feeding domesticated animals; and assisting at family and community gatherings. Elder children usually helped their mothers in these tasks, and their husbands helped with some of them at times. Some women wove clothing, blankets, and craft articles in their homes, as well, while others worked on finishing wood carvings made by the men of their family or community.[2] One lower class, married peasant woman, the mother of six children, described a normal day in her life:

> When I awaken, I cook and eat, feed the animals, and wash clothes. My children pound rice. Then I usually go to my rice fields, where I weed, plant or harvest. Both I and my husband clear the swidden field. When planting sweet potato, we work in a group, planting with men and women. The men dig the hole and women plant the sweet potato cutting. We work especially in groups for distant swidden fields, only as *ubfu* [reciprocal labor, not for pay]. I have a garden sometimes. My husband helps in the garden, especially in cutting the sticks for the beans to climb. I carry water.
>
> I return at any time, three or four p.m. If we are working as *ubfu*, I always return at five p.m. When I arrive home, the food is already cooked by my children. At night, I cook food for the pigs.[3] After eating, I finish wood carvings made by my husband,

or any other person. I also fix paddies in the fields.[4] During harvest season I carry rice home on my head, especially when you harvest your own fields. Even bundles of rice in a sack or large basket is carried on our [women's] heads, because bundles of rice carried on a stick is too painful.

A married upper class, business woman, and mother of four children, described an average day in her life:

> I wake up, cook, prepare breakfast, feed the children, and prepare them to go to school. I awaken at about five a.m. I wash clothes, dishes, and clean. Then I open the store at six thirty a.m. or seven a.m. I can wash clothes at home. It is difficult to be helping my children go to school and watch the store. My girl [domestic helper] helps me to do my work.[5] She is my relative. She is in fourth year high school, but she's a scholar, so she has no tuition. We provide her room and board and an allowance for her needs.
>
> I cook lunch, manage the store, and then cook dinner in the afternoon. I purchase goods for the store. I can't go out now because I have no other companion [domestic helper] during the day. So the stores deliver. . . . At the end of the evening I watch Beta Max and relax before sleeping.[6]

Keeping in mind the cycle of women's lives, the daily life of younger, lower class peasant women who had a number of babies was focused mainly on child care and domestic tasks. One young, lower class peasant woman described, "I get up at about five a.m., I cook and we eat. I feed the animals, wash clothes, wash the dishes, then sit down, babysitting. I do not go to the fields now because I have three small children. Then I cook for lunch. . . . I pound rice in the afternoon, and cook again. Then we eat, and after we sleep."

For some women, child care was juggled between themselves and their spouses, or other relatives, as this lower class, peasant woman with two babies explained:

> When I wake up I cook, and wash clothes if there are dirty clothes. Then I go out to work in the swidden field or rice fields. I bring my lunch if it is far, always, but I will come home to eat if it is near. Or, I stay home and babysit. I clean the area for swidden fields also, and work on government projects if there is a babysitter. Whoever stays home [I or my husband] pounds rice, but sometimes our parents take care of our children. If I come home from work and no one has pounded rice, I will pound. Whoever stays home will feed the animals. We both babysit about the same amount of time. Sometimes, late in the afternoon, noon or morning, we bathe the children, either of us depending on who stays home. The first one who comes home from work will cook. After eating in the evening, we sleep.

Some women worked as business women and craft producers, as this lower class, married woman with two children described:

I begin working in my store after seven or nine a.m., depending on my home work. I am sanding, varnishing, and selling woodcarvings, and others. People come here and sell to us [for resale in her store]. Sometimes the carver doesn't bring my order, so I have to look for them. Or, some customer orders something special, so I look for a carver. . . . Mostly I work all day. I have little time to relax.

Most elderly, lower class peasant women still worked diligently at home and daily in their fields. They were often asked to babysit for young children of their relatives, as this sixty to seventy year old married, lower class peasant woman, who had no children, said:

I wake up early in the morning, cook food, eat, sweep, pound rice, fetch water, and wash the dishes. This is the usual work, morning or afternoon. If I have no viand I go out to look for some, like shells [shellfish, snails, etc.] in the rice field. Whenever I see that it is a sunny day, I wash my clothes in the morning before going to the fields. When I come home from the fields in the afternoon, if my clothes are very muddy, I will wash them in the afternoon. I work cleaning [weeding] the fields. But before I start weeding, I see if there are shells. I will collect them before beginning weeding. Or, I may weed first, then collect shells in the afternoon to bring home. If there are no shells, I go home with no viand or use only salt [to eat with rice or sweet potatoes]. If I am going home very late in the afternoon from the rice fields and I didn't get shells or other viand, like *gabi* leaves, then I have no viand.[7] Sometimes I don't mind to get *gabi* leaves because I'm the only one to eat it. My husband doesn't like them. Sometimes, whenever I go to the field and I don't have betel nut ingredients and I see someone in a distant field, I will go and ask that other woman for the ingredients.[8]

I work planting and harvesting rice fields. When there's no sweet potato in the house I will go and dig for sweet potato. Yesterday, when I finished digging sweet potato, I saw that in the mud there were mice footprints. So I cut the weeds in the field, then covered the walkway of the rat so it would have difficulty getting to the sweet potato at night. Then I got sweet potato leaves for the pigs. Today, I am removing the shells from the fields because they will eat the seedlings, the leaves of them, and destroy them. If I notice that the leaves are rotten [weeds placed in a pile to rot for compost], then I spread them around the field [for fertilization].

I make a garden for vegetables after planting, when I will finish all the field work. When I was young, there were no gardens. Instead, they planted vegetables in the swidden or rice fields. It's only now that people have gardens and vegetables for sale. I first made a garden two years ago when I saw other people make them. For beans, I need to plant a garden, but for squash, I plant it in the rice fields or swidden fields. Before, there were native beans, but for those they were very long and the peel was harder than the new variety. Those beans were only planted in the rice fields. You could plant the new varieties of beans in the rice fields, but only when the field is dry [during the dry season].

In the afternoon, sometimes I wash clothes, feed the pigs and animals, go inside the house and build a fire for cooking. Sometimes my nieces ask me to take care of their children, but I don't like to do this. I like to go out to work in the fields instead of staying home and babysitting. Even my niece, I will not babysit for her so that it will be fair for all of my nieces. They may say, "Oh, you only love her, what about us?" Sometimes, my nieces' children are all gathered in my house, and I will feed them all. And what I don't like is when they are quarrelling with each other. I want the children to stay with me, but they don't like to sleep with me at night. . . . Sometimes I will babysit when the children all have colds, are sick.

I fetch water if none. I cook the pigs' food, after cooking our evening's food. To prepare food for pigs I chop the sweet potato leaves, and the large sweet potatoes. Even in the late evening, if there's no sweet potato for the pigs to cook, I am forced to go out and get them, to cook them in the evening. I go to work every day and rest on Sundays. After mass [on Sunday], I go to work again. I work even when it's raining; only not during typhoons. I'm afraid that I will fall during the typhoon. I go to bed around nine p.m. Sometimes if I feel very, very tired I have a hard time sleeping, so I fall asleep only around eleven or twelve p.m.

Single, lower class women (including widowed women, women separated from their husbands, or women who never married) comprised about 15 percent of the Ifugao adult female population. Single, lower class women who had children had many demands made of them and had the greatest difficulty supporting their family financially. Many of these women received no child support from the fathers of their children. I learned of at least five cases of fathers not providing financial support to their children born out of wedlock, and one case in which the father gave material assistance occasionally. Two reasons suggested by Ifugao women for why fathers did not support their children either born out of wedlock or following divorce were that the father was already married to another woman or that he denied the child was his. Another reason was that the father did not love the mother of his child and "was only playing with her." He did not want to marry the mother and broke all ties with her and the child. One other reason offered was that a father may not support his child if he judged the mother to be sexually promiscuous or if she was a prostitute.

Single women with children were compelled to take on the roles of both mother and father, engaging in work culturally designated for both. A single, lower class peasant woman, the mother of three young children, described her daily life as follows:

I get up [in the morning], then cook, clean the house and fix it, sometimes. Then when the food is cooked, we eat. I feed the animals. Sometimes they [my children] will cook. If there's no firewood, I will go to gather firewood, come home and chop it. Then I gather the tools I will use in the field and go to the field. In the field I cut the straw, weed, and plow using a spade. After that, I do something different the next day, like if it's time to plant seeds, I prepare the fields before setting the seeds. Every afternoon, I get sweet potato and sweet potato leaves for the pigs. Sometimes, I build things at my house, like a pig pen. Sometimes I do sanding of wood carvings in [the center of the municipality]. I wash the pigs. I also wash clothes, either early in the morning or late in the afternoon. Sometimes the boys [her sons] will wash their clothes.

They will help me by pounding rice, fetching water, sometimes getting food for
the pigs [in the fields], cook, catch Japanese fish [in rice fields or fish ponds] for
viand, and shells, and get firewood, but only a little, whatever they can carry. In the
afternoon, when I return home, if the boys did not pound rice, I pound rice, cook
food, cook sweet potato leaves for pigs, feed the pigs. That's all; always work, always
the same. Then I eat, sweep the floor, prepare the beddings, then sit down for awhile
before sleeping. The children go to sleep earlier than me.

In this case, the single woman engaged in work culturally designated as men's
work by collecting firewood, building pig pens, and plowing rice fields using a
spade.[9] This single woman also had built her own small wooden house for her
family.

Children helped their parents, according to their age and abilities, sometimes
missing school days or quitting school entirely to do so. One woman said that she
had observed adults who were unsupported by their fathers growing up to be very
successful, as though it was their "blessing" after the hardships endured as they
grew up. She also offered that some of the fathers attempted to reconcile with their
children when they had become older, but most children rejected their fathers who
had given no support to them or their mothers during very difficult periods of their
lives.

Other activities participated in by women included local religious rituals (*baki*)
related to illness, agriculture, or other life events (e.g., introduction of a newborn
baby to spiritual beings, funerals, and house blessings); Christian church services
on Saturdays or Sundays, and weekday evening prayer or Bible study services;
Christian celebrations (e.g., baptisms and house blessings); secular community
celebrations (graduations, national holidays, municipal fiestas, etc.); community,
government, and development related meetings; and occasional travel to other
locales to purchase family needs. Women spent much of their time participating in
these activities.

Lower class Ifugao women developed and maintained networks of assistance,
especially among their relatives and wealthy patrons, to aid them on a daily basis
and particularly when they experienced extreme financial difficulties. Women
maintained very heavy work loads, working throughout the day and often into the
evening, accomplishing multiple types of work both inside and outside of their
homes. This was referred to by some Ifugao women as their "double burden."[10]
Some women said that they only had time to rest when they went to bed in the
evening.

Work that was culturally constructed as men's work included plowing irrigated
rice fields, either by hand using a spade or with a water buffalo drawn plow;
carrying the majority of newly harvested bundles of rice from fields to homes;
collecting and chopping firewood; butchering and dressing large domesticated
animals; building and maintaining rice fields; fishing, and sewing and maintaining
fishing nets; building and maintaining houses, stone walls, and fences; carpentry;

weaving baskets; driving public transportation vehicles; blacksmithing; masonry; wood carving; working on community infrastructure projects; and, less frequently in recent years, hunting.

Work that was not culturally gender specific, but was not always equally shared between men and women or performed in the same manner, included pounding rice, collecting firewood, child care, butchering small domesticated animals, cooking, fetching water, maintaining irrigation canals, clearing swidden agricultural fields, non-skilled wage and migrant labor, and professional employment.

Despite the existence of cultural gender codes regarding work, they were regularly broken. Single people and married persons whose spouses were ill or away from home performing migrant labor most frequently broke the codes. More women than men remained at home with children without a spouse (as single mothers, wives of husbands who had migrated for labor, or widows), and were more commonly required to perform opposite gendered tasks than men.

Sometimes single women paid men to assist them in certain tasks, such as plowing rice fields. But the single women whom I interviewed accomplished many male designated tasks on their own, out of necessity. Their participation in opposite gendered activities was culturally accepted by the community. However, it would have been less acceptable for a married woman to participate in male gendered activities. A married woman's husband would be harshly ridiculed and his masculinity would be diminished for allowing his wife to perform what was considered to be his culturally prescribed duties. For example, more men than women worked on government infrastructure projects. One woman said she had never tried this type of work because it was difficult labor, "because I cannot do it; and because our husbands, they do not want their honor to become low. Because if a woman goes to do that kind of work, what other people will think is that the man is not feeding us. The men say [to their wives], 'You can go earn [money] if really you don't have anything to cook for food.'" Nevertheless, some married women did perform culturally defined men's work at times. As one woman said of Ifugao women generally, "sometimes she will work the work of a man, like making rice fields . . . and go to the swidden field and make one field for the sweet potato."

The cultural gender codes varied from one Ifugao municipality to another, such as women regularly plowing rice fields using a spade in some areas. The acceptance of single women performing male designated labor, the engagement of some married women in male designated labor, and the variability of gender codes among the different Ifugao municipalities, exemplified the socially constructed nature of the gender roles and the variability of women's roles within Ifugao society as a whole.

Social Class and Gender

Conceptions of social class were culturally constructed in Ifugao, specific both to their local ideology regarding wealth, status, and prestige, and to modern ideologies of wealth and power. Ifugao women's and men's gendered positions were intertwined significantly with their social class positions, as well as their ages, ranks, and educational levels. Ethnicity also played an important role in constructions of Ifugao persons' statuses, mainly in relation to people and institutions outside of Ifugao.

Social class distinctions among Ifugao people were acknowledged overtly and felt on a daily basis. There were specific local, and some imported, terms to identify people of the upper, middle, and lower classes. These terms were used openly and regularly in daily conversations. Many Ifugao adults had a keen knowledge of the socioeconomic status of the other members of their immediate communities. This information was necessary for the survival of the majority of lower class Ifugao people, since the upper class landowners and businesspersons mainly employed the poor and provided them with loans (with interest) in times of need. Inversely, the members of the upper class were dependent on the lower class for labor to produce rice, often resulting in patron-client relationships.

Before delineating the social class distinctions in Ifugao, I will describe Ifugao kinship and inheritance patterns, related to wealth and status. The Ifugao kinship system was bilateral, meaning that a child was related equally to family members of both parents; relatives of each child's parents were addressed by the same kinship terminology; and an individual's most important social groupings were relatives of both parents (Errington 1990). Historically, the family unit was the primary social unit. Local ties among kin were very strong and important for participation in social life, including domestic, religious, agricultural, other economic, and political activities. Prior to and during colonization, Ifugao people developed an extensive and clearly defined traditional system of personal law regarding property, inheritance, water rights, and family law (Barton 1919). In the contemporary period, through bilateral inheritance, both women and men can inherit property possessed by either parent through a system of primogeniture. With primogeniture, the eldest child inherits the largest amount of terraced, irrigated rice fields (usually of either the mother or the father, whomever owns the most rice fields) and other inheritable items such as Chinese vases or gold jewelry. The second child inherits the second largest amount of rice fields and inheritable items, and so on. In some areas of Ifugao, the youngest child usually inherited the parents' house. Sometimes, especially for poor families who owned small rice fields, only the first or second child could inherit their parents' rice fields. This was necessary to keep the area of land large enough to support at least one family. If they continued farming, the remaining children usually labored or sharecropped on other landowners' rice fields, unless they purchased rice fields of their own. The system of primogeniture may have been instituted to maintain the strength of Ifugao extended families. It was also one mechanism by which a distinct social class and status organization, based primarily on ownership of terraced, irrigated rice fields, was reproduced, though it had been altered to some extent with the introduction of cash in the Ifugao local economy.

During the early 1990s in Ifugao, while some families did not own any irrigated rice fields, there were no families who were absolutely landless. All families had access to community lands on the mountainsides where they could plant dry rice, sweet potato, and other crops on swidden fields. (A farmer could claim land on a mountainside on which she worked until abandoned.) As was commonly pointed out among the Ifugao people, although the poor may not own terraced irrigated rice fields, no one remained without food in Ifugao since there was land available for cultivation on the mountainsides. Swidden farming on mountainsides, however, was more strenuous than agricultural labor on terraced rice fields. Also, a farmer generally could not become wealthy through swidden agriculture but only exist on a subsistence level. With other forms of labor opportunities available in recent years, many Ifugao people turned away from swidden agriculture. This was due, in part, because the labor required for swidden agriculture was very difficult, strenuous, and time consuming for little gain, whereas wage labor could be more profitable and sometimes easier. Also, with increasing population, deforestation, and overuse of swidden fields, the fertility of the fields had decreased along with its productivity. The increase in rice available for purchase in Ifugao markets and Ifugao people's preference for eating rice over the sweet potato also influenced the reduction in swidden farming. Another contributing factor was the introduction of hybrid pigs, usually as part of a development project. The hybrid pigs were fed commercial feeds by families, instead of the sweet potato and leaves fed to so-called "native pigs."

Women maintained ownership of their property even after marriage or separation from a spouse. This offered women some economic security in the event of separation. Land purchased after marriage was owned equally by husband and wife. Land could be sold, purchased, and mortgaged in Ifugao, yet it was primarily sold among family members. However, this pattern was changing slowly, with greater accessibility to and need for cash.

Differences in wealth and status were assessed very intricately in Ifugao. When I asked Ifugao men and women in the three communities to classify families within their barrios into ranked economic groups, from wealthy to poor, some people delineated ten distinct groups. For the purposes of this analysis, I will outline my respondents' conceptions of three social classes.

The families who comprised the upper class group were viewed as distinct from the most wealthy families in the Philippines at large, in that the Ifugao wealthy could not compare to the elite billionaires of the Philippines. Nevertheless, there were wealthy families in Ifugao, some of whom owned hotels, sizable rice fields, restaurants, large trucks to transport goods, and dry good stores, and or had substantial cash savings.

Since Ifugao's incorporation into the market economy, there had been a distinction made between the wealthy who were indigenously termed *kadangyan* and those called *bacnang*. *Kadangyan* were the traditional wealthy, those who had become wealthy through their inheritance of large areas of irrigated rice fields and valuable heirlooms. *Bacnang* (sometimes called *bfwatnang,* an Ifugao version of the Ilocano *bacnang*) was an imported Ilocano term which identified upper class who acquired their wealth through their own economic activities, such as business or agricultural ventures, and who generally retained large amounts of cash.[11] *Bacnang* may also have owned large areas of irrigated rice fields, the majority of which they purchased either inside or outside of Ifugao.

In the early 1990s, *kadangyan*, and some *bacnang*, possessed sizable areas of irrigated rice fields (at least more than one quarter of a hectare). But the actual land possessed was not the most significant factor in determining the wealth of families among Ifugao people. Rather, it was the ability to produce enough rice for one's family to be able to eat rice for three meals per day, every day, until the next harvest, and possibly to have rice left over to pay people for labor, to loan, to sell, and to use for rituals or community events. Rice was the most highly valued food product in Ifugao. Rice had only recently become the main staple food for the majority of Ifugao people. Prior to the middle of this century, when rice began to be imported into Ifugao, the sweet potato was the main staple crop of the lower class in Ifugao. The sweet potato was still regarded as the food of the poor during my research period.

Bacnang, and some *kadangyan*, invariably had large cash savings, which they often loaned out with interest.[12] Some *bacnang* may have owned large businesses (hotels, restaurants, dry goods stores) within or outside of Ifugao. They were also able to offer cash for labor in the rice fields, while other families more commonly paid workers in kind with rice.

Kadangyan and *bacnang* usually could afford to pay for their children's college education. They often had a large, so-called "modern house," constructed out of wood or cement, rather than a "native house" (*bfwaley*) built on wooden stilts or a nipa hut (*aphong*).[13] Some owned many large animals, such as cows or water buffalo. Ownership of vehicles also signified wealth, since only a very low percentage of Ifugao families owned vehicles.

One person observed that upper class persons had a "high well-being" overall. Eating a wide variety of foods (especially rice, meat, and expensive canned foods) and being overweight were usually associated with wealth. *Kadangyan* and *bacnang* were able and expected to butcher many pigs, water buffalo, or cows at rituals or family and community events, signifying great wealth and offering the upper class prestige and honor.

Both men and women were considered to be *kadangyan* and *bacnang*, and each had high status in Ifugao. Yet, female *kadangyan* and *bacnang* were usually not considered to be the head of their household unless their husband had died. Also, male *kadangyan* had been considered historically as community political and social leaders, and decision makers on community councils, who attained their position through birthright, possession of property, and performance of specified ceremonies (Scott 1982:135). This perception has continued to some extent today. Historically, female *kadangyan* were not allowed access to this leadership role.

Women's participation in leadership positions still remains limited, although this has been changing. Generally, male *kadangyan* and *bacnang* were accorded a higher status than female *kadangyan* and *bacnang*. However, female *kadangyan* and *bacnang* had high status in relation to poor men and women. Since the upper class officially comprised only about 4 percent of the Ifugao population, there were not many Ifugao women who were accorded high status based on their economic wealth.[14]

The middle class was formerly, but rarely today, indigenously referred to as *natumok* (Barton 1919). During the 1990s, the middle class was considered to be better-off than the lower class. Most of the middle class possessed some terraced, irrigated rice fields, but fewer than the upper class, and they may not have produced enough rice to last until the next harvest. If they did not own rice fields, they had enough money to purchase their needs from employment or wage labor. Many of the men, and some of the women, had full time employment, some professional and some skilled and non-skilled labor, or they owned a thriving small business. Some middle class men were woodcarvers, who sometimes migrated for labor.[15] Some middle class families received a pension, from the Philippine government or the U.S. government (for veterans of World War II), or received financial assistance from a relative working overseas. They usually had modern homes made of wood, concrete, or galvanized iron. Middle class families could afford to purchase all of their basic needs, and most could afford to formally educate their children. Some owned one or two water buffalo, which they could rent for plowing. Still, the middle class of Ifugao did not really approximate the middle class of the United States, since most had no cars, plumbing in their homes, or products such as flush toilets, washing machines, clothes dryers, or televisions. The middle class officially made up approximately 21 percent of the Ifugao population.[16] High status usually was accorded to middle class women who were highly educated and employed in professional positions, rather than for economic reasons.

The lower class poor were indigenously identified as *nawotwot*. They comprised the majority of the Ifugao population, as approximately 75 percent of the residents of the province had incomes falling below the official government designated poverty line.[17] In some Ifugao barrios in 1992, the average income of lower class families fell far below the poverty level set by the national government for Ifugao Province. In one barrio, for example, the average annual income of all families (the majority of whom were lower class) was only 14,091 pesos compared to the government determined poverty line of 27,396 pesos for a family of six in the province (CECAP 1992).

Ifugao people distinguished between different degrees of poverty within the lower class. Those in the upper levels of the lower class usually possessed one to six small irrigated rice fields, while those in the lower levels had few or no rice fields. They had irregular additional cash income. At times they lacked basic necessities; and they could not always send their children to high school, and more rarely still to college. They usually had to work on other people's fields for cash or rice, or sharecrop, from which they obtained one-half of the harvest. In one Ifugao municipality, many of the men carved wood. Many of the children also earned money by wood carving (for boys), working as a domestic helper (mostly for girls), agricultural labor, or engaging in other work. They often contributed to their families' incomes. The lower class' rice harvest was never sufficient to provide enough rice throughout the year until the next harvest, since they did not own enough rice fields. So they had to earn cash to purchase rice, earn rice in kind, or cultivate sweet potatoes for their staple food. Most raised small animals, such as chickens, pigs, ducks, and—for fewer families—goats and turkeys. They often had to borrow food or money to survive, especially during the months prior to the rice harvest.

The poorest of the lower class families had no irrigated rice fields. They earned their main incomes by sharecropping or by performing agricultural or other wage labor. The men depended on wood carving (in one municipality), wage labor on government projects, migrant labor, or any other source of cash income. Women earned cash less often, but they could earn some through agricultural labor. Some women finished wood carvings, washed the laundry of the upper classes, wove, sold small amounts of vegetables, or engaged in other work in which they could earn cash. They also raised small domesticated animals.

Many lower class people noted they were living from "hand to mouth," as they were always running out of rice. One poor man commented, "We have no rest. We have to work continuously. You have to run after rice." Although the poor ate more sweet potato than the middle or upper classes due to lack of rice, they strove to earn or borrow money to purchase rice, since they preferred both the taste of rice and the feeling of fullness in their stomachs rice provides. Many parents of the lower class perceived their children to be their wealth and to accord them with at least some degree of status in the Ifugao community.

The most insecure among the poor tended to be the elderly (persons over sixty years old), single (usually widowed) women, and families who had an adult member with a serious or long-term illness. Of the fifteen poorest families in one barrio, ten had principle adults who were sixty years old and above. Of eight widows residing in this barrio, six were among the poorest families of the barrio. Ifugao people tended to become poor as they grew older, mainly due to the cultural practice of giving their children inheritances of rice fields upon their marriages. This depleted older Ifugao people's primary material resources. However, constant interaction remained between the majority of married children and their parents, in terms of food production, sharing of economic and food resources, child care, and continued parental advice. Since elderly people's active engagement in agricultural production became more physically difficult as they aged, this inheritance practice and mode of continued interaction between children and parents ensured their being provided for in their old age. This clearly signalled one important reason for the great desire and need of Ifugao parents to bear children who could support them in their old age. If elderly people were initially poor, they could become members of the most impoverished group as they aged. Single women became members of the most impoverished group for many reasons, including the low wage rates for women.

Power and Prestige

Power and prestige in Ifugao was most heavily dependent on wealth. Power was also derived from holding high level political office (congressman, governor, mayor, councilor, barrio captain, etc.). Most commonly, those who held positions of power were members of the upper and middle classes (except for position of barrio captain). This was a continuation, to some extent, of the historical practice of *kadangyan* community leadership, though operating within a very different political system. Ifugao people could also attain prestige from displaying strong oratory skills; from offering many animals and rice to spiritual beings, and sharing the offerings with other community members during ritual ceremonies; and from providing many animals and rice for secular community events. Power in Ifugao was also displayed by militarization, weapons, and violence, depicting the power of individuals (e.g., the wealthy or political office holders who retained private armies), the state, or the rebelling forces (members of the NPA). Historically, men could acquire prestige through bravery and success in warfare and headhunting expeditions.

Dress and material products displayed social status. Local dress, such as the *torkay* (or *tapis*, woman's skirt) or the *wanoh* (man's loin cloth), identified the social class of the wearer through the colors and patterns, and the place and community to which a person belonged. Wearing expensive western styled clothing also signified wealth and prestige. Specific styles of woven blankets were used during funeral rituals, depending on the social class of the deceased. Religious leadership also accorded status, and some degree of power.

Age ranking was an important source of status in Ifugao. Persons older than an individual were accorded a high degree of respect. The use of honorifics was embedded in Ifugao discourse, such as the use of *manang* (elder sister or woman) or *manong* (elder brother or man), both imported Ilocano terms, when addressing an older person. Conversely, elder siblings were responsible for aiding their younger siblings' development, both morally and financially. Providing this assistance accorded elder siblings high social status and respect from their younger siblings. In the realm of age ranking, women were accorded higher status and greater respect than men in situations where they were older than the men concerned.

In the Philippines at large, ethnicity influenced social status and ethnic stratification could generate discrimination. Ifugao people, particularly of the lower class, faced problems related to their ethnicity in Philippine society at large. A coalition of ten women's organizations in Metro Manila, called the Group of 10, noted: "For women from indigenous non-Christian groups, there is the additional bind of ethnicity, i.e., their marginalization through subordination, neglect, and stigmatization by the dominant lowland Christian culture" (Group of 10 1989:6).

As an ethnic minority group in the Cordillera region, Ifugao people have faced problems related to their cultural practices which have been in conflict with national government plans and policies. Ifugao people were active in the Cordillera Peoples Alliance (CPA), seeking regional autonomy in an effort to overcome these conflicts. Examples of conflicts in the Cordillera region included resistance to the implementation of large state and international development projects, such as dams, geared toward meeting the needs of modernization and industrialization of the Philippines (Cordillera Resource Center 1996). For Ifugao people, ethnic inequality also was demonstrated during the last decade by the Philippine government's attempt to control the Cordillera people's opportunity for regional autonomy prior to the 1990 plebiscite for approval of Republic Act 6766, or the Cordillera Organic Act. This manipulation was seen as an attempt by members of the government to maintain access to resources in the Cordillera region and impede the Cordillera people's drive to gain control over their own resources and land (Cordillera Resource Center 1990).[18]

Agrarian reform also had specific meaning for Ifugao people. The mandates of the agrarian reform law regarding land redistribution did not affect many Ifugao landowners, since the average size of rice fields in the province was less than five hectares. A few large landowners in Ifugao were affected, however (Nolledo 1987:122). Also, much of the agricultural land in Ifugao was protected by the right of indigenous communities to control their ancestral lands and the exemption of lands with at least an eighteen degree slope under the 1987 Philippine Constitution, although these rights may be superseded by other national laws.[19] But a genuine agrarian reform law could improve the lives of many Ifugao peasants, since many were migrating out of Ifugao for the last few decades in search of agricultural lands to purchase, especially in neighboring provinces in Cagayan Valley such as Isabella and Nueva Viscaya. Other migrants had searched for regular employment in both rural and urban Philippine areas. This increased migration was due to many factors, such as increasing population growth, inadequate agricultural land to support the population, inadequate food supply, decreasing soil fertility, and high unemployment within Ifugao. Also, some Ifugao families had purchased agricultural land in the Cagayan Valley, while still residing within Ifugao Province. Redistributed agricultural lands in the Philippine lowland areas, which conceivably could be distributed or sold at low cost to Ifugao migrants, might benefit many Ifugao families.

For Ifugao people, as well as other residents of the Cordillera mountain region, one of the most significant aspects of the Comprehensive Agrarian Reform Law was the recognition by the Philippine government agency implementing the Comprehensive Agrarian Reform Program (CARP) of the Cordillera mountain people's right to their ancestral lands and its resources. Although the Philippine constitution acknowledged this right, almost 87 percent of the total land area of the Cordillera Mountain Region was declared government property, particularly as "forest land," despite the fact that much of this land was referred to as "ancestrally owned lands" by Cordillera people, land that had been cultivated for generations. The government allowed large-scale logging on these lands by large businesses and politicians, leading to soil erosion and the drying up of fertile agricultural lands. The government also allowed expanded mining operations in Benguet Province of the Cordillera region. Land titling processes involved in CARP were also problematic. I heard discussion of cases of abuse of this system by persons who had extensive knowledge of the bureaucratic processes involved in land titling, affecting persons who had little or no knowledge of these procedures. Proponents of Cordillera regional autonomy from the national Philippine government wished to have the question of the recognition of their ancestral domain resolved before any land redistribution took place (Batangantang 1989:31-34).

Ifugao Women's Position Considered

Gender relations and the social position or status of Ifugao women were issues discussed and contested among Philippine state agents, development agents, members of national and Cordillera regional women's organizations, Cordillera region scholars, Ifugao women and men, and members of religious organizations.[20] Some scholars proposed that Cordillera gender relations, including those in Ifugao, were primarily egalitarian, while other women, especially those involved in feminist activism, stressed Cordillera women's inequality with men. Although assigning a single level of status, high or low, to women is problematic, the social position of Ifugao women is important to this study of malnutrition in Ifugao society because many of the development programs operating in Ifugao had as part of their ideology the view that women's social status in Ifugao was lower than that of men's, both within Ifugao and in Philippine society in general (UNICEF 1992b). Further, they proposed that raising women's economic status could aid in raising their overall social status.

Advocates and practitioners of women in development historically have assumed that work outside of the home enhanced status for women (Tinker 1990a:9). National and international health program personnel have asserted that with the raising of women's economic and social status, the health and nutritional status of both women and their children will improve. The UNICEF and CECAP programs in Ifugao sought to identify and incorporate in their plans strategies that would meet the needs of women (Women Development and Technology, Inc. 1992:69). As noted earlier, academic researchers have also proposed a strong relationship between women's nutritional status and their social status (Senauer 1990; Schoepf 1987).

Most western scholars historically, and some Filipino scholars currently, have stressed the relatively high status of Filipino women.[21] In a recent study of women in the Cordillera region, Filipino researchers dismissed feminist arguments regarding the oppression of Filipino women, stating that they found that there was "little evidence of systematic oppression of (Cordillera) women either by socialization or through social institutions associated with agriculture" (Casambre et al. 1992:93).

The idea of Filipino women having high status usually has been based on comparisons of Filipino women to women of other cultures, such as Indian or Middle Eastern women. High status for women usually means they enjoy economic opportunities, suffer few legal restrictions or damning stereotypes, and participate in cultures where the sexes are construed in terms of complementarity and balance rather than differential worth in comparison to men (Atkinson and Errington 1990:viii).[22]

Historically, scholars often attributed their evaluation of women's high status and equality between men and women in societies designated as indigenous in Southeast Asia (including Ifugao) to their bilateral kinship systems. Also, some scholars have viewed Filipino women's management of the family's finances as proof of women's high status and power within the family (Alvarez and Alvarez 1973). Differences in work patterns have been viewed simply as differences in gender roles, roles that scholars described as being complementary to each other. Complementarity, as defined by Errington, is an ideology of difference between the sexes, even opposites, but the opposites are parts that always reunite to form an undifferentiated whole. The opposites complement each other rather than compete against each other (Errington 1990). For example, in rice production in areas of Ifugao, men built, repaired and plowed rice fields, while women planted, weeded, and harvested rice—all of which were necessary tasks for the production of rice. The different roles enacted by insular Southeast Asian men and women have been viewed historically by scholars in terms of complementarity and egalitarianism. Only recently have scholars begun to inquire into power relations involved in gender roles.

To say that women in the Philippines traditionally enjoyed high status does not inform us empirically about what actual power they have in society, nor of the actual conditions under which women live. It is important to look at local cultural constructions of gender relations on their own terms, rather than primarily in comparison to western or other societies (Errington 1990; Ong 1988). It is also important to take into account differences in women's social position within each society, depending on different variables such as their social class or their educational attainment, in relation to the meanings that are attributed to these variables in each society (Eviota 1986). Ifugao women's position was not categorically low or high in the early 1990s. As will be shown, women's status in Ifugao was situationally variable, depending on the women and men involved, the social position of each, and the arena of status being considered (e.g., social class, age rank, or educational attainment). Nevertheless, in some very significant areas of life—especially economic, political, and domestic—the majority of Ifugao women experienced lesser power in relation to men.

Cultural Conceptions of Women

Ifugao women have of late experienced increasing modernization, incorporation into the Philippine market economy, and national and international development efforts in Ifugao society; conditions of widespread poverty; internal war; increased migration; institutionalization of Christianity; and greater numbers of Ifugao youths attending college. All of these phenomena have had an impact on Ifugao gender ideology and women's social position. Additionally, the rise of a national Philippine women's movement since the 1960s, having roots in women's struggles for suffrage at the turn of the century, is just beginning to have an impact on Ifugao women. The women's movement in the Philippines had its inception in the urban areas, where it developed its greatest organizational strength. Women activists only began consciousness raising activities in Ifugao in the late 1980s, after the women's movement blossomed in the mid-1980s in Metro Manila during Marcos' fall from power (Angeles 1989; Jayawardena 1986).

Ifugao women held a variety of conceptions of what it meant to be a contemporary Ifugao woman in the early 1990s, interpreted here as Ifugao cultural construction of female gender roles. The following were some of their conceptions of the cultural ideal of an Ifugao woman. One lower class, widowed woman said:

> She goes to the field and weeds, plants rice, harvests, goes to the swidden field, then burns the field and plants with mongo or rice. When the mongo is ripened she will harvest it. Then weed again and plant the sweet potato. When it is grown, she will get sweet potato. She should feed the chickens and pigs. She will go and get cogon grasses for roofing of the house. She loves other people. She loves her family and children. She is a good Christian, believing in God. She doesn't steal. And she shares, especially vegetables if she has.

Another married, lower class Christian woman said:

> She only marries once. She doesn't divorce and commit adultery. She respects all relatives of her husband, the same as her own relatives. She is working. If she is a farmer, she is really a farmer. She must go to work in the fields, swidden fields. She is not extravagant, buying unnecessary things. That is always the talk of the people, like bread and candies. Most especially, she is not supposed to be a drunkard. And a woman who is not a slanderer and gossiper.

Other lower class women stressed women's role as health providers: "She would help, especially for those who will give birth; and the sick, they will help to watch.

Teach the children what is good, good manners and right conduct." Or, "Like meetings about nutrition, they [women] will join." Other lower class women emphasized women's role in their community: "We will work our own work and work of others, as *ubfu* and at the same time for payment. We have to cooperate with other organizations and other people. To share our knowledge or opinion in the community"; or, "She would be helpful; she would help solve the problems of the community."

Other women spoke about what women should not be, some depicting the value placed on women repressing their anger and stressing cooperation with other family and community members. Responses included: "They will not quarrel with their husband. They are very kind, even if their husband has a hot temper"; "She is very kind. She will not have a hot temper. She should know how to care for herself. She knows how to care for her house"; "She is not a gossiper, doesn't have a hot temper. She doesn't quarrel. She works, she helps her neighbors and relatives, like *baddang*"; "she shouldn't go with many men, not be a nagger, not steal," and "You have to ask permission before you get something in others' fields, like vegetables."[23] The last woman added, "Here, they expect women to get married."

The majority of the women stressed women's work and the cultural prescription for women to be "industrious" in their work: "She will make a swidden field, work in the fields. Just always working. She helps others"; "They will take care of their children"; and "She will work for her food." One woman emphasized that women should not be dependent on their husbands, saying, "She knows everything to do. She knows how to work, and knows what she is doing, unlike other women who don't know what they are doing and only depend on their husbands for everything."

Other women stressed the importance of a woman's relation to her family, her desire to have children, and her responsibility to provide care and work for them. It is important "that you would have children. Most Ifugao people like to have many children; that is their prayer"; "produce children and be married. Because in Ifugao way, even if you are married a long time, if no children, you separate because you have no children"; "She knows how to care for her children, her husband, and her house, and the animals. Clean the house and the children. And work"; "the woman manages the money of the house." Some women discussed a woman's relation to her husband, saying, "During work they will help the men also. She respects her husband," and "A mother does her ordinary activities, like cleaning the fields, carrying her babies, cooking the food, and getting the food, like sweet potatoes, and offers service to her husband." Some women discussed a woman's role in sharing food among community members, especially among her children and relatives: "They will share, give food if you will ask for food if you are in need."

One woman commented upon the heterogeneity of expectations of women among community members, saying, "Some will say, 'Oh, she has done a good thing.' And sometimes, even if you do a good thing, they will say, 'Oh, you did something wrong.' So, there are different expectations among different people."

One woman stressed women's need to repress their feelings if they did not conform to cultural expectations of women's gendered role. This also relates, as will be seen, to the expectation that women should always share food with their family members and sometimes sacrifice their own nutritional needs for that of other family members:

> Women should be industrious. But even if she is industrious and has a bad attitude, then she is not considered to be good. Bad attitude means stealing or if you ask her for something she gets mad; or goes with other men when she's married. And even if she is industrious, but she gets something and hides it from her family, like a good type of viand and eats it herself. But seldom women will do that.

Beauty was not a primary attribute demanded of Ifugao women. As one woman commented, "A woman who is pretty but has a bad attitude, that is not good. But even if she is ugly and she has a good attitude, that is good. She should respect her companions, her husband. She is not selfish, helps other people, shares food with other people and does not quarrel with other people." One man's response depicts the value placed on women's work over beauty: "she should really go to the fields instead of protecting her fingers. When it is Ifugao work, she will really work and not be afraid to get her hands dirty, like those Manila girls who never want to get dirty. . . . They [Ifugao people] still judge you on how you work in the field. . . . How can you scold her if all the work that she will do she is doing it?"

Ifugao women were expected to dress in a conservative manner. As one middle class woman responded, "How you dress yourself; you see to it that you wash your clothes to look nice. Longer dress length, not low cut blouses. Everyone should have a *tapis* for special occasions."

The greater cultural value placed on women's work over their beauty depicted a cultural ethos of hard work for women in Ifugao, and it may be explained by the tremendous amount of work that was required by both women and men for basic survival in this predominantly subsistence level agricultural community. It also pointed to the complementary nature of Ifugao work patterns between men and women, in that each sex relied on the other to perform the activities involved in food production. Therefore, men valued women's hard work very highly for their own and their children's basic survival. Still, it will be seen that an even higher value was attributed to men's work in Ifugao culture, as it was perceived to be more physically strenuous and demanding.

The responses of women of all social classes did not vary greatly. It is striking that Ifugao women of the upper class continued to work outside of the home despite their financial security, again depicting the strong Ifugao value of women working hard, both inside and outside of the home. Many middle aged and elderly upper class women continued to carry out agricultural labor due to their love of farming, while younger upper class women usually engaged in business or professional work. To construct Ifugao women primarily as mothers, which most international aid—especially health—organizations tended to do, was culturally inappropriate in Ifugao.

Although a woman was expected to share everything with other members of her family and not to buy extravagant things, a father could use family money for his gambling and drinking of alcohol, which, although not necessarily approved of by his wife, was generally accepted in the Ifugao community. Also, despite the stress on working industriously, women were thought by Ifugao men and women to be inherently the weaker sex, more suited to "lighter" work. They were also viewed as less likely candidates for social positions of leadership and power. Characteristics similar to the cultural constructions of Ifugao women also were found in other areas of the Philippines, as noted by Carolyn Israel-Sobritchea (Israel-Sobritchea 1992:22).

Gender Relations

Women usually maintained autonomy in their work, both in agriculture as well in other types of work and employment outside of the home. For example, of thirty-five married peasant women interviewed, 86 percent (thirty) stated that they could decide independently how they would conduct their work without consulting their husbands, and may even be consulted by their husbands regarding agricultural work. Ifugao women had an extensive knowledge of agriculture, which was not necessarily shared by their husbands. As one woman explained, for agricultural work she made the decisions "because the men don't know about planting, only the women. They [men] come only to make the rice paddies." Another woman said that it is only in the area of agricultural work that she made independent decisions in her household, "because the men don't know about the work of women."

Women's work outside of the home and their decision making ability in their work did not necessarily translate to full equality with men, however, particularly for women of the lower class who had little education. Some men and women who did not own irrigated rice fields worked on other owners' fields as tenant farmers, usually acquiring one-half of the rice harvested, while other men and women worked as seasonal day laborers for either a cash wage or payment in kind of rice. Many did both. Some women worked as day laborers to pay off debts previously acquired.

Virtually all peasant women worked on other people's rice fields during the planting and harvest periods, since it was too difficult to accomplish this work alone. Relatives and friends were requested to work on a rice field by the owner or tenant farmer on a specific date. This system rotated until all of the rice fields were planted or harvested. There were at least four modes of payment for women's group agricultural labor. One mode was called *ubfu*, which was a pattern of reciprocal labor. Through *ubfu*, a woman or a man worked on another's field for one day, and the owner or tenant farmer of that field had to return the labor on that worker's fields on another day. Written or mental records of labor accomplished and owed were maintained by each peasant or land owner. Laborers could be paid in cash instead, or in kind with rice, or they could work to pay off a previous debt. The mode of payment for each laborer (which may be as many as forty laborers in one day) was negotiated with the owner or tenant farmer of the rice field until both agreed. This practice of networking for mutual assistance and paid labor was integral to agricultural production in Ifugao and demonstrated the need for sustained relations among Ifugao people, both within and between social classes.

Women's labor was not valued equally with men's labor, however. One day's pay for women's agricultural work in Ifugao, which was culturally rather than legally prescribed, was only one-half that of men's and only one-half the regional daily wage rate. Ifugao women, therefore, did not even earn a minimum wage for their agricultural labor. Women performing government paid manual labor were sometimes paid less than men for performing the same work, as women told me was the case for two government reforestation projects in the early 1990s in two different Ifugao municipalities. Women who did finishing work on wood carvings, as a part of craft production, were paid less than men who carved the wood.[24] Despite the fact that a national law mandated that men and women's salaries should be equal, the cultural system in Ifugao of paying women less than men persisted, as gendered work designated for women was valued less highly than gendered work designated for men.

Ifugao women held varying opinions on the reasons for this pay differential and the fairness of the unequal pattern. One lower class peasant woman said, "Men earn more because that is the rate here. It's not the same with men and women. Like in harvesting, five bundles of rice for women and ten bundles of rice for men. It's not the same. I don't know why. That's how it began before. It's fair." Another lower class peasant woman said:

> I don't know why women's rate is lower than men's. It is already established that it is lower for women than men. Because even before, you could earn only thirty pesos while men can make seventy pesos. Half/half. Now, women can make forty pesos and men eighty pesos. It's been like that for a long time. In the olden days, women earned fifty centavos while men earned one peso for one day's work. This is unfair because they both work together for the same number of hours. We cannot do anything because it depends on the type of work. I worked before in IRRI, and I earned thirty-five pesos, and we asked to add five pesos to make it at least forty pesos.[25] So when IRRI raised it to forty pesos, that's when the people raised it to forty pesos.
>
> In the government forestry nursery, forty pesos a day for women and fifty pesos for men for the same type of work. Probably it depends on the employer [contractor for government work], because they are the ones getting the money and they will pay them. We complained to the Department of Agriculture worker that we will not work unless you raise the pay [mostly women complained, and one man]. He said he would check, but we got no response until now.

But mostly here, they pay you low because you are a woman and the standard here is that the salary of the men should be higher than the woman. But in the office it's not the same. Sometimes, the woman is earning more than the man. It depends on their course or degree. It is common practice here to pay women less for the same labor as men.

One woman said, "I think men are more powerful than women." An upper class businesswoman said Ifugao women earned less than men, "because the man works harder than the woman here in our custom. No, it's fair, because we are not working so hard; but the man is working hard." Another upper class business-woman disagreed, saying,

> They keep saying that it's in agricultural work that the men's work is heavier than women's. Women just weed but men's work is heavier, since they carry rice bundles from the fields to the homes and use their strength. That's not fair, because they [women] work the same hours. They stay under the sun the same hours, and they really exert effort. I don't know how to equalize men's and women's pay because it's not the government or an agency paying men and women for agricultural work. It's the rich who are doing that to them, because the people go to ask them to work. The wages are not necessarily standardized; it's what they [the rich] say.

A married couple, who are professionals, held the following conversation with me:

> Husband: As we consider the weaker sex [women], that they will be underpaid in the usual way, they can't compare their work to men. Their work is lighter than men. Like harvesting, they are just harvesting, whereas the men are carrying rice from the fields to the houses, which is heavier. It is not fair, but it is a tradition, custom.
> Wife: It's not fair because it's the same hours. But the problem there is the kind of work. The men work harder, but the women work lighter. The same. But if we see the classification of work, there is a difference. Cleaning, planting, lighter. Making stone walls, men can do because it's heavier. Men can first clean swidden fields.[26] People don't like to hire women to do men's work, because they think they're slower and won't do the job as well. If the husband is away from home or dead, the women can do men's work, but the lighter men's work. But men can also do better the work of women. If a man's wife died, and there are no other women to hire, men can do it. Men do it better. Plus it's easier than being a single woman, because women's work is easier for men to do than vice versa.
> Husband: Women have more work than men because men's work is seasonal. But women work day in and day out. Not like in the lowlands where the men are doing the work. There's a great difference in [one Ifugao municipality and another Ifugao municipality], that women can do men's work in [one municipality where] women are the one's preparing the fields and planting the seedlings. In [the other municipality], men prepare the fields before planting. For those fields with water, women can do, but in dried fields men will plow.

The majority of the women explained that there was a wage differential between men and women primarily because that was the *ugali* (tradition or culture) among the Ifugao. One Ifugao woman said, "I think that this is traditional, that they are still following. Because otherwise, if not for that tradition, women's pay should be increased. Because before, the men were hardworking, and they often look that cleaning and weeding is light work. But actually, they [women] are tired, just like the men, so it should be equal." Some Christians claimed that the differential wage pattern between men and women was a commandment of Moses, thereby validating the practice through the use of the Bible.

As seen from these comments, Ifugao women were divided about the issue of the inequality of agricultural pay rates for men and women, as some women expressed their wish to equalize the pay and others preferred that the rates remain as they were. Of fifty-one women interviewed, 67 percent (thirty-four) said that they thought the pay differential was fair, 31 percent (sixteen) thought it was unfair, while one woman was unsure. The view of some women that the gendered pay differential was unfair represented the changing ideologies of women regarding women's value and rights in Ifugao society, as well as the changing work patterns in Ifugao. One Ifugao feminist (who had attempted consciousness raising work in Ifugao in the late 1980s but who quit due to her feeling a lack of support from Ifugao women) stated that the view that women are inferior to men was "very strong in the [Ifugao] culture." The women who thought the pay rates for men and women were fair predominantly gave the following reasons: men did heavier work than women; it was the custom of the Ifugao people since agricultural labor payment has always been this way; and the employers refused to pay men and women equally, so women had to accept what they were offered, since they had few other options for employment.

Ifugao people evaluated the difficulty of men's work in terms of the physical effort men exerted in performing labor culturally designated for them. For women's work, Ifugao people evaluated its difficulty in terms of the longer length of time spent by women in accomplishing the work tasks culturally assigned to women than spent by men. One woman expressed the following during an interview:

> That is our problem, why? Why are women being paid lower than men? Maybe on the types of work. In my opinion, this is fair for some types of work, but not all, so that women and men have different pay. Like in working in road widening, men and women are the same rate. Our farming work, harvesting and planting, it's fair for me because in planting the women can just not exert more effort. But for men, they are using the spade and exerting more effort. But all pay for work is unfair when it comes to the time of the work. But if it is for effort, then it [women's lower rate] is fair also for men and women. For the lower rate of women, it is for effort. But if they work the same amount of time, they should get the same pay. To make it fair, women and men should be paid the same, not considering the effort.

> Even if you have no money . . . you need to pay someone just for labor. . . .
> Because we are poor we only provide that low rate of women; and women also accept
> it because of lack of work. Even if they need a higher rate, if there's no work for that
> higher rate, they have to do it at the low rate. It's better to have a lower rate than
> nothing.

This last statement exemplified the important structural reason why women accepted their low agricultural pay, which was below the official minimum wage. By the early 1990s, Ifugao people were actors working within a capitalist labor market, created only within this century. Within this capitalist labor market, there were very few other employment opportunities in Ifugao for non-professional women who had no access to capital to initiate a business. While there were still inadequate numbers of cash paying job opportunities available for men, there were even less culturally designated jobs available for women, as expressed by both Ifugao women and men. Another peasant woman said, "Women are paid lower because if she is going to spend time going to look for other jobs that will pay a higher wage and there are no jobs that pay higher than that, you might as well just take the low paying work. . . . I don't know if this is fair. I think I am not satisfied, but I cannot do anything. If I think to go and work for cash paying labor, I should go away from the community." Another landless peasant woman depicted the bind that women felt they were in and their perceived lack of power to change the situation:

> And men have a higher pay than women because their work is harder. Actually,
> it is unfair, but we have to be patient, because that is the only work we can do, and
> there is no other work. It depends on the person who will give the amount. If you will
> ask them to change it, the owner might say, "But you are not the one who is paying
> them." If I was the one paying, I might do that. They [owners] will say, "Oh, and you
> are only the laborer and you are telling me what to do?" We just be patient with the
> work in our place. Even if it's not enough, we just say nothing. We don't say
> anything because they might say, "This is how we give the rating. What do you
> know? You are only the laborer." I'm also afraid that if I speak out I won't get any
> work. The owner might say, "Have you been doing that [paying women equal pay]?"
> That is why I'm ashamed to ask.

Two women did state that they had asked employers to raise women's agricultural pay rates in the past, but to no avail. One woman said that she would like people in her barrio or at municipal meetings to discuss an increase in women's agricultural pay rates.

While many women responded that men were given a higher pay because their work was harder than women's, many women also complained that, overall, women worked much more than men in terms of time spent laboring and the number of tasks required of them. Some women related this to women's poor nutritional status. While discussing nutritional status with one Ifugao woman health volunteer, who was a peasant, she said, "The men are stronger [more well nourished], because the women are harder workers in the field. . . . If you are going to observe the mothers here, they look very old compared to the men." Ifugao women also related women's lower nutritional status to their spending less time in recreation compared to men. Overall, women viewed themselves as more hardworking than men, since men spent more free time socializing with their male companions (commonly referred to as *barkada*) than women did with their female companions. One woman said, "Women are more hardworking here in [our Ifugao community] than men. . . . Women work day and night, day and night." One Ifugao woman, who was a government social worker, said:

> At nighttime, usually the man sleeps well, but women are the ones to take care of the children when they awaken during the night. When men finish their work outside, they can rest sometimes, but women come home from their work outside of the home and do most of the house chores and care for their children. Although there are some men who help in the household; but many men say the work in the household and caring for the children is the work of the women. The men only take care of children when women are away working in the fields. In most cases, both are working, men are out working for money, but women are growing vegetables. More men work for cash than women; when men wood carve, they sell it for cash. There are not as many opportunities for women to work for cash.

The claim that Ifugao women work longer hours than men was verified by a 1992 study funded by UNICEF. It was conducted by a research group called Women Development and Technology, Inc., which carried out a time allocation study among women and men in one municipality of Ifugao.[27] The study found that Ifugao women work longer hours than Ifugao men through their combined reproductive and productive tasks. They also found that on many occasions women's labor tasks overlapped, that is, these tasks were conducted simultaneously, placing greater strain on women physically and emotionally (Women Development and Technology, Inc. 1992:70).

Women's work (planting, weeding, harvesting, and other work) was also viewed as more repetitious than men's work, having to be carried out on virtually a daily basis from early morning until dusk. Men's work was viewed as more short-term and more varied. Women described their work as never-ending, both within and outside of the home, while men's work seemed to women to have distinct initial and terminating phases. A few women also said that women never had enough time during each day to accomplish all of the work they needed to do.

In professional work, although women were paid equal salaries with men, over time men were given preference for promotion to higher positions according greater authority and power. The majority of high-level positions in Ifugao government offices were filled by men, except in health care where there were approximately equal numbers of male and female doctors in Ifugao. Professional women were employed primarily in lower-level governmental teaching, secretarial, and health positions, while the majority of elected and hired or appointed government officials were men. Although some women did hold positions of authority, they were a small minority.

One reason given for these differences was that there was an association made between the level of professional position and the expectation that women maintain primary responsibility for child care in their families. It was assumed that women would have reduced ability to travel away from their families, which was often required of persons holding higher positions. This construction of women persisted as part of the Ifugao gender ideology, despite the professionalization of women's work, and hindered women's professional advancement and level of power. Another reason given for fewer promotions of women was that it may have been dangerous for women to hike to distant villages alone, for fear of men's violence against them. One married couple, both professionals, explained their view of why professional women were promoted less often than men. The wife said, "Sometimes women are talkative, so they aren't promoted." Her husband added, "The ladies are vocal, and they may expose corruption." Having internalized their culturally assigned role of primary child care provider, some women requested to be assigned to an area that was near their homes so that they could be closer to their families, thereby participating in the limiting of their professional advancement.

Using western derived terms and ideology, men were considered to be the "head of household" (*ulun chi pamilya*) by most Ifugao people. "Head of the family" is understood by some Ifugao women to be the one who disciplines the children; the "bread earner" (again a western concept); the decision maker; the planner and manager of the family; the one responsible for "getting all of the needs of the family"; "he will teach and correct the woman if you are lacking in something," and "He directs us in what to do, like in work. . . . Because the men, you have to obey; do not override your husband." One woman said her husband was the head of the family because her Christian religion taught her that this was natural. She said, "it says in the Bible that the man is the head of the family. So that is nature, for all husbands to be the head of the family. But only if the husband is still there; because if he is dead, the wife is the head of the family." A professional man said that while male dominance in the family and community was historical in Ifugao culture, another reason for this could be the influence of the teachings of the Catholic Church, which became influential in Ifugao during the twentieth century. He said that in his experience, the Catholic Church taught its members that women must be subservient to their husbands. As will be seen later, contemporary Protestant churches offered the same message to Ifugao people.

Of forty-four married women interviewed, 61 percent (twenty-seven) said that they considered their husband to the "head of the household"; 36 percent (sixteen) said that they were equal to their husband and there was no single head of the household; and one woman did not understand the term. Ten single women interviewed headed their households alone, the majority of whom had children.

Some married women who identified their husbands as heads of their households still shared decision making with their husbands, however.

The devaluation of women's labor, both outside and inside the home, was depicted by the use of the term "bread winner" to describe men's labor, despite the fact that women also worked long hours each day inside and outside of the home, providing the bulk of the family's food. In Ifugao, women were associated with producing food and men were associated with earning cash, as one Ifugao woman commented: "The problem here is food. So the wife must be the one to provide food by working in the fields. Men will provide cash."

In Ifugao men generally had a greater opportunity to earn cash for a number of different reasons. First, as I previously stated, men usually earned a higher daily pay than women due to differential pay rates for men and women. In part for this reason, as well as the ideology of women as the primary providers of child care, men participated in wage labor or migrated from their homes to earn cash for short or long periods of time more often than women. While only 2 percent (one) of forty-seven married women whom I interviewed worked away from their homes in a one-year period (1991–1992), 32 percent (fifteen) of their husbands worked for cash away from home, performing migrant labor for an average of 5.6 months during that time.[28]

A second reason for men bringing more cash into the family than women was that peasant women were engaged in agricultural labor in their own or others' fields almost every day throughout the year. Men, on the other hand, were usually engaged in agricultural labor only on a short-term basis, mainly just prior to rice planting and harvesting seasons (although some men worked in vegetable gardens as well). The time women had available to work for cash, either within Ifugao or as migrant laborers, was more limited than men's. One man stated, "Men have been migrating out [to work] for a long time, even permanently. Many have migrated out because of lack of food and limited space for agriculture." In the past, men used to venture away from their communities on hunting, trade, and headhunting trips, and also used to spend time guarding their communities. Today, however, there are few wild animals to be hunted in Ifugao Province, and headhunting is no longer practiced (although revenge murders still occur and Ifugao men participate in the LIC). Craft production, wage labor, and migrant labor were some of the activities men engaged in which replaced hunting expeditions and headhunting. Third, as noted earlier, men earned more cash because there were more cash paying jobs available designated as male jobs. Some women had been hired for these jobs, especially in the past decade, but still fewer than men.

Women earning less pay than men and their having less employment opportunities in wage labor jobs had the effect of keeping most women within their homes (providing child care and domestic labor) and working in their fields. This was because, strategically, as wage rates were then organized, it was more profitable and possible for a man to work earning money than a woman, since he potentially could earn double the amount she could within a particular time period. All of the lower class peasant women interviewed stated that they originally chose to work as farmers because, having been poor when they were young and having had no finances to provide for their education, there were few other employment alternatives for non-professional women within Ifugao.

One lower class Ifugao man expressed his views about men, women, and gender roles in Ifugao:

> People don't think women work as hard as the men. They [women] are just standing there all day in the rice fields during harvest season and cut rice and bundle them. . . . I have three sons and one of my children is a girl. She is useless to me without an education, unless she marries a man. But what if she marries a poor man? Then life would be nothing, only poor. He would easily get a job, like today we have this wood carving industry. My boy this summer can help me with carving. But for girls, she has only to go as a domestic helper, but she does not have the same pay as a boy. She cannot earn what a boy can earn in a month. Jobs for women are only rarely found here.

These problems were heightened for single women, particularly uneducated single mothers, many of whom were the sole economic and emotional providers for their children. They had great difficulty finding cash paying labor and often had to leave their children with relatives for long periods of time when they migrated to work in distant municipalities or cities where they located employment. They also were forced to work almost double the amount of time as men in order to earn the same pay, since men were usually paid a higher wage. While only 2 percent (one) of forty-seven married women whom I interviewed worked away from their homes as migrant laborers during a one-year period (1991–1992), 56 percent (five) of nine single women interviewed worked away from their homes as migrant laborers for an average of four months during the same time period.

One single peasant woman, a mother of three young children who had built her own wooden home and pig pen, said that she tried to find any kind of cash paying work that she could. She worked on government projects constructing cement stairways in the community, finished wood carvings, washed other people's clothing, and raised pigs for sale. She said she must continue looking for jobs, "because I have no money." She had to borrow money to feed her hybrid pigs because her salary from a government project was delayed. She did not even plant a garden because she was alone to care for it, and "that is not enough because then my other work will not be done." She wished that her mother, who lived in a distant city, would return to Ifugao to live with her and help her with her family, "because then she could do some other work, like cooking or going to the swidden fields, and I could plant a garden."

For some people, the differential pay rates created a differential in power between men and women, both within the household regarding the spending of family cash resources and in the community in terms of leadership roles. Within the household, although Ifugao women usually managed all of their family's cash resources, women were highly conscious of the money they themselves had earned versus the money earned by their husbands. Some did not always feel they could freely spend the money that their husband had earned. Errington and Filipino scholar Delia Aguilar have argued that women's active management of money does not necessarily signify women's power in insular Southeast Asian societies, but rather women's responsibility for managing family finances (Errington 1990; Aguilar 1988). In Ifugao, women's management of the family cash did not mean that all Ifugao women had control over how the cash was spent, though they may have had some input into how it was spent.

One woman stated she was often reticent to ask her husband for money that he had earned for items or services that she felt she needed, or that she would have liked to give to her relatives in crisis. Another peasant woman said she had to ask her husband's approval to buy things, usually large items, since she had no money. She referred to herself as "just a baby-sitter," despite the fact that she worked as a full-time farmer, a volunteer community health worker, and a community leader. In a less common case, a woman spoke of her friend, a teacher, whose husband was also a professional, who had difficulty spending her own money for herself or her children without her husband questioning her about her purchases or expressing dissatisfaction with her spending money.

Ifugao men tended to spend money on themselves more often than women spent money on themselves. In many cases, the men's personal money was spent on drinking with their male *barkada* or gambling. Women, on the other hand, tended to spend money on their family needs, again stressing the value they placed on their relationship to their family, rather than on their individuality. An increase in women's income could possibly aid their own and their children's nutritional status, if women spent more money on purchasing nutritious food for their families.

One lower class peasant woman expressed that many Ifugao women felt inhibited about asserting themselves with regard to earning and spending family money. Ifugao women, she said, discussed their problems about freedom and their problems with men among themselves, but did not talk about these things with their husbands. She said, "We cannot say to men that we wish to earn our own money. They will say, 'Why, you are not eating? I am not feeding you?'" She explained that since Ifugao men were expected to provide the main financial support for the family, if a married woman worked to earn money as a migrant laborer rather than her husband, he would be looked down upon by other people as not being capable of supporting his family. He would experience a loss of pride. She added, however, that women criticized their husbands if they spent their money foolishly.

A woman government social worker also stated her view that Ifugao women were not always very assertive in expressing their needs and wishes to their husbands. She described the difficulties that arose between wives and husbands when women did assert themselves, especially in regard to contraception use and sexuality. She said:

Ifugao women are not so assertive. They always give in to their husbands' decision. They always see their husband as the head of the family and they should always submit to the husband. Regarding contraception, it's usually the decision of the husband that prevails. If women use pills or tubal ligation it creates problems between husband and wife. Men don't like them to use any contraception. Men like to have many children; it is prestige for the men, it proves their virility. Before, they still believed in the economic value of children. Before when we relied mainly on agriculture, they wanted many children for many workers, helpers. But they should see today that life is different. Husbands are also afraid of the side affects for their wives of using pills or tubal ligation. There is a belief that if the woman has tubal ligation she will never be able to do heavy work again. For pills, husbands are afraid of side effects because of experiences of some women who complain of headaches, irritability, and many discomforts. Women also believe these. Sometimes, women, even if they would like to go for tubal ligation, they will not have the tubal ligation because men may get jealous, because they think women want to have sex with other men. They always want their wives to be very faithful.

[For the spacing of pregnancies for women, it is] yearly for some women. This is because when they do not give in to their husbands to have intercourse, they [husbands] get suspicious or get angry if they are not satisfied. Men are always bothering them at night. The women give in so they can sleep. Women feel pressured from men. Women said that even if they tell their husband that it is painful or they don't feel well, their husband insists. So all they have to do is give in. That's the reason when we give Family Planning sessions, that's why men don't attend, because they don't want to hear what is to be learned. They [husbands] say, "the Bible says go ye and multiply."

Regarding overall decision making within the household, of forty-three married women interviewed, 72 percent (thirty-one) said that they usually discussed issues on an equal basis with their husbands before both agreed or disagreed on a decision, while 28 percent (twelve) stated that their husbands always had the final say in household decision making.

There was some resistance to husbands' authority among wives, as women did not necessarily always submit to their husbands' wishes or practices. One example was described by a poor peasant woman, who had a high school degree. Early in her marriage, when her first child was still an infant, her husband criticized her child care practices. She said she became so angered by his criticism that she left him to live with her parents. Upon leaving, she defiantly said to him, "See how well you can take care of your son!" She stayed with her parents for three days, then finally returned after deciding that his criticism was not reason enough to end the marriage. After arriving at her home, she discussed the issue openly with her husband and they resolved the problem. Another example was of a woman who was drunk when her husband criticized her. She yelled at her husband, "I will divorce you tomorrow, and then we will see how you can feed yourself!"

In a more extreme case, a woman turned to violence to confront her husband. A friend of this woman told me that early in her marriage, she would become enraged when her husband became drunk, which was frequent at the time. Once she ran after him with a knife, screaming at him, and threatening to hurt him if he did not stop becoming drunk. On other occasions she hit him. The woman's friend never heard of the husband beating his wife. He eventually changed his behavior, so that, while he still drank liquor once in a while, he no longer became drunk. This was one of two cases described to me in which a woman threatened her errant husband with a knife. In the second case, the husband left his wife, then tried to reconcile years later after not having supported his wife or children, except for his family paying the wife just over half of what they had agreed to pay in a marital separation agreement.

While not necessarily the norm, these examples of wives' resistance to their husbands' criticisms or practices illustrate the complexity of the notion of household authority in some cultures. While some women may perceive their husbands to be the authority within their household, they may still assert their own needs or frustrations within their households. In Ifugao, this occurred in a society and culture wherein women participated in labor inside and outside of the home, contributed to their families' cash and material incomes, owned property, and where violence against women was viewed as highly improper behavior.

When asked who had the primary responsibility for child care within their families, 68 percent (thirty-two) of forty-seven married women who had children replied that they had the primary child care responsibility in their families. A substantial number, 26 percent (twelve), stated that child care responsibilities were shared equally between themselves and their husbands. Only 6 percent (three) stated that their husband had the primary child care responsibility. All of the married women with children said that their husbands did share in child care at times, especially when they were working in the fields. One of the reasons offered for why women were primarily responsible for child care within their families was that the mothers were breastfeeding. Following breastfeeding years, women said that some of the reasons why women retained primary responsibility for child care included: children "naturally" or biologically feel closer to their mother; men are often out working; and women "naturally" provide better child care than men, since they are more patient with and more attentive to the children than men.

Regarding responsibilities concerning the nutrition and health of their families, of forty-nine married women interviewed, 51 percent (twenty-five) said that they were primarily responsible for these concerns, while 45 percent (twenty-two)—again a substantial number—said that these responsibilities were shared equally between themselves and their husbands. Only 4 percent (two) said that their husbands were primarily responsible for the health and nutrition of their families. All women said their husbands cooked for their families intermittently and did so regularly during the postpartum period. Thus, many Ifugao men did share some family responsibilities with their wives.

There was a connection between men's labor, women's agricultural and child care responsibilities, and community leadership. Men's work outside of the home and the farm was said by Ifugao people to provide men with greater experiences and knowledge than women. These experiences were said to make them more capable as community leaders. Men's work experiences outside of the home and farm were more highly valued than women's work experiences within the home, on the farm, and in the Ifugao community. Men were also believed by many Ifugao people to have innate superiority in oratory skills over women, enabling them to be more capable and effective community leaders.

The ideology that men were better suited for leadership positions because of their greater experience outside of the home and farm, which then accorded them power in the community, was perpetuated and reinforced through national political propaganda displayed within Ifugao. During a pre-election period in May 1992, I read a political election poster hanging on a lower class Ifugao family's native house in a barrio while people were gathering for a community meeting.[29] The poster read: "The World Needs Men—Who cannot be bought; Whose word is their bond; Who put character above wealth. . . . Vote" (Political Poster, Ifugao 1992).[30] Although the moral intention of the political theme was positive, the message being relayed to men and women in the community was that political leaders were "men," neglecting to seriously consider women as political leaders.

To counter this kind of message, however, a national organization, the Research Committee of the National Movement for Civil Liberties of Quezon City, Metro Manila, produced a political poster promoting women holding political office. I found the following message on the poster, which was hanging on a bulletin board in the local municipal hall in the center of the municipality where the above cited barrio was located:

> Woman Power. There are 32.2 Million Females in the Philippines—49.7 percent of the population. But:
> Out of 24 Senators only 2 are women.
> Out of 201 representatives, only 18 are women.
> Out of 75 governors, only 3 are women.
> Out of 60 city mayors, only 5 are women.
> Obviously, women are grossly underrepresented. Electing more women will correct this imbalance and could result in more initiatives to improve the status of women in the Philippines—*if* we elect women who firmly believe in gender equality (NMCL Research Committee 1992).

Although there were some women in high level government leadership positions in Ifugao (such as mayor and barrio captain), some of whom were voted into office because voters judged them to be highly capable for the position (among other reasons), women's access to political power within their communities and the nation as a whole was more limited than men's.

Regarding sexuality, contemporary Ifugao men were given more sexual liberties than women. Women were more harshly condemned for sexual expression before or outside of marriage than men. Still, it was not uncommon for women to become pregnant before marriage. They were not severely criticized if they married the father of the child, or in some cases even if they did not. It was also an accepted practice for couples to become engaged and raise a family before getting married, especially if their finances could not yet accommodate a wedding. However, while a woman was harshly criticized for engaging in sexual relations with numerous men, little criticism was offered to her sexual partners. Men were said to have affairs outside of marriage more frequently than women. An Ifugao man said that some Ifugao men visited prostitutes, and that a small minority of Ifugao women worked as prostitutes, for a long or short period of time, for a variety of reasons such as to provide money to pay for their college education. But prostitution was not highly visible within Ifugao Province in comparison to its greater visibility in a nearby province and in larger cities outside of Ifugao.

One woman described the precautions married women had to take to prevent gossip from damaging her reputation and her marriage:

> It is expected that she [an Ifugao woman] does not flirt because we have a custom; it is really imposed. For example, if I am alone without my husband, I should not be seen alone with my brother-in-law. I talk to men outside of my house. If I did this all the time [be seen alone with other men] they would all talk and would really destroy everything. First the parents would talk together, then agree on *ucat*, wherein you are being forced to buy a pig to resolve a problem in marriage. The couple could stay married or separate.
>
> Or, also, if I am widowed, it is expected of me that I should mourn for him for one or more years, because there are some women here who marry before one year. The in-laws say that "you are wrong," that "you flirted with him even while you were married." So you have to buy a pig for them again. You wouldn't refuse. This would make things even worse.

Married couples did separate in Ifugao, although divorce was not officially or legally sanctioned. After separation, it was common for men and women to unofficially remarry. Women who owned property retained their property after the separation. In most cases, the children remained with their mother, although sometimes the fathers cared for some or all of the children. Some men who had separated from their wives or had fathered children with women who were not their wives provided child support; but many did not, which was generally frowned upon. Nevertheless, in one case a woman separated from her husband, who was in the process of providing for herself and her three children single-handedly, defended her ex-husband who was not providing regular child support. She stated that he could not provide anything because he was poor and had another family to provide for since he remarried. She perceived it to be her sole responsibility to provide fully for her children.

Ifugao women's social position had a dynamic quality in relation to men. Ifugao women were not always considered to be innately inferior to men, and their social position was not categorically lower than Ifugao men's social status. In some areas of social life, such as leadership and power within the community, women were considered to have lesser ability and lower status due primarily to the practices they engaged in or did not engage in, such as work experiences outside of the home and farm (Atkinson and Errington 1990). Yet, women's social position was not conceived of independently of their social class, educational status, or age rank. Some women, such as those of the upper class, in certain situations retained a higher position than some men, such as men of the lower class. Or women of an age higher than men held a higher position than them and commanded respect due to the cultural value placed on age ranking in Ifugao society. Women maintained control over decision making in their work. A few Ifugao women had begun to transform their limited role in the larger community by taking on leadership roles, such as political positions or positions of authority within government agencies.

Still, within their own homes and among men of their own social class, an upper class woman may have been considered to have less power than men of the same rank. Upper class women may have been perceived to have less power than men generally in a situation where leadership ability was being considered. Since the majority of the population were poor, the majority of Ifugao women were poor and accorded a low social position based on their intersecting gender and economic situation. Also, women were usually considered to be physically weaker than men, naturally superior child care providers than men, and their labor was devalued both monetarily and ideologically.

Everyday Tribulations

Problems poor women faced were expressed to me during a discussion among a group of about fifteen women, aged approximately between twenty to sixty years old, in March 1992. As farmers, they experienced much difficulty hiking on foot paths, carrying heavy loads of rice, sweet potatoes, vegetables, fruit, water, firewood, or clothing on their heads, or in baskets with the handle draped over their foreheads, day after day, in a province that lacked roads. This also inhibited their cultivating more agricultural products for sale, since they could not carry these in large quantities from their homes to sell in markets. Walking was quite difficult through the muddy mountain paths during the rainy season. They complained that their clothing and bodies would become very dirty from the wet soil. They also found walking to their fields wearing only inexpensive thongs to be painful, as they stepped on stones and sticks, and their feet burned from the soil that became hot from the strong sun. Their arms and backs would become sore and their hands blistered as they pounded rice, almost every morning and evening. They said that women pounded rice more than men, yet they never grew accustomed to it over time. They also said they had greater difficulty acquiring medicines, since more free medicines were available during the Marcos presidency.

PHOTO 3.2 While the majority of Ifugao men participated in agricultural labor, they also typically supplemented their incomes by working as wage laborers for cash. These men are building a stone wall that lines a paved mountain road.

When women became pregnant, the baby felt very heavy, making work especially difficult. Pregnant women worked until delivery, and then returned to work at various times, some after ten days and others after two months. If a woman felt good, or if she was very poor, she returned to work soon after delivery. Women expressed that their being the main providers of child care in their families was a hardship for them. Some women experienced a problem of having little breast milk for their infants or had difficulty in accomplishing breastfeeding. They then had to buy milk for their infants. If they had no money for milk, they had to look for work. A woman said, "It is very hard to find work. During the harvest season, we will harvest for money, or make swidden fields for others after the planting season is finished." They said more men worked for cash than women, because the pay rate for men was higher than for women. When I asked if they would like their pay rates to be higher, many women exclaimed, "Of course! We would like to work [for cash] more if it was higher. [But] if the rate of the women becomes higher, of course the rate of the men will become higher." When I asked if the rates could be equal, some women said no, because "it is the rule of the people," and "because the work of the men is harder than that of the women. But for us women, we say that the work of the women is also very hard."

Although not stated initially, the women of the group agreed with the words of one woman, who said that "our number one problem is that we are poor." One fifty year old woman, who was a farmer, discussed her life:

> Me, I have a husband. I was very young when I got married. I started working when I was very young because there was no food, only sweet potato, and only a little rice. I have been working like that until now. Before, there were no water buffalo, so we had to plow the fields ourselves. And there was no safety irrigation before [when there was no rain]. We were always afraid there wouldn't be enough food. We mostly ate sweet potato.
>
> When I was pregnant, I carried a heavy load, and I gave birth in the afternoon. The placenta couldn't come out because of the heavy load. I had to go to the hospital; that was in 1964 or 1965.

Another woman said, "Today it is better because the government helped us to buy cement for irrigation. If there is no rice we can buy some in the center of the municipality. We can get money to buy rice by borrowing from our neighbors, and paying them back with cash from work on government projects. If there is no work, we can sell animals." In response, a third woman commented, "Our food is not enough for us, because our fields are very small. If there is no rain, it becomes dry, and the rice dies or we get a small yield. Now the rice is dying here, in our *sitio* [a cluster of homes, a subdivision of a barrio], because of no water." They said they had to buy rice every year in the center of the municipality or in Isabella Province, bordering Ifugao, since their rice harvest did not provide enough rice for their families to eat throughout the year. They said this practice began many years ago. Some people migrated to the lowlands; a few people could afford to buy fields there, by selling their land, animals, and houses in Ifugao.

On another day in May, I met a woman at an elementary school in a distant barrio, during a weighing survey clinic and distribution of food supplements. She was a farmer, in her late sixties, and was very thin. That day she had walked approximately twenty-four kilometers from her home to the center of town and back again. She traveled in order to buy a basket full of bread to resell in her barrio and to people she encountered on her journey. She said she did not ride the *jeepneys* that occasionally passed in and out of the barrio because she did not have enough money for the fare, which would have depleted all of her profits. She bought 100 pesos worth of bread and sold each small bag of bread she bought for two pesos more than she had paid for them. She said she earned only about twenty to thirty pesos of profit (approximately U.S.$1.00) for one day's effort. The amount was so low, in part, because she ate some of the bread as she walked, since she had become hungry, and she had met a few of her children and grandchildren on the way and shared bread with them. She said she was not ill, but she remained very thin even though she was able to eat. She believed that she was thin because she had become old and her food supply was limited, and because she worked very hard. She still had a ten year old daughter to support, as well as grandchildren to help raise.

Thus, in contrast to many scholars' attribution of high status to women in the Philippines, Ifugao women's position was socially constructed in many important areas of their lives as being lower than men's, yet higher than men's position in some other areas of their lives.[31] This assessment of women's position in Ifugao is significant to this study of malnutrition for a number of reasons. As seen in Chapter 1, recent studies have shown that women's social position in societies can influence their own and their children's nutritional status. The stereotype of Filipino women having high status in Philippine society disregards the extent of the impact of their often degraded position in their communities, and how their lesser power may negatively influence their own and their children's nutritional status, as well as their overall health and well-being.

It is important to understand how gender relations were construed in Ifugao to understand contemporary development programs operating in Ifugao, that either focused on or had as one component of their programs the raising of women's social and economic status to enhance their own and their children's health and well-being. As will be seen in the following chapters, national and international development organizations, while attempting to raise women's social status, neglected to delve deeply into the specific arenas in which Ifugao women experienced social inequality with men. Because of this, the programs inadvertently reinforced women's low social position in specific areas, including domestic labor, child care, and economic spheres.

To better understand Ifugao women's and their families' daily lives, the next chapter depicts the difficulties and problems experienced by Ifugao women as they lived in the midst of the Philippine LIC in the early 1990s. It also explores how the conflict relates to and has an important influence on Ifugao people's nutritional status.

Notes

1. *Tagalog* (or English) song learned in Ifugao elementary schools (1992). When planting and harvesting rice, women worked in groups, usually from early morning until lunch without break. They ate lunch for about one hour, sometimes still under the strong sun, then worked again without break until five or six p.m. This work was accomplished while continuously bending to plant or harvest rice, and standing barefoot or only wearing stockings in cool, wet, and sometimes leach infested mud paddies.

2. Finishing work on unfinished wood carvings includes carving to refine a carved object, sanding, and staining or painting. Sanding on sanding machines generates a great

amount of dust from the wood, necessitating that women cover their noses and mouths with a protective cloth, lest they develop health problems from the dust.

3. Pigs were commonly fed boiled sweet potatoes and sweet potato leaves.

4. "Fixing" rice paddies was more commonly designated as a gendered male activity, involving repairing and maintaining terraced rice paddies.

5. It was common practice for middle and upper class Ifugao (as well as other Filipino) women to have one or more "helpers," or domestic workers, to provide domestic labor. Most often the helper was a relative, a young woman attending elementary or high school. Most upper and middle class families lived in the *poblacion*, or central, area of municipalities, where some schools were located. The helpers were school age boys or girls, or women in their late teens or twenties. Payment for the helpers' services could include school tuition, room and board, money for personal needs, or a combination of these.

6. Beta Max is a Sony Video Cassette Recorder (VCR).

7. *Gabi* is a root crop, which has edible roots and green leaves.

8. Ifugao people commonly referred to betel nut as "the chewing gum of the Ifugao," when they characterized it for foreigners. Betel nut is a nut that can be chewed with other ingredients, always with mineral lime and *hapeed* leaf, and sometimes with tobacco. Ifugao people said that chewing betel nut staved off hunger and it acted as a stimulant. Betel nut also served an important social function, as sharing betel nut and chewing ingredients was a demonstration of sociability, kindness, courtesy, respect, and friendship. Ifugao people also said that sharing betel nut is our "good morning" to each other.

9. Women did plow rice fields using a spade in another Ifugao municipality, however, where water buffalo drawn plows could not be used due to the steep terrain.

10. This was a phrase borrowed from the United States and most likely introduced to Ifugao women by members of Filipino feminist organizations from urban areas.

11. Ilocano is the ethnic group and language of the majority of lowlanders in the northern part of Luzon island. It is also the lingua franca of the Cordillera region. Virtually all Ifugao people understand and speak Ilocano.

12. Poor people preferred to borrow money from individuals rather than banks since borrowing from banks required collateral and having an account with the bank, neither of which the majority of Ifugao people had.

13. What was usually meant by "modern house" among Ifugao people was a square, western-style house. This contrasted with the "native house," which was a one-room wooden house raised from the ground on four sturdy, wooden stilts, having a cogon grass or galvanized iron (GI) sheet pointed roof. Inside of the native house, above the room, were rafters on which bundled rice and other materials were stored.

14. This figure is based on 1988 Ifugao family income figures from the National Statistics Office report of 1990. Upper class, in terms of income, is defined here as families whose annual income is 60,000 pesos or more.

15. Due to shortages of appropriate carving wood, many wood carvers had to migrate to work in other provinces where wood could be obtained.

16. This figure is based on 1988 Ifugao family income figures from the National Statistics Office report of 1990. Middle class, in terms of income, is defined here as families whose annual income is more than 29,999 pesos and less than 60,000 pesos. As of October 1992, the poverty line for a family of six in Ifugao was set by the Philippine government at an annual income of 27,396 pesos (National Statistics Office, Republic of the Philippines 1992a).

17. This figure is also based on 1988 Ifugao family figures from the National Statistics Office report of 1990. With the poverty level set at 27,396 pesos in 1992, using 1988 statistics, approximately 75 percent of Ifugao families fell below the poverty line, with 20 percent earning an annual income of less than 10,000 pesos.

18. A majority of the Cordillera people voted against this Act in January 1990, after the process of creating the proposal for regional autonomy had been virtually taken over by government officials from Cordillera residents. Ifugao was the only province in which the majority voted for the Cordillera Organic Act in 1990, likely because the Ifugao people may have still benefited from the Act since Ifugao was the poorest province in the region.

19. For example, in 1993 the Department of Agrarian Reform announced that all rice terraced fields in the Cordillera region should be given a legal title, according to Philippine government regulations. This was announced despite the fact that these rice fields were considered by the Ifugao and other Cordillera people to be ancestral lands that should not be subject to national Philippine law, as provided for in the 1987 Philippine Constitution.

20. Such as Casambre et al. 1992:93; UNICEF 1992a, 1987; Women Development and Technology, Inc. 1992; Manazan 1991; and Group of 10 (1989).

21. See Fox 1963; Macaraig et al. 1954; Mendoza-Guazon 1951; and Keesing 1937.

22. In recent years, numerous scholars have addressed the issue of the position of women in the Philippines, as well as women and gender in insular Southeast Asia. See Ong and Peletz 1995; Angeles 1990; Atkinson and Errington 1990; Blanc-Szanton 1990; Lopez-Rodriguez 1990; Agarwal 1988; Aguilar 1988; Torres et al. 1988; Nolasco 1987; and Esterik 1982.

23. *Baddang* was a cultural system of assistance to other family or community members. It took many forms and could occur at any time of the year. See Chapter 7 for a more extensive discussion of *baddang*.

24. One Ifugao woman said that her husband could earn 150 pesos for one day of wood carving, while she averaged from eighty to 100 pesos per day for finishing wood carvings.

25. IRRI is the International Rice Research Institute, which had a rice production research project in Banaue, Ifugao, for at least two decades. Ironically, their research was popularly known among Ifugao people to have never benefited them. The IRRI project hired Ifugao people to labor in its rice fields.

26. "Cleaning swidden fields" involved burning and cutting trees, bushes, and other plant life on a mountain slope, thereby readying the area for planting crops.

27. The 1992 unpublished report was entitled "A Gender and Development Framework for the UNICEF Assisted Third Country Programme for Children in the Philippines."

28. The one married woman who did work away from her home was working on her own property in another province, feeding her pigs for one month. She later brought the pigs to her home in Ifugao.

29. In May 1992 an election was held during which Philippine voters chose a president and local government officials.

30. The political poster for the May 1992 election read in its entirety: "The World Needs Men—Who cannot be bought; Whose word is their bond; Who put character above wealth; Who possess opinions and a will; Who are larger than their vocations; Who do not hesitate to take chances; Who will not lose their individuality in a crowd; Who will be as honest in small things as in big things; Who will make no compromise with wrong; Who will not say they do it 'because everybody else does it'; Who are true to their friends in adversity as well as in prosperity; Who do not believe that shrewdness, cunning, and hard headedness are the

best qualities for winning success; Who are not ashamed or afraid to stand for the truth when it is unpopular; Who can say 'no' with emphasis, although all the rest of the world says 'yes'; Whose ambitions are not confined to their own selfish desires. Vote" (Political Poster, Ifugao, 1992).

   31. See Fox 1963; Macaraig et al. 1954; Mendoza-Guazon 1951; and Keesing 1937.

4

Violence and Uncertainty

For more than twenty years, Ifugao people have negotiated the uncertainties and complexities of life disrupted by armed conflict. Daily life in the rural mountains of Ifugao is generally quiet and serene. Nevertheless, in the early 1990s Ifugao people lived day-to-day with a keen underlying awareness of the continuous movement of state soldiers and communist revolutionaries (the NPA) on their mountain footpaths and of the possibility of sudden outbursts of violence.[1] Ifugao inhabitants were also aware that their own movements could be observed and scrutinized by members of both sides of the warring groups, and that they were subject to the possibility of reprisal depending on the ideology and assumptions of the surveillant. At times, community life in Ifugao was disrupted by the occupation of a barrio by state or NPA soldiers, for short or extended periods of time, or by an eruption of violence.

By 1992, Ifugao had become heavily militarized with state soldiers. This had not been the case during most of the 1980s. A Philippine state army's infantry brigade command headquarters was installed in one Ifugao municipality, and platoons and companies were stationed in municipal centers and villages throughout Ifugao. Military operations were carried out on a regular basis in the communities where I conducted research. These were a part of the state army's "intensified counter-insurgency (COIN) campaign" to "destroy the CPP's [Communist Party of the Philippines] Ifugao Provincial Party Committee within a period of six months" (702nd Infantry [SOT] Brigade 1992b:1)

By June 1993, a second army infantry battalion camp had been established on the border of Ifugao and the neighboring province. Truckloads of uniformed, armed soldiers passing through municipal centers and remote mountain roads were a reminder and symbol of the state's military power during 1992 and 1993. Soldiers were also stationed within barrios. Ifugao civilians often met these soldiers as the civilians traveled on mountain trails or worked in agricultural fields and the soldiers patrolled the area or engaged in military operations.

In one Ifugao barrio during 1992, military soldiers periodically visited and held meetings among the residents to convince them of the state's interpretation of democracy and communism. The soldiers then moved on to other barrios to hold similar meetings. In another Ifugao barrio, a series of groups of soldiers stationed themselves within the elementary school in the center of the barrio, during both the school year and summer recess. Other soldiers, riding in trucks or hiking on foot, frequently passed through the barrio on the local dirt road. Military presence and power was felt on a daily basis in this barrio.

ɔome Ifugao people viewed their problems of poverty and lack of adequate food and other basic needs as being caused by social structural and political forces. A number of these people joined the revolutionary NPA in an attempt to change their desperate situation. NPA soldiers tried to raise the conscience of other Ifugao community members and organize them to action. At the same time, while occupying many areas of Ifugao and other Cordillera region provinces, the Philippine military enticed or coerced some poverty stricken Ifugao men to join their ranks as government military soldiers or as civilian defense soldiers in the Citizen Armed Force Geographical Unit (CAFGU) through promises of steady work and salaries.[2]

The problem of hunger in the Philippines must be understood by assessing the relationships among the ongoing LIC, the condition of hunger experienced by Filipino people, the conflicting cultural constructions of the causes of hunger among different groups in the Philippines, and the local resistance to state imposition of national ideologies and policies on local communities (including health ideology and policies), sometimes forced through militarization. It is necessary to analyze the configuration of these social processes since none exist in isolation of the others, and each reciprocally influences and generates the others. The relationships among these social processes have too often been neglected in previous studies on hunger in the Philippines. The internal war often is not discussed in literature focusing on hunger in the Philippines, although there are exceptions. Yet, the war was significant to the analysis of hunger for a number of reasons. There is a relationship between hunger and the inception of the war. Ifugao people have experienced problems obtaining and retaining food resources during the war. The state military has played a role in repressing cultural constructions of the causes of and solutions to hunger that do not conform to state sanctioned ideologies.

To further a gendered analysis of hunger, the impact of certain state policies on women must be brought to the fore in order to fully understand why hunger persists. This is integral since, historically, Philippine state policies, including military, political, economic, and health, have affected both women's lives and the social production of hunger in the Philippines. These policies have generally failed to significantly change social and political structures that maintain asymmetrical power, social class, and gender relations.

In the early 1990s, Ifugao women were confronted in their everyday lives with the risks and dangers of war as they attempted to produce food, earn incomes for their family members, and provide health care to their families and communities. Ifugao women had to negotiate the war as they labored as volunteer and paid health workers to alleviate hunger and other illnesses experienced by their family and fellow community members.

Historical Experiences of Violence in Ifugao

In Ifugao, uncertainty and fear were generated not only from the violence of the contemporary internal political conflict but also from historical experience. Everyday life in Ifugao was not characterized by constant overt physical violence stemming from war, but the society was marked by a long history of episodic violence which had broken the calm and routine of peasant life. As a result, contemporary Ifugao people felt an underlying anxiety related to the real possibility of violence, as confirmed by their experience of periodic eruptions of violence within their communities. This communal experience included warfare among villages now comprising Ifugao Province and warfare by Ifugao against other indigenous groups during the pre-Hispanic colonial period, conflict against colonizing powers during the Spanish and American colonial periods, warfare during World War II, and low intensity conflict throughout the contemporary war.

The Pre-Hispanic Colonial Period

Tribal wars were fought within the area now designated as Ifugao Province between men of different villages, particularly in times of drought and poor harvest seasons, often involving culturally sanctioned headhunting. During these times the people experienced hunger, malnutrition, and famine. Men who survived these difficulties raided nearby villages for food and animal resources. In earlier periods, the taking of a single head was adequate to complete a battle. By the late nineteenth century, however, after having acquired guns from the Spanish colonizers, these raids often led to bloody battles and numerous deaths, sometimes devastating entire villages (Dumia 1979). Historically, internal violence was linked to hunger, as battles involving headhunting were sometimes fought because of the need for food. Battles and headhunting raids were fought between upland people and nearby lowlanders as well.

Spanish historical records indicate that by the 1800s lowland communities near Ifugao Province were inhabited by the Christianized *Gaddang*. This area, which was considered to be agriculturally prosperous, had earlier belonged to villages in the Ifugao region. It is unclear when they were driven out by the *Gaddang* people, but the uplanders continued their attacks on them until at least the 1800s (Scott 1974:203).

The Spanish Period: 1565–1898

Battles for defense of territory and society against Spanish incursions into Ifugao occurred into the 1700s (Scott 1974:3). Numerous fierce battles were fought as Spanish colonizers attempted to gain control over Ifugao territory. The Spanish first arrived in the Cordillera region in the 1500s and tried to control gold and other resources found there. They also punished Ifugao people for raids in the lowlands. The Ifugao resisted the Spanish for more than two hundred years. Finally, in 1841, a section of Ifugao territory came under Spanish administration (Dumia 1979:26, 28).[3] By the late 1860s, after a forty-day expedition with rifles, the Spanish succeeded in winning the submission of most Ifugao villages (Scott 1974.:238). Yet, violent Ifugao resistance continued during the Spanish occupation.

One man in Ifugao remembered an elder man's friend's tales of Spanish occupiers forcing Ifugao people to work as slave laborers building roads and performing other work within Ifugao. Another Ifugao man, who died in 1992, was said to have been assigned to feed grass to the Spanish "black people's" (called this because their uniforms were black) horses as a young boy.[4] Of another Cordillera ethnic group, a Spanish priest wrote: "They have not been able to make up their minds [that] they have lost their independence, so they consider having to work on public projects for the [Spanish] State an abuse" (Father Angel Perez 1902:236, in Scott 1974:291).

In addition to labor, the Spanish imposed taxes as high as one-third of an Ifugao family's income, derived mainly from food production. This tax would usually be collected in the form of rice in areas where cash was not available, causing great difficulty for both subsistence level rice farmers and the many families who ate mainly root crops for their staple food. Many Ifugao families who did not own irrigated rice fields were forced into debt peonage.[5] They labored in the irrigated rice fields of wealthier families, or requested loans with interest from these families to pay taxes, as did families in the lowland areas of the Philippines. This further reduced poor Ifugao people's incomes and food resources (Scott 1974). Not all Ifugao families actually paid tribute, however, creating difficulties for Spanish soldiers and priests (Scott 1974).

During this period of Spanish military occupation of areas of Ifugao and continued violent and nonviolent resistance of Ifugao people, the Spanish used the tribute to feed themselves and their conscripted soldiers, as occurred elsewhere in the Philippines. In 1890 in the Ifugao municipality of Kiangan, the Spanish occupiers forced each family to provide forty bundles of unpounded rice at harvest time, a great amount to surrender considering most families did not produce enough rice to last for an entire year (Villaverde 1879, in Scott 1974:323). Spanish Acting Commandant Juan Alicart wrote in 1896 that there was an "absolute need of this detachment, like the others in this district [Ifugao], to obtain rice from the villages for distribution to the troops." At times, the military forced families to sell their rice at low prices, thereby necessitating the import of food from the lowland areas (Scott 1974:285-286, 296). Ifugao people resisted the Spanish appropriation of their food resources. One elderly Ifugao woman recalled stories she heard from her parents about the Spanish soldiers within Ifugao:

> I do not know about the Spanish because I was very young. I only heard stories. Only the very old people saw them. The Spanish would take their food, so the people were hiding their rice. The Spanish did not pay them. Whenever the Spanish would see animals, they would take them. Whatever their horse could carry, that is what they would take. That is why some people went to the mountains. . . . when I was young, I asked my mother, why do my grandparents go to the mountains? My mother said they had to hide their rice there. Some hid animals also in the cave. So, when they knew the Spanish were coming they would hide them in the cave. Then when they would leave, they would feed their animals.

The Spanish militarization of Ifugao, therefore, had an impact on the food resources and the overall economic status of those Ifugao people whom the Spanish forced into submission. This also occurred elsewhere in the Philippines among groups who could not resist the Spanish, and from a much earlier period than had occurred in Ifugao.

The American Period: 1901–1946

The Philippine revolution against Spain, beginning in 1896, and the Filipino national resistance movement's defeat of the Spanish colonizers (with the aid of the U.S. army) in 1898, ended the Spanish occupation of Ifugao. However, U.S. colonization of the Philippines, beginning with the Philippine-American war in 1899, brought more violence to Ifugao. During the early years of the twentieth century, American policies of pacification and "civilizing" created more hardships for Filipino people (Scott 1974:33). The American presence in Ifugao began in 1901 with the establishment of an American colonial military government in the area of Kiangan. By 1902 Ifugao was incorporated into the Province of Nueva Vizcaya. Later, in 1908, Ifugao was incorporated into the Mountain Province.[6]

The Americans, like the Spanish, required Ifugao people to build more trails and roads to facilitate the American supervision of the region and to open more areas to a market economy. American military administrators also collected taxes from Ifugao people in the form of rice, other material products, or cash. Besides the use of force during the Philippine-American war and their military presence in Ifugao, the Americans tried to win the "hearts and minds" of Ifugao people through cultural, political, religious, medical, and economic means. The United States encouraged American and foreign missionary instruction and medical services, incorporated Ifugao men into official government positions, established schools, occasionally sponsored large feasts and peace pacts among warring Ifugao tribes, and began the economic development of Ifugao. American military officials also implemented a strategy of enlisting Ifugao men into local militias to police their own communities (Fry 1983:59).

American officials made an effort to end headhunting practices and tribal wars, which had become disastrous to communities attacked with guns. One of the ethnic Cordillera groups, the Kalingas, developed a peace-pact system at the turn of the century. This followed the opening of trails under the Spanish and increased travel and trade opportunities among formerly warring peoples (Fry 1983:56-57). With these increased opportunities, and the encouragement of peace among the ethnic groups by American occupiers, headhunting and tribal wars virtually ceased.[7] The American pacification campaign was much more successful than Spanish attempts to pacify the Ifugao and other Cordillera ethnic groups. Ifugao people generally accepted the American occupiers (Dumia 1979:37).

Because of a drought in the early 1900s, famine struck Ifugao during the American occupation. Hunger affected some families so greatly that parents resorted to selling some of their children into slavery in nearby lowland areas. Parents likely hoped their enslaved children would be well fed by their owners and thus would survive (Dumia 1979:40). The children were sold for rice, pigs, water buffalo, or cash. Some lowland Filipinos took advantage of the Ifugao people's desperate situation by traveling through Ifugao to buy people, with money or animals, to use for labor. One Ifugao woman recalled an incident which occurred right after World War II. She said that one family was very hungry, having had no rice fields or other means of income except swidden farming. The parents decided to sell their twelve-year-old son to a woman from a nearby province, who had only one son. She bought him for his labor, though she is said to have grown to love him and treat him as if he were her own son. His parents sold him for one cavan of rice. The boy survived, inherited some property from the woman who bought him, married, and later reunited with his family when he was in his sixties. The extreme hunger experienced during this period facilitated the selling of children into slavery as a viable alternative to starvation since outside assistance was not readily available.[8]

World War II: 1942–1945

Contemporary elderly Ifugao people have clear memories of World War II. These memories were animatedly related to me by many Ifugao elders, as they told stories of fighting and working side by side with American soldiers against the Japanese invaders. Japanese soldiers forced their way into Ifugao in January 1942, and they occupied various areas. They established a government and schools where Ifugao children were instructed by Japanese soldiers in the Japanese language (Dumia 1979). Some Ifugao elders remembered spending months or years learning from their Japanese teachers.

During the battles between Japanese soldiers and American and Ifugao soldiers, many Ifugao people were killed, interrogated, maltreated, or threatened by the Japanese. Others died of hunger or illness, as did many other Filipinos. Houses were burned, and food and animals were stolen by Japanese soldiers. Numerous Ifugao families evacuated from their homes, often for months or years, to escape the violence. Families who had rice reserves were more likely to survive, but most people did not have such reserves. To survive they ate sweet potatoes, which they cultivated in communities the Japanese had not yet overtaken, and wild plants gathered in the forest.

Hunger was widespread during the war, since many Ifugao people were forced to flee from their homes and farmlands. When the Ifugao left their homes, Japanese soldiers raided their rice granaries and stole their animals. Although there was food available for people who could find refuge in villages not occupied by the Japanese, there was not always adequate supplies or variety of food available to the evacuees.

In the face of hunger, evacuees continually shared food during the war among people not normally considered to be kin or neighbors. The Ifugao moral code of sharing food with those who were without was maintained and possibly strengthened during this period. Numerous elderly Ifugao people commented that the sharing of food was one of the most positive aspects of their wartime experience. It was a period of great cooperation among people who found themselves in the same desperate situation.

However, this, was also one of the most traumatic periods of Ifugao people's lives. Those who experienced the war related stories of death, hunger, disease, battles, fires, escapes, hiding, and fear. One elderly Ifugao man remembered:

> The people fled for one year, only returning when World War II ended. Whenever the Japanese went from this place, we would come home, then flee if we thought the Japanese would come. There was no food [meaning rice], so even some people would dig sweet potatoes at night. The way we ate was whatever food we could eat we would eat. We didn't eat well. We could not work because of the war. After the war, the rice fields, swidden fields, and homes turned into grasses. We would come for five days in our own house and the Japanese would come. We would run again to the mountains. Those people had rice who had hidden some of their rice. There were many swidden fields then, so there was a lot of sweet potatoes, unlike today when there are few sweet potatoes. During the time we were in the mountains there was much *gabi* [root crop], corn, bananas, ginger, pineapple, brown peas, and sweet potatoes. But some people would steal others' crops just to survive. . . . When we fled we went to the mountains where the Japanese could not see or find us from here. We slept in a temporary house in the swidden field, and the highest priority was letting the children sleep in the house and the adults kept guard. We made a little shed for us to sleep.
>
> We would eat by group, different families in one group. If one family lacked food and others had extra, we would share with them. We would all cook by each family. We did not share food between groups, but we would give food to some friends. We

used our old fields and went to dig sweet potatoes at night, especially when it was moonlight, because if it was daytime the Japanese would shoot us. Some of the [community] people invited some of the Japanese to eat with them because they [the Japanese soldiers] were hungry. While eating, one man and others planned to kill them . . . when they got to the river, they killed them and cut their heads. They only began headhunting the Japanese soldiers after the Japanese started killing them. They would invite the Japanese to eat, then kill them because some Japanese would just see Ifugao people and then shoot them. No Ifugao people died of hunger, but some died of sickness, as did some Japanese.[9]

Ifugao men who fought against the Japanese soldiers were locally called "*bolo*-men."[10] Ifugao women also played an important role in the struggle against the Japanese, though their efforts often go unrecognized in historical accounts. Women gathered, carried, and cooked food for the male soldiers and washed their clothing (which at that time was commonly loin cloths woven from tree bark fibers). Women had no soap, so they washed the clothing with firewood ash. When mixed with water, the ash became highly alkaline and bruised the hands of the women. Until recently, these women's efforts went unrecognized financially, although Filipino male veterans were compensated by the U.S. government. Currently, Filipino women can receive a pension from the U.S. government as compensation for their contributions during the war.

An elderly Ifugao woman was married and had seven children during World War II (called *gkufat*). She told me her of experiences during the war:

The Japanese burned our house. During that war, we kept on roaming around here for food. Then my son-in-law told us to go to another Ifugao barrio where we had relatives. We stayed in there for one year, when our rice was beginning to ripen. When we came back, it had already been eaten by the Japanese and other Ifugao people here. . . . My daughter would sometimes go with people to buy food in two distant municipalities in neighboring provinces, buying sweet potatoes. When we· came back there were no seeds for rice, so we planted sweet potatoes and had to harvest them after three months, when it was still small. When we came back we had to mortgage some of our rice fields so we could buy food from a neighboring Ifugao municipality. We had a small sweet potato field. I and my son-in-law went to get sweet potatoes. When the Japanese were going home, they gave us money and blankets for sweet potatoes. After this some of the Americans dropped food from airplanes for us, so the people would get them. . . . It was good that we had relatives in another barrio who had food. I had seven children at that time. I worked and earned in others' fields in my barrio because the rice was ready to harvest when we got there. I also had my own swidden field and worked in others' fields, sharecropping. . . . My husband guarded us against the Japanese. He brought us to the other barrio, then returned to guard against the Japanese. We were not hungry because some of our relatives called us to get sweet potatoes. One man went during the nighttime to harvest . . . sweet potatoes in another barrio and brought it to us.

Japanese General Tomoyuki Yamashita surrendered in 1945 to U.S. officers in Kiangan, Ifugao, ending the war for the Ifugao people (Dumia 1979).

The Philippine Political Conflict and Health: 1969–1993

The period before World War II was usually referred to by Ifugao elders as "peacetime." Their use of this idiom exposed how the only time in their memory when they felt that there was relative peace in Ifugao was more than fifty years ago. By 1993 the political conflict between the Philippine government and the CPP had been waged within the Philippines for more than twenty years. The Philippine government, with the aid of the United States, employed a military strategy of LIC in the rural areas, including Ifugao, which had a tremendous impact upon Filipino lives.

During the 1950s campaign against the *Huks*, the U.S. Army, while assisting the Philippine army, developed and refined its LIC strategies. Bello wrote that the U.S. LIC strategy in the Philippines developed through four major confrontations: the U.S. colonization of the Philippines between 1899 and 1903; the campaign to defeat the *Huk* insurgency from 1950 to 1953; the struggle to contain the NPA during the Marcos period from 1966 to 1986; and the recent counterinsurgency effort attempted by the Aquino (and Ramos) government(s) and the Armed Forces of the Philippines (AFP) (Bello 1987:1). American advisors for counterinsurgency warfare trained a 1,200-man Philippine Battalion Combat Team during the 1950s in an attempt to eradicate the *Huk* rebellion (Rosaldo 1980:164). Bello argued that the Philippines "has enjoyed the dubious distinction of serving as America's principle proving ground for developing and testing strategies and tactics for low-intensity conflict." LIC strategies were also employed and further developed by the U.S. Army during the Vietnam conflict (Bello 1987:3).

LIC is a war doctrine derived from U.S. military strategy, which evolved in response to growing popular movements throughout non-industrialized countries. It is a form of war which requires the reevaluation of traditional war tactics. In addition to armed offensives, military strategists implement a total war at the grassroots level on economic, social, political, and psychological fronts. LIC in the Philippines integrated military science with all aspects of government policy (Davis 1989:10-11). This included the provision of government services and the incorporation of international and missionary health and development services as part of an overall LIC strategy. The use of health services in LIC provides one example of the interconnectedness of hunger, health services, international development, women as the primary providers of health care in Ifugao, and LIC. Soldiers of both sides of the war (AFP and NPA) used health services in their LIC strategy for political conversion.

Attempts also were made by the military to coerce health workers to conform to government ideology, including health ideology. The Philippine government health program during the early 1990s neglected to address adequately the relationship between illness and social inequality in Philippine society, exemplified by economic stratification, widespread hunger, and unequal international relations. Government nutrition programs in particular were structured to focus on the individual, the family, and to some extent the community. Attempts to go beyond this health care focus were sometimes repressed by the military.

From 1991 to 1993, the Philippine state under President Aquino, and later President Ramos, waged a stepped-up LIC strategy against the NPA. The Aquino and Ramos administrations attempted to resolve the war through peace talks with the NPA as well, but to no avail.

Ifugao People's Experience and Memory of Political Violence

In recalling early experiences of the LIC, one Ifugao woman said:

> I remember when we were still little, we went for an evacuation and there we got sick; we had diarrhea. We were in the field and they evacuated all those people in the far barrios. The army forced us to come in the school there so they could shoot in those far places. And we were afraid to be hurt. Food was a problem . . . because we could not get food. We could not go to our fields; we had to stay in another area. They gave us food but our gardens and fields could not be cared for. So our crops died. And when there was fighting, I remember my sister who nearly got shot during those periods of fighting. A person told people that there were NPA in that place, so the soldiers just shot, shot, shot, and my sister had to go away.

A woman from another barrio related that, "About fifteen or twenty years ago there was fighting between soldiers and NPA. We were afraid to go out, so we went to hide in a friend's house. No one went to the field. It was noon. This was the problem." Another woman expressed how her family had been affected by the war: "before [about fifteen years ago] when the soldiers and NPA met here in our place, surely we were affected. Just the other year, we were shocked when they were firing all of their guns and machine guns, and they were bombing in the mountains with their helicopters. We would go with the little children and hide in the mountains, for about one week."

Through this contemporary violence, uncertainty and fear were generated by both sides of the war. This was influenced by how often soldiers of opposing sides met in their communities and fought, whom the state military suspected of being members or supportive of the NPA, whom the NPA suspected as being supportive of the state military, and how soldiers of each side treated the civilians on a daily basis.

In 1990 an Ifugao woman fled from her home due to incursions between the state military and the NPA. She identified the LIC as one of the main health problems in her community. She said that some of the effects of the war for Ifugao people in her community had been nervousness and stress. When barrio members evacuated from her community, four families stayed in one house for two weeks. Most became ill with diarrhea, and they had no medicines.[11] They had carried rice to their evacuation site, but it was not an adequate amount. The government Department of Social Welfare and Development provided some food for the evacuees, but it was insufficient. She and other evacuees sometimes risked going to their homes to get food, but they feared being hurt by soldiers and would not travel in the evening. They did no work in their fields for the two weeks of their evacuation, because of fear of being hurt in crossfire. She stated that three women in the community had spontaneous abortions following this period of violence.

In another barrio, a woman's husband was killed by NPA soldiers in 1978. She explained that before the killing, her neighbors were jealous of her family because her husband was intelligent, industrious, and had more wealth than they did. She said the neighbors told the NPA negative tales about her family. NPA soldiers brought empty rice sacks to the woman's house, and told her and her husband to fill the sacks with rice and return them to the NPA. The woman and her husband complied for a time. But when "they got tired" of this, they stopped giving rice to the NPA soldiers. After that the NPA soldiers shot her husband. Another community member offered a different interpretation of the reason for this man's murder. She thought the NPA soldiers suspected that he had divulged information to the military about the NPA's activities.

The Politics of Food and War

Access to, distribution of, and control over food are important processes to consider in analyzing the impact of LIC on people's nutritional statuses. Food, and the sharing or relinquishing of food to soldiers, take on multiple meanings in the context of LIC. Feeding soldiers on both sides of the conflict has had some impact on Ifugao people's nutritional status. This impact was felt most strongly in communities where state military or NPA presence was long-term, and where providing food for soldiers was requested, subtly required, or forcibly imposed.

NPA soldiers survived in part through the support of communities in which they were present, including Ifugao. The NPA soldiers requested food from poor families and at times "taxed" wealthy families. State soldiers in the past stole food from Ifugao people or requested that food be given or sold to them. In the early 1990s, state soldiers in Ifugao usually supplied their own food, although they sometimes requested to purchase food from community members. While some people actively supported soldiers of either side by giving them food, some people perceived themselves to have been forced or coerced into feeding them, as they felt threatened by the sight of military weapons.

In this political context, feeding soldiers took on multiple meanings and acquired significant symbolic value. One meaning involved the high cultural value that has long been accorded to hospitality and sharing food with visitors among the Ifugao people, particularly with those with no food. Since soldiers were perceived to be visitors rather than community members, it was culturally proper to feed them. Other meanings included the provision of support for the state or the communist movement, fear for one's life and that of family members, insecurity related to the lessening of a family's already limited food resources, danger, threat, and stress. Danger was derived not only from the soldiers' demands for food, but also from the state military's potential retribution for presumed support of the NPA if one shared food with them. Danger was also derived from the possibility of being ambushed by the NPA or AFP while soldiers of the opposing side were eating in one's home. During the early 1990s, under the Aquino and Ramos administrations, state soldiers were usually provided with adequate supplies of food or money to buy food in Ifugao, although during the 1970s and 1980s this was not always the case. Ifugao people remembered that state soldiers stole animals and crops from them during that time.

In 1990 the state military held meetings in Ifugao barrios during which they requested that people submit their names if they had ever supported the NPA by feeding them. In one barrio, government soldiers had been living in the elementary school for five months. The majority of community members complied with this request because the soldiers promised that no retribution would be taken against persons who submitted their names, a promise that they kept. Still, the soldiers remained a threat to those who would not comply with their request. Moreover, the soldiers' continued surveillance of Ifugao people's activities maintained a threat of retribution against those who continued to feed the NPA.

One female farmer said that the war affected her family's food supply at times, because, "we cannot work during fighting, and both state and NPA soldiers come and stay in your house and eat your food even when there's no fighting. Today, not so with the state soldiers but it is so for the NPA because they have no food. This is difficult for us, because if we have food only for one day, and they eat all of it, we go hungry for the rest of the day . . . if we have no more pounded rice." The NPA and the government soldiers at times became a burden to community members, reducing their limited food resources. Another lower class Ifugao woman said, "Only the NPA will eat with us. The army brings their own food. This is a problem because they will come and eat our food until they leave. It's better for the army because they will come in group and eat their own food, and buy their own viand."

One Ifugao woman described her fears of the violence and explained how the feeding of NPA soldiers affected her family and other community members. She added:

> because we are afraid . . . even if they are very far from here and the war is going on
> on the road, we are afraid because we are thinking of the other people on the road,
> wondering if something will happen to them, or the bullets might come to our house

even if it's intended for others. One time they were trying to shoot my husband, maybe because they thought he was NPA, or just for revenge, because for the state soldiers, if the soldiers are killed, the other soldiers may just kill anyone for revenge. And because they think that the people are the ones feeding and supporting the NPA, so the state soldiers might kill them just to get back at them.

When the military enters a community, many people think that the army is searching for NPA soldiers among them. Women expressed being afraid of "flying bullets," or being caught in crossfire, even if they were not actually targeted. This is particularly the case when soldiers of either group slept in or near the people's homes. One health worker expressed her great nervousness when soldiers of either side slept on the porch of her clinic and other people's houses, because, she said, "the bullet does not know who it is supposed to hit; and the houses are only nipa or wood."

Regarding the relationship between LIC and the production of food, many women said they had problems producing food during conflicts. One woman commented, "Yes, because we are afraid. Because one time when we were harvesting and the fighting was in another *sitio*, and the sound of the bullets was very strong, we were uncomfortable working, we wanted to run, and some went home just to see their children." Another woman said, "I feel lazy because I am afraid, so I will not go to the fields. And I have no appetite to eat." And another woman expressed how the war affected their health through danger, threat, and stress: "sometimes we are disturbed. A woman who lives nearby did not eat for three days because of her nervousness. Battles have happened three times here, up and down, and the people don't eat because they run because of their nervousness. They just go to the small caves to hide themselves."

Another woman reflected on the conflict: "it affects our health a lot. Because we are afraid. Like if you are in the swidden field digging, and the helicopter comes and there is fighting on the ground, and you hear the bullets, you don't even take your sweet potatoes, you just run home, see your family and go hide in the caves."

Fear and Uncertainty

Ifugao people's experience and evaluation of the war and soldiers on each side were not consistent among individuals or communities, nor were they consistent over time for the same people. There was an irregularity of position or feeling among Ifugao people toward the groups on either side of the war, as it transpired over the last decades. For Ifugao people who found themselves caught in the middle of the war, their personal experience with soldiers on both sides was one important determinant of how they perceived each warring group. Ifugao people's level of fear, their socioeconomic status, and their perception of the government also influenced their political stance.

A woman living in a barrio where a government RHU was located expressed her experience of the war and of the soldiers:

> [For example,] the NPAs, because they will come here and they just say "Suppose we will just butcher any kinds of animals" that they want, and we are afraid, so of course we will butcher the animals. And from those community members who have wide pastures and have water buffalo, the NPA ask for a donation, to give one water buffalo. And of course they give because they are afraid. This always happens here. Only when the government soldiers come here we are not afraid because they do not force us to butcher any animals. They bring their own food and if their food supply is consumed they will buy. It is not like the NPA. They will just come and eat with us, with no pay and they will ask to butcher any animals with no pay. But now the NPA are not always coming here convincing the people to join them. They have meetings. . . . Before there were only a few women who joined them. State soldiers always paid for food, only the NPAs did not. Each year the NPA ask for one water buffalo. Every year, even this year. That's why when the time that the state soldiers came and they convinced the people to join the CAFGU the people wanted to join . . . it is bad, though, because the soldiers never organized them. They said it is because of a lack of funds for them. . . . If the NPA comes here we feel afraid, but if soldiers come here we do not feel afraid because we know they are helping us.

This woman lived in a municipality in which NPA soldiers attempted to burn two municipal buildings in the center of the municipality in 1986. They did not follow through with the burning, though, after an Ifugao woman begged them to stop, explaining that the fire would spread to approximately thirty civilian homes and businesses in the vicinity.

By November 1992 there had been increased militarization in one municipality through the intensified recruitment and training of CAFGU members from local communities. Men were being asked to work in their own communities as a form of home defense. The men were given uniforms and guns to keep in their homes. Each man would patrol through his barrio for one hour each night. Their pay at that time was 900 pesos per month, but they had heard that it might increase to 2,500 pesos per month the following year. Many men who joined were poor men, who needed more income. One day in late November, three CAFGU recruits attended a *baki* ritual for one of the recruits in an attempt to ensure his safety in his new work, as well as to bless his family. As his wife searched for a *mumbaki* ("native priest") to conduct the ritual earlier that morning, relatives of the man had disapprovingly commented to her, "So your husband is now a CAFGU. Maybe the NPA will come to kill him in your house and you will not be able to fight back because your children are there. Then what will you do?" In another situation, while walking through the center of a municipality, a woman commented to her friend, "Here come the dogs," upon seeing the newly uniformed CAFGU recruits. Hearing her comment, another woman whose friends and relatives had joined CAFGU, became very upset. The woman told her she was wrong to call them dogs.

Thus, the recruitment of CAFGU members, predominantly among poor men, generated fear and derision for some people and conflicts among relatives and community members.

Another woman in the same community said, "Yes, of course it affects our health when they are near, because where will you go if they are here? So, we are affected. When the army comes here we are not affected. Even NPA, if they come here and you didn't do anything bad to them, they won't hurt you. NPA will come and ask for food, and because we are afraid we have to give. The army usually has their own food." Another woman of the same barrio added:

> It's good when the military are here and there are no NPA. If NPA is here also, they will fight. It's better if neither will come here so that it is peaceful. Because if the military come, you are expecting that the NPA will come and fight them. And it's dangerous for the children at the school because the military lives there. . . . Once they were fighting here and I was so sick of nervousness. If I did not overcome my nervousness, I thought I might die.

Another woman in another community said, "Even when the state soldiers are here we are not affected because the NPA are not here. They have no enemies [NPA] here. Because if the enemies are here hiding in our place, that's dangerous, but maybe they are hiding in other places."

These narratives contrasted starkly with the responses of some women who lived in a barrio in which a health NGO was operating, rather than a government health clinic. This barrio was also located near a former NPA stronghold, which was stable during the 1970s and early 1980s. Some women in this barrio expressed greater fear of the state soldiers and less fear of the NPA soldiers. While there were numerous reasons for this, one significant factor was that state soldiers suspected the activities of the female NGO health volunteers to be anti-state. In one barrio discussed previously, the presence of the government RHU generated no such suspicions among state soldiers, and the people there received better treatment from the government soldiers than those in the second barrio. Also, the women in the barrio with the health NGO had long-term, daily interactions with government soldiers that were often abusive, especially during the Marcos era. For example, women in this community told of prior experiences of community members who were continually monitored by state soldiers under President Marcos. Civilians were stopped on the road or trails and asked for their identification cards. The state soldiers sometimes slapped Ifugao people for not responding adequately to requests or questions, usually due to language barriers between soldiers who came from other provinces and Ifugao people who did not speak the soldiers' dialects. Elderly people, who commonly only spoke the Ifugao language, were most often abused for this reason. Also, in the past state soldiers stole animals from families in this community. And some people suspected of being NPA supporters had been killed by state soldiers. Many women said the people felt powerless to act against these abuses, and the women complained of being "attacked with nervousness" due to the militarization of the area.

Some women only feared soldiers when soldiers from both sides of the war were present in their community at the same time. One woman explained, "If by chance they come here and fight we will be affected. If one comes and not the other we are not affected. The community members are afraid that they will be hit by the bullets. They would go and hide, because if you will stay in your house the bullet might hit your house and you'll be inside." This woman expressed many people's fear that even one's own home was not a safe haven from the war. Soldiers of either side entered people's yards or homes uninvited, and community members had little recourse. Many women spoke of running to hide in caves during battles, the only place where they felt well hidden and protected.

There was also a silencing of dissent by the military. Community members of one Ifugao barrio feared the state soldiers living in their elementary school, located near families' homes, especially while their children attended classes. One man voiced the sentiments of many community members when he commented during a community development meeting sponsored by the EC, "If we say we don't want the military in our community we will be called subversive." This man did not feel he had the freedom to voice directly his opposition to the soldiers' choice of living quarters, for fear of being imprisoned, tortured, or killed by the military, as had happened to people in his and other communities in the past. The soldiers were sitting in a nearby classroom while the meeting was being conducted at the elementary school when he made his comment. The soldiers did not appear to be directly monitoring the meeting. At another community meeting, Ifugao people said the state military is "all-powerful," and "They have all the power." The fear of military retribution against persons contesting military practices inhibited the members of this barrio from actively trying to terminate the soldiers' occupation of classrooms within the elementary school.

A female teacher, who taught health, nutrition, and other classes in this elementary school, approached me in 1992 on a Saturday morning in the busy, crowded outdoor marketplace in the municipal center as she shopped for her family. In exasperation she exclaimed, "I don't know what is happening to my life!" She went on to describe how during the previous evening she had fainted in the teachers' quarters of the elementary school due to her extreme nervousness over the resident state soldiers' activities that evening. The soldiers were residing in one classroom of the school, located only three rooms away from the teachers' living area. That evening the soldiers had become heavily intoxicated and boisterous. The teacher was terrified of being shot if shooting erupted among the soldiers, a common occurrence among drunken soldiers in these upland communities. Two specific violent incidents involving drunken soldiers occurred within a six-month period in this teacher's municipality in 1992 and 1993.

PHOTO 4.1 The NPA ransacked and partially set this government office on fire in 1986. The NPA soldiers put the fire out after they learned that it might spread to civilian homes and businesses.

The school teacher held conflicting feelings about the state soldiers' presence at her school. At times she was afraid to express openly her true feelings to me about the soldiers' living at the school. She based her immediate assessment or judgment of state soldiers on their individual personalities, rather than their ideology. Prior to her fainting experience during the soldiers' drunken revelry, she expressed to me:

> Well, for this army now, we have no complaints. Not like the other years when they always come and peep, two years ago. Now they are quiet, stay in their room. Before, they were very noisy and drunk. During the first year they were bad, but this time they're OK, very quiet. Because I told them on the first day they entered the school, I will accept you but don't drink liquors because it will be a disturbance on our part. Sometimes they give food for us, and everything we tell them they do it. They even help us in cleaning the grounds every day. . . . Their discipline improved a lot even within two years. It's up to the leadership of the higher-ups.

When this teacher spoke highly of the soldiers, she was referring specifically to a group of soldiers who lived at the school prior to the group who had become drunk before her fainting. Following her fainting experience, she explained that she did not like the soldiers now living at the school, but felt that there was nothing she could do about it. She explained that the building was a public building, and that the military had a legal right to occupy public buildings. The soldiers had acquired permission to live in the school from local politicians, to the dismay of local residents. However, other residents claimed that the soldiers should not occupy school buildings but rather were supposed to reside at least thirty meters away from school buildings.

In this community, groups of soldiers were rotated to different stations every few weeks, creating uncertainty and stress for residents each time a new group of soldiers arrived. The people had to adjust to each group and worry about how the soldiers would treat them. They needed to rebuild their trust of state soldiers each time they were replaced. This resulted in a heightening of community awareness and vigilance each time a new group came in. To many community members, based on previous personal experiences and stories told by other people, soldiers generally could not be trusted. Neither professionalism nor respect could be assumed from state soldiers.

This uncertainty resulted in increased stress and wariness for community members. The uncertainty blurred the distinction between the state military as protector and abuser of Filipino citizens. The drunken, disrespectful soldiers were considered to be more dangerous and threatening than those who were respectful and did not drink. The teacher focused on the individual personalities of the soldiers, giving instructions to the first group regarding her expectations of their behavior in the school. She may have presumed her interaction with the soldiers on an individual level, through her instructions to them, to be a means by which she could maintain some degree of control or influence over the soldiers. She may have felt less of a sense of control if she had focused on the soldiers being a segment of a larger state supported military institution. In the latter case, any control would have been beyond her reach. She never discussed issues of ideology regarding the state military or the NPA with me. Her main concerns seemed to be her everyday experience of life under militarization and her responsibility to protect her young students who attended classes while the soldiers were stationed inside the school.

The power of the military was exerted over this community and felt by community members on a daily basis. This was the case despite the fact that the soldiers asserted that they had entered and occupied the community to maintain peace and order. One woman asked some military soldiers why they had moved into her barrio. One soldier replied, "To guard the people here." She contested him, saying, "Guard us from what? Now there is no fighting, why do you have to guard us?" He answered, "It is just better that we will guard you." Instead of maintaining peace and order, the soldiers created a sense of disorder, loss of control, and unpredictability for many community members.

International Development and Low Intensity Conflict

Historically, western states have had a strong influence on the social construction of health care in non-industrialized states and its use as a strategy in LIC. This was particularly true of U.S. operations in the Philippines. Biomedicine was introduced widely to Filipino people during the American colonial period, especially by Christian missionaries. In more recent decades, international development organizations (such as USAID, UNICEF, EC, and the World Health Organization) have coordinated with the Philippine state and influenced Philippine national health policy. International development organizations worked in specific Filipino communities such as Ifugao. By 1992 and 1993, Ifugao provincial officials had accepted the implementation of UNICEF and EC health and development programs within Ifugao. Western cultural ideologies also influenced community-based NGOs, since most were funded with money from western states or private organizations in western nations. One complaint expressed frequently by NGO members in the early 1990s was that they felt forced to conform to the dictates of western funding organizations in order to retain the organizations' financial support.

Regarding the link between international development and state militarization, most development organizations avoid overt involvement in military and political activities. Yet in the Philippines, they usually were supported and protected by the Philippine armed forces. There were multiple reasons for these practices. One reason was that the Philippine government served as host to the international development organizations, and government officials thus felt some obligation to protect their guests. Another reason was that international development organizations were typically implementing programs closely aligned with the ideological orientations and goals of most government officials.

Generally, within Ifugao international development agents (including Filipino agents employed by international development organizations) attempted to create an image of political neutrality among people with whom they interacted. They tried to depoliticize international development programs through their discourse during community development meetings in Ifugao. Related to militarization, this practice was exemplified by community development meetings sponsored by the EC in Ifugao. At one of these meetings, after a development agent requested participants to identify their community problems, one Ifugao person raised his hand and said, "presence of military at the school." The following discussion then transpired:

Ifugao woman: Because of the insurgency, many people will not go to work. None. There's no fighting now, but there was fighting in the past year.
Ifugao woman: It's the military, an outside force.
Ifugao man: If we say we don't want the military, we will be called subversive.

> Development agent (a Filipino man): This [the threat of violence due to the military occupation of their community] is not an existing problem, because future problems are not allowed in this activity.

With this comment, the development agent ended the discussion of the problem. He chose to ignore the real and existing problem of the military occupation of the community by stating that the military's presence did not constitute an "existing problem." Yet, the military occupation of the school was perceived by community members to threaten the lives of school children, school teachers, and community adults on a daily basis, each of whom could have been caught in crossfire if a battle erupted. Soldiers' weapons lying in close proximity of children, and the frequent drunkenness of soldiers, posed real and "existing" dangers to community members. In 1992 a woman told me that in another Ifugao barrio, the NPA was staying with the people and holding nightly meetings with them. Soon, state soldiers became aware of the NPA presence there. One night the soldiers came and began shooting at the NPA. The ensuing battle involved many local people, since it occurred in the middle of a residential area. She further said,

> That surely affected the people there! In our barrio, we like the soldiers to stay here, but only if they stay away from the *sitios* and schools. When they are staying at the school and the children see their guns, it makes the children very nervous. Some of them like to play with the soldiers, but what if their guns are laying around and a child picks it up? That is something bad for them. Many times we have asked them not to stay at the school, but you know that it is a good location for the soldiers because it is safe there, and they cannot be attacked there.

The development agent in the meeting cited above avoided any discussion of why the military personnel were stationed in their community and inside the school, why the war was being waged, and what community members could do to remove the soldiers from the school. The practice of international development agents neglecting to deal with existing social and political problems involving power relations, such as imposed militarization of communities, combined with their strong emphasis on community projects, served to redirect potential political action on the part of local people toward development activities. Participation in these development activities, in turn, left the existing social order unchanged, a practice that was supported by the state and its military. The development agent may have dismissed the anxieties of community members in order to distance the international development organization from activism geared toward resisting the state military. This was an example of how international development organizations subtly, if inadvertently, supported the social and political status quo in Ifugao, and how they became intertwined with the violence of LIC.

Members of the grassroots Cordillera Peoples Alliance (CPA), some of whom were Ifugao people, noted the links between hunger, Philippine state development goals and programs, and state militarization in the Cordillera mountain region, including Ifugao. A CPA petition letter submitted to President Ramos in 1993 read in part:

> Why is it that the Total War Policy is still being implemented despite its massive ill effects on civilians and its failure to solve the insurgency problem?
>
> If the soldiers are here in the Cordillera to sow peace and instill order in our midst, why are the civilians being terrorized?
>
> Fear, not peace, is what militarization has brought to our villages. Bombings, strafing and mortar shellings are the order of the day. Torture, rape, looting, mass evacuation, arrests, killings and other forms of human rights violations are very much prevalent. The CAFGU's murder of Cris Batan, a human rights worker, is yet to be given justice.[12]
>
> Hunger, not order, Mr. President, is the result. We are hindered from roaming our own forests for game. We can no longer freely tend our swidden fields, where we grow basic crops. We hesitate to go to our rice terraces because of the bombings. Mr. President, we will surely starve. Even your soldiers will have nothing to take from our granaries anymore.
>
> Ethnocide, not peace and progress, is the impending result of militarization and your development agenda. The disrespect of our sacred rituals and the undermining of our indigenous socio-political systems, and the outright intrusion on our ancestral lands, and the direct assault on our environment characterize the conduct of military operations.
>
> Our land is rich in natural resources. Through the years, government laws and policies have always outlined the Cordillera as a resource area for extractive industries, such as mining and logging, and for infrastructure support, such as hydroelectric dams and other energy projects.
>
> We know, Mr. President, that we have time and again opposed government policies and programs. Is this why we are being heavily militarized? Is this why you have to ask for "emergency powers" so you can impose your will and forcibly implement your energy projects? Unless the Cordillera people are the direct beneficiaries and the projects are environment-friendly, we oppose these programs and policies because they threaten our very existence.
>
> We oppose these projects, Mr. President, because land to us is not just a commodity. Land to us is life itself. And not just any land, either, for we are rooted in only one: the Cordillera. To separate us from it would be to deprive us of our existence and identity as a people. We belong to this land and to no other (Cordillera Peoples Alliance 1993).

State Militarization and Right Thinking: Power, Control of Bodies, and Low Intensity Conflict

With regard to healing in the context of LIC, in everyday discourse, the concept of healing implies the practices of restoring an individual to health, or making an individual sound or whole.[13] In the context of political conflict, however, healing is invested with additional, multiple meanings, which are often ambiguous, shifting, and contested. This has been the case in the Philippines, where multiple meanings have been attributed to healing by participants in the political conflict, including the state military, the NPA, and Filipino citizens.

Repressive state militaries are often viewed as appendages of the state which inflict terror and physical harm on individual bodies, to manipulate them to conform to the dictates of the state (Amnesty International 1993). However, the Philippine state military, viewed by many as having historically been repressive, has also manipulated the body through biomedical healing practices to gain support for the state among citizens enmeshed in political violence and power struggles.[14]

The Philippine state practice of military healing generated a contradiction when placed alongside the broader destructive effects of the military on the civilian Philippine population. The Philippine state military was accused by many Filipinos and non-Filipinos, since at least the rule of former President Ferdinand Marcos, of being an institution which "salvages" (or "disappears"), tortures, and imprisons individual civilian bodies. Yet, it simultaneously engaged in healing and making whole the bodies of civilians (Carling 1996). The contradiction is more easily understood if we consider the goals of the state military in healing, that is, to aid in constructing individual bodies which were ideologically aligned with the state—in other words, a form of political conversion.

Furthermore, the manipulation of the body through healing for purposes of political conversion was not limited to the state military; the Philippine revolutionary movement also long engaged in a similar practice of healing civilians. This practice was both an integral aspect of its proposed political agenda, implemented prior to the success of the movement, and a strategy of construction of bodies ideologically aligned with the revolutionary movement, that is, the political conversion of civilians in the midst of political conflict.

Foucault argued that power is "a strategy, that its effects of domination are attributed not to 'appropriation,' but to dispositions, manoeuvres, tactics, techniques, functionings" (Foucault 1977). He viewed the body as being the product of classificatory knowledge and power. Healing the body has been used by the Philippine state military and the resistance movement during political conflict as a form of power, a technique used in an attempt to manipulate, produce, or reproduce political subjects aligned with their respective ideologies. Variable meanings have been attributed to healing in Ifugao by different healers, depending on the intentions of the healers and the context of the healing practice.

In the 1990s, healing was taken up by numerous diverse groups in the Philippines. These included the free state biomedical institutions at hospitals and clinics across the country, private biomedical institutions, international development organizations such as UNICEF, international and national medical mission groups, international and national religious organizations, local non-governmental health organizations, Ifugao *mumbaki* (indigenous *baki* religious specialists), Christian leaders and community members, more recently the state military, and historically the NPA and the NDF. Despite what appears at first glance to be an abundant and wide-ranging set of healing resources, the majority of Ifugao people experienced inadequate access to health care due to poverty, poor infrastructure, and lack of adequate biomedical facilities, equipment, medicines, and personnel. Problems associated with the LIC also limited health care, such as inaccessibility of medical services during military battles or with military hamletting, also known as "reconcentration."

Most poverty-stricken Ifugao people not directly involved with the war were not politically discriminating in their choice of biomedical health care services. Ifugao people were discriminating in their choice of biomedical health care services, however, if their choice would put their lives in danger (such as placing them in the line of crossfire), or if finances did not allow them access to certain private or public services. However, most poor Ifugao people used whatever biomedical health services became available to them when they were in need, regardless of the political or religious orientation of the health care provider. Poor Ifugao people's experience of inadequate access to health care provided a prime avenue for the manipulation of the body through healing by the state military and the NPA.

As discussed earlier, in many Ifugao communities there was an intensification of militarization and military instruction given to civilians in the early 1990s. In 1992 and 1993 the military engaged in "total war" against the NPA in Ifugao, as well as in the rest of the country. The Philippine LIC included state, military, international, and missionary health and development services as one component of an overall strategy. This included the coordination of the army with all local state officials and agencies, including health, education, agriculture, political officials, and police (702nd Infantry [SOT] Brigade 1992c:1).

Part of the Philippine's LIC strategy was psychological warfare, enacted in part through the military's institutionalizing a discourse of state ideology during military sponsored community meetings where state health care was discussed, as well as other topics. The military conducted municipal level seminars, called "Live-in Seminars," as well as barrio meetings, as techniques of repressing "wrong" thinking, that is, thought critical of or different from the government's ideology and critical of structures of inequality. These seminars were also used to impress upon people what "right" thinking was, according to the state.

The Live-in Seminars lasted for one or two days. They were called "live-in" because people hiking from distant barrios to the center of the municipality to attend the seminar were required to live in the center for one or two evenings. The Live-in Seminars included instruction on government health care ideology, among other topics. For example, the military group stationed in one community held a reeducation seminar in 1992 which discussed the merits of democracy, the evils of communism, and the benefits of government programs of health care and education. One session taught by a government official was entitled "Filipino Values—Reorientation on the Bad and Good Values." The health session, delivered by a government doctor, was entitled "Personal Hygiene and Sanitation." Although the doctor may not have intentionally been promoting the military's ideology, the emphasis on "personal" responsibility to achieve good health ignored the social causes of illness and malnutrition. In this example, the military, performing under the guise of democracy, engaged in the social construction of "appropriate" or "right" conduct as they defined it, including the construction of an appropriate or acceptable form of health care which ignored political and economic causes of illness and hunger. The soldiers also were backed by their weapons, which could be used against those who contested their modes of thought and authority (HAIN 1992:304).

One state soldier stationed in an Ifugao municipality told me that when he visits Ifugao barrios, he holds meetings with the residents. He and his fellow soldiers tried to convince the people to side with the state and to deny support to the NPA. He talked to people about communism and democracy because "the people don't know about communism. They only know about [the NPA's] work fighting the government. The communists attack the government because that is what their higher-ups in Manila tell them to do." He instructed the people that "communism is no good, because they are fighting against the government and because they are like the people in Vietnam. When you work, there is only one person who is telling you what to do."

A 1992 local military newspaper asserted that the state's "civil military operations program [was] another subtle way of winning the hearts and minds of the people to the government side" (702nd Infantry [SOT] Brigade 1992a:5). The army's civil military operations program included the provision of health services to community members by soldiers, involving a number of dental and medical civic action programs within the Ifugao community. The civil military operations programs also included soldiers serving as "Army para-teachers [in the community] in support of the government's education for all (EFA) program" (702nd Infantry [SOT] Brigade 1993b:2); working on infrastructural development of roads and bridges; and playing in musical groups, providing "concerts at the park" (702nd Infantry [SOT] Brigade 1992a:5, 7).

The state's attempt to construct a political ideology that was acceptable to its civilians through military engagement in community programs, including health care, can also be observed through the following segment of a 1992 article in the Philippine army's local Ifugao newspaper, "The Central Luzon Tribune, Defender of the People." The article, entitled "Unity and Cooperation: Solution of Insurgency Problem Seen," read as follows:

> [A Brigadier General] informed the same [government] officials that just like in Mt. Province and other provinces in Central Luzon where the brigade successfully operated in the past two years and 9 months, the military now in Ifugao intends to carry out the campaign in close coordination with other government agencies and the people to insure success.
> He said the campaign is primarily centered on the deployment of Special Operations Teams (SOT), a pro-people and community-based strategy which

> concentrate on the enlightenment of the citizenry on the ills of communism, the programs of the government to alleviate their plight [including health care] as well as military efforts as their real soldiers and protectors, in order to gain support and cooperation in the most peaceful means rather than the usual search and destroy concept.
>
> ... [He] however hinted that the military will not hesitate to initiate full combat operations against the armed components of the underground movement if only to clear the province of insurgents to make it free and safe for progress and development ... (702nd Infantry [SOT] Brigade 1992c:1, 2).

Following this dual strategy in its military operations, at the same time that the Philippine military introduced its community health care programs in Ifugao, as well as in other regions of the country, it stepped up its warfare activities. During the early 1990s it increased its military presence in Ifugao Province greatly, moving a brigade of soldiers into Ifugao that remained there until at least 1993. The soldiers stationed in Ifugao conducted aggressive operations against the NPA, often involving civilians in their violent maneuvers. In a contradictory fashion, these operations sometimes inflicted physical harm on civilians at the same time that the military was engaged in healing practices among other members of the civilian population. There was also constant surveillance of the Ifugao population by state soldiers, who stationed themselves in the middle of Ifugao villages and patrolled the mountainsides, seeking the NPA and keeping a watchful eye on the activities of Ifugao people. This led to a feeling of wariness on the part of many Ifugao people, and a silencing of open dissent in front of the soldiers.

A contradiction, involving the military's practice of simultaneous warfare against and healing of individual bodies, arises when the population they are attacking and healing is one and the same, that is, the civilian population. The Philippine military did not limit its maneuvers and techniques to the communist rebels; the AFP involved thousands of civilians in its operations. For example, the Philippine state military utilized the strategy of hamletting civilian populations in Ifugao, as well as in other communities of the Philippines, to deny material support to the NPA. Hamletting in Ifugao and elsewhere resulted in illness, anxiety, miscarriage, and malnutrition of civilians (HAIN 1989c). Numerous deaths of internal refugees were attributed to hamletting in areas outside of Ifugao. Food blockades were enforced in communities by the state military, placing people at greater risk of becoming malnourished and acquiring illnesses (Adiong 1989; HAIN 1989b, 1989c). Amnesty International and the NGO Philippine Task Force Detainees documented numerous human rights abuses of civilians perpetrated by the Philippine military and police, including illegal imprisonment, torturing, and killing of civilians (Task Force Detainees of the Philippines, Baguio, 1993, 1992, 1991).[15]

The military also targeted civilian NGO leaders and members in Ifugao and elsewhere, including members of health NGOs, suspecting them of being members of the NPA (Dumlao Jr. 1996a; HAIN 1989b). While the state provided health services to some civilians, it denied health services to other civilians through the military's harassment of health NGO personnel.

In 1989, on the southern Philippine island of Mindanao, the military instituted a food blockade among an indigenous group to reduce the chances of the villagers providing food to NPA soldiers. The Philippine military announced that food and medical missions would not be allowed in the community, and that rationing of food and medicines could be done only under military supervision. In this case, the military regulated individual bodies and the body politic by simultaneously denying and controlling food and healing practices for civilians, and by denying NPA soldiers access to these resources. Also, the military in this situation was engaged in healing the same civilians which it had injured or made sick through its military operations.

In many other cases, the state's public health institutions were tasked with caring for the injured and sick casualties of the war, again placing the state in the position of both inflictor and healer of illness in the context of political violence. In fewer cases, members of health NGOs assisted victims of the LIC.[16]

New People's Army and National Democratic Front Healing Strategies

While the Philippine military increased its healing activities in Ifugao in the early 1990s, the revolutionary NPA historically had been engaged in such activities with Ifugao community members, including health education. As noted earlier, the CPP and NPA were members the National Democratic Front (NDF). The NDF described itself in 1990 as, "an alliance of revolutionary organizations and individuals with roots in the various sectors and regions of the Philippines. Its long-term goal is to build a society characterized by national sovereignty, authentic democracy, social justice, progress and peace. It seeks to unite with all forces willing to fight to achieve these goals" (Liberation 1990:2). As described by the 1989 "National Democratic Front 14 Point Programme for National Liberation," the goals of the NDF included:

1. Unite the Filipino people to overthrow the reactionary rule of US imperialism and its local allies.

2. Advance the people's revolutionary struggle to achieve genuine democracy, national freedom and lasting peace.

3. Establish a democratic coalition government and a people's democratic republic.

4. Establish a national revolutionary army at the service of the people.

5. Uphold and promote the free exercise of the people's basic democratic rights.

6. Terminate all unequal relations with the United States and other foreign entities.

7. Complete the process of genuine land reform, raise rural production through cooperation, and modernize agriculture.

8. Carry out national industrialization as the leading factor in economic development.

9. Guarantee the right to employment, raise the people's living standards, and expand social services the soonest possible after establishing democratic state power.

10. Promote a patriotic, scientific and popular culture and ensure free public education.

11. Respect and foster the self-determination of the Cordillera people and all ethnic minorities.

12. Respect and support the continuing struggle of the Moro people for national self-determination and promote their national democratic aspirations.

13. Guarantee the equality, partnership and co-operation of women and men in all spheres of life.

14. Adopt and practice a revolutionary, independent and peace-loving foreign policy (Davis 1989:54).

The provision of social services and resources to meet the basic needs of all Filipino people included a comprehensive health care program. Their planned health program emphasized primary health care, traditional and modern medicine, and a national health care system that would be universally accessible. It would be a mass-based health system, both self-reliant and comprehensive (*Makabayang Samahang Pangkalusugan* 1987).

The NDF began to implement these goals in some areas of Ifugao during the LIC by engaging in Socio-Economic Work during the 1980s. The 1990 chair of the NDF People's Welfare Commission stated in an NDF official publication that,

> providing basic social services to the people was considered part of agrarian revolution and mass work in the countryside. With the guerrilla fighters as the primary implementors . . . much of the revolution's socio-economic work was geared towards addressing the immediate needs of the masses. Comrades helped in raising agricultural production, improving health and sanitation and instruction on reading, writing and arithmetic (Felipe and del Fuego 1990:3-4).

Revolutionary health work included the provision of primary health care and education; medical, dental and minor surgery consultations; and preventive campaigns (such as sanitation and agro-nutrition) in local villages and for the NPA soldiers (NDF National Executive Committee 1991:3). Agricultural development was emphasized to improve nutrition. According to the 1990 chair of the NDF People's Welfare Commission, the NDF Socio-Economic Work priority in 1990 and 1991 was to increase the production of staple and survival root crops, and high-nutritive vegetables and other farm products in guerrilla zones and bases

(Felipe and del Fuego 1990:6). The NDF's nutrition program, as well as its overall program of revolutionary change, involved the implementation of a genuine agrarian reform program and a restructuring of the existing unequal class structure in the Philippines. The NDF asserted that the transformation of Philippine social structure would lead to the improvement of the health of poor Filipinos, as well as their quality of life generally.

The NDF included the *Makabayang Samahang Pangkalusugan* (MSP), or the Patriotic Health Association, established in 1979. This was a revolutionary organization of health professionals and workers that developed a Marxist analysis of the social causes of widespread poverty, illness, and hunger in the Philippines:

> The relationship between poverty and health is well accepted. But poverty should be recognized as the product of gross social inequality and of exploitative social relations. In the Philippines, poverty and underdevelopment are the direct results of foreign subjugation and widespread landlessness. The crisis of the health care system is in fact, the crisis of a semi-colonial and semi-feudal society in the throes of total disintegration.
>
> At the root of the health problem lie the same basic evils that have plagued Philippine society through its entire modern history—US imperialism, feudalism and bureaucratic capitalism (*Makabayang Samahang Pangkalusugan* 1987:2).

The Proceedings of the Second National Congress of the MSP (January 1987) acknowledged that malnutrition afflicted the majority of Filipino children, citing a government food consumption survey which showed a decline in both quantity and quality of nutritional intake over the last decade. "As a result, nutritional -deficiency diseases, such as goiter and Vitamin-A blindness, remain endemic in many regions of the country" (*Makabayang Samahang Pangkalusugan* 1987:3). In 1987 the MSP, in addition to supporting revolutionary workers, saw the following as its objectives:

> Playing the lead role in the health sector, the MSP mobilizes health professionals and students, workers in health institutions and agencies, traditional healers and trained health workers at the grassroots level, to actively participate in the people's war for national liberation and democracy. Specifically, it plays a key role in developing the revolutionary health mass movement that will ensure the people's inalienable right to health and lay the foundation for a new health care system (*Makabayang Samahang Pangkalusugan* 1987:11-12).

Women, as well as men, led the NPA war against the Philippine state. *Malayang Kilusan ng Bagong Kababaihan* (MAKIBAKA) was a mass organiza- tion of women established in 1970 and influenced by the CPP. MAKIBAKA means "to fight, to struggle" (Davis 1989:139). MAKIBAKA's first chairperson, Maria Lorena Barros, sought to link the emancipation of women to class and male oppression and the struggle for national liberation. MAKIBAKA's objectives included the mobilization of Filipino women towards greater participation in society and the liberation of women from social discrimination and sexual exploitation (Davis 1989:139). They raised gender issues within the CPP and NPA, but these often were not taken seriously. Women fought as guerrilla soldiers, served as leaders within the NPA, and worked as health workers or doctors within the NPA health structure. Women also were involved in NPA intelligence operations, worked as education officers, organized mass protest movements for peasants and workers, and brought gender issues to the fore in a movement that had traditionally subsumed gender issues under nationalist and class issues (Davis 1989:132). Ifugao women fighting as NPA guerrilla soldiers sometimes were referred to as "Amazons" by the Philippine army, and women from other Filipino ethnic groups also fought with the NPA within Ifugao (702nd Infantry [SOT] Brigade 1993a:1).

A 1987 NDF publication revealed that the provision of health services by the NDF was not strictly geared toward improving the health status of Filipino citizens:

> The practice of bringing health care to the people can be traced to the very beginnings of the revolution's expansion. Health care was considered important as a direct service to the people, who were deprived of effective health services by the reactionary state. But it was also used as a means to arouse, organize and mobilize the masses in the countryside for the armed struggle (*Makabayang Samahang Pang-kalusugan* 1987).

In this example, as in the case of the Philippine military, the body, through revolutionary health work practiced by members of the NDF and NPA, was used as a site of political conversion, involving the construction of ideologies aligned with those of the NDF and NPA. In the case of the NDF, health services were used for political conversion, as well as for the accomplishment of the NDF's goals of providing health services to those deprived of them.

The ideological splits experienced by members of the CPP, NPA, and NDF in the early 1990s may have influenced the health policies and practices of these groups. According to one source, by the mid-1990s, members of a Rejectionist group were more interested in using health issues to "conscientize" people than to mobilize them for armed struggle. Nevertheless, health care based on this new ideology was still being used as a political vehicle to help people recognize the issues and concerns of the left movement.

The contradiction between the NPA's practices of warfare and healing was not as great as that of the Philippine military, since the NPA focused its attack primarily on the state government and military and was attempting to revive the body politic through a fundamental change of the existing unequal social class structure in the Philippines. However, there were cases in Ifugao, as well as in other areas of the Philippines, of NPA soldiers implementing their own form of social justice, often involving civilians. Local, usually wealthy, civilians were targeted,

harassed, victimized by extortion, or killed by the NPA, due either to their social
class position and their exploitation of the poor or their criminal and abusive
activities (Alconaba 1993). These civilians were most likely perceived by members
of the NPA to be oppressors and powerful elites perpetuating the unequal social
class structure which the NPA was attempting to eliminate. Or, the civilians may
have been perceived to be a threat to the community due to their criminal activities.
Some civilians were killed by the NPA after being accused of aiding the military
in its war against the NPA, such as by informing the military of the location of
NPA soldiers.

Health Care as Political Weaponry

The historical use of biomedical health services and other social development
activities as a strategy of low intensity conflict continued in the Philippines, in a
context of structural social inequality, as late as 1993 (Carling 1996; Cordillera
Human Rights Commission/Cordillera Peoples Alliance 1996). The state strategy
of using health and social development activities as a tool of repression in low
intensity conflict to subtly coerce people into accepting state ideologies defused
some overt political action which could have contested the Philippine state. This
political strategy used by the state and its military influenced civilians as they
"crafted" their "selves" in a field of power (Kondo 1990), including their political
identities, beliefs, and alignments.

Members of the military used healing as a tool of power, as well as other social
services such as international development activities, to validate, strengthen, and
maintain their political agendas and ideologies. This occurred within a society
where state policies geared toward creating social equality and justice had at times
lost credibility and was challenged both violently by the NPA and peacefully by
numerous non-governmental organizations.

The state's ability to coerce people into supporting its ideologies was suggested
by the slow turning of local political support from the NPA toward the state
military from the 1980s to the 1990s in some Ifugao communities. This occurred
for a variety of historical reasons, but it was due in part to the perception that the
military was newly involved in assisting the poor through the military's health and
social development practices. This shift in political support provided some
evidence that the manipulation of the Ifugao people's political allegiances by the
state through healing and other social development techniques was effective to
some extent. The military soldiers were also perceived as being generally more
professional and respectful in their interactions with civilians during the 1990s than
they had been during the Marcos presidency, a change which came about during
the Aquino and Ramos presidencies. Also, the government Department of Health
(DOH) had attracted some members of the left movement during the Aquino
period, and DOH programs appeared to be more progressive under former

Secretary of Health Juan Flavier during the Ramos presidency. These changes may have influenced Ifugao people's perceptions of the government's health programs. Still, the focus of government and military sponsored biomedical health care remained the curing of the individual body rather than a radical restructuring of social relations as a means of restoring health, even under a more progressive administration.

The military's new efforts toward providing social and medical assistance to the poor can be contrasted to the NPA's slow movement away from social and medical assistance to Ifugao people during the early 1990s. This may have occurred for a number of reasons, including the significant reduction in the numbers of NPA soldiers located in Ifugao by the 1990s, in part due to the increased presence of state soldiers in the area. Also, with the removal of President Marcos from office in 1986, the subsequent installation of Corazon Aquino as President of the Philippines, and the ratification of the 1987 Constitution, numerous NPA soldiers resigned from their war efforts to return to civilian life, thereby reducing the NPA's presence in Ifugao. This process was facilitated by the state's amnesty program for NPA soldiers, begun under the Aquino administration, which encouraged NPA soldiers to return to civilian life. With Ramos' election and the end of the cold war in 1992, the power and legitimacy of the NPA were decreasing (Druckman and Green 1995). Another possible catalyst for the reduction in NPA health workers in Ifugao in the early 1990s may have been the ideological splits occurring within the CPP, NPA, and NDF.

During the early 1990s, some Ifugao people stated that the NPA soldiers' treatment of local people had changed from the 1980s. NPA soldiers were evaluated by many Ifugao people primarily on their treatment and respect of community members. For example, during the Marcos period, the NPA presence in one Ifugao community was stronger than it was in 1992. During that period, most members of the community were said to have accepted the NPA and appreciated their contributions to the community. The NPA engaged in community activities, including helping residents with their agricultural and household labor, and conducted community meetings about health education, leadership skills, community organization, democracy, and NPA ideology. The NPA were said to be very respectful, polite, and always ready to help residents. They generally were also perceived as pursuing goals that would benefit the Ifugao and Filipino people at large. Additionally, the NPA taught local people organizational and leadership skills. One Ifugao woman attributed the remarkable community oriented organizational skills of residents of her community to training conducted by the NPA ten years previously.

By the early 1990s, however, the NPA soldiers' treatment of the people in the same community had changed. The NPA was no longer perceived to be helpful, respectful, or hardworking by many local Ifugao people, in large part because the soldiers did not help in the same way that their predecessors had. Some viewed the new NPA soldiers they encountered as being lazy, consuming too much of the community members' food without contributing anything. Some community members' evaluation of the NPA had become somewhat negative by the early 1990s, at least in regard to their treatment of local people. Thus, the reduction in NPA health services and other social development activities for Ifugao people may have resulted in a lessening of support for the CPP, NPA, and NDF movement.

Indigenous Healing Resisting Politicization of Biomedical Healing

For some Ifugao people, and for many other Cordillera people and organizations, the historical and continued government militarization of the Cordillera region and the military practice of health and other social development activities were linked to the government's pursuit of control over and usurpation of valuable natural resources in the Cordillera region (Carling 1996; Cordillera Human Rights Commission/Cordillera Peoples Alliance 1996; Nanglihan and Fianza 1996). State health practices were linked both to the war and to the exploitation of indigenous people's cultural and political rights. In light of this perspective, the indigenous healing process, *baki*, may have been practiced by some Ifugao people as a partial response—of which they may not have been fully conscious—to the overt politicization of biomedicine by the state military and the NPA, in an attempt to resist state and revolutionary control over their lives.

Still, Ifugao people commonly engaged in multiple forms of healing without being politically discriminating. This reflected either a lack of political involvement or a desperation for much-needed health services, or both. It also reflected contradictions people often display as they engage in activities and create identities which conflict with each other (Kondo 1990). Yet, while accepting biomedical services from both the NPA and state military soldiers appears to be contradictory ideologically, both aided in achieving the same goal of good health in the face of poverty. The lack of political discrimination in acquiring health care by many Ifugao people also pointed to the reality that state and revolutionary attempts to control bodies through health care, or other social institutions, as strategies of power, were not always entirely successful, despite the intentions of groups asserting their power. Nor were their ideologies hegemonic, as people acted in ways that countered their mandates.

Local Non-Governmental Community-Based Health
Organization and Militarization

Despite the numerous health programs operating in Ifugao, improvements in the nutritional status of children and women had been minimal by the early 1990s. In light of the shortcomings of these health services, local Ifugao women actively attempted to provide health services to their communities, usually in conjunction with the health programs. The women's health work in Ifugao, though, was layered with multiple meanings since it was conducted in the context of LIC and increased militarization in their communities. Notions and meanings attributed to the provision of health care were constructed, sometimes violently, by social forces.

Male health workers faced similar dangers in carrying out their work, some of whom were killed while serving as health workers. Yet, the majority of health workers in the Philippines, both paid and volunteer, were women. In large part this was due to the gendered construction of biomedical health care in Ifugao as women's work, both within families and communities. It is important to assess how women as health workers in their communities, and as primary health care providers within their families, experienced the effects of LIC in their daily lives.

Attempts were made by the Philippine state military to stifle deviation from the government defined health care system and to silence critical historical analyses of health problems through military intimidation, surveillance, and, in some cases, interrogation, detention, or "salvaging" (killing) of health workers (Task Force Detainees of the Philippines, Baguio 1993; Collins 1989; Estrada-Claudio 1988; Permanent Peoples' Tribunal Session on the Philippines 1981). To be an NGO health worker in the Philippines meant both providing health care services to fellow community members and risking one's life if red-baited by government and military officials. This double meaning attributed to health care was found most often within communities where state social institutions and health services did not meet the basic nutritional and health needs of the poor.

Civilian health processes were a site wherein conflict, violence, and everyday resistance were played out in one Ifugao community, generating changes in cultural and social constructions of health care and illness. The state form of biomedicine limited its explanation for the causes of and solutions for illness to the individual, family, and community. When the state construction of hunger and other illnesses was criticized by health workers, the state at times attempted to repress and change the alternative ways of understanding and alleviating hunger and illness, sometimes through military intervention.

Militarization had a significantly negative impact on health NGOs in the Philippines, as well as non-health NGOs. In contrast to the state health system, one domestic community based health NGO did address issues of economic and political relations, inequality, and justice within their health program. The NGO workers viewed these as factors integral to health, nutritional status, and health care. This NGO attempted to raise community members' nutritional status. It also advocated less dependency on costly western drugs. It aimed to "establish and understand the links between social, economic, cultural, spiritual and political interrelations in health and disease" (Health NGO 1990). It was the only health organization in this community that analyzed, with community members, both macro- and micro-level sources, or "the root causes," of poverty, illness, and hunger, including gender relations. Its method was based on Paulo Freire's notion of facilitating the development of a critical consciousness among community members. It received the majority of its funding from a European NGO, specifically a church organization.

The experience of the health workers of this NGO illustrates a second example of the government construction and education of community members in acceptable forms of health care in the context of LIC. One health worker reported she attended a meeting in a nearby town sponsored by government soldiers, who were discussing the meaning of democracy and the evils of communism, among other matters. She heard government soldiers say that some NGOs were really communist front organizations, and the soldiers named the health NGO she worked with and another community development NGO working in Ifugao as examples. In 1992, an individual speaking during a radio program listened to by the majority of radio listeners in the Ifugao area publicly branded this health NGO as being communist-led, stating that the clinic would be used by NPA soldiers. Military officers and a member of an international development organization also were heard to say that they suspected the NGO health clinic to be a communist front organization, which would ultimately treat the health needs of NPA soldiers. The mayor of another municipality said that the health NGO and the health workers were communist. After hearing these accusations, many local community members questioned if this NGO health clinic was indeed communist. One health worker said, "the military tells the community 'Be careful of NGOs coming to barrios because they are front liners of communists.' That is what they are always telling us." These discourses inspired rumors and fear in the community in which the health clinic was located.[17]

Despite the Philippine government's being a signatory to a Geneva convention which allows health workers to provide health care to any person regardless of their race, creed, or political affiliation, the Philippine Congress passed a law requiring health providers to inform the state military or police if they treated an NPA soldier. Yet, as one government document stated, "The government strongly affirms that health is a fundamental human right" (Philippine National Economic Development Administration 1986:22).

The Philippine and U.S. governments had a history of red-baiting Filipino citizens and grassroots, or "people's," organizations as a strategy of LIC since at least World War II and the development of the *Huk* and other early peasant organizations (Davis 1989:41). Ben Kerkvliet wrote about the American colonial government's relationship to the *Huks* after World War II: "To Filipino elites and American officials, any popular organization with determined leaders, many of whom were peasants themselves, threatened the established order. The political system in the country had never experienced such a phenomenon. It ran contrary to elitist politics, which had tolerated only a moderate amount of non-elite participation" (Kerkvliet 1977). U.S. military intelligence personnel in the Philippines reported to their superiors that the *Huk* leaders were primarily communist-inspired (Davis 1989:41).

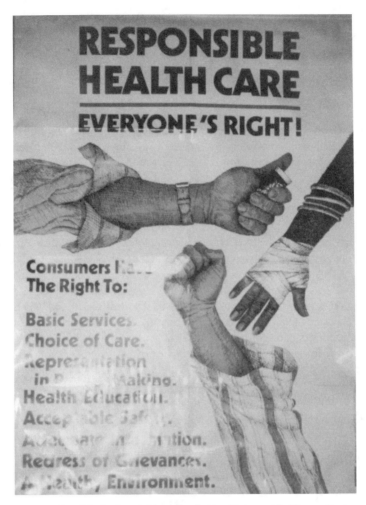

PHOTO 4.2 A health NGO displayed this poster in its office outside Ifugao. It advocates a universal right to responsible health care, including: basic services; choice of care; representation in policy making; health education; acceptable safety; adequate information; redress of grievances; and a healthy environment.

A few months after the radio broadcast mentioned above, it was rumored within Ifugao that the establishment of the health NGO clinic in the Ifugao barrio was one important factor prompting state military officers to station soldiers in the community. The military stayed in the barrio for several months between 1990 and 1993. When health workers of the NGO or other community members walked past the state soldiers, they usually asked the people where they had been and where they were going. The state soldiers maintained a surveillance of local activities and evoked a constant edge of uncertainty from the community members as they went about their daily affairs, including health work.

The branding of this health organization as communist served to educate the community members that the health NGO's social analysis of health problems and health care activity at the community level was unacceptable to members of the state, and possibly threatening to the social order. State officials accomplished this through the red-baiting of the NGO by the military. The NGO health workers had facilitated a broader social analysis with community members regarding health and illness than the state normally promoted. The community was educated about "appropriate" health care through militarization of the community and the development of fear among community members. These processes reinforced the state's construction of malnutrition and other illnesses as being primarily the responsibility of individuals at the family and community levels, since an analysis which went beyond this was branded as being communist or subversive. It also reinforced the state's construction of an acceptable form of health care practice at the community level, one which did not question or analyze social institutions. In Ifugao, as well as in other parts of the Philippines, when a health organization did try to conflate social relations and illness, viewing them as inseparable, members of the state sometimes tried to terminate this critical social analysis of health, illness, and social relations. In the Ifugao case, the state tried to create its hegemony through its modes of discipline enacted by the military. As Jean and John Comaroff have noted, the power of hegemony "has so often been seen to lie in what it silences, what it puts beyond the limits of the rational and the credible" (Comaroff and Comaroff 1991:23).

The military also reinforced the domination of the government political and organizational structure in the area. An NGO health worker said:

> Anyone outside of the government structure is suspected of being communist. Communists are defined as those groups who go to far barrios and work for little money. The military is planting this notion in the minds of the people. The politicians often say that a place is "peaceful" because the military is there. The government's focus is just to wipe out the insurgency by violence rather than resolving the social problems.

Health work, as gendered activity in Ifugao, placed women health workers at particular risk. They often conducted their home visits by hiking alone to distant or nearby homes of the ill, usually with no protection or defense against abuse by the military such as sexual harassment, rape, torture, or murder. Reports of sexual abuse of both men and women by government soldiers were widely known in the Philippines. One Ifugao woman and her male companion, each of whom worked with a national human rights organization, were arrested and tortured in the early 1990s by state military soldiers outside of Ifugao, after being accused of passing information to a prisoner. Both she and her male companion were sexually abused during their imprisonment (Interview with an Ifugao woman 1993; Dizon 1993a). One day in February 1992, an NGO health worker said that she learned that three members of a "people's" NGO in a bordering province had recently been under arrest and had just been released the day before. She heard that one member had a broken rib. She commented that this situation poses a danger to the future of small NGOs.

According to Foucault, punishment "leaves the domain of more or less everyday perception and enters that of abstract consciousness; its effectiveness is seen as resulting from its inevitability, not from its visible intensity; it is the certainty of being punished and not the horrifying spectacle of public punishment that must discourage crime" (Foucault 1977). In this Ifugao community, where state soldiers stationed themselves near the NGO health clinic for eight months in 1992, and again for some time in 1993, women volunteered their time and energy to learn about and provide health care for their community. The female health workers' knowledge of torture and imprisonment of political prisoners (including at least one member of their community), combined with the presence and surveillance of the soldiers living near their clinic, imposed a consciousness of wariness and uncertainty within some of them.

NGO health workers often expressed confusion due to inconsistencies in state policies and directives. On one hand, since the presidency of Corazon Aquino, the Philippine state has encouraged and welcomed the participation and linkage of NGOs with government agencies. The state has specifically encouraged NGO cooperation in improving health and nutrition in the state's goal of "developing" the Philippines (Nutrition Service, Republic of the Philippines 1991:40-41). The members of the health NGO in Ifugao had initially met with and been accredited by the mayor and governor of the municipality in which they would conduct health work. Despite these factors, this organization still had been branded by the military, on at least two occasions, of being a communist front organization. One NGO member from a nearby province stated that since local executives in her area have close ties with the military, she could not see any possibility of a government-NGO partnership (Arao 1992:1).

These forms of intimidation and labeling by the military also had an impact on the women health workers' sense of their identity in the community. As a woman, to be a health worker was to be a respected leader in the community. This respect was derived not only from her knowledge of biomedical and other health care practices, but also from her willingness to dedicate her time and efforts to assist those in need in her community. Yet, to be labeled a communist when one's activities were not linked to the communist insurgency led to the mystification of her role as a health worker and leader in the community. This resulted in confusion among some health workers. When I asked a health worker how she felt about being labeled communist because she was a health worker, she said, "Very bad. It gives (us) a bad reputation." The government, military, and international development program members' labeling also resulted in mistrust of the health workers by other community members. They may have felt uncertain of the health workers' primary motivations, or they may have judged that their associating with persons red-baited by the government and military would be dangerous.

In the face of uncertainty, in terms of health, basic everyday survival, food resources, and possible victimization from the forces operating in the LIC, many Ifugao people clung to religion to provide some amount of certainty and stability in their lives. Although the local religion differed in many respects from the Christian religions operating in the region, both seemed to offer a degree of security to believers about the causes of and solutions to adversity and hope for good fortune in an atmosphere of tremendous unpredictability. It was not unusual for people to attend religious rituals four or five days or nights each week in the rural barrios, for reasons of healing, mourning a death, placating a disturbed ancestor, or studying a bible. In addition to fulfilling religious beliefs, these rituals provided some security and regularity in the face of forces that Ifugao people could not readily or easily control, including the war.

By the end of 1992, state military soldiers were intensively recruiting local Ifugao men to join CAFGU to aid the military in their surveillance of Ifugao communities. In spite of the military and CAFGU surveillance of the health workers' activities, and the fear that it had generated among the women, they continued to pursue their health work. One health worker defiantly stated, "Even if our purpose or goal is for the welfare of the people, there's a difference for the government who claim we are communist. When we had training, there were many rumors about our being communist-led that we heard. But, as long as they [red-baiters] have no evidence of our being communist, then they can find nothing of what they predict." Another health worker related to me:

> For us trained health workers now, even if they say that the health NGO is communist, they [NGO educators] have taught us and even found an agency to fund that health clinic and pharmacy. Even if they say that ["Is that communist?"] we don't mind that because we know the clinic is helpful, but they call it communist. . . . As for me, no I am not afraid, because the people were trying to prevent us from accomplishing our goal, because maybe they saw many NPA here and they think that health NGO belongs to their [NPA] companions. But, with our trainings, we know that is not true. It is to help us and our community to be sustainable.

There was no effort among these health workers during my research period to overtly confront issues of social inequality or to organize people to revolutionary action while the military was present. There was, however, some discussion of the LIC during at least one leadership training session of the health NGO. A local health worker said that during the meeting:

> I tried very hard to reach people's emotions in discussing our community problems. I asked them how they felt with the coming of the NPA and the health NGO, and later the military soldiers. They told me that they were nervous about the

> NPAs presence in the barrio before, since it could attract fighting between them and the soldiers. With the health NGO, they never believed that it was communist since they saw no evidence of this and only observed the health workers assisting the people with their health, going to far *sitios* to visit sick persons. Still, the report that the clinic was a communist front made them nervous. And the coming of the military to camp in our barrio for long periods of time made them more afraid and nervous, fearful of encounters with the NPA. We decided to request from the government and military that the soldiers be removed from the school and housing areas of the barrio.

The women's resistance to the military's intimidation, through their continued participation in health care training and providing health services for community members in the face of red-baiting, effectively prevented the closing down of their clinic. The women were ambivalent about their fear of the male military presence and threat. One female health worker often said that she was not afraid of the military. She related that, at the time, people in the barrio may not have hesitated to request services from the health NGO clinic because "in our experience the people like the health NGO and they trust us. And they understand that the clinic is for the people." Still, at other times, she expressed her fear of violence erupting in the community with the military presence. It was unclear what the women's response would be to stepped-up military violence within their community, as had occurred in another province near Ifugao with the murder of an NGO health worker.

In 1992, months after the military had spread rumors about this health NGO being a communist front organization, during an inter-agency government meeting held in the center of the municipality, a local government official encouraged the local government health agency to coordinate their work with this health NGO. His encouragement of state cooperation with the red-baited health NGO demonstrated some acceptance among state officials of the viability of the health NGO. Later, in 1993, an EC development program operating in Ifugao, in coordination with the Philippine government's Department of Agriculture, contributed funds for medicines and material development of the NGO clinic. The women's resistance to the military threat and their continued daily health work had been effective to some extent in gaining the trust of both community members and some government officials. The Ifugao government officials' actions supporting the health NGO also demonstrated that the state did not operate as a monolithic force against critics of its policies and practices. There were divergent positions and viewpoints among actors within the state. The officials' support of the health NGO countered the state military evaluation of its being a communist threat.

The Politics of Food and Health Care Amidst Political Conflict

Historically, militarization has affected the production of food and access to food resources, either because of evacuation, hamletting, or generation of fear of working in fields with soldiers present or during battles. Militarization also affected the retention of food by civilians, since soldiers stealing food and the coerced or voluntary sharing of food with soldiers reduced community members' food resources. In some cases, these problems were short-term, while in others they appeared to be long-term. Overall, militarization created a strain on already limited food resources for some poverty stricken people.

The historical use of biomedical health services and other social development activities as a strategy of LIC, in a context of structural social inequality in the Philippines, effected some diffusion of overt political action which could have contested the Philippine state. Some members of the state used health care and international development agencies to validate and strengthen their political agendas. These health and development activities did not improve significantly the lives of the poor. Instead, they in some cases maintained or increased social stratification, resulting in the reproduction of widespread hunger.

The strategy of healing the body for political conversion was attempted by both the Philippine military and the NPA to win the "hearts and minds"—and bodies—of Filipino citizens to their respective ideologies. In these instances, class and power discourses and practices were played out on the body through the use of healing as a technique of persuasion, coercion, and control. Thus, healing and hunger should not be viewed in isolation from the LIC in the Philippines, since healing practices, for hunger and other health problems, were integral to the political and ideological strategies of each side. Widespread hunger in the Philippines was also an important impetus for the inception of the LIC, as members of the NPA and NDF sought to solve this problem through social structural change. Although the Philippine state also promoted and implemented programs to solve the problems of hunger and malnutrition, it did not effectively alter existing unequal structures of power and control over resources in the Philippines toward this end.

Yet, in the same location, the practice of healing bodies was also used as a tool of empowerment for poor Ifugao women who were attempting to resolve the many health problems within their communities by addressing both the social and biological causes of illness and hunger. These cases reveal the importance of understanding the multiple meanings invested in healing in political conflicts, and the conflicting and contradictory uses of healing in a field of power. Healing, then, cannot be understood apart from its historically specific cultural and social context, from the intentions of its practitioners, and the conceptions of its recipients.

Contemporary constructions of malnutrition, and of health care which addresses malnutrition in Philippine society, must be analyzed within the context of the war. In this context, concern should not only focus on how LIC may inhibit the provision of health care services or how military battles create illness among community members. Concern should also focus on how the state military can be used to enforce a construction of health care among people at the community level which does not directly address power relations and economic and political causes of different forms of inequality and its manifestations, such as hunger.

In the next chapter, I will look closely at the range of local Ifugao understandings of malnutrition, thinness, illness, and healing in order to depict the complexity of meanings attributed to thinness and malnutrition in Ifugao society.

Notes

1. "Violence" used in this chapter does not refer only to state sponsored violence. Instead, I am referring to violence in the broadest sense of the word, including physical and emotional abuse, restraint, armed conflict, and repression.

2. The Citizen Armed Force Geographical Unit (CAFGU) was a state institutionalized civilian militia, implemented by President Aquino on July 25, 1988. At that time, Aquino was faced with widespread human rights abuses perpetrated by both the state military and vigilante groups (which she at one time personally supported). In 1988, she ordered the vigilante groups disbanded, replacing them with CAFGU, the new state army-trained militia. CAFGU replaced the Civilian Home Defense Force (CHDF), created by Marcos, which had been accused of widespread human rights abuses (Davis 1989:181). The CAFGU and CHDF were part of the "total war" on the NPA in the Philippine government's LIC strategy.

3. Although England gained control of the Philippines for two years, from 1762–1764, the English did not have a great impact on Ifugao people's lives.

4. Even if this was not entirely accurate, it is important that this historical memory of the Spanish within Ifugao remained through 1992.

5. Those who did not own irrigated rice fields worked for pay in kind on irrigated rice fields owned by other community members. They also had access to swidden fields on the mountainsides.

6. Ifugao was considered to be a subprovince of Mountain Province, which also included the subprovinces of Bontoc, Benguet, Amburayan, Lepanto, Apayao, and Kalinga.

7. The concept and practice of revenge murder for reasons of kinship honor and spiritual appeasement have remained to the present.

8. Slavery was outlawed by 1911, when the Philippine Commission enacted Act No. 2071 on August 7, 1911.

9. Many of the dead were found to have bloody diarrhea on their clothing.

10. A *bolo* is a machete.

11. Diarrhea has been shown to have an important influence on nutritional status, since during diarrhea episodes nutrients are lost through excrement, and nutrients are not well absorbed by the body.

12. Cris Batan, a worker in the human rights organization Task Force Detainees of the Philippines, was murdered in barrio Betwagan, Sadanga, Mountain Province in 1993, allegedly by CAFGU members.

13. The next two sections of this chapter were originally part of a conference paper, presented at the 1995 94th American Anthropological Annual Meeting in Washington, D.C., and a version of the sections was published in *Urban Anthropology and Studies of Cultural Systems and World Economic Development*, 25, 4 (Winter 1996):385-417. I am grateful to the journal for granting permission to incorporate sections of that article in this chapter.

14. Linda Buckley Green cites a similar case in which members of the Guatemalan ruling state government, during the 1970s, used international development programs, specifically

primary health care programs, as one of a number of strategies to legitimize or enforce their control over the government (Green 1989).

15. In 1995, after the period in which this research was conducted, the NGO Cordillera Resource Center reported that the human rights group KARAPATAN found that the number of human rights violations committed by police and military men in the Cordillera from January to June 1995 had decreased, although they were still being committed (Dizon 1995).

16. The cases of NGOs assisting victims of the war were likely fewer due mainly to the smaller number of health NGOs and personnel in comparison to the widespread Philippine state public health system.

17. By 1992, President Ramos legalized the Communist Party in the Philippines. But with heavy militarization of parts of Ifugao, and a government pledge of "total war" against the NPA, to be branded a communist still placed an individual at risk.

5

Spirituality and Hunger

Many Ifugao people retained dynamic local healing beliefs and practices during the early 1990s, stemming from the Ifugao religion and forms of the *baki*, an Ifugao religious ritual.[1] These varied by locale within Ifugao. *Baki* was not only performed for healing, however, since it was a core feature of the Ifugao culture. Different forms of *baki* were performed for all important life events of Ifugao people, including illness, stages of agricultural production, funerals, weddings, headhunting (in the past), and other life events (Dulawan n.d.:ix). *Baki* was also performed simply to validate a person's prestige and position in a community, such as the *bumayah baki* performed only by the wealthy. Or, the validation of prestige could be disguised as another kind of *baki*, such as a healing *baki*.

Baki were also important for building, rectifying, and maintaining social relations, as well as for the functional purpose of benefiting a family sponsoring a *baki*. Sponsoring *baki* could demonstrate respect for one's family members, reciprocation for *baki* one has attended in other homes, and gratefulness for the kindness of friends. *Baki* was also important in regard to sharing food resources, which symbolized prestige, honor, and abiding Ifugao social morality. *Baki* was additionally significant for propitiating spiritual beings to whom it was offered.

However, Ifugao society was a religiously and medically diverse society, since biomedical and numerous forms of Christian healing practices operated in Ifugao as well. Christianity (Catholic, Protestant, and nondenominational) had been established in Ifugao since at least the beginning of this century.

In this chapter I will first explore Ifugao local religious healing beliefs and practices. I also describe the Ifugao construction of malnutrition, and how the local religion addressed the Ifugao category *na-ong-ong*, or extreme thinness. I will later explore the practice of Christianity and Christian healing in Ifugao. Some theories of religious conversion are discussed and an assessment made of how the body can be central to the process of religious conversion and control through healing. Finally, I examine some Christian discourses and practices which have a bearing on nutritional status among Ifugao people. Although there were numerous Christian organizations in Ifugao, for the purposes of this chapter I focus on three Christian organizations: a Catholic food supplement program, an Evangelical clinic and hospital, and a Methodist church. My focus here is on Christian individuals who actively pursued Christian conversion among followers of *baki* or who denigrated *baki* and the local Ifugao religion. However, I would like to emphasize that there were many Ifugao Christians who maintained great respect for the local Ifugao religion and its followers and who participated in *baki*.

Historical Context of the Local Ifugao Religion

Healing in Ifugao can only be understood by situating healing practices within their historical, cultural, and social context, as political, economic, religious, and ideological processes affect the changing structure and content of healing practices (Turner 1984). The Ifugao healing ritual was said by one *mumbaki* (a male "native priest") to have existed since the beginning of Ifugao society. The creator god *Muntalug* created human beings.[2]

Popular Ifugao oral history about the inception of the Ifugao people began not with the first humans created, but with the repopulating of Ifugao following a massive flood. The flood was believed to have covered and refigured the earth, creating the mountains and plains. The Ifugao woman named *Bugan* and her Ifugao brother, *Wigan*, were the sole survivors of the flood on earth. Although they were siblings, they conceived a number of children, who were distributed around the world. The children of *Bugan* and *Wigan* later conceived their own children together.

According to one legend told to me by a *mumbaki*, the learning of *baki* by Ifugao men and women happened only in later generations, after *Bugan* and *Wigan* died. Another woman named *Bugan*, a descendent of the original *Bugan*, had refused the courtship of all males. A god named *Maingit* heard this and visited earth to impregnate *Bugan*. After doing so, he told her to call their son *Balitok* when he was born. When *Balitok* had grown, his mother became ill, but he did not know how to help her. His grandfather told him to seek *Maingit*. He asked *Maingit* to help his mother. *Maingit* came to earth and taught him and the people in Kiangan, of Ifugao, the home of *Bugan*, how to perform *baki*. He told *Balitok*, "Say my name and all gods will be there."

As all cultural processes do, *baki* has changed over time. Jules DeRaedt argued that the introduction of wet rice cultivation in Northern Luzon initiated a change in the pantheon. He argued further that the introduction of wet rice was "causal in the development of ancestor worship due to changes it brought in the importance of descent for economic position and rank in the society" (DeRaedt 1964). Contemporary Ifugao people to whom I spoke also commented on changes they observed over the years in *baki* practice, such as a reduction in the elaborateness of dress and dance during the rituals and a reduction in the knowledge of *mumbaki* of the *baki* prayers. These recent changes were in part the result of Christianization and westernization in Ifugao, a shift to the poor as the main followers, and the influence of formal education.

During the colonial period, Spain's Catholic mission system in the Philippines sought to convert and pacify indigenous Filipinos, while simultaneously capitalizing on Philippine labor, land, and resources. However, Spain was only able to penetrate successfully the Ifugao territory in the late nineteenth century (Scott 1974). At about the same time, beginning around the 1840s, U.S., European, and Canadian Protestant Christian overseas missions began expanding into Asia. This religious movement was one facet of a process of expansion of political and economic power of western societies in Asia (Kenyalang 1990:60). Intensification of U.S. and European Catholic and Protestant missionary efforts in the Philippines began with the U.S. colonization of the Philippines in 1898, and it included the penetration of biomedical knowledge and practices into the Philippine countryside. Both were introduced in Ifugao during the early part of this century.

Religious healing practices in Ifugao during the early 1990s operated within a social context of widespread poverty, increased international development activities, and LIC. Additionally, they were practiced in conjunction with two forms of biomedical health institutions: the Philippine government biomedical health care program which strove to provide free health care services to all Filipino citizens, but which could not always accomplish this; and private biomedical health care services, which could be expensive and were sometimes linked to religious organizations and ideologies.

Government and privately operated biomedical services in Ifugao were accepted by followers of both Ifugao local and Christian religions, and these services were at times integral to the practices of Christian conversion and retention of Christian followers. Followers of *baki* also often utilized the services of Christian biomedical institutions. Some tried to perform *baki* outside of hospitals while their family members were hospitalized. One Evangelical clinic/hospital in Ifugao was perceived as providing better treatment than the nearest government hospital. The government hospitals usually serviced large numbers of patients, whereas the Evangelical clinic/hospital had fewer patients. Additionally, there was no government hospital located in the municipality in which both the Evangelical clinic/hospital and a Catholic mission clinic/hospital operated. While government medical services were free for all patients, other expenses were involved in obtaining biomedical treatment, such as purchasing medicines, travel costs, food for a family member or friend assisting the patient, and time spent away from work while traveling to the government hospital.[3]

Illness can never be regarded as a state which is dissociated from human agency, cultural interpretation, or moral evaluation (Turner 1984:4). In Ifugao, disease and illness were interpreted in numerous ways, depending upon a number of physical and social factors involved in specific illness episodes. In the following section, I will explore aspects of Ifugao local healing beliefs and practices, assessing theories of illness causation and treatment practices, and, specifically, modes of treatment of extreme thinness, or *na-ong-ong*.

Baki as a Healing Ritual

In accordance with Ifugao local healing beliefs and practices, specifically *baki* for healing, there were a variety of theories of illness causation. Gods of varying ranks, spirits, and ancestors composed the Ifugao pantheon. *Muntalug*, the creator god, was considered the highest male god. Second to *Muntalug* was the god *Maknongan*, who was actually a number of male gods who bore the same name and who mediated between human beings and *Muntalug*. *Maknongan* gods had wives, who were also considered gods to be prayed to.

Numerous spirits played important roles in the Ifugao religion, such as *aninito* (spirits living above the earth) and *fee-fee-o* (evil spirits living on the earth). *Fee-fee-os'* activities could harm human beings. *Aninitos'* actions could benefit human beings, but even they had a potential for evil if provoked. Ifugao animist beliefs included the existence of spirits of the *Luta*, or earth, which inhabited all things (such as stones, trees, and the forest), and spirits and gods of *Kabunyan*, the world above, *Dalom*, the underworld, *Lagud*, the eastern world, and *Daya*, the western world.[4] These locations comprised the five worlds of the Ifugao religion.

Ancestral spirits were ever present in the daily lives of many Ifugao people, as they were considered to be living among the people and to be active participants in their lives. The ancestors sometimes interacted directly with their descendents through dreams, or they served as mediators between gods, spirits, and Ifugao people. Ancestors still retained bodily needs, such as food, warmth, and clothing, and they sought good burial locations. One method ancestors used to signal their needs to their living relatives was to inflict illness on a living descendent.

All of the spirits, gods, and ancestral beings could cause illness, such as *na-ong-ong*, or they could cause other forms of misfortune.[5] However, gods did not inflict illness on children, although ancestors and spirits could. At times, a spirit "played" with a child, and then could cause him to fall ill.

The local Ifugao religion purported that if all things in nature were not respected and social codes were not adhered to, illness or misfortune could befall the errant individuals. There were other causes of illness as well. Although there was a local concept of an underworld, it was not similar to the Christian concept of hell as an evil and feared punishment after death. If a person transgressed social morals and codes, they were believed to be punished while alive on earth. As one former *mumbaki* explained, "People fear gods (spirits and ancestors). There is no fear of hell. If you do a bad deed, the same deed will happen to your children." Ancestors existed among both the living humans and spirits, interacting with the living as they desired.

PHOTO 5.1 *Mumbaki* ("native priests") praying over sacrificial offerings during a *dinupdup baki* healing ritual to cure an ill man.

Baki was often divided into two categories: *hongan di tagu*, or rituals for humans, and *hongan di pagke*, or rituals for rice culture (Dulawan n.d.:ix). *Baki* was performed by a *mumbaki*, and sometimes with a *mama-o*, or female spirit medium, as well, especially in the case of illness. A patient often consulted either a *mumbaki* or a *mama-o* after an unsuccessful initial *baki*. A *mama-o* then performed a divination ritual to specify the cause of an illness. The *mama-o*, like women in many societies (Nourse 1996; Steedly 1993), acted mainly as a spirit medium. She called on all the gods, spirits, and ancestors who may have caused an illness, until the spiritual being who inflicted the illness possessed the *mama-o*. Without the *mama-o's* awareness of what was being spoken, the spiritual being spoke through her, relating to other people present the reasons for causing the illness and the spirit's requests (such as performing a *baki,* or providing a blanket or clothing). *Mumbaki* did not become possessed.

Although female *mama-o* played an important and complementary role to *mumbaki* in performing *baki,* their overall role in the *baki* religion was more limited than men's. While male priests could perform almost all rituals, female spirit mediums were limited to performing divination rituals and participating in illness rituals. They could join rituals led by male priests, but they could not lead other rituals except divination. For example, during a *dinupdup* healing *baki,* *mama-o* joined the ritual prayers, but in a separate area from the *mumbaki,* singing special prayers that were only sung by *mama-o.* However, there were other rituals, such as blessing a dead relative's bones, where *mumbaki* and *mama-o* prayed simultaneously in the same location. The status of *mama-o* was evaluated by Ifugao people to be somewhat lower than the status of *mumbaki,* although the *mama-o's* ritual knowledge and activities were considered to be important, necessary, and highly respected among those who believed in *baki.* This is one example of how healing practices reflect social structures in the society in which they operate, in this case specifically unequal gender relations.

Once the cause of an illness was determined, a *mumbaki* was consulted and informed of the result of the initial ritual. This *mumbaki* then prescribed an appropriate ritual to be performed, specific to the type and cause of the illness. If a patient and his or her family agreed to sponsor the prescribed ritual, one or more *mumbaki* from the community performed the ritual, with one *mumbaki* serving as the head priest. All community members usually were welcome to attend *baki,* and many people still attended *baki* during my period of research.

The rituals included prayers invoking all gods, spirits, and ancestors of the family of the ill person, and inviting the spiritual beings to partake of the sacrificial offerings made to them, including rice, meat, rice wine, betel nut, tobacco, and sometimes other offerings.[6] The spiritual beings were also requested to provide a favor, such as the cure of an illness, a good harvest yield of rice, or good fortune for a family. The words of the prayers usually were not standardized, but rather they were created as prayed or sung. After praying over and butchering the animals, the *mumbaki* "read the bile" of the sacrificial animals to determine if the *baki* would be successful. If the bile appeared normal (i.e., full and green), the outcome would be positive. If the bile appeared abnormal, the *baki* had to be repeated at another time. After the *mumbaki* read the bile, the spirits were believed to eat and drink the soul of the offered food and wine, while the human participants consumed the material food and drink.

The number of animals sacrificed during any particular *baki* was prescribed by a *mumbaki,* based on religious prescriptions learned from their forefathers or directions provided by a spirit or ancestor. The rules had been passed on through the generations by means of an oral tradition of *mumbaki* training from father to son, or elder male to younger male relative.[7] For any ordinary butchering of animals, even outside of the ritual event, if a *mumbaki* was present he would recite prayers, since *mumbaki* always had to offer the soul of a butchered animal to the creator god. After performing *baki*, *mumbaki* received select cuts of meat to take home with them, with the head *mumbaki* receiving the best.

Vegetables, fruit, and fish were taboo for followers of *baki* at certain designated times. This was because spiritual beings disliked the odors of vegetables and fish. These foods were restricted at rituals, at meals serving ritual meat after the ritual, sometimes for periods of time following funerals or other rituals, and during the rice harvest season. Only foods such as rice, sweet potato, bread, noodles, milk, rice wine, mongo beans, eggs, and meat could be eaten during those periods. If the tabooed foods were eaten during any of these restricted periods, the *baki* would be ineffective and the *mumbaki* who performed the *baki* could die. For the rice harvest season, if the foods were eaten, the rice yield could be low and the rice could "be easily consumed."[8]

Mama-o, or women of the household in which a ritual was performed, were often consulted about the genealogy of their families during *baki*, so that *mumbaki* could invoke the family's ancestors during rituals. Women thus played an important role during *baki* rituals. Ifugao myths were also chanted during *baki*. As sacrifices were being made to numerous gods, spirits, and ancestors during each *baki*, the spiritual beings were propitiated for an individual's or family's well-being, such as the curing of an extremely thin family member (*na-ong-ong*).

There were a series of *baki* for healing illness, beginning with the simplest in terms of prayer and small sacrifices, and ending with the most elaborate. A patient would stop sponsoring healing *baki* at any time during the series when his or her illness was cured.

Illness Causation

For the followers of the Ifugao religion, illness had a number of underlying causes, which instigated gods, spirits, or ancestral spirits to inflict the illness. Examples of these were breaking social codes, not meeting the needs of one's ancestors, or neglecting prescribed rituals (such as rituals for agriculture, weddings, ancestors, births, and deaths). Ancestors sometimes interacted with their descendants in dreams to make them aware of the ancestors' needs. These could include needing another ritually offered blanket because the ancestors were cold, or being ritually moved to another burial site because they were not comfortable in their present site. Also, an ancestor's bones had to be removed periodically from the gravesite and ritually washed. Neglecting to perform these rituals could bring illness to family members. Residents of one Ifugao community believed that if an illness was caused by a supernatural being, a spirit entered the body of the afflicted human being.

Spirits of the natural world could cause illness if a human being disturbed their habitat, such as when a person overturned a stone in which a spirit lived. One woman explained to me that:

> if a person goes to the field, and she does something to a spirit there and she feels sick, her family will go to a priest to ask what they will do for her. So the priest says, "the spirit of that field touched her; that's why she's sick. You go call her spirit because it is held in the field." Her mother really believes that if she doesn't do that she will die. So they go to the field, hold offerings, chickens, pigs, and blankets, because their faith is if they will not go and call she will die. They perform *baki* because they believe.

There were roaming good spirits who could protect against illness and who lived, for example, within an entire *sitio*. There were also preventive rituals, such as *baki* before traveling. During divining, if the bile of the animal was not good, the traveller postponed his or her trip. In the past when hunting and headhunting were common, *baki* was performed to test for enemy aggression, predict success, and protect the hunters. In the 1990s this *baki* was still performed for men preparing to carry out revenge murders.

When a person fell ill, a spirit was sometimes said to be "holding" a person, or grabbing on to his spirit. In order for *baki* to cure this cause of illness, it had to be performed at the exact place where the person fell ill, or had his "soul held," so that the spirit could be asked to return the human spirit. Ifugao people did not believe that the spirit took a person's entire soul, because if it did she would die. These spirits were not ancestors but rather evil spirits of the earth, who usually resided in the forest, on a mountain.

Children were particularly susceptible to being "taken" or "held" by a spirit, since children appealed to spirits and were perceived to be more vulnerable than adults. When a child was crying, he could easily be taken by a spirit. These spirits were often the spirits living above the earth, called *aninito*. Pregnant women were advised to stay indoors during the nighttime because *aninitos* could place spells on their fetuses, causing an abortion. If parents abused or neglected their baby, the gods or goddesses pitied the child and spirits could decide to kill the child, believing it better to take the baby's soul with them so that they could care for it properly. As a result, Ifugao parents had to be very protective of and care for their infants at all times.

Illness could be caused by sorcery or a curse (*muniyak*, or curse ritual), usually inflicted communally through a *baki* or sometimes inflicted by an individual either inside or outside of Ifugao. Curses most commonly served as revenge for a major infraction such as murder. Illness could be caused by a spirit of a living relative, called *linawa*, a general term used for the souls of all things. This form of illness could occur if a person neglected to invite a relative to a *baki* when she should have been invited according to kinship norms. These illnesses could be cured by inviting the relative to a *baki* performed in the future. Illnesses could be caused by a yawn or an "evil eye" from another person. In these cases, the person responsible for the illness was not aware of his or her infliction. The illness could be cured by having the person who yawned visit the ill person.

Contagion was another cause of illness. In one case of contagion, an Ifugao woman who died of kidney failure had a greatly bloated body. Usually before a deceased person was buried, an extended wake period ensued, often lasting up to ten days. However, the woman whose body was bloated was buried the day after her death because of fear that exposure to a dead person whose body is bloated would cause sickness or death. *Baki* would be performed to cure an illness caused by contagion. Another cause of illness was a spirit's falling in love with the spirit of a living human being. The spirit may then cause illness in the human to take the human's spirit. [9]

Finally, illness could result from organic causes. In seeking a cure from such recognized causes, a person could visit a local Ifugao herbalist, bonesetter, masseuse, or biomedical personnel. Biomedical care was very well accepted by the majority of believers of the Ifugao religion, even most *mumbaki* and *mama-o*. This was because some illnesses were believed to have purely organic causes, unrelated to spiritual beings.

Treatment of Illness

In some cases, there was an overlapping of healing practices. For example, even if an illness was diagnosed by biomedical personnel as being a particular biomedically classified illness, such as tuberculosis, and the patient accepted this diagnosis as being correct, he might still have believed that the tuberculosis was originally caused by a displeased ancestor. Treatment may then include both drugs and *baki*.

Sometimes Ifugao people experienced difficulty in determining the exact cause of the illness. They would try different treatments, either serially or simultaneously, in order to cure the illness. A single illness could be viewed as multi-causal; and individuals then would use multiple treatments, such as performing *baki* while the ill person was being treated in a hospital. One of the most important times for Ifugao people to conduct *baki* for illness was when biomedical doctors failed to provide a diagnosis for a disease or biomedicine had not cured the illness. In these cases, illness was presumed to have been caused by gods, spirits, or ancestors of the local Ifugao religion.

There were also many special rules for pregnant women and newborn babies, which were predicated on both personalistic and naturalistic theories of illness. Pregnant women and postpartum mothers were advised to eat ginger and mung beans, because mung beans produce "soup." Food that can be cooked in water to produce a broth, or has "soup," was believed to help mothers produce milk. Ginger was also believed to give rosy cheeks to babies, produce more mother's milk, and help babies to become strong. Another example was the belief that when a woman was six months pregnant she should conduct a *baki*, sacrificing two chickens. Through this ritual, the gods and spirits would be made aware that she was pregnant and they would prevent a natural abortion.

Baki and Na-ong-ong

Baki was historically performed for children or adults who were perceived to be *na-ong-ong*, translated as extremely thin, a practice that continued through the early 1990s.[10] *Na-ong-ong* was the local Ifugao classification of severe undernourishment or a state of being severely underweight. *Na-ong-ong* could be caused by malevolent spiritual beings, a curse, illness, lack of adequate supplies of food due to poverty, natural catastrophes (such as typhoons, earthquakes, pests, or drought), or, in cases when a person was born thin, just the natural state of a person's body. In some cases, *baki* was performed to cure *na-ong-ong*, since *na-ong-ong* was sometimes understood to be caused by supernatural beings. One lower class, older *mumbaki*, who was highly respected for his extensive knowledge of and skill in performing *baki*, explained some possible causes of *na-ong-ong*:

> The causes why a person is thin is probably because he did something wrong and a person probably cursed him to become thin. The family of the ill can call a priest to perform against the curse. Then you could be cured. If it is a child who is very thin and they perform *baki*, it will be cured. Those who became sick and very thin, they will be cured. But if a person was born very thin and remains that way to adulthood, *baki* cannot cure this because that is their body. Sometimes if a family did not perform *baki* for a long time, the spirit comes and takes the child and the child becomes very thin, and then the family performs *baki*, the child will become cured. . . . The person may have done something wrong to a *fee-fee-o*, or the spirits of your ancestors, or *Maknongan*.

Usually in the case of extreme *na-ong-ong* one of two types of *baki* were performed, although there were other *baki* for thinness: *tanig* and *lawit,* especially for thin children. These were also the names of the spirits that caused thinness. One *mumbaki* said that at least three chickens had to be sacrificed at these forms of *baki*. The prayer said at the *tanig* and *lawit baki* requested that the spirits *tanig* or *lawit* remove the sickness of that person and make her grow normally.

Another *mumbaki* and a *mama-o* said that *lawit*, or *inlawitan*, could be performed with one chicken. The *mumbaki* tied a chicken and then brought it to any place. When the chicken pecked at a stone, they returned to the home of the thin person and continued the *lawit*. They did not butcher the chicken that had pecked the stone because that chicken would "get the spirit that is inside the sick person." The person who was thin could not feel the spirit, but the *mumbaki* could feel it. The day following the *lawit,* the spirit would leave the body. According to these religious leaders, the relatives of each parent must perform four *baki* each, either *tanig* or *lawit.* These rituals could only be performed for three different episodes of thinness for each individual.

Both old and young people could be "attacked" by these spirits. In some cases, *na-ong-ong* was caused by the spirit of a *mumbaki* who had not been invited to *baki.* "His spirit will get the spirit of one of the people in that house. . . . Even if a child is eating a lot, she will stay thin," explained a *mumbaki.* He further stated:

> If an elderly adult is thin and if they perform *inlawit*, they will die after one day, because the person is very thin, cannot work, is tired of sleeping. He will want *inlawit* so he will die, because he thinks he is useless. For adults who want to get better [for thinness or any type of sickness] there are many *baki* that they can perform. If they cannot use *inlawit*, they will perform *honga* with ten chickens.[11] If this *honga* does not cure illness, they will use five pigs or six for *chinupchup*. If this does not work they will perform *inyapoy*—one pig. If this does not work, they will perform *hutlik* or *hagoho*—one pig.[12] If this does not work, they will perform *inakum*. If this does not work, they give up and wait for the person to die.

For some cases, if the child was very thin, felt and looked sickly, and did not eat well, the illness could have been caused by a female goddess, *Na-ina.* *Na-ina,* which means old woman, (or it could mean old mother, since *ina* is the Ifugao term for mother) would be the spirit possessing the child, causing thinness. The spirit was not always female, however. *Lawit* could cure this form of thinness. If the person was an adult, *pahang,* another form of *baki,* was performed. When a person had no appetite to eat, he was considered to be *munlamhit.*

In one case in the late 1980s, a male child was said to have been cured of extreme *na-ong-ong* through *baki.* The parents were so grateful to the *mumbaki* who performed the ritual, having feared that their child might die, that they renamed their child after the name of the *mumbaki.* Two women who were members of my interview sample witnessed *lawit* for thin children, one for her own child and the other for another person's child.

In another case, in 1992 a man studying to become a *mumbaki* had a two-year-old child who became sick. She was coughing, had a weak and thin body, and could not walk. Her parents brought her to the hospital numerous times, but she still had not been cured. Her father had a *munhapud* ritual (divination ritual) performed by an elder *mumbaki* to diagnose the cause of the girl's illness and determine which ritual should be performed. The *mumbaki* called for some *anitos,* then he got a stone and a machete. The *mumbaki* called the names of *anitos* and named types of *baki* until the stone stood upright on the machete. The *mumbaki* prescribed the performance of *lawit* and told the family which *mumbaki* to request to perform the *baki.* *Lawit* was chosen because the stone stood on the machete when the *mumbaki* named that ritual. No animals were sacrificed nor was rice wine drank at the *munhapud*, since they were not regularly included in divination rituals.

The parents sponsored the *lawit,* at which four chickens and one pig were sacrificed, and rice, rice wine, and possessions (usually betel nut, rice on a stalk, tobacco, *tikom* leaves, and a chicken feather that had been offered at a previous *baki*) kept in the *kintib* (priest's ritual box) were offered to spirits, ancestors, and gods. A number of *mumbaki* performed the *lawit,* which lasted one day, from early morning until late afternoon.

To begin the *lawit,* a number of *mumbaki* and family members brought rice wine, one female chicken, and a sugar cane stalk to a river in the morning. At the river they called the spirit of the child. The *mumbaki* told the family that the spirit of the sick stayed in the river. The *mumbaki* called many kinds of *fee-fee-o* which may have been "holding" the child's spirit, in order to request that they release it. The *mumbaki* did not know specifically which spirit caused her illness, so they called all of them. After this short ceremony of calling the *fee-fee-o,* the *mumbaki* called the spirit of the sick child. They released the chicken so that the chicken would peck a stone in the river. Then they took the stone the chicken had pecked and placed it in the *kintib.* This stone represented the spirit of the child, which they had gotten back from the *fee-fee-o* and brought home with them. The *mumbaki* prayed, "Come, and we will go home, so you will be well."

The group returned to their home and continued the *lawit,* sacrificing one pig and some chickens. The ill child ate much meat that was sacrificed at the *lawit.* Her parents related that they did nothing else different for her from what they normally had done. By 1992 she was no longer on medication (her father could not recall what medication she had taken). Her father said that his daughter was doing well at the time of our interview, although the BNS had recently told him that she was second degree malnourished. He added that she was trying to begin walking.

This man continued to tell me about another case of *na-ong-ong* in his family, saying that he and his wife had the same problem with his four-year-old elder child when she was two years old. She would only drink breast milk, did not want to eat other foods, and always had diarrhea and many other sicknesses. Her parents brought her to two local hospitals, but "medicines did not cure her. So the only remedy was *lawit.*" They performed *lawit* two years ago and she was cured. This man's son, on the other hand, was also ill as a child, but for him medicines from a pharmacy were effective.

A thirty-five-year-old woman was identified as being *na-ong-ong* by Ifugao friends and relatives in 1992. She was a farmer, married, and raising five children. She was very thin and had been diagnosed by biomedical personnel as having a kidney illness, hepatitis, an ulcer, and tuberculosis. She was given medicine for these illnesses, but she did not take them because she said they hurt her throat when she swallowed them. One week in August she did not eat for five days because she had no appetite. She had many *baki* rituals performed for her to cure her illnesses, but her conditions only worsened. Following the week of abstinence from food, she had planned to have *lawit baki* performed to cure her, or at least to help her regain the weight she had lost. *Lawit* was commonly performed for people who were both very thin and sickly. She seemed to have much faith in the effectiveness of *baki* to cure her illness. Unfortunately, she died one evening before the *lawit* could be performed for her.

Feter was another indigenous Ifugao concept related to hunger. It was translated as a period when there was absolutely no food nor any means to acquire, cultivate, or purchase food. An abbreviated translation of *feter* can be "famine." *Feter* could also refer to *anitos* who eat a family's rice, therefore reducing the family's rice supply. During these periods, great hunger (*na-akang-an* or *munhinaang*) was experienced by Ifugao people. *Feter*, as famine, could be caused by spirits, drought, pests, typhoons, war, or other forces. *Baki* was performed to end *feter* or to drive the *feter anitos* away from one's rice stocks. *Feter* and *na-akang-an* were often experienced by lower class people during the months prior to the rice harvest, when they had eaten all of their rice supplies and did not feel physically or emotionally satisfied with eating sweet potatoes as their staple food.

In the early 1990s *baki* still remained significant for seeking cures for *na-ong-ong,* severe thinness (or what would be biomedically classified as severe undernutrition or third degree malnutrition) for some Ifugao people, especially children, and for *feter*. However, there was usually no perception of, nor were there local classifications for the biomedical constructs of first or second degree malnutrition. These stages of malnutrition would not culturally be considered severe cases, and the affected children may not appear to be extremely thin to Ifugao people.

Illness and Social Relations

For many Ifugao illnesses, *baki* causation theories related to circumstances in Ifugao social life and social relations. Most of the local explanations for illnesses can be understood, in part, as a discourse of social control. If a person broke societal rules, treated their children, spouses, or relatives badly, did not carry out prescribed rituals, or did not respect nature, then he must risk the consequences of becoming ill or dying. In Ifugao, illnesses symbolized these human relationships, and this ideology served as a preventive strategy. However, some illnesses did occur even if a person did nothing wrong; these were caused either by an evil spirit, a human, or organic causes.

Healing illnesses through *baki* were usually communal affairs, wherein all community members were welcomed to attend. However, it was of primary importance that one's relatives be invited. Food, offered as sacrifices to gods, spirits, and ancestors, was shared among all persons attending rituals. Wealthy community members were expected to provide more food offerings and were expected to host more *baki* than the poor, for a variety of occasions. For example, the poor could provide chickens for a *baki* while the wealthy had to provide pigs or, in recent years, water buffalo. It was expected that attendees of *baki*, especially relatives of the sponsors, would bring an offering to *baki* to assist the sponsoring family. Offerings included such things as money, animals, rice, rice wine, or gin. Only purely physical treatments, such as massage or bone setting, were carried out individually, although they also were sometimes carried out in conjunction with communal spiritual rituals. *Baki* could be performed to prevent illness and misfortune, or to ensure proper health and good fortune, such as *hogop* (house-blessing) or *bagor* (the introduction of a newborn baby to spiritual beings) *baki*.

Although numerous types of *baki* were still practiced by Ifugao people, the majority of *baki* ceremonies were intended for illness and funerals. There were still *baki* performed for agricultural production, but much fewer than in the past. This may have been due to the influence of formal education regarding agricultural production, sponsored by the government agriculture agency's outreach program, and formal education obtained from the school system. It also may have reflected the significance of bodily experience in illness and death which influenced religious practice and belief and solidified kinship relationships and ethnic identification.

Christian Healing Practices

According to a 1970 census, 49 percent of Ifugao people identified themselves as "Christian," 32 percent were identified as "Others" (religions which may have included the local Ifugao religion), and 21 percent identified themselves as having "no religion" (National Statistics Office, Republic of the Philippines 1970). By 1990, 54 percent of the Ifugao people identified themselves as Catholic, 26 percent identified themselves as Christian of Protestant or nondenominational churches, for a total of 80 percent Christian. Some followers of *baki* may have been included in the 11 percent of Ifugao people who were placed under the category "Others" or in the 9 percent of people under the category "Not Stated" (National Statistics Office, Republic of the Philippines 1992b:16).[13]

Although these statistics were quite unreliable, particularly since a high percentage of people were not included in the reports, and since the category of "Others" was not descriptive, it did point to the great influence Christianity had in the lives of Ifugao people. However, the number of people practicing or participating in the Ifugao religion was much higher than these statistics indicated implicitly, since numerous Christians practiced or participated in *baki* in conjunction with their Christian practices. In many societies, religious conversion is not always complete, as converts sometimes accept some aspects of Christianity which serve them well but reject those that do not, while simultaneously retaining beliefs and practices of their local religions. Similarly, not all groups of a particular society convert at the same time nor to the same degree (Hefner 1993).

Christianity was strongly associated with modernization, development, progress, and educational enlightenment.[14] Catholic churches historically established schools in Ifugao. Education was viewed by many Ifugao people as a means to upward mobility, as it was in other ethnic societies (Mountain Movers 1993:2; Mullings 1984:30). Christianity was accorded high status among Ifugao people, as it was among the majority population of Filipinos. The majority of people in most areas of the Philippines (though not all) practiced Catholicism. These factors helped explain Ifugao people's preference for identifying themselves primarily as Christian in a public forum such as a census, despite the fact that they may have simultaneously practiced *baki*.

Christianity was also typically associated with power, high social class, and prestige in Ifugao. Still, there were cases of individuals in powerful political offices who identified themselves as Christian, while they publicly practiced *baki* as well. Stereotypes existed, categorizing Christians as formally educated individuals and people practicing *baki* as illiterate and uneducated. While these stereotypes may have been true on record or through self-identification of religious affiliation, in everyday life both educated and uneducated people of *baki* and Christian religions practiced or participated in *baki*. I found that those who identified themselves as practicing *baki* fully were generally of the middle to lower economic classes, or were elderly, while self-identified Christian individuals were members of all economic classes.

Ifugao people were affiliated with many different religious organizations, including Catholic, Protestant, nondenominational, and—to a lesser extent—Islamic and Buddhist (National Statistics Office, Republic of the Philippines 1992b:16).[15] Although in recent years foreign Christian missionaries still lived in Ifugao for extended periods of time (such as Catholic priests and nuns) or visited Ifugao for a few months and then moved on (such as "Youth With A Mission" members), most contemporary Christian leaders in Ifugao were Ifugao men and women, or Filipino persons of another ethnic heritage.

Christianity in the Philippines

The Christian mission encounter with people indigenous to the Philippines is a set of discourses and practices paralleling those of contemporary development organizations. Historically and contemporarily, most agents of both Christian and development institutions have assumed western superiority in both ideology and practice. Conversion of Filipino people to western ideologies and practices was one of the primary objectives of each institution. Furthermore, these institutions have historically operated symbiotically in an attempt to achieve a hegemony of western cultural orientation among non-western peoples.[16]

The historical spread of Christianity in Ifugao, and in the Philippines generally and more broadly in Asia, was linked to the advancement of the political and economic objectives of western societies in their intervention in non-western societies (Kenyalang 1990:60). Many missionaries of the nineteenth century based their work on the paradigms of scientific racism and social evolutionism. These paradigms situated caucasian peoples and their societies at the apex of a hierarchy of human races. Nineteenth-century European Christian racist notions, such as the Theory of Degeneration,[17] and popular scientific racism theories, such as the Teutonic Origins Theory,[18] Herbert Spencer's social Darwinist "survival of the fittest" theory, and the eugenics movement, were the ideological bases for the drive to practice mass religious conversion of peoples unaware of western beliefs and knowledge of Christianity. Most western Christian missionaries sought to save or enlighten "pagans," or non-believers of Christ, viewing peoples of other societies as childlike (Scott 1974:261), primitive, lower than themselves on a religious and social evolutionary scale, and in need of instruction and guidance to organize their societies and enlighten their modes of thought. "Pagans" needed to emulate westerners in order to be civilized, as missionaries perceived themselves to be, to know their understanding of the "truth."[19] For example, Scott cited a Spanish priest, Father Juan Villaverde, who attempted to convert and pacify Ifugao people in the late 1800s. In 1879 he wrote the following to Spanish military officers, in an attempt to move all Ifugao people out of their native, ancestral mountain homeland into the lowlands so they could more easily be converted to Catholicism, pay tribute to the Spanish colonial government, and be better managed by the Spanish missionaries and military:

> In view of the existence and results of this mission of Ibung [in the lowland area], I believe that without wasting any more time, for time is precious, the suggestion should be made to the Igorots of Kiangan [in Ifugao] that they start to come down [to the lowland areas]. The Governor of the province could do it by summoning the most important leaders of the villages already pacified, or whatever other means he should find convenient, explaining to them on behalf of the Central Government that they could live in Ibung safely, protected and free of all duties except a small *recono-cimiento* such as they were used to in Kiangan, but in no way should it be implied that the sum will later be increased. Following this suggestion and the offer of land in the mission should come the threat that if they don't come down themselves, a military expedition will go up, not to kill them since they have made no resistance, but to destroy their houses, fruit trees, and fields or terraces. . . .
>
> When they get accustomed to paying this minimum tribute for two or three years and when they are then living in some greater comfort, will it not be possible to add another *real* and another ganta of rice, etc., increasing it painlessly, and making them see they should give evidence of their love and gratitude to our Senor *Patul* [as they call the paternal government of Spain] who loves and protects them like children, spending great sums to sustain their missionary and the authorities, officials, and soldiers, etc.? (Villaverde 1879, in Scott 1974:261).

The propagation of scientific racism through the conversion of non-western peoples to Christianity suited the political and economic objectives of the governments and elites of colonial societies. The more westernized the conquered peoples became, the easier it was to manage and control them for the colonial powers' political and economic benefit. Missionaries were not always direct agents of governments, nor were their conceptions of treatment of indigenous peoples always in accord with those of colonial officials. Still, missionaries' conversion activities historically supported the efforts of colonizers through their facilitation of the conversion of non-western peoples to western cultural ideologies, spiritual values, knowledge systems, and practices (Steedly 1993; Comaroff and Comaroff 1991). Again, Scott wrote that in the mid-1800s, the Spanish colonial government was experiencing great resistance to their penetration of the Cordillera mountain region, of which Ifugao is a part. He wrote:

> The central [Spanish] Government, however, considered [Catholic] conversion both a means and a goal of conquest, and so wanted missionaries on the advancing frontier. . . . The Government accordingly expanded its regular requests in 1877 to include missionaries "to reduce to towns and parishes the tribes in the Island of Luzon who live without fixed homes, or paying tribute, or practicing the Catholic religion" (Scott 1974:248).

And in the early 1900s, during the American occupation of Ifugao, efforts were made by European Episcopal missionaries to imbue a Protestant work ethic among indigenous people in the Cordillera region ("Igorots"), since the missionaries considered their cultural approach to labor to be too casual (Clymer 1986), not suited to capitalist expansion.

Christian missionaries continue to place great emphasis on providing both western-style education and medical service in the Philippines, as did the U.S. government in its colonial policies, particularly in education (Schirmer 1987; Constantino 1987). Fred W. Atkinson, the first General Superintendent of Education in the Philippines, stated at the turn of the century:

> The Filipino people, taken as a body, are children, and childlike, do not know what is best for them. . . . In the ideal spirit of preparing them for the work of governing themselves finally, their American guardianship has begun . . . by the very fact of our superiority of civilization and our greater capacity for industrial activity we are bound to exercise over them profound social influence (Atkinson n.d., cited in Schirmer 1987:43-44).

Reciprocally, such practices aided in converting peoples to western Christianity and ideologies. They provided the transition necessary for economic and political westernization, such as the contemporary Philippine political and the economic systems which are based on U.S. models, at the expense of important aspects of local cultures and values. The U.S. government viewed the use of an American-controlled educational system in the Philippines during the colonial period as a technique of pacification, as General Arthur MacArthur stated in reference to an appropriation of funds for a Philippine educational system: "This appropriation is recommended primarily and exclusively as an adjunct to military operations calculated to pacify the people and to procure and expedite the restoration of tranquility throughout the archipelago" (MacArthur n.d., cited in Constantino 1987:45).

The Philippines retained a "Special" relationship with the United States since the end of the U.S. colonization in 1946. Western ideologies and material products were promoted through the western-style educational system, media, market, and political system. The hegemony of western culture resulted in a commonly held assumption in Ifugao that anything western was superior or true. These assumptions were sometimes referred to as reflecting a "colonial mentality" by nationalist Filipino intellectuals.

The educational system in Ifugao was highly valued among the elite, a value shared by many in the middle and lower classes as a means to upward mobility, especially among those who could acquire the funds to support their children to attend schools. A July 1993 publication of the UNICEF ABCSD included an editorial written by an Ifugao person about the perceived value of western-style education among Ifugao people: "For others [in Ifugao], education provides the needed prestige and honor that they crave from society" (Mountain Movers 1993:2).

The perception that western-style formal education provided prestige and honor carried over to Christian religious instructions, particularly that offered by foreign missionaries who either were from or assumed to be from the United States. Christianity also became associated with prestige, modernization, and status within the general Filipino population, while local religions such as *baki* were often looked down upon and referred to as "superstitions" by people of majority groups in the Philippines, as well as by some Christian Ifugao people. This association of Christianity with high social status facilitated the conversion of Filipino peoples to Christianity, both historically and contemporarily.

Viewed as a specific historical cultural construction and practice, nineteenth- and twentieth-century Christian conversion of non-western peoples can be understood as a variant of the contemporary neocolonial development paradigm created and practiced by western peoples today. Kenyalang (1990) draws a parallel between the purposes of Christian missionaries and foreign aid in Asia, viewing both as ultimately securing a pro-western orientation among Asian peoples. He states that neither were requested by members of Asian societies, but they rather were imposed on them from without (Kenyalang 1990:63). Foreign aid did not originate from requests from non-western countries but was instead organized by western powers in 1949, in part as a strategy against the spread of communism during the cold war period (Kenyalang 1990) and to expand capitalist markets and exploitation of resources.

In contemporary Ifugao, Christianity was indirectly linked to the discourse and practices of modernization and development. Most international development agents in Ifugao allied themselves with local Christian leaders in their efforts to convert people to the ideologies of their development programs. Government and development agents usually included Christian prayer, songs, and discourse in their meetings and seminars. For example, in 1992 one government sponsored seminar, entitled "Family Life Development Module," was facilitated by a government employee in a distant barrio. It was held in the Catholic church, even though there was a public barrio hall in that village. Throughout the seminar the government employee, who was Catholic, quoted phrases from the Bible to support her positions. For example, while discussing conjugal relationships she stated, "The Bible says, 'Love is not indecent or immoral,' and 'Love does not look for its own interest.' If you love your spouse you want them to be happy."

Reciprocally, conversion of Ifugao people to some Christian sects (such as Methodist) included a promise of personal and familial economic prosperity with acceptance of Christianity. Development agents raised similar hopes of economic prosperity through participation in their development programs. However, as has been demonstrated over the past decades of both development and Christian practices in the Third World, including Ifugao, economic prosperity of the majority of the people of non-western societies does not necessarily follow from acceptance of these paradigms. This is particularly true in the case of women and the poorest people. At the same time, elites of western and non-western societies continue to benefit from economic and political structures and practices introduced in or imposed upon non-western countries by international development and lending institutions.

In practice, many contemporary Ifugao Christians attempted to convert other Ifugao people to Christianity out of concern for their spiritual welfare, particularly following death, and because of their belief that this was their Christian duty. One female Christian lay practitioner said, "We believe that in some years to come all of the people of [our barrio] will believe in Christianity, because that is our goal and our work. Because you cannot enter heaven without believing in Jesus Christ."

Finally, the Christian paradigm historically had been a patriarchal construct in Ifugao. Although many Catholic missionaries were female, few women held positions of power in the churches' hierarchical structures. Although there were female missionary instructors, the content of their teaching often emphasized a submissive role for women. But with the increase in Protestant activities in Ifugao, and some Protestant churches' acceptance of female religious leaders, more Ifugao women held positions of religious leadership in Christian churches.

Historical Development of Christianity in Ifugao

Ifugao people's first experiences with Christian missionaries included their encounter in 1767 with Spanish Dominican missionaries, who visited Kiangan (currently an Ifugao municipality). The Spanish missionaries established a mission in an Ifugao community in later years. While Spanish missionaries did convert a high number of Ifugao people to Catholicism for a short period of time, most of them returned to the exclusive practice of the Ifugao religion. The most successful early conversion of Ifugao people to Christianity began in 1907 by Belgian missionaries of the Congregation of the Immaculate Conception Missionaries, who still operated in Ifugao in the early 1990s (Dumia 1979:24, 38).

Biomedical practices were first established in Ifugao, mainly through the work of these Catholic Belgian nuns, during the American regime in Ifugao (Dumia 1979:32). One older Ifugao man remembered that the nuns did not teach about health education or the biomedical theory of illness causation. Instead, the nuns only dispensed basic medicines, taught about the beliefs and practices of Catholicism, and began to influence people to stop performing *baki*. Ifugao people at that time experimented with the medicines. If they were ineffective, the ill would then sponsor a *baki*. In Ifugao, biomedicine, development, and Christianity operated symbiotically, resulting in the diminishing of local Ifugao religion and culture.

In some areas of Ifugao, the strongest missionary and biomedical activity and conversion came in the 1950s. This was related to the intensification of western nations' international development activities following World War II. The Ifugao man cited above remembered that, during the early 1940s, people in his municipality were aware of biomedicine and hospitals, but neither had yet been established in their immediate vicinity. In that municipality, a Christian evangelical clinic was built in 1949 and government health services blossomed in the 1950s. Another Ifugao man said that Filipino Espiritista missionaries first came to his barrio in 1951. Filipino Catholic missionaries came to his barrio in 1958 and Filipino Pentecostal missionaries visited in 1989.

Religious Conversion

Religious conversion from the local religion to Christianity was still occurring in Ifugao in the early 1990s, mainly attempted or carried out in recent years by Ifugao Christian religious leaders or Ifugao Christian activists, although Christian leaders from other locales (either from within the Philippines or from abroad) were also working in Ifugao. Some Ifugao Christians shifted from one Christian organization to another.

There were many reasons for conversion to Christianity. Some groups or individuals converted for reasons of protection; access to resources, power, or status; acquiring a new identity; or coercion (Merrill 1993; Yengoyan 1993). Conversion also could be accomplished to protect and retain one's resources, such as food required to be sacrificed during ritual feasting in local religious practice (*baki*), as occurred in Ifugao and other areas of the Philippines (Pertierra 1988). Religious conversion was often accomplished through healing illness, changing the processes and structure of healing prayer, and promising earthly prosperity (Keyes 1993). In religious conversion the body can serve as the site of a symbolic battleground among religious groups (Turner 1984:191). Each of these factors played a role in Ifugao people's decisions to convert to Christianity. In Ifugao, great focus was placed on "Healing bodies and winning souls to Christ" by liberal and fundamentalist Protestant groups.[20] The body, through illness and healing, can play an important role in religious conversion.

Contemporary Foreign Missionaries in Ifugao

Ifugao hosted a number of Christian aid and development organizations.[21] Contemporary foreign missionaries exerted a strong influence in diminishing the practice of *baki* in Ifugao and, for some, in stigmatizing *baki* as an evil practice. During my stay as a Peace Corps Volunteer, one American Christian missionary woman living in an Ifugao municipality asked me if I was afraid to travel to and live in a barrio located at a distance from the center of town. She believed there were many evil spirits lurking everywhere in these communities, brought there by the cultural beliefs and practices of Ifugao people. Another foreign Christian missionary woman, living in the same Ifugao municipality, advised me in 1992 that I must pray for God's help when reading literature about *baki* (which she let me borrow) because, she said, it is "very powerful . . . the spirits are present [in Ifugao] and they are evil." Through these discourses, the Christian missionaries were participating in the Ifugao religion by accepting some of the premises and beliefs of the Ifugao religion, although in a distorted manner. Not all foreign Christian missionaries propagated such strong judgments about the Ifugao indigenous belief system, however.

Christian Healing in Ifugao

My research of Christianity and healing primarily involved Catholic, Methodist, and Evangelical Christian healing practices. Most Christian healing practices had certain characteristics in common. They involved prayer to God, Jesus, or the Spirit of God for cure of illness. Many Christians prayed to saints as well, to request that they intervene between themselves and God on their behalf. Prayers for the sick could be individually said at any time, or they could be communally shared at scheduled times. At communal Christian prayer gatherings, serving food was usually optional. When food was served at prayer gatherings, it was not considered to be a sacrifice but rather was viewed as an offering to God. At prayer rituals where food was served, its main function was to provide sustenance for the sponsoring family's guests, who usually came from both near and distant areas to assist the patient in becoming well through prayer. The majority of Christian healing practices included the acceptance and use of biomedical treatments.

PHOTO 5.2 An internationally-sponsored Christian health clinic in Ifugao.

Espiritista healing events usually were conducted at the end of a regular Sunday service, or at gatherings specifically for healing. Some Catholic healing prayer services took place in the evening, or during the daytime, some with food served. Other Christian healing services involved women "speaking in tongues" over an ill person. There were Methodist healing prayer services conducted in the daytime or evening. Some exorcisms were performed in the Evangelical Christian operated clinic/hospital.

Catholicism and the Politics of Food Supplement Programs

As stated above, approximately 54 percent of Ifugao people identified them-selves as members of the Catholic Church in the early 1990s. The Catholic Church had the highest membership of all Christian religious groups in each Ifugao municipality. At least one Catholic clinic operated in Ifugao, as well as Catholic supported high schools. In distant barrios, where priests only visited occasionally, lay Catholic members held their own weekly masses and prayer services.

During the Marcos era, some Catholic priests in Ifugao questioned state policies, particularly out of concern for the poor. One Catholic priest gave sermons which denounced injustices inflicted by the Marcos regime on the Filipino population, despite the danger this entailed. The Philippines is well known for its Catholic liberation theologists and their struggle for social justice. The activities of Fr. Conrado Balweg were infamous in the Cordillera region. Balweg was a renegade former Catholic priest who joined forces with the NPA during the Marcos period in the Cordillera region. He later parted with the NPA, having formed his own Cordillera People's Liberation Army, which later aligned with the Philippine government. The Catholic Church's participation in the Metro Manila EDSA revolution against Marcos was also a significant force.

In the past, some Catholic priests in Ifugao were said to have advised patients for whom biomedical treatments were not effective to sponsor *baki* at their homes. One Ifugao woman, a former *baki* follower and Catholic, who became a Methodist, said that the Protestant leaders were more strongly against *baki* in contemporary Ifugao than the Catholic leaders. In contrast, a former *mumbaki* related that some Catholic priests had encouraged the Ifugao people to stop practicing *baki*, having informed them that they would go to hell after death if they continued.

With admirable intentions, the Catholic Relief Services (CRS) operated a Food Supplement Program for malnourished children in Ifugao, as well as in other parts of the Philippines. CRS had been operating in the Philippines since 1946, three years after its founding in the United States. In 1992 CRS spent U.S.$13.3 million in the Philippines on food supplement programs for the malnourished and some community activities in poor communities to effect "profound economic changes" (Catholic Relief Services 1993:13).[22] The formal policy of CRS stated: "The policies and programs of the agency reflect and express the teaching of the Catholic Church. At the same time, CRS assists persons on the basis of need, not creed, race or nationality" (Catholic Relief Services 1993:i).

The CRS program provided an example of the implicit connectedness between U.S. Christian organizations operating in foreign countries and U.S. government political and economic objectives in the same countries. In 1992 the U.S. government provided 76 percent of CRS' total funding (U.S.$220 million), some of which came specifically from USAID (Catholic Relief Services 1993:22, 25, 29). CRS did not overtly promote U.S. political ideologies, however. Additionally, in 1992 CRS also received U.S.$5 million in material resources (mostly food) from the EC (Catholic Relief Services 1993:30). As noted earlier, the EC funded and managed a large development project in the Cordillera region, including Ifugao, which began in 1988. The other sources of funding for CRS in 1992 were as follows: 19 percent in material resources donated by individuals, groups, corporations, and foundations, and including revenue from investments; 5 percent in material resources from the EC and cash from international organizations and "various governments" (Catholic Relief Services 1993:22). The total amount of funding for CRS in 1992 was U.S.$290 million.

A CRS food supplement program that operated in Ifugao also provided an example of the use of one biomedical approach to healing malnourished children and pregnant women to subtly aid in Christian conversion and education, in addition to trying to improve their health. In one Ifugao municipality, a CRS program operated through a Catholic church to provide food to malnourished children and pregnant women of all religious affiliations, limiting the number of children receiving food supplies to one per family. Local program personnel decided on this one child per family policy "because of limited supplies," according to the Catholic woman tasked with distributing the food supplements, who happened also to be the local government BNS.

In contrast, the parent recipients of a CRS food supplement program operating through a Catholic church in another Ifugao municipality and providing food supplements to malnourished children between the ages of zero to five, were mostly, but not all, Catholic. All three months or less pregnant women also received CRS food supplements. A government health worker in a barrio of this municipality, in which there were CRS food supplement recipients, stated that the CRS program was "targeting Catholic families." The CRS began its program there in 1990 after the Catholic community members applied to CRS to establish a food supplement program in their municipality. CRS provided food supplements, such as corn meal, bulgar, and dried milk, once a month to the parents. However, the supply was not always provided regularly, sometimes limited to only one of these foods.

The Catholic nun administering the CRS sponsored program in this municipality was a Filipina of another ethnic group. She stated that the criteria for receipt of the food supplements were age, malnutrition status, and "Catholic affiliation." She explained:

> Malnutrition is a great problem, not only for food supplies but also for nutrition education, Christian formation, and training for self-reliance for the mothers. The Catholic Church formed a . . . mother's class. . . . Mostly women come to receive the food supplements, but if the mother is sick the husband comes. In order to get food they are required to attend the class. We have to train them, educate them because some are just after the food.

She stated that the food supplement program was mostly for Catholic parents because it was a religiously sponsored program involving Basic Ecclesiastical Communities (BEC). She said the limited program could supply food supplements for all Catholic families in the program area. She added, "We are also educating them for BECs; and that [the food supplements] is also one way of them coming together." She thought the food supplement program had helped Ifugao children since many had "graduated" (attained a normal weight), but she acknowledged that the percentage of malnourished children was still high.

> Because that is only a supplement. They [parents] must do the rest. That is why we must educate the mothers not to be depending on the supply. Education on how to prepare the local food. Food supplements are only a part of the solution. . . . The parents, they prefer to take the supply rather than take the education part of it. So that is why this year we required that they come to education class before we give the supply, to discipline them. Pity, we also pity, pity. But we must educate and discipline them. . . . In the mother's group, I teach about health and self reliance, and Christian living. We have education on health, Christian values, economic sufficiency, and social stability.

This Catholic church was also organizing and educating people about cooperatives for food and other basic necessities to assist the community members.

Although the practice of religious prioritization of Catholics for receipt of food supplements did not correspond with CRS official policy, this particular case which went against this policy was an example of religious power relations operating around the problem of malnutrition. It also demonstrated that individuals or groups administering aid programs at the local level can reappropriate and refashion the construction and dictates of the aid programs at the international level to accomplish their own objectives.

In this example, although expressing commendable goals and physically aiding malnourished children and pregnant women, the food supplements were used as a means to achieve the ends of disciplining and educating poor Catholic or non-Catholic parents, especially women, in both their dietary practices and Catholic religious values and practices. In this context, foreign donations of food supplements served multiple purposes: the nutritional fortification of malnourished children and pregnant women; the education of parents regarding health and nutrition; and religious indoctrination. In this discourse, parents were seen as needing to be "disciplined" to acknowledge that their lack of biomedical nutrition and health knowledge and appropriate child care practices were the primary causes of the malnutrition of their children. They were instructed to fall in line with a notion of personal responsibility for the proper health of their children. This form of discipline exerted a subtle form of control over the dietary and religious practices of Ifugao people and inadvertently resulted in an internalization of blame for the problem of malnutrition. The nun expressed the participant parents' resistance to this disciplinary technique when she sensed that they would prefer to receive the food supplements rather than participate in the education program.

The targeting of the food supplement program to mostly Catholic parents may have also served as an incentive for poor parents of other religious groups, who had malnourished children, to convert to Catholicism. In this example at the community level, the body served as a site of religious conversion and indoctrination, as the promise of bodily health, through the use of food supplements and nutritional education, was, to a degree, used as an incentive to accept and reinforce Catholic beliefs or religious conversion.

Evangelical Clinic/Hospital: *"Healing Bodies and Winning Souls to Christ"*

An Evangelical missionary clinic/hospital located in Ifugao was established and staffed by an American missionary doctor and his wife in 1949, but in the early 1990s it was run by a Filipino doctor who migrated from the Manila area. Financial support for the clinic/hospital came from Christian partners in the United States, the "Far Eastern Gospel Crusade," later called SEND International. By 1974 it became a non-stock, non-profit organization and had expanded over the years. In the early 1990s it was supported by private and group donations in the Philippines, as well as by donors from the United States through SEND International. Additionally, fees were charged to patients for services.

According to the resident doctor, the clinic/hospital was staffed by one doctor and six or more nurses. It had the capacity to perform surgery, but it did not have a full-time anesthesiologist. The clinic hosted visiting surgeons and an anesthesiologist from a nearby government hospital in 1992, who performed eye surgeries in the clinic while participating in a free eye clinic in which I was involved. It had an X-ray machine, incubators, a laboratory, and a pharmacy. The clinic/hospital provided only curative services, not preventive or primary health care, due to lack of staff and an intentional avoidance of duplication of the primary health care services provided by the government RHUs. The Evangelical clinic/hospital coordinated with the local government health providers, however. The staff informed Ifugao people when medical specialists planned visits to Ifugao, frequently from the provincial government hospital (such as goiter specialists, optometrists, and ophthalmologists). The doctor of the Evangelical clinic/hospital pointed out that its services were available for all persons, without regard for their religious affiliation. Generally, however, the clientele were Christians due to their personal desire to be treated there. Patients often used services of multiple health institutions in the area, according to the doctor. The clinic/hospital's biomedical services were well respected among people within and outside of Ifugao, and it was regularly frequented by Ifugao inhabitants.

The doctor's perception was that there was not much malnutrition in Ifugao, compared to the Metro Manila area where he previously worked. He stated that there was no severe malnutrition, only very minor malnutrition. One Ifugao nurse working at the clinic disagreed, however, saying that she thought there were many cases of malnutrition in Ifugao, especially in the distant barrios.

The chaplain or staff conducted prayer services, open to all of the patients, during the daily chapel service. According to their brochure, "As patients are treated for physical needs they are given the opportunity to hear the Gospel of Jesus

Christ in the daily chapel service being handled by the Chaplain and staff." One stated objective of the clinic was "Healing bodies and winning souls to Christ." The clinic's brochure stated: "In a place where pagan practices are still deeply rooted in people's lives, the ministry of the . . . Clinic and Hospital is being used to change lives through the healing of bodies and winning souls to Christ . . . Mark 13:10 'And the Gospel must first be preached to all nations.'"

One follower of *baki* commented that, without his request, "When one of my children was in the hospital the Christians came to pray for us. Often Christian prayer warriors would come to our hospital room to pray for us."

A Methodist Christian pastor related this story of a form of exorcism in this Evangelical clinic/hospital:

> Last week a child was sick and the doctor could not find any finding. And he was always spitting, and there was a physical change in his appearance. The doctor requested pastor because he believed it was the work of the devil. Pastor rebuked the devil and it didn't work; and also some believers went in group to pray and it didn't work. But another pastor went and other pastors. They sang a Christian song and then the devil manifested. The child was shouting "No! I do not want to hear those songs that you are always singing!"; and other words. So pastor laid his hands on the child and rebuked, "In the name of Jesus, I tell you to get out!" And then there was a change in the child's physical appearance, and he was brought back to normal. The doctor could not diagnose the illness, another sign that it was the work of the devil. When they were singing Christian songs, he was shouting, "Mama, I will go!" or "I will die!" So the mother will have fear and will make them stop singing Christian songs. That is the strategy of the devil. The mother is an unbeliever. But doctor recommended pastor to save the child to rebuke the evil spirit.

In contrast to this Christian religious healing practice, the doctor of this Evangelical clinic/hospital expressed his view of *baki* for healing:

> Many people here still practice the pagan religion. This is a problem for us since they perform *baki* when a person gets sick then wait a few days to see if it will work. This delays our providing our services. So usually non-Christians would not go to the . . . clinic/hospital. . . . [The clinic personnel discourage the use of *baki*, although] sometimes we find them practicing it outside of the hospital when a patient is being treated in the hospital.

He continued saying that sometimes, even if the patient was Christian, the elders of her family persuaded the patient to perform *baki*. Because of family values and respect for elders, the children did what their elders requested.

Again in this example, the body was a site of religious conversion and cultural change in contemporary society, whereby biomedical healing of the body was used to influence people's beliefs and attitudes toward accepting Christianity. Christian healing ceremonies and biomedicine were viewed by Christian medical personnel as superior to *baki* for healing, and this ideology was propagated among Ifugao people through the services and practices of the clinic/hospital's personnel.

Methodist Church

One Methodist church entered a distant Ifugao barrio approximately two years prior to my research. The membership of the church ranged from fifty to one hundred Ifugao persons, mostly of the lower economic class since all of the people in this barrio were of the lower class. The pastor of this church in many ways resembled fundamentalist Protestant Christians found in the United States, although he did not identify himself as such. By fundamentalist Christian, I am referring to a person who believes in "unqualified acceptance of and obedience to the Scriptures," and who defends the Bible as the absolute, inerrant, and authoritative word of God—although interpretation of the Bible can vary among fundamentalist Christians (Beale 1986:3). I also mean a person who judges all things by the Bible, and "endeavors to preach it to every creature" (Beale 1986:348). The pastor of this Methodist church was an Ifugao man, trained to be a Methodist pastor in a city outside of Ifugao. He frequently spoke at community events outside of the church, as he was invited to Christian dedications of babies (a Protestant ritual similar to a Catholic baptism), community meetings, development meetings, funerals, birthday parties, Bible studies, and *baddang* (communal assistance) for the harvesting of rice.

Illness for Methodist Christians of this church could be caused by the devil or by the natural environment. God did not directly inflict illness on people, but God could allow the devil to inflict illness and allow natural causes of illness to develop among human beings, sometimes for testing or chastisement. One Methodist woman related:

> We have one person who is possessed by the devil. Every few days she is like she is crazy: one eye is red; she doesn't like to eat; and she keeps quiet. This is the sign of the bad spirit. One of her children wanted *baki*. Another child, a Christian, wanted to drive out the bad spirit through Christian prayers. She did this. Her mother tumbled down, did not wake up for a few hours. When she woke up she was cured well. The bad spirit wants to get the person in a bad appearance so you will perform *baki* to give him offerings. But when you utter Jesus Christ, the devil is frightened, because Jesus Christ is higher than the devil.

The Methodist pastor further stated:

> When it [an illness] is caused by the devil it is coupled with fear. And in order for them to be healed, they will play *baki* and it will be healed. So that's how we know [that the devil caused the illness]. For most believers in Christ, the devil's work will not work. But if you doubt, the devil may come. Signs [of the devil causing illness]

are physical, you can see it in the eyes, like a lion, and a tiger look. His appearance is: eyes are reddish and full of lies. Those who visit or administer to them, you can feel it because you also feel fear and your hands will stand. These are a few signs, but there are many illnesses which can be caused by devil. A person has no peace of mind, wants to kill or be killed, rebuke Jesus Christ. . . . What I have encountered when they are demon possessed is they want to die, to kill. It seems that they are very strong; you cannot hold them even though they are very weak. All that comes out of their mouth is devilish. . . . Child illness can be caused by devil. . . . Even disorderly children can be the work of the devil.

For Methodist Christians, illnesses caused by God were viewed as a test of an ill person's, or his or her relative's, faith in God. The pastor affirmed,

God is not a God who lets us suffer. God, who is loving, is merciful, so I don't believe that God causes sickness. To unbelievers, they are actually sick physically and spiritually because of sin in this world. Because sickness comes from: first, the work of the devil; second, the environment, water, air, food; third, sickness for believers is chastisement. This is sickness coming from God, but it is chastisement because He cares to make us sick in order to revive us. . . . Child illness can be caused by devil. But not by God because they are only children. For believers only, God will allow illness of children as chastisement to parents to make them realize that they are going away from their faith.

For signs that God caused an illness, the pastor said,

It depends on the person concerned. It is not me who will say that is caused by God. The individual will discern. When a person accepts Jesus Christ, God will give that person a discernment spirit from which they can discern if the illness is devil or God. Only some people will have a discernment spirit. They can tell you if it is the work of the devil or God, or you yourself will know.

Sometimes illness causation can be multidimensional. For example, illness caused by the devil can be disguised as a physical illness. Regarding cause and treatment of illnesses, in the words of one Christian woman:

If we have sickness, we do both hospital and pray to God, or we just pray to God. If we know the sickness is the work of the devil, prayers will work. If a sick person is frightened then we know it is the work of the devil. Physical sickness is through air or foods. As a Christian, you have faith in God that God will work through the doctor and bless the medicines that you will take.

Another significant determining factor of the cause of illness was inefficacy of the biomedical system. One Christian woman said, "If the hospital doesn't work, then illness is always caused by the devil. If the family is Christian, and the doctor says 'no illness,' then it is caused by the bad spirit." The pastor explained, "If illness is caused by the devil or God, medicine will not work. The cure is to drive the devil out by rebuking illness. If it is caused by God, the believer must repent and ask forgiveness. . . . I think that is the experience of many doctors and that's how they will be converted." Followers of the Ifugao belief system believe a similar notion regarding the failure of biomedicine.

So, for Methodist Christians, whether the cause of illness was believed to be natural or supernatural, prayers to God or rebuking the devil aided in curing illness, independently or in conjunction with biomedical services. The pastor validated his belief in the power of prayer to cure illness when he said, "In here we have experienced miracles with illness. In [our barrio] there are many who say they have headaches, stomach aches; they say when they pray it will go away. Those demon possessed during Bible studies faint as if they will die, and want to run away. Demon possessed are only those who are unbelievers or believers who doubt."

When I asked about the relationship between Methodist beliefs and hunger, the pastor said that he had never experienced thinness or malnutrition caused by the devil or God, but he stated that this was possible. Otherwise, the cause would be a "lack of nutrients." He said: "When a child is thin or abnormal it is never the sin of the child but rather the sin of the parents. If it [child malnutrition] is caused by the devil or God, and the parents are believers, they must ask forgiveness from God. Proper foods would not help in this case. If only physical cause, proper food would help."

As in *baki*, malnutrition and thinness for Christian Methodists could have supernatural origins, either caused by the devil or God, as well as natural causes (i.e., "lack of nutrients"). In both *baki* and this Methodist church, children were particularly vulnerable to the evil intentions of bad spirits or the devil, or to the sins of their parents and the resulting chastisement of gods or God for those sins. This may have reflected the actual physical vulnerability Ifugao people experienced their children to have, as evidenced by the frequency of illness and malnutrition among Ifugao children.

For followers of both religions, cure for malnutrition caused by supernatural beings required prayer. Only in the case of *baki* did it additionally require the sacrificing and eating of food (animals, rice, rice wine) during communal rituals, wherein food was eaten by the malnourished person and shared among all community members who wished to partake in the ritual. However, throughout the duration of *bakis*, no vegetables, fruit, or fish could be eaten by participants.

Christian Views of Baki

Many newly converted Christians, and many pastors, nuns, priests, and missionaries, did not dismiss *baki* beliefs as being fictional or untrue. Instead, they experienced the evil spirits believed in by followers of the Ifugao religion. But Christians believed that they were protected from these evil spirits by their belief and faith in their Christian God. Also, as previously noted, many Christians sponsored or participated in both Christian services and *baki* for healing. Some explained that they sponsored *baki* out of respect for their older parents or grandparents who insisted on conducting *baki*. Others explained that they had to do everything they possibly could to cure their ill family members. Many Ifugao Christians had a very broad view of religion, finding no conflict in believing in and practicing both the Christian and Ifugao religions simultaneously.

One Christian woman only began sponsoring *baki* for healing in early 1992, due to a serious illness of her now deceased baby, for whom she sponsored a healing *baki*. She explained that when there was an indication of serious illness among members of her family, she used biomedical services, *baki* for healing, and Christian prayers. She had no standard order of utilization of each of these modes of healing, saying in our interview:

> Christian Woman: If we will go to the hospital and the illness is not yet cured, we perform *baki*.
> Lynn: Do you ever perform *baki* first?
> Christian Woman: Never first, especially diarrhea, we would not perform *baki*. We will perform *baki* first if they think that the illness cannot be cured by medicine. When there is sickness and then you have a dream (indicating the cause of the sickness is ancestors, spirits, or gods), you would perform *baki*. . . . We also go to hospital and perform *baki* at the same time. We would not pray Christian prayers and *baki* at the same time. Because if you are performing *baki*, then Christian prayers are useless. There's a contradiction if you do that because in Christian prayers you are praying to God, but in *baki* you are not asking all to God but to other spirits as well.

Additionally, there was some acceptance among Christians who denounced *baki* as evil that *baki* could cure illness. A Christian woman, who was also a BHW, said "Their faith will come true if they believe it. For sickness, if they really believe (in *baki*) it will be cured, because faith is very powerful." There seemed to be some ambivalence on this point since the same woman also said that although one illness episode may be cured through *baki*, the spirits would keep returning for more offerings, causing future illnesses. This woman found more security in Christian prayers, though she did not offer an explanation for why Christians may also acquire a series of illnesses. At yet another time, she said that if an individual sponsored *baki* for illness, he would not ultimately be cured because *baki* was evil:

> because the spirit that they [*baki* followers] believe in is the spirit of the bad spirit. Christians say it is evil because it will give you something. You will spend more for the ritual and you will still have that sickness. A spirit will call you and you will give something to her and you will be cured. But next time again, she will come back again and ask for something more. So if you will not give you will die. It will continue. She is always asking, and asking, and asking.

Multiple Treatment Strategies

Ifugao people often relied solely on *baki* or Christian prayer services to cure illness, especially in three cases: the failure of biomedicine (if a biomedical doctor could not offer a biomedical diagnosis for an illness, or treatments were not effective); prohibitive costs of biomedical treatments; and the wishes of the patient or a family member to use religious healing practices. Prayer and home remedies were then the only modes of treatment feasible. Reasons for use of multiple treatment strategies for a single illness episode may have included the wishes of the patient or family members to use every means available to cure an illness, the need to accommodate a variety of medical and religious beliefs held among family members, or a delay in healing while using one form of treatment.

A married Christian woman in her thirties became ill in 1988. She visited four hospitals for treatment in three different municipalities of Ifugao and in one nearby province. In the nearby province, she spent seven months in an herbalarium for treatments. She was told at a hospital that there was a problem with her arteries. She began having a difficult time walking, then in urinating, and later in defecating. Her whole body was paralyzed by April 1992, and she was severely underweight. Her family said they were no longer bringing her to the hospital because "it is too expensive." This family had already exhausted all of their available resources to provide for biomedical and herbal treatments for her over a four-year period. Although the government hospital services were free, poor families still sometimes could not use them due to the cost of medicines and the need for a family member or friend to assist the patient at all times during the hospital stay. Her husband sold his rice field for money to purchase biomedical treatments and medicines. By April 1992 she was becoming more ill. Every evening Christian community members, both men and women, gathered at her home with her extended family to pray and sing Christian prayers for her from Catholic prayer books. Non-Catholics were also welcomed and in attendance at the prayer services. When I asked if they would perform *baki*, a neighbor replied, "No, there is no *baki* here (in our *sitio*) anymore."[23] No food was served at these prayer services. In this case, when the patient and her family had no more money to spare, they resorted to individual and group Christian healing prayer services. The woman died a few months later.

Christianity and Food Production

Food production was an integral aspect of Ifugao life and was viewed by many as their primary means of survival. Prayers for food production had been incorporated into Christian practices and could be viewed as a refashioning of the Ifugao religion's *hongan di pagke* (rituals for rice culture). Ifugao Christian people regularly recited prayers, both individually and in group, for planting and harvesting rice, requesting assistance from God in food production to ensure a good harvest. Christian prayers were also recited for thanksgiving and supplications (asking for "blessings," which could include large rice, vegetable, and fruit harvests, as well as many animals and children, good health and general good fortune). The prayers for rice production were narratives of the insecurity surrounding food production, the means of livelihood for the majority of Ifugao people, in the face of natural forces which they could not control or had difficulty controlling (i.e., pests, plant diseases, typhoons, drought, irrigation problems); some human created problems (i.e., deforestation, reduced fertility of soil due to chemical use); and a sociopolitical system which was not able immediately and adequately to meet the needs of all communities struck with disaster.[24]

Food, Body, and Christianity

The body in Ifugao was often perceived in terms of work, particularly be women. Work was, in turn, usually viewed (especially by Ifugao peasants) as something undertaken to acquire food. One Christian woman's view of a particular set of Christian prayers for food was that

> for everything that is here around us that gives us strength on the body, there are Christian prayers. . . . If you believe in Him, ask and you shall receive . . . Matthew 6:33: The kingdom of God is in you, strength of the body. . . . God created you and gave you different functions in your body and you use those different functions to work, to plant food to bring back to give strength to the body.

There was a cyclical pattern to her belief, with the functioning of the body being the source of production of food as well as the receptacle for food produced. God was viewed by this woman as being an integral source of food, bountiful harvests, strength of the body, and work, and as the human body's internal strength.

If food was lacking in a household, Christians might pray to God for assistance in obtaining it. The same Christian woman said:

> We have experienced whenever we need something, we pray. God will send other people to give you. If you need rice and you look upward, God won't send rice from the sky. . . . At harvest time, I prayed that I didn't have food for tomorrow; I asked Him. So what come to mind through the power of the Holy Spirit in my mind, I thought of a person to work for, and in the evening she would give me rice for my food.

The Ifugao cultural norms and values of sharing food and maintaining networks of assistance, for those in need, was depicted here as the intentions of God.

Religious Alterations

As noted earlier, the spread of Christianity did not fully alter the meanings and forms that Ifugao people gave to prayer, illness, or healing. Christianity in Ifugao incorporated aspects of Christian beliefs and practices into Ifugao religious beliefs and practices, as is commonly found in other local communities where Christianity has been introduced. In one community during a group interview with former *mumbaki,* the *mumbaki* stated that they often compared *baki* to Christianity and viewed the two religions as being parallel. For example, they compared the statues of Catholic saints to the *bulul*, rice gods carved out of wood used for rice harvest *baki* and the protection of rice.

For both Christians and believers in *baki*, illness could be caused and cured by supernatural beings, as well as by natural causes. Prayers regularly were recited to cure illness for both Christians and believers in *baki*. For followers of both religions, the healing power that religion was believed to elicit was attributed to the depth of belief of the individual. Many Christian prayer services for the ill, as well as other services such as baptism or dedication of a baby, house blessing, and funeral, retained a similar structural form as the *baki*, although the prayers were Christian. For both religions there were community gatherings and extensive prayers recited or sung by individuals or groups led by male or female religious leaders, with the objective of curing illness. Christian saints could intervene between God and human beings, as ancestors could do during *baki*. Animals were prepared and served to people gathered, sometimes at the end of Christian healing services and always at *baki*. While there were important differences between the two religions, some aspects of the practice of *baki* had been retained among some Christian Ifugao practitioners. As mentioned previously, many Ifugao families practiced both *baki* and Christianity for a variety of reasons.

In these healing beliefs and practices, malnutrition was constructed as being caused either by supernatural beings or natural causes (lack of nutrients or food, or caused by a related illness). Each religious healing belief process conceived of malnutrition as potentially stemming from a social problem as well, in the sense that malnutrition or extreme thinness could be caused by a supernatural being due to a personal or familial transgression of social and moral codes, or, for *baki* followers, by the curse of another human being. Although extreme thinness was viewed as a social problem at the individual, familial, or community level, both *baki* and Christian religious healing beliefs lacked an understanding of malnutrition that would include a broader analysis of its macro-level political and social causes. As discussed throughout this chapter, biomedicine also played a significant role in defining causes and providing treatments for malnutrition. In the next chapter I will assess Ifugao women's experiences and interpretations of the biomedical construction of malnutrition in relation to gender and social class.

Notes

1. The word *baki* was used only in some areas of Ifugao. People living in other areas used linguistic variations of this term (i.e., *bfuni*).

2. *Muntalug* was referred to in other Ifugao communities as *Kabunyan*.

3. Filipino patients in government hospitals were urged to have at least one family member care for them while in a hospital. This was an institutionalized practice in government hospitals. The Philippine government Social Service agency had only limited funds for indigent patients and could not provide for all of their needs. Nor could the Health Department always meet all of its patients' medical needs, due to lack of personnel and resources.

4. These five Ifugao terms were from a different Ifugao dialect than the one used primarily in this book.

5. Extreme thinness was also termed *napikot* or *nakotong* by Ifugao people speaking different Ifugao dialects.

6. Ritual meat could be obtained from chickens, ducks, pigs, or water buffalo.

7. There had been cases of male *mumbaki* teaching their female children all of the rituals designated for male priests and female priestesses. This was particularly common in one municipality of Ifugao, though it had occurred in a municipality where the norm of males teaching males, and females teaching females held fast. In one case, a *mumbaki* only had daughters, so he taught one daughter rituals performed by both *mumbaki* and *mama-o*.

8. This was a phrase commonly used by Ifugao people, meaning that the consumption of a rice harvest will extend only over a short period of time rather than long. All *hongan di pagke baki* included a prayer requesting that supernatural beings allow the family's rice not to "be easily consumed."

9. All things on earth were believed by some Ifugaos to have spirits, including humans, plants, stones, houses, etc.

10. This classification is similar to the biomedical classification of severely malnourished or underweight. This is differentiated from biomedical classifications of mildly to moderately malnourished or underweight, which Ifugao people usually did not culturally perceive to be particularly problematic, until told to consider them as such by biomedical health care providers.

11. All rituals were called *honga*.

12. *Hutlik* and *hagoho* were the same ritual.

13. In 1970 and 1990 Ifugao census statistics, less than 1 percent of respondents identified themselves as Islamic.

14. Although the use of these terms is problematic, modernization and development among Ifugao people commonly referred to access to new, nontraditional, or nonlocal services and technologies which were perceived to enhance life and facilitate everyday living (such as easily accessible potable water supplies, concrete roads, forms of healing processes, formal education, and markets; adequately paying employment; new forms of irrigation systems; etc.). For Ifugao people, modernization did not necessarily involve a distinct separation of rationalization (as an aspect of modernization) and religion (as irrational, traditional behavior), as it has for many western social scientists in defining modernization (Von der Mehden 1986). Instead, Christianity in Ifugao was closely associated with modernization.

15. More specifically, these included Catholic, Evangelical, Espiritista, Jehovah's Witnesses, Church of Jesus Christ of the Latter Day Saints, non-denominational, Iglesia Ni Cristo, Aglipay, United Church of Christ in the Philippines, Lutheran Church in the Philippines, Philippine Benevolent Missionaries Association, Seventh Day Adventist, Born Again Christians, Philippine Episcopal Church, Presbyterian, Baptist Conference of the Philippines, Bible Baptist, Southern Baptist, other Baptists, Iglesia Evangelista Methodista en Las Filipinas, Lutheran Church, United Methodist Church, other Methodists, Alliance of Bible Christian Committees, Assemblies of God, Four Square Gospel Church, Nazarene Church, other Protestants, Islam, and Buddhist (National Statistics Office, Republic of the Philippines 1992b:16).

16. Although development agents in recent years have perceived and acknowledged some local cultural practices to be good, beneficial, or environmentally sound, the development agents usually ultimately judged which local cultural practices were to be considered bad or good (generally meaning in line with their development objectives and plans).

17. The belief that all contemporary indigenous peoples are descended from peoples who once enjoyed civilization prior to the construction of the Tower of Babel (Harris 1968:54).

18. A doctrine of white supremacy that posited that all Anglo-Saxon institutions of any worth had historical roots in the Teutonic tribal institutions of ancient Germany and that only they retained the ability to build and maintain stable governments and high civilization (King, Jr. 1967:73; Stocking, Jr. 1968:50).

19. See Comaroff and Comaroff 1991; Horsman 1981; and Scott 1974.

20. The title of a 1990 pamphlet produced by an Evangelical mission in Ifugao that operated a health clinic.

21. These included an Evangelical hospital and clinic; a Catholic hospital and clinic; Catholic Relief Services food supplementation programs; a Christian Children's Funded Development Program (an organization which provided aid to poor children); Catholic sponsored high schools; and Christian "Youth With A Mission" aid programs (including medical relief programs).

22. The exact description provided in the CRS 1992 Annual Report was "an effort aimed at helping local church counterparts affect [sic] profound economic changes in poor communities throughout the Philippines" (Catholic Relief Services 1993:13).

23. *Baki* was sometimes performed in this barrio, but rarely since only two families of approximately 400 residents still believed in *baki*.

24. Filipino people and the Philippine government had to cope with numerous large scale disasters during the early 1990s, including the 1990 Northern Luzon earthquake, the 1991 Mount Pinatubo volcanic eruption, the 1991 flooding disaster in Ormoc, Leyte, and the 1991–1994 nationwide energy crisis.

6

Interpreting Hunger Biomedically

As seen in Chapter 5, malnutrition, as the biomedical construct of inadequate nutrient and food, or calorie, intake, was only one construct of inadequate food intake held in Ifugao. Since malnutrition was not a concept indigenous to Ifugao conceptions of eating, bodily size, thinness, illness, and health, the use of the concept of malnutrition by biomedical personnel posed some problems of interpretation and understanding among many Ifugao adults. As discussed in the last chapter, the local Ifugao concept of extreme thinness was *na-ong-ong*, believed to be caused by lack of food, illness, or supernatural intervention.

In this chapter I assess cultural meanings attributed to food and eating in Ifugao; biomedical conceptions of forms of malnutrition; how social class and gender influenced malnutrition within Ifugao; and women's ideas, perceptions, and practices surrounding malnutrition. I also explore poor Ifugao people's everyday practices geared toward coping with their lack of access to adequate food resources for their families and how they coped with their poverty.

Deconstructing the Concept of "Malnutrition"

When considering the concept and use of the term malnutrition, care must be taken to contextualize it within the broader biomedical paradigm from which it emerges. Biomedicine is commonly viewed as a scientific, rational and technological approach to and practice of preventing and curing illness.[1] It also has been conceived of as a cultural system, or process, particularly by anthropologists and other social scientists.[2] Western biomedicine is a culturally constructed medical process that emerged in western culture since at least the Greek period. Foucault (1994) argues that modern western biomedicine began in the early nineteenth century with the introduction of the clinic in medical practice. Also at that time, government authorities, health officials, and medical practitioners became concerned about "public health." Foucault contends that biomedicine operates through historically specific cultural and social assumptions, and that it reflects prevailing ideas of the society from which it stems. Biomedicine shapes people's perceptions of their bodies and the world around them. It influences "what can be said, what can be seen, and what is considered to be true about the body." A clinical "gaze" emerges with modern biomedicine, focusing evaluation and treatment on the individual body, specifically inside the body, rather than on the disease in isolation or abstraction from the body.[3]

The biomedical model also rests on the Cartesian legacy of duality which assumes a split between the mind and the body (Scheper-Hughes and Lock 1987). Historically, modern biomedical conceptions and treatment of disease have focused on the physical body, as distinct from the mind and emotions. Furthermore, biomedicine perceives individual bodies in isolation, separate from the social relations in which patients are embedded.[4] The perceptions have begun to change to some extent, with biomedical personnel increasingly considering the influence of the mind on disease. In addition, some practitioners have begun to consider the impact of social and political conditions—such as poverty, racism, and violence—on the health of individuals. Yet few serious interventions have been made by biomedical personnel to improve the social relations within which people live, as part of a comprehensive approach to preventing or curing illness.[5] Interventions of this sort are difficult and complex, as they threaten existing powerful social relations in the global capitalist system, within which biomedicine operates and supports (Waitzkin 1986).

A biomedical conception of the category of malnutrition, as primarily a condition of inadequate intake or retention of calories and specific nutrients, has led to biomedical treatment strategies tending to focus on individual malnourished bodies, providing specific calories and nutrients as food or vitamin supplements. While poverty commonly is cited as one cause of malnutrition by biomedical personnel, social relations generating conditions of poverty are rarely addressed, thereby reproducing existing relations of power and concealing sources of social injustice leading to illness (Waitzkin 1986). This stems from the limitations of the biomedical perspective, rather than the intentions of biomedical personnel, which tends to exclude social relations from conceptions of causes of disease and treatment approaches.

Biomedicine also involves a notion of disease as a natural fact, a pathological condition existing independent of culture and society, thereby neutralizing what are actually social problems.[6] Malnutrition is a culturally specific concept that has been exported from western to non-western societies through the expansion of biomedicine globally, beginning during the colonial period (Doyal and Pennell 1981). One problem with the cross-cultural use of the term is that it disguises the historical social power relations generating patterns of widespread hunger in non-western societies. These power relations are international, national, and local, and often involve western nations.

A second problem with the use of this term is that it is often poorly understood by and has created confusion for members of non-western societies, who have not necessarily been immersed in the many cultural assumptions with which biomedicine operates (such as disease being caused by germs, or an understanding of the concept of nutrients).

Finally, there are problems with the seemingly arbitrary manner in which categories of malnutrition are defined, thereby influencing conceptions of the nutritional condition of individuals and of the extent of malnutrition in societies. Standards of nutritional well-being change over time and vary from society to society, making the determinations of malnutrition and cross-cultural comparisons complex. For example, as discussed in Chapter 1, the anthropometric tables and charts Ifugao health personnel and volunteers and I used to measure children's weight status in 1992 were based on data collected in 1985 in a nationwide survey among more than 23,660 clinically and physically healthy Filipino children (Florentino et al. 1992:2). These standards replaced older standards which were published in 1971 and which had been based on 1958–1968 data collected on a regional basis (Florentino et al. 1992:1).

It is important to note again that the weight-for-age standards for Filipino children were actually lowered with the new 1992 standards, so that some children who previously had been considered second degree malnourished were in 1992 considered only first degree malnourished, and some children who previously had been considered third degree malnourished were in 1992 considered only second degree malnourished. This change significantly reduced Philippine government reported rates of second and third degree child malnutrition. Michael Lim Tan, M.D., medical anthropologist of the University of the Philippines, Diliman, also pointed out that even the Philippine FNRI and Department of Health's 1971 growth standards had been lower than those agreed upon by international organizations such as the World Health Organization (Tan 1991:24). Additionally, the category of first degree malnourished, while biomedically identifying a state of malnutrition, was rarely included in definitions of the extent of malnutrition in Philippine society.

There were also significant problems related to the collection of data to assess malnutrition, particularly involving weighing programs, which added to the lack of reliability of biomedical measurements of malnutrition. For instance, I found many inconsistencies in reported figures for malnutrition in Ifugao. I also found many problems with the weighing process itself, such as instruments in poor condition being used for weighing, and heard that some weighing technicians created numbers for children's weights to meet their job's requirements, even though some children were not actually weighed. In light of these issues, it is difficult to assess definitively the extent of biomedically defined malnutrition in societies.

In this analysis, I make use of biomedical categories of hunger. In some areas, I analyze hunger from a biomedical perspective. I also assess how biomedicine operated as a cultural process in Ifugao society in regard to malnutrition. My use of biomedical categories is not meant to assert a definitive assessment of malnutrition in the Philippines, or in Ifugao specifically, but rather to provide one framework by which to evaluate the extent of hunger in these societies. Another important guide to understanding this issue is to learn poor Ifugao people's assessments of their access to adequate amounts or variety of food on an everyday basis, and the hardships they face as they perceive themselves to live from "hand to mouth," having to "run after rice." It is also important to understand cultural conceptions of food and the body held by people within Ifugao, to comprehend how these conceptions influenced their health perceptions and practices, and how they varied from biomedical conceptions of the body.

Food in Ifugao: Availability, Symbolism, and the Body

Food Availability and Symbolism in Ifugao

There was a wide variety of food available for people within Ifugao Province, although a family had to have the finances to purchase the foods they could not grow, raise, or gather themselves.[7] Foods that could be cultivated were usually only seasonally available, making it difficult to acquire certain types of foods—specific fruits, vegetables, and rice—during the dry and monsoon seasons.

Food in social life is given cultural and symbolic meaning by members of a society.[8] In Ifugao the most highly valued, desired, and sought after food was rice. Most Ifugao people preferred to eat rice as their main staple energy food during each meal of the day. Most people did not feel emotionally satisfied that they had eaten a complete meal unless rice was included. One woman commented, "This is how we eat here in Ifugao. Even if we eat a very heavy snack, like [sweet] rice cakes in the afternoon, we are not satisfied unless we eat rice for dinner in the evening, even if we are not hungry."

Rice had great social significance in Ifugao, as well. Rice was prescribed as an offering to spirits, gods, and ancestors during *baki*, in the forms of boiled rice and rice wine. Another social significance of rice was the honor that serving it to relatives and community members accorded to an Ifugao family in their role as host during social events such as weddings, funerals, baptisms, and so forth. Not to serve rice at a community gathering would have brought shame and dishonor upon a family sponsoring the gathering.

As noted earlier, rice was also symbolic of wealth and prestige. This had to do, in part, with the greater labor investment involved in building and maintaining terraced rice fields on the Ifugao mountainsides, the need for limited irrigation water, and the need for organized communal labor to plant and harvest rice. Also, rice fields were the only landed properties owned and inherited, apart from the land that houses or businesses were built on and some forest areas. All of these factors resulted in the increased value of rice. Eating and sharing rice provided one with status in Ifugao society, while eating the sweet potato symbolized poverty. The sweet potato historically was viewed as the food of the poor, although most Ifugao people of all social classes still ate it as a snack during the early 1990s. The sweet potato and its leaves were also important foods for "native" pigs.

One practical reason why Ifugao people preferred to eat rice over the sweet potato, or recently available bread, was because of the physical sensation they perceived when they ate rice. Ifugao people commented on numerous occasions that eating rice allowed them to maintain a feeling of fullness for a longer period of time while they were physically laboring than did the sweet potato, even if their stomachs felt full immediately upon eating sweet potatoes. Although not fully physically deprived, if people of the lower class ate the sweet potato as their main staple food, they sometimes felt emotionally deprived and socially disadvantaged. As explained earlier, the trend in Ifugao was to reduce the size of sweet potato fields or to stop growing sweet potatoes altogether, and instead to seek wage labor, especially for men, in order to purchase rice.

Meat was considered to be another food highly desired by gods, spirits, and ancestors during *baki*. They were thought to dislike vegetables and fish and to prefer eating meat. The Ifugao religion dictated a restriction on eating vegetables or fish throughout the harvest season, except for *mongo* (mung) beans. The harvest season could last up to two or three months. Spiritual beings were thought to dislike the strong odor of fish. Vegetables did not have blood in them, which the spiritual beings desired. Some Ifugao people stated that vegetables symbolized weakness because, before being cooked, vegetables were large and firm, but after vegetables were boiled they became small and soft. *Mongo* beans were acceptable since they expanded in size after being boiled. Another reason for the higher value placed on meat was that animals raised to provide meat required a greater long-term investment of both labor and inputs (sweet potatoes, other vegetables, or, of late, commercial feeds) than either vegetables or fish. Meat was also symbolic of wealth, since it was not often eaten by people of the lower or middle classes, due to the expense of raising animals and high cost of meat. Meat was eaten by the poor primarily during ritual and community events. Only the wealthy could afford to eat meat every day, which in Ifugao was considered to be a healthy, desirable, and prestigious practice.

As seen above, meat was associated with strength while vegetables were associated with weakness, particularly in the realm of ritual. Nevertheless, the normal diet of the lower class included regular meals of at least one vegetable and rice or sweet potato, unless there were no vegetables available due to the season. Other foods eaten irregularly included dried or fresh fish, eggs, fruit, and meat. Although the eating of vegetables, fish, and fruit was restricted during the harvest season by the Ifugao religion, very few families abided by this rule in the early 1990s.

Fresh fish was available to persons living near rivers and to those who raised small fish or shell fish in their rice fields or fish ponds. Dried, salted fish was commonly eaten in Ifugao. Although not very expensive, the lower class could not always afford to buy fish or did not have access to a store or market to purchase it on a daily basis. Wild plants and some small creatures such as insects or birds supplemented the diet of the lower class, especially lower class children who foraged in the forest during play, picking up wild fruits and vegetables. Most lower class children had an extensive knowledge of these.

The traditional and most common method of cooking food in Ifugao, as in other areas of Northern Luzon, was boiling, usually with salt. Foods were also fried, but not as frequently by members of the lower class who did not always have enough money to purchase oil or did not live near a store. Soy, vinegar, *bago-ong* (fermented, salty fish paste), *patis* (salty fish sauce), and sugar were other foods regularly used in cooking and eaten with meals by middle and upper class people, and irregularly by lower class people, depending on their cash availability and access to the foods. The most common meal composition for lower class families was rice or sweet potatoes (sometimes corn) as the staple food, with only one viand such as a vegetable. Some of the poorest people commented that the sweet potato was good to eat for a meal when they had no viand, because the sweet potato could be eaten alone with only sugar or salt.

Food, Eating, and the Body in Ifugao

Literature on the body has posited that the body is socially constructed to symbolically represent social, natural, supernatural, and spatial relations.[9] The body is inscribed with notions and understandings about the world and the societies in which people experience their everyday lives. In Ifugao, a variety of symbolic meanings were attributed to body size by Ifugao people, who regularly observed, scrutinized, and commented on physical attributes. As mentioned earlier, the stout or overweight body (*matabfwa*) was symbolic of health and wealth in Ifugao. The thin body (*na-ong-ong*) was symbolic of a number of social and physical conditions. Symbolic meanings attributed to thinness, as well as other poor or painful bodily conditions, included economic deprivation and hard work. A bodily manifestation and internalization of poverty was starkly exemplified by one poor, Catholic Ifugao peasant woman's solemn comment to me, after I had asked her why she thought many people were poor in Ifugao, "That is the question that we are asking our bodies, 'why do we belong to the poorest of the poor?' After a few minutes, we think that maybe this is the will of God; and, sometimes, we accept that and we say that, 'this is the will of God.'"

Ifugao people associated a loss of weight with illness, due either to supernatural intervention, a curse, or natural causes. In recent years, with the penetration of biomedicine in Ifugao, many people associated a severely thin child with "malnutrition." For women, a loss of weight was commonly associated with having become married, having delivered children, performing labor continuously, or having a chronic or short-term illness.

PHOTO 6.1 A child being weighed during a government-sponsored, weight-monitoring program for children under six years of age. Use of older scales may have sometimes resulted in inaccurate weight readings.

The poor nutritional status of the population in the Philippines was the embodiment of unequal social relations, both within the Philippine nation and in relation to other nations. During my initial interviews with families of the lower class, when I asked why some of their family members migrated to other municipalities, the most common responses were "to look for food" and "to look for work." Poor Ifugao people spent the majority of their waking hours "looking for food," as reflected both in their actual daily activities and their discourse and thoughts, depicted by this common response. Work in Ifugao was closely associated with food and eating, as other common phrases heard among Ifugao people were: "we are working in order that we can eat" and "we are working from hand to mouth." In frustration, one lower class, peasant woman once said to me, "We work and work in our fields and still we do not have enough food." Primary concerns of the lower class, who made up approximately 78 percent of the Ifugao population, were acquiring enough food to feed their families and, relatedly, locating a variety of means to obtain food through such activities and things as work, improved seed varieties, and new irrigation systems. Although the migration of Ifugao people entailed looking for employment or land on which to farm, it was significant that many women's discourses and perceptions were that they or their family members left their homes to look specifically for food.

In addition, in recent years with the introduction of wage labor, there had been disinterest on the part of Ifugao men and women to exert the time and effort to repair irrigated rice terraces damaged by poor weather conditions or other causes. Also, with the increase in the cost of labor in the Ifugao market economy, many families could no longer afford to hire laborers to repair damaged terraces, which in some cases would have cost thousands of pesos. This was also related to the men's desire in some Ifugao areas to perform nonagricultural labor, such as craft production, to earn a higher income. The reluctance of Ifugao people to repair damaged rice terraces was also, in some cases, related to deforestation and the drying up of irrigation sources, making the repair of rice terraces that no longer had an irrigation water source unfeasible. These trends made it difficult for families, especially those headed solely by women, to hire male agricultural laborers to work for them. The introduction of a capitalist market economy, the increase in (although still limited) wage labor opportunities, the disinterest in repairing damaged rice terraces, and the loss of irrigation water through deforestation combined to alter agricultural patterns, food production, and social life in Ifugao. Many lower class Ifugao people's problems of limited access to resources and employment were directly linked, in many Ifugao people's conceptions, to their problem of inadequate food resources, food insecurity, and malnutrition of their children. They did not perceive the problem of malnutrition to be primarily a matter of lack of nutritional knowledge and poor management of their children's diets, but rather a lack of adequate access to a variety of food.

Malnutrition in Ifugao

Using biomedical constructions of inadequate nutrient, food, and calorie intake, malnutrition in Ifugao was manifested mainly as protein energy, or calorie, deficiency,[10] primarily found among children under six years old in Ifugao, and with lesser frequency among school age children.[11] There were some severe cases of undernutrition among Ifugao children under six years old, and among fewer school age children and adults. Still, the most common form that child malnutrition took in Ifugao was chronic, long-term protein energy deficiency, with first degree malnutrition being most prevalent, followed by second degree malnutrition, and, lastly, by third degree malnutrition.[12]

That there were much fewer cases of third degree malnutrition in Ifugao than in other areas of the Philippines can most likely be attributed to both the prevalence of breast feeding among Ifugao women and to the Ifugao situation wherein even the poorest families, who had no rice fields, businesses, or professional or full-time employment, could obtain a subsistence level of living by cultivating root crops, dry rice, vegetables, and fruit on the communally shared mountainsides within Ifugao; working on others' rice fields; sharecropping; engaging in craft production; raising small, domestic animals; or finding some form of wage labor. The poorest families usually pursued a combination of these livelihood activities. Cases of severe or third degree malnutrition were more prevalent in other areas of the Philippines where both absolute landlessness and higher rates of unemployment and underemployment were commonly found.

Despite the fact that severe hunger was not prevalent among Ifugao people, chronic protein energy malnutrition, in the forms of first and second degree malnutrition, was widespread and could have had detrimental effects on Ifugao children physically, intellectually, and emotionally.[13] Chronic protein energy malnutrition among children can lead to poor physical growth, short stature, poor muscle growth, weak teeth and bones, and a weak immune system. In one Ifugao barrio, a 1992 survey taken of the heights of eighty-six children who were seven to ten years old showed that 43 percent (thirty-seven) of these children were stunted in height (Ifugao Provincial Office 1992). Although Ifugao children did not often die of starvation, their poor nutritional status increased their risk of contracting other diseases due to their diminished resistance, some of which could result in child death (such as pneumonia, measles, diarrhea, etc.). All of the women interviewed stated that their children were frequently ill with diarrheal diseases, "cough and colds," and skin diseases. This may have reflected their low resistance to illness due to their poor nutritional status.

Of the ten leading causes of infant mortality in one Ifugao municipality in 1991, the first and largest category was "unknown" reason for death. This can be interpreted, in part, as meaning that the majority of infant children who died in this municipality were dying in the absence of medical attention, depicting how the government health service could not adequately serve all of the poverty stricken people at that time. Other leading causes of infant mortality, which occurred at the same rate, were severe malnutrition, "born extremely premature," severe broncho pneumonia, liver disease, bleeding on the base of the umbilical cord, sepsis neonaturom, harelip and cleft palate, and tetanus neonaturom.

The ten leading causes of morbidity for all age groups in this municipality in 1991 were respiratory infections (or cough and cold); parasitism; skin problems; diarrhea; bronchitis; gastrointestinal disease; goiter; headache; musculoskeletal disease; and early pneumonia (Ifugao Rural Health Unit 1992). Many of these diseases are more easily acquired by persons having nutritional deficiencies and weakened immune systems. Some, like forms of diarrhea which were frequently acquired by Ifugao children, exacerbate nutritional deficiencies and are an important factor contributing to malnutrition. Intestinal illnesses acquired by Ifugao people were linked to poverty, malnutrition, poor sanitation practices, and inadequate sources of potable water.

Severe protein-calorie malnutrition can lead to impaired brain and behavioral development, as well as negative changes in personality and emotional behavior of children. Children with marginal (first degree) to moderate (second degree) malnutrition may not have impaired brain development, but their nutritional deficiencies may result in their being handicapped in learning by having a shortened attention span and responding less actively in school classes. Added to these problems experienced by malnourished Ifugao children were very poor conditions for learning in the hinterlands of Ifugao, where instructional materials were lacking and teachers often had to juggle teaching students of two or more grades in one classroom.

Children living in the most remote barrios were at the greatest educational disadvantage. In addition to chronic malnutrition, these children often received less attention than students living in the municipal centers. One barrio was located at a great distance from the center of the municipality and could only be reached by a rigorous three to six hour hike through narrow and steep mountain footpaths. Although the majority of Ifugao school teachers were dedicated to their work and students, in this barrio the newly assigned teacher did not arrive to teach her classes until a few months after the school year began in 1992. The young students became very discouraged after hiking far distances up steep hills, for days on end, only to find their teacher repeatedly absent. This was not an isolated incident in this barrio. These nutritional and social problems hindered many Ifugao children's intellectual and emotional development, and may have had an impact on their ability in future years to attend secondary school, to acquire employment as adults, or to understand biomedical concepts of nutrition, which may in turn influence their own and their children's nutritional status.

Being identified by biomedical personnel as having malnourished children led to great shame among many Ifugao parents, some of whom felt blamed for the nutritional status of their children. As Nancy Scheper-Hughes shows in Northeastern Brazil, hunger, largely caused by political and economic forces, can influence mothers' responses to their own children. Brazilian mothers sometimes "suspend[ed] the ethical" toward some of their weak, hungry, and sickly infants, choosing to neglect these infants, who were perceived to be born "wanting to die," for reasons of self-survival and survival of their stronger children (Scheper-Hughes 1992:20).

More commonly found in Ifugao were cases of severely ill adults, whose poverty stricken families had to decide whether to allow them to die or continue purchasing expensive biomedical health treatments. This was related to hunger and nutrition, since most Ifugao families survived only at a subsistence level. Spending a great deal of money on medical treatments, and usually thereby becoming highly indebted, created a situation wherein their ability to feed themselves became even more precarious. I observed two cases in 1992 of two ill women, one in her thirties discussed in the previous chapter and the other in her forties, who suffered from serious illnesses and had received biomedical, Christian, and herbal healing treatments. Their family members finally had to decide discreetly that the women's illnesses would be allowed to take their natural courses without further biomedical treatment. They made these decisions due to their lack of economic resources to continue costly biomedical services without posing risk to the survival of the remaining members of their families, especially in the absence of health insurance for poverty stricken families in the Philippines. The relatives and friends of the ill women diligently and fervently continued practicing Christian healing prayer rituals, on a nightly basis over a period of months for one family, and kept daily vigils with the sick women. In the case discussed Chapter 5, the husband of the ill woman sold his rice field before her death to pay for her biomedical and herbal treatments, thereby risking his own future survival and ability to feed himself. This woman's extended family members were forced to decide if they would give up their own means of livelihood and source of food—their rice fields—to attempt to save her while risking their own survival in the future. Since her illness was very severe, they chose to retain their resources and practice their less expensive religious healing rituals.

That many families of ill persons were forced to make these moral and often painful decisions to ensure their survival, primarily their ability to feed themselves in the future, depicted how poor families in the Philippines lived at the edge of existence, depending mainly on subsistence level agriculture and limited employment opportunities. It also depicted the failure of international aid programs to improve significantly the lives of the Filipino poor, despite the numerous years of international aid agencies' involvement in the Philippines. Finally, it depicted the difficulties faced by the Philippine government health department, which attempted to provide free and adequate health services to the poor, but which, in the face of limited funding, could not meet all of the health needs of its poverty-stricken population.

Returning to hunger and nutritional deficiencies in Ifugao, vitamin and mineral deficiencies were prevalent among all age groups, though some were more prevalent among particular groups, especially women and children. Some Ifugao children had vitamin A deficiencies, affecting their eye development and vision. Although I have no figures for rates of occurrence of vitamin A deficiency among children in Ifugao, it appeared to occur at a relatively low rate. However, when it did, the effects of Vitamin A deficiency could be traumatic and crippling, with some children becoming blind and some having one or both eyes surgically removed.

PHOTO 6.2 Women were highly susceptible to developing goiter, a noncancerous enlargement of the thyroid gland. It is visible as a swelling at the front of the neck, and it is often associated with iodine deficiency. Men and children also sometimes developed goiter.

More prevalent nutritional deficiencies, especially among Ifugao women, were iron and iodine deficiencies, causing anemia and goiter respectively.[14] Although Ifugao men also experienced these deficiencies, more Ifugao women were deficient in these two nutrients. Living in an inland area, with no local sources of iodine, Ifugao people have had difficulty acquiring adequate amounts of iodine in their diets. Rates of iron deficiency were unknown among Ifugao children, since they were not regularly tested for this deficiency. While not all Ifugao women were regularly tested for iron deficiency, clinical examination of many women's physical appearance had been undertaken by biomedical personnel to determine a presence of anemia, especially among pregnant and lactating women who usually were examined for anemia during prenatal clinic visits.

Malnutrition in Three Ifugao Barrios

In 1991, 23.3 percent of Ifugao children under six years old were found to be moderately (second degree) and severely (third degree) malnourished, a figure which did not include first degree malnourished children (Ifugao Provincial Nutrition Committee 1991:2).[15] The following are the malnutrition rates of children zero to six years old living in the three Ifugao barrios in which I conducted my research. I have included in the figures the rates of first, second, and third degree malnourished children.

In Barrio A, 43 percent (179) of children from zero to six years old, of a total of 413 children, were underweight for their age in 1992.[16] This barrio was the central barrio of a municipality, having a large market where an abundance of different foods were sold (particularly on Saturday "market days"). Located where health services were easily accessible, it was a barrio where most upper and many middle class persons resided, although many lower class families lived there as well. Only native rice varieties could be grown in this barrio, however, and only one crop of rice could be grown each year due to the climate and water supply.

Vegetables were also cultivated in this barrio, some recently being grown as cash crops with the encouragement of local development programs. A few trees bore fruit. Wild plant foods were gathered by people in this barrio, particularly by lower class people. As many as 12 percent (fifty) of the children zero to six years old in this barrio were overweight for their age, most likely due to the accessibility of food generally, and foods high in calorie and sugar content specifically (such as cakes, cookies, "junk foods," and soft drinks), and to greater opportunities for wage labor in this area and the subsequent use of earned wages to purchase food. The majority of the people living in this barrio were Christian, and some were believers in and practitioners of the local Ifugao religion.

In Barrio B the nutritional situation was very different, wherein 59 percent (seventy-one) of the children zero to six years old, of a total of 120 children, were underweight for their age in 1992.[17] Nine percent (eleven) of all children under six in this barrio were overweight. The majority of the people in this barrio were members of the lower class. A number of residents were engaged in craft production, especially wood carving and finishing, in addition to farming. Located quite a distance from the center of the municipality, approximately nine kilometers, this barrio was accessible by vehicle from the center of the municipality on a one lane, dirt mountain road, about a half-hour drive. Still, mobility was difficult, since there were few vehicles that traveled to and from the barrio each day except in the early morning hours and late in the afternoon. A person could wait for a *jeepney* (public transportation jeep) for hours in the center of the municipality before it would begin its daily journey back to the barrio, losing much needed work time. During the rainy season, the dirt road became a puddled and thickly muddied road. These conditions made transportation by *jeepney* very difficult, and sometimes impossible. They necessitated hiking by foot, which could also be dangerous due to the possibility of mud slides during the typhoon season. In addition, most of the residents of this barrio lived a further distance from the road, requiring them to regularly hike through the mountains from a *jeepney*, sometimes carrying heavy cargo, slung over their backs or shoulders for men, or on their heads for women. So access to the public market was not always easy.

There was an NGO health clinic in this barrio, but by 1993 it had not yet acquired medical supplies, medicines, or equipment due to difficulty in locating funds to support the clinic's needs. The clinic hosted several health education classes for women health workers, though, who then offered their free services to their community members. The nearest staffed and somewhat better supplied government RHU was located in the barrio contiguous to Barrio B. The RHU could be reached by hiking for about twenty-five minutes or riding in a *jeepney* for about fifteen minutes. Vegetables were grown in this barrio, but they were available only seasonally. Very few varieties of fruit could grow in this area, and few were cultivated. Wild plant foods were gathered by most people in this barrio. Only native rice varieties could be grown, and only one crop of rice could be grown each year due to the climate and water supply. Small, domestic animals were raised (including pigs, chickens, turkeys, dogs, and ducks), and shell fish were gathered in the rice fields. Families had access to the not-too-distant fresh market in the municipal center, but they had to have cash on hand to purchase the food. Approximately one-half of the people living in this barrio were Christian, and approximately one-half were followers of the local Ifugao religion. Many people practiced a combination of the two.

In Barrio C, 84 percent (thirty-eight) of the children zero to six years old, of a total of forty-four children, were underweight for their age in 1992.[18] Only one child (2 percent of the children zero to six years old) was overweight for his age. The majority of the people in this barrio were also members of the lower class. It was the furthest of the three barrios in which I conducted my research, being a twelve kilometer hike from the nearest road and approximately twenty-one kilometers from the center of the municipality. The footpath leading to Barrio C was narrow and steep in many areas. Travel to and from this barrio was very strenuous and tiring, particularly when residents carried heavy cargo over their shoulders or on their heads. In 1993, with the aid of an EC funded project, the residents of this barrio began to widen their footpath so that a water buffalo-drawn cart could be used to carry cargo into or out of the barrio.

There was a government RHU located in Barrio C, which had a midwife staffed in the clinic and limited medical supplies. The municipality in which this barrio was located did not have a regular fresh market, except for Sunday mornings when there was a small gathering of approximately five to fifteen women near a church in the municipal center who sold vegetables they cultivated. There were dry goods stores located in the center of town, though, which irregularly sold fresh vegetables. However, Barrio C did have many fruit trees; vegetables were grown as well. However, the fruit and vegetables were seasonal, and there were periods when they were not available. Wild plant foods were gathered by people as well. Barrio C also had a river where fish could be caught, and small animal husbandry was practiced. High yielding varieties of rice could be planted and harvested in this barrio on irrigated fields twice each year, due to its low elevation and warm climate. The people living there were predominantly Christian.

Among these three barrios, the one located furthest from the center of a municipality and a fresh market, having the highest percentage of self-identified Christians residing in the barrio, having no local regular wage labor or craft production opportunities, and made up of primarily lower class peasants had the highest rate of malnutrition in the first quarter of 1992, despite the fact that it did have a variety of local sources of nutritious foods. However, these foods were not always available since they were seasonal. Their food supply (including rice) was not always adequate, and there were few opportunities available for wage labor in the vicinity of this barrio.

Malnutrition: Social Class, Gender, and Religion

Ifugao Household Members

During my interviews with members of sixty-two households in these three barrios, I weighed all of the individuals within each household. I weighed most of these individuals three times throughout 1992, at three-month intervals. However, some individuals were weighed less than three times due to their unavailability on the date of the weighing. My main purpose in measuring the weights of these individuals, combined with open-ended interviews, was to look at the nutritional status, practices, and understandings among people of differing social class groups, genders, ages, and marital statuses, and among people within similar social groups.

I chose a range of varying household compositions for my research sample in an attempt to obtain a representative sample of Ifugao households. In choosing the families to participate in my research, I considered social class, marital status, age, the presence of children in the household, and the location of the home. I also considered the nutritional status of their children under six years old, based on existing recent government weighing reports, in an attempt to locate a range of the nutritional status of children under six among the households.[19]

My household sample was composed of fifty-one married couples, ten single female-headed households, and one single male-headed household.[20] Five of the households were located in the upper class, seven in the middle class, and fifty in the lower class.[21] Of all the households, fifty had children living in their households, including eight of the single female-headed households and the single male-headed household; twelve had no children living in the household. Two married couples were childless, and two single women had no children currently living in their households. One single woman had been married when I selected her household, but she separated from her husband just prior to our first interview. The ages of the primary adults in the households ranged from the teens to eighty years old, with the majority falling between twenty and forty years old. Of a total of 113 primary adults of the households, 14 percent (sixteen) had no formal education at all, 43 percent (forty-nine) had some elementary school education, 23 percent (twenty-six) had some high school education, and 20 percent (twenty-two) had some college education.[22] Eighty-nine percent of the women and 83 percent of the men had acquired some formal education.

Regarding their social class, four of five upper class families interviewed owned irrigated rice fields. Although one did not own irrigated rice fields, she was considered to be very wealthy through her daughter, who was a successful entrepreneur and who owned irrigated rice fields. Each upper class family had a substantial amount of cash available to them, either through a regular salary, business transactions, savings, or relatives. The upper class families owned much larger and more expensive houses than families of the other two social classes, although one upper class family was still renting a house while they were in the process of building their own. All of the upper class families owned a modern house, most of which were made out of cement and wood, and one family owned two native houses as well. The primary occupation of three of the upper class women was business, and two were farmers. The upper class men were business-men and professionals.

All of the upper class families had toilets, with all but one having a flush or water seal toilet. Sixty percent of the upper class families had Catholic family members, while others had Evangelical and Pentecostal family members. Fifty-six percent (five) of the upper class adults in my sample attended some college, 11 percent (one) completed high school, 22 percent (two) attended some elementary school, and 11 percent (one) had no formal education.

Of a total of seven middle class families interviewed, four owned irrigated rice fields, two did not, and I do not know if one family owned irrigated rice fields or not. Five of the middle class families in my sample also owned modern houses, made of wood and cement. One middle class family rented an apartment in a modern house, and one owned a native house with a cogon roof. Two families owned more than one house, and one rented an apartment in addition to owning a house. The primary occupation of three of the middle class women was business, while two were professionals, and two were farmers. The primary occupation of three of the middle class men was professional work, while two of the men were drivers of public vehicles, and two were farmers.

Seventy-one percent (five) of the middle class families had toilets, most owning water seal toilets and one owning an open pit toilet; 29 percent (two) of the families did not own or use a toilet, using the nearby forested area instead. Fifty-seven percent (four) of the families had Catholic family members, while others had Pentecostal and Espiritista family members. Forty-three percent (six) of middle class adults in my sample had attended some college, 29 percent (four) of middle class adults had attended some high school, 21 percent (three) had attended some elementary school, and 7 percent (one) had no formal education at all.

Of the lower class families in my sample, 50 percent (twenty-five) of the lower class households, of a total of fifty, owned irrigated rice fields, while 50 percent (twenty-five) did not. Four of the twenty-five families who did not own rice fields had owned fields in the past, but had given them to their children by 1992. The average number of rice fields owned by lower class households was three, a total of approximately one-quarter to one-half hectare.[23] Lower class families owned a wide range of housing types, with 34 percent (fourteen) living solely in a native house, most having a cogon roof. The other families owned modern wooden, GI sheet, or cement houses, *campos* (small, wooden houses), or nipa huts. Twenty percent (ten) owned two small houses, while 12 percent (six) were renting (with one living in a house paying no rent). The majority of lower class women, or 76 percent (thirty-seven), were farmers, while the remainder, 24 percent (twelve), were small businesswomen, craftswomen, full-time wage laborers, and homemakers. The majority of lower class men, or 63 percent (twenty-six), were farmers, while 37 percent (fifteen) had other primary occupations, including wood carver, full-time wage laborer, carpenter, mason, small businessman, and homemaker (mainly chronically ill men).

The majority of lower class families, or 72 percent (thirty-six) did not own or use toilets, although one of these families was in the process of building one. Twenty-two percent (eleven) owned open pit toilets, while only 6 percent (three) owned water seal toilets. Forty-nine percent (twenty-four) of the families had Catholic family members (one inactive), while other families had members who were Jehovah's Witness, Evangelical, 7th Day Adventist, Pentecostal, Ifugao Local Religion, Methodist, or Espiritista. One person engaged in independent Christian study, and one was agnostic. Twelve percent (eleven) of lower class adults in my sample had attended some college, 23 percent (twenty-one) of lower class adults had attended some high school, 49 percent (forty-four) had attended some elementary school, and 16 percent (fourteen) had no formal education at all.

Malnutrition, Social Class, and Gender

Child Malnutrition of Zero to Six-Year-Old Children. Malnourished children were found among all social classes in my sample.[24] While I did not acquire rates of malnutrition of all households in Ifugao Province by social class, it was not unusual to find one or more children in households of all social classes who were underweight for their age. However, upper class households tended to have fewer and less severely malnourished children among their children than middle and lower class households. There were a number of intersecting factors that explained this phenomenon and that demonstrated that malnutrition was not only influenced by social class.

One reason for the presence of malnutrition among upper class children may have been unequal gender relations in Ifugao society. This influenced malnutrition because of the relationship between women's gender position, both within their society at large and their households, and their own and their children's nutritional status. While my sample of upper class households was very small, I will provide an analysis of women's position and status in two upper class households, in which two children within each household were first or second degree malnourished, in order to try to understand why upper class children were malnourished.

In these two upper class households, each woman's position within her household was lower than that of her husband. A woman's position was assessed in terms of her decision-making power within her household, and her responsibility for child care. Although the women in these upper class households were full-time businesswomen, each responded that while she discussed family decisions with her husband, he ultimately had the final say in decision making within their family. Each woman held primary responsibility for child care, despite the fact that both she and her husband worked full time. Both women also stated that they spent more time providing child care than their husbands, although their husbands provided child care sometimes. Both husbands were professionally employed full time outside of the home, and they traveled occasionally for business meetings for a few days at a time. One of these women had a domestic helper, yet both women still performed all household tasks as well.

While upper class Ifugao women had more money than middle and lower class women, most still attempted to meet the culturally gendered expectations of Ifugao women by working full time and taking on primary responsibility for child care and household labor, while their husbands participated in child care when they had time. Some also had less authority than their husbands regarding family decision making. Like lower class women, these two women may not have had the time or energy to attend closely to their children's nutritional needs, despite the fact that they could provide more than adequately nutritious food for their children at each meal. In other words, they may not have had time to make sure that their children actually ate nutritious food, or they may have given them less nutritious food when they were in a hurry. Their lower position within their families may have influenced their ability to meet their children's and their own nutritional needs, while their husbands spent less time directly monitoring their children's food intake. As cited earlier, a number of scholars have argued that women's social position influences their own and their children's nutritional status.

A related factor influencing malnutrition among children of upper class households was the prevalence of refined sugar and junk foods within and in the near vicinity of their homes, and their greater access to cash to purchase these foods. These children may have filled up on highly sugared, oily, and starchy junk foods, only to neglect eating nutritious foods because of their dislike of them or because after eating junk foods they no longer felt hungry at meals. These practices could lead to either an underweight or overweight status, and usually an undernourished one.

Combined with this was a common practice among Ifugao parents of all social class groups of allowing a child to eat whatever he wished as long as he ate some type of food. For upper class families this might take the form of eating junk foods between or during meals. Again, this problem was related to women having the multiple burdens of being primarily responsible for attending to their children's nutrition needs, while at the same time trying to attend to their other child care responsibilities, being employed full time, and engaging in household labor, thereby having little time to closely monitor their children's diets. It also reflected a particular understanding among parents of the relationship between eating food and good health.

The important influence of sugar in generating malnutrition among children of all social classes in Ifugao was related directly to international and national development activities since the period of U.S. colonization. These activities effected modernization processes and social changes within Ifugao society, including dietary changes, mostly imposed by outsiders. This specifically included the development of markets in the centers of municipalities, the establishment of small *sari-sari* stores throughout Ifugao communities, and the development of roads to transport imported, inexpensive refined sugar and sugar laden junk foods and beverages from the lowland areas and from other countries (i.e., Coke). These foods and drinks were sold to Ifugao children and adults at low cost. Prior to the 1940s, before the development of local modern markets, sugar derived from sugar cane was the only sugar eaten by the majority of Ifugao children and adults, and then only occasionally. Sugar cane did not grow in great quantities in Ifugao. Also, after the development of markets in areas outside of Ifugao before the 1940s, refined sugar was purchased by some in a nearby province, but this involved a few days hike or ride, as well as money to purchase sugar. Few people had the time or money available for that kind of travel. The foods eaten prior to the introduction of refined sugar and sugared products for sale in Ifugao were natural and had greater nutritional value (although it is not known definitively if Ifugao people's diets were well balanced nutritionally prior to the opening of the market). Men's increasing participation in wage labor, due to greater demands for cash with development and modernization for such things as education, clothing, household items, and medicines, also meant less time spent by men in household food cultivation. This resulted in more food, including refined sugar and sugared food products, being purchased in markets.

Another reason for malnutrition among upper class children was that they lived in unsanitary conditions in public areas of Ifugao, where animal feces were scattered on the ground and where diarrheal diseases could be easily acquired by children, thereby reducing their nutritional status. Additionally, government and international health programs tended to focus on the poor. Upper class women and men did not usually become involved in health programs to the same extent that poor women did. Health personnel did not usually analyze the unique issues related to each social class group's experience of malnutrition. They were, however, beginning to address gender-specific problems. Yet, as will be seen in the following chapter, there were still complexities involved in the issue of gender stratification which were not considered by health programs by the early 1990s. To reiterate, the problem of malnutrition for upper class Ifugao children was related to the complex interactions of unequal gender relations, international and national development and modernization, the increase in refined sugar and sugared foods in children's diet replacing other nutritious foods, and unsanitary conditions found in Ifugao contributing to diarrheal diseases. There surely were other factors that influenced malnutrition of upper class children, but these were some of the most significant ones.

Many middle class households also had malnourished children, of mainly first or second degree. These families usually had access to nutritious foods, as did upper class families, although their access was more limited than the upper class due to their lower incomes. The issues surrounding malnutrition for the middle class households were very similar to the upper class, although the lower educational attainment of some middle class parents also influenced their children's nutritional status.

Among lower class families, malnutrition was found in most families; and the most severe cases of malnutrition were found within this social class group. An important point to be made here is that the problems described above for upper and middle class families were also found among lower class families. But the problems of malnutrition among the lower class were exacerbated by a lack of availability of nutritious food during certain periods of the year and a lack of cash to purchase food, especially during these periods. When I asked lower class women a general question about what they perceived to be their greatest problems, a common response was that they did not have enough food. For much of the year, particularly during the monsoon and dry seasons and the period prior to the next rice harvest, lower class people felt insecure about their ability to meet even minimal food needs. After health and nutrition education classes, one of which I facilitated in a barrio as a part of a series of health classes offered by the government Department of Social Welfare and Development Office, women invariably remarked: "It is very nice to learn all of these things about nutrition and a well-balanced diet. But, if we do not have the food in our barrio and no money to buy it, the information is useless." One poor peasant woman, who had severely and moderately malnourished children, said that when she learned from the volunteer BNS that her children were malnourished, "I said, 'What will I do then?' The BNS told me, 'You feed them with different kinds of food.' But where will we get them? We have no money to buy them, so where will we get it?"

These women perceived the problem of malnutrition to be due not to their lack of nutrition knowledge or education, but rather inadequate access to a variety of nutritious foods to feed their families. The UNICEF ABCSD program tried to address this problem by promoting and offering agricultural training sessions on backyard gardening and animal husbandry, which many families participated in. Yet, the poorest families sometimes had difficulty maintaining these projects due to lack of capital, continuous access to resources, and time, as well as general indebtedness. In addition, some vegetables simply could not be grown during certain periods of the year.

Unequal social class relations were the most significant factors in lower class Ifugao people's inability to meet the nutritional needs of their family members. First, the traditional inheritance pattern—through which some family members did not inherit rice fields—reproduced poor families, although this pattern was beginning to change among families who allowed all children to inherit some rice fields, if possible. Second, the pattern of sharecropping—wherein one-half of the rice harvest was given to the rice field owner—and the pattern of agricultural wage rates in Ifugao—by which women were paid one-half the minimum wage—contributed to malnutrition among the lower class by limiting the produce or wages earned by these laborers. Third, middle and upper class persons charging high interest rates on much needed loans borrowed by members of the lower class, sometimes for food, also exacerbated poverty and malnutrition. Fourth, the lack of implementation of a genuine agrarian reform program affected Ifugao peasants who did not own rice fields. Although very little land would be redistributed within Ifugao itself, many Ifugao people have historically migrated out of Ifugao to seek land, as well as employment, and could do so with land redistribution. Fifth, the inability of lower class Ifugao people to always purchase foods during periods of the year when cultivated and wild foods were less available related to structural adjustment programs which resulted in less opportunities for employment, depicted by high unemployment and underemployment rates; low wages and restrictions on raising minimum wage rates; higher food prices; and higher prices of other commodities and services.

Although lack of irrigated rice field ownership had an impact on both a family's income and nutritional status, consistent with finding malnourished children in all social class groups, I found that owning irrigated rice fields in Ifugao did not in and of itself appear to be the most significant factor influencing the incidence of all degrees of malnutrition within Ifugao households. This was likely due to the fact that Ifugao people who did not own irrigated rice fields could instead cultivate crops on the Ifugao mountainsides. However, the ownership of irrigated rice fields among Ifugao families may have played a significant role in the incidence of third degree, or severe, malnutrition of Ifugao children. In my 1992 sample, among twenty-two households having first and second degree malnourished children (underweight for their age), 59 percent (thirteen) owned some irrigated rice fields, with half (seven) owning more than two irrigated rice fields, while a lesser percentage, 41 percent (nine), owned no irrigated rice fields. However, among six households in my sample having third degree malnourished children, some also having first and second degree malnourished children, 67 percent (four) owned no irrigated rice fields, while 33 percent (two) owned some irrigated rice fields. All were lower class households. Of the two households with third degree malnourished children that owned rice fields, one was a single woman headed household, and the other had only one small rice field. In each of two of the households that owned no rice fields, one parent was not working full time, increasing the number of dependents in the family (one due to the father's chronic illness and the other due to the mother's full-time child care for her three young children). This made their economic situation and access to food more insecure. Also, the poorest families tended to own land that was not the most fertile or did not have the best access to irrigation water. Ifugao peasants' ownership of irrigated rice fields may have been a significant factor in alleviating third degree malnutrition among Ifugao children, although it was not the sole factor influencing malnutrition, as indicated in the previous discussion of upper and middle class households.

Regarding unequal gender relations and malnutrition, one reason given repeatedly by Ifugao people, mostly women, for Ifugao children's poor nutritional status was the lack of time women had to give proper attention to their children's nutritional needs because of the heavy work load of all women. While this was certainly true, a related significant factor was women's low social position within their households and society. Ifugao men, women, and health workers never criticized the men of these households for their lack of participation in caring for their children's nutritional needs, since they all viewed women as primarily responsible for child care and nutrition. The more common comment regarding men and child care was men's lack of attentiveness toward their children even while they were providing child care. That phenomenon was interpreted by Ifugao people as one reason why women should engage in more child care than men. (Elderly parents, female relatives, and elder siblings also participated in child care when both mother and father were working outside of the home.)

While there were calls for men to share household duties equally with women during development program meetings in Ifugao barrios, only women were subtly blamed for their children's malnutrition. Women were criticized for rushing out of their homes to go to work before attending carefully to what their child was or was not eating. This accusation placed women in a problematic position. On the one hand, Ifugao women culturally were expected to work outside of their home, and, further, to work industriously to provide food for their children and their husbands. On the other hand, when women did work diligently, leaving their homes early because their employment began at an early hour or because they were supposed to meet their agricultural coworkers at a designated time, they were criticized for not providing proper nutritional care for their children. No criticism was attributed to the men of their households for leaving their homes for work outside of the home. One lower class peasant woman, a mother of six children whose family did not own irrigated rice fields, expressed her feelings about this bind women found themselves in:

But sometimes even if you know what to do [regarding proper nutrition], it is hard to do it because of work. Every day I go early to work, in [the center of the municipality] or the fields, because if you do not work you do not produce anything, like food. That's why even if we are tired we have to work [farming] because we have no [full-time wage labor or professional] job; we are jobless. We come home late at night. I leave my children here, and I cannot clean as I should.

She blamed herself for her children's malnutrition, having internalized the cultural expectation that women produce food and provide the majority of child care, "I don't know why my children are malnourished. They always eat. But I accept that there is a lack of nutrition because of what I produce, what I provide, because I cannot provide all that they need because of lack of means. Like milk, except when there's rations [food supplements], that's when they can taste milk." When I asked her how she felt when she learned from a BNS that her children were malnourished, she said, "I am affected [emotionally], but you cannot do anything. I'm affected because I am the mother and they are under your care." This woman took full responsibility and blame for her children's nutritional status, without ever mentioning her husband's role in providing care for his children. This was an example of a woman who had internalized the notion that she, as the mother, was to blame for child malnutrition. This woman did not consider the larger political-economic factors that profoundly affected her situation of poverty; instead, she accepted the full, individual responsibility for her children's poor nutritional status.

Another lower class businesswoman expressed the cultural expectation of women having primary responsibility for child care, when I asked how she felt when she learned from a BNS that her children were malnourished:

A little bit disgusted because, as a mother, if you know the [poor] health of your child you are a little bit hurt. Because in general, they [other community members] may say that you are not doing something for your child that you're supposed to be doing. That should be the responsibility of the mother. Mostly the mother, rather than the father, because when the father is working he has no time to look after the health of the child, so she should be the one. If the mother is also working, it is the combination of both parents to overlook the child. Sometimes the fathers are ashamed to go to health classes, especially if there are so many women, they are ashamed to mingle with them. That's why mostly "Mothers' Classes," no "Fathers' Class." Maybe health care is defined as women's work.

One lower class peasant woman, who had five malnourished children in 1992 (two of whom were severely malnourished), rejected the accusation that her children's malnutrition was her fault, when she was criticized by a BNS for her children's undernourished status. "I wonder why my children are always underweight and I keep feeding them. [A BNS] got mad at me and said, 'Why is it that your children are always underweight?'" At another time she said, when we went to harvest [rice] one time and . . . [a BNS] was there [also harvesting], and . . . [the BNS] kept talking about malnutrition, the women asked, "Why do you keep talking about malnutrition?" [The BNS] said, "Oh, ask [the woman being interviewed], all of her children are malnourished." I said, "No, they are not malnourished. It is not my fault."

The BNS criticized her another time: "the BNS said [to me], 'Oh, you keep on sanding [wood carvings, as part of craft production] and all the kids are malnourished.' I said, 'Yes, if someone will take them and feed them so they are not malnourished, then I will take them back.'"

This woman was criticized for attempting to work to provide food for her malnourished children, with the implication that she was thereby neglecting her children's nutritional needs. Women were accorded the majority of the blame for the poor nutritional status of their children, even from international development organizations. Women also took on more of the blame for malnutrition than their husbands in the face of greater migration of men, wherein women stayed at home and were forced to take on all of the responsibilities of child care and household labor.

The primary point of this discussion is that women's lower position relative to their husbands' within the household (as women were expected to both take on primary responsibility for child care and household labor, work full time outside of the home, earn less pay than men, etc.) was subtly reinforced by biomedical programs that placed most of the blame on mothers for the malnutrition of their children, instead of altering the situation by consistently attempting to equalize nutritional and general child care between working mothers and fathers.

Feeding sugar to children, with rice or sweet potato instead of vegetables or proteins, was a common source of malnutrition among lower class Ifugao children. One example of this occurred during my interview with a woman of a lower class family that took place inside of her native house. When it was time to feed the woman's two-and-one-half-year-old son, his grandmother quickly prepared a plate of rice and a bowl of chicken for him, which they had simmering over an open fire. As he started to eat his rice, he began to scream because he did not like the chicken. His mother immediately arose from her seat, pulled out a bag of dried, sweetened cocoa mix from a shelf above her child's head, and placed the bag near him. He immediately stopped crying, pulled the bag next to him, dipped his tablespoon into the bag, and spread a heaping spoon full of the sweetened cocoa over his rice. He then quickly scooped tablespoon after tablespoon of sweetened rice into his mouth, now and then digging into the cocoa bag to spread more over his rice. At one point he picked up the back of the chicken, bit into it, and immediately put it down again. He continued to eat more rice and cocoa, sometimes eating spoonfuls of cocoa between bites of rice. He stopped eating abruptly, arranged the cocoa bag, his plate of rice and the plate of chicken by his side, jumped up, and walked to the door to climb down the house ladder to play outside. This boy was first and, at another weighing, second degree malnourished during 1992. Since he preferred the taste of sugared cocoa over vegetables and meat offered to him, his mother and grandmother allowed him to substitute it for the more nutritious food he could have eaten. They did this in part to coax him to stop crying and to eat at least something, while not fully realizing the nutritional value of the vegetables and meat.

There were a number of interrelated reasons for this practice. One important reason was the desire to use sugar or salt as a substitute for other healthy viands (such as vegetables) when they did not have access to these. At times, these vegetables could not be grown during particular seasons, and often poorer families lacked the resources to eat animals they were raising or to purchase other food such as milk products. Many women offered comments similar to this one from a lower class peasant woman: "If we have no viand, we all eat sugar." Another lower class woman, who was employed full time in a low paying job and had a moderately malnourished daughter, said:

> Those very rich people, they will not experience like this [malnutrition among their children] because they can afford to buy those nutritious foods and they will eat them everyday. And those poor people like me, sometimes if I have no money, I just give sugar to my children, even though they tell us sugar is not good for children. Because if we have no viand, they will ask for some [sugar]. I read this [sugar is not always nutritious for children], but sometimes I give sugar to my children.

Many women said that they did not know that feeding their child only sugar and rice for meals was not healthy. Instead, they thought that as long as their child ate something, and was satisfied, the child would be healthy. A common understanding among Ifugao people was that filling the stomach during a meal will maintain one's health, regardless of the type of food eaten. One lower class peasant woman said that in order to have a healthy meal, "It's good to eat until we are full."

Many lower class women also made comments similar to the following one, made by a lower class woman who was a wage laborer: "Sometimes the food the children eat is different from us [she and her husband] because sometimes they eat sugar with rice at meals, or they don't like the vegetables if there are no additional ingredients to make it delicious, like meat."

Some women, unsuccessful at breastfeeding and who lacked money to buy milk for their growing infants, fed them rice gruel mixed with sugar instead. These infants usually became severely malnourished. Most of the women interviewed said that rice gruel fed to infants, even in addition to breast milk, was always mixed with sugar—if it was available—and sometimes with salt. One college educated woman trained her infant son to eat sugar with his rice and milk gruel, even when he did not want to eat sugar, because she thought his food should taste sweet. She said, this boy doesn't want sweets. I started to give him sugar at seven months, and he vomited. But now I try to force him to eat a little; I put sugar and milk on his rice and I force him. Because if I just put milk and rice it doesn't taste so sweet, so I add sugar. He is still eating the rice and milk, but I just think it doesn't taste so sweet.

A lower class woman peasant, two of whose children were second and third degree malnourished, thought that sugar was good for her children. She said they ate more sugar than she and her husband, "because we always sacrifice for the children. We reserve the sugar for the children." A few women did say that they limited the amount of sugar that their children ate.

Many men and women lacked the education they conceivably should have acquired from the free government school system and did not have a good understanding of a biomedically defined nutritious diet. Many lower class children dropped out of school, or stopped their education after completing elementary school, due to poverty and the inability of their parents to pay for their clothing and school needs. This can have an impact on the nutritional knowledge of both women and men, and directly affects their future livelihood possibilities, as many women interviewed pointed out. While the government offered free public schooling for all children, it was not able to solve the problem of poor children having to discontinue their education due to lack of finances. Although there were government and NGO sponsored health classes covering nutrition education, which mainly women attend, I found that there was never a direct discussion about the practice of substituting sugar for vegetables or proteins at meals. When I discussed this at one nutrition education seminar, many women informed me that they had never known that this was not a nutritionally sound feeding practice.

Regarding gender and nutritional knowledge, according to the UNICEF ABCSD program, a criteria for families at risk for malnutrition among children in their families was an "illiterate mother." Again only "mothers" were blamed for their children's malnutrition because of their illiteracy and not having a good understanding of biomedical conceptions of proper nutrition. Members of the program did not seem to perceive that an illiterate, or even literate, father had an influence on their children's nutritional status (Ifugao Provincial Nutrition Committee 1991).

Another interesting reason children were readily given sugar to eat for meals was that Ifugao parents did not like their children to cry and preferred to give them what they requested in order to halt their crying. This pattern was also observed by Guthrie, Masangkay, and Guthrie in their study in the early 1970s of fifty-six children six to thirty-six months of age in another upland village in the Philippines (Guthrie et al. 1976). Thinking that eating sugar was good for a child's diet, parents easily gave in to their children's crying demands for sugar at meals, instead of convincing them to eat more nutritious foods. Ifugao women said that they pitied crying children and that it could be shameful if one's own child cried often. Women also revealed that if a child refused to eat a meal unless given sugar, and the parents were in hurry to leave the home, then giving the child the sugar became the easiest means to get the child to eat her meal. Again, development and modernization, with the creation of markets, the greater accessibility and low cost of sugar, and the increase in wage labor, has facilitated the development of this source of malnutrition for Ifugao children of all social classes.

Another reason often given by Ifugao biomedical personnel, social workers, and development program personnel for child malnutrition among lower class children in Ifugao was the widespread practice of young children babysitting younger children during the daytime, usually elder siblings caring for their younger siblings. Children served as "baby tenders" historically, at least since the turn of the century (Barton 1930). In the early 1990s this was practiced, in part, due to inadequate numbers of low cost child care facilities in Ifugao or other systems of child care. Also, on certain days, and especially during the planting and harvesting rice months, both women and men had to work during the same days. Some upper and middle class parents in the center of one municipality had access to a child care center, but it was quite expensive for lower class parents. Women of the lower class often asked their relatives, especially their parents or sisters, to care for their children. However, women did not often ask friends to care for their children. This was because they did not want to impose additional work upon their friends, who already had their own work to accomplish.

Ifugao children as young as five years old often carried infants slung over their backs in a blanket all day long, while other younger siblings trailed behind them. Some school children brought their infant brothers, sisters, nephews, or nieces to school with them while their parents worked, necessitating divided attention between their school lessons and child care responsibilities. These child babysitters did not always understand the nutritional needs of the children under their care—or their own needs for that matter—and often did not feed them properly. One lower class peasant woman explained the problem, commenting on how children could become well nourished. She said, "feed your children properly [so that they will become well nourished], feed them three times a day. But when the elder children care for younger children they will not feed them three times a day. They will just play and play, and they cannot remember to feed their sister or brother."

Sometimes, children four to six years old stayed home all day without child care, as one four year old girl who lived with her laboring grandparents did in one Ifugao barrio. Finding herself alone at her home one day at lunch time, she dug out a handful of cold rice from a pot hanging outside their native house, which had been cooked earlier in the morning. The rice, eaten from her small, dirty hands, was the only food she ate for lunch, since there had been no vegetables or other viand prepared for her.

The woman who had five malnourished children described her frustration with her children's malnourished status, and an average day for her children:

> My children do not eat much. And I keep scolding them to eat more, but they still eat little. They prefer to eat fruits, bananas, corn, or bread at any time. At meals they

don't eat much. Even if I spank them to eat, they still won't eat well. I even cook early to let the children eat early. Sometimes the children will eat alone, because sometimes I am not here. Most of the time I am out working, sanding wood carvings, and I will work when there is work [available]. I go out to work after breakfast. Sometimes I do not come home for lunch. My husband is out working also. My sister helps watch the children [she was twenty-eight years old]. There is always someone to watch them. But, at lunch the children go into the house and get their own lunch. Most of the time for lunch there is no viand, so they eat sugar and salt [with rice or sweet potato]. Most of my children eat sugar with rice, even if we have vegetables as viand, my children want to eat sugar.

The UNICEF ABCSD program attempted to address this problem by instituting day care centers in a number of barrios. Although ideally this was a positive movement forward for women and their families, in practice it did not always benefit women, as I will discuss in the next chapter.

Women's low pay also influenced lower class children's nutrition, since an increase in women's pay, at least to the minimum wage, may have provided peasant families with more money to purchase more nutritious food when it could not be raised due to weather conditions. Many Ifugao men were said to spend a portion of their money on alcohol or gambling, which could have been spent on food, while women rarely engaged in these activities and tended to spend money on their family's needs. Although an increase in income did not always translate into better nutrition, as seen in the cases of upper class households, it may be viewed as one aspect of a broader solution to the problem of malnutrition.

Many lower class children's nutritional problems were again related to the low status of women of the lower class in Ifugao society. This was exemplified by the fact that poor women were overburdened with work, yet they were expected to be the primary providers of child and nutritional care for their children, an expectation reinforced by national and international health programs. They were subtly blamed when their children were malnourished by community members and health program personnel, even when they were attempting to support their children by working outside of the home, usually to provide food. The establishment and operation of day care centers for children, which would greatly aid both women and children, was not considered a priority by the national government. Also, women's low pay reduced their ability to purchase more nutritious food for their families.

Regarding intra-household eating practices, all of the women interviewed reported that they and their family members ate simultaneously at meals, which I also observed, unless they had very different work or school schedules. All of the women reported that there were no restrictions on the amount of food that each family member could eat. Many women reported that if there was only a small amount of viand, both parents would save it for the children. The majority of women also said that their children ate more sugar than the parents. Children often ate sugar with meals as their viand even if other viand was served, but they especially ate sugar when no other viand was available.

Although there were no great gender differences in weight status among Ifugao children or adults, one gendered difference in eating patterns at meals was that some young boys could be more aggressive in taking more of the viand served in a communal plate than the young girls. In the three barrios in which I conducted research, 55 percent (159) of all of the girls under six years old (of a total of 289) and 49 percent (134) of all of the boys under six years old (of a total of 273) were malnourished in the first quarter of 1992. More boys were overweight than girls: 7 percent (twenty) of the girls were overweight while 12 percent (thirty-three) of the boys were overweight. Nationally, according to a 1989–1990 malnutrition statistic based on a Food and Nutrition Research Institute National Nutrition Survey, 17 percent of preschool females were second and third degree malnourished (underweight for their age), while only 9.8 percent of preschool males were second and third degree malnourished (underweight for their age) (Tan 1991:67).

A lower class Ifugao businesswoman expressed the general perception that Ifugao boys' weight status was higher than that of girls when she said, after learning that two of her female children were malnourished, "That's why I said probably they are underweight because of a lack of vitamins and because they are girls. That's what the old men told me. They said that men are heavier than women, and I believed that because they are not sick even."

Another explanation offered for these differences was, as a forty-year-old man recalled, that when children were young, boys were allowed to roam around the community more freely than girls, who tended to stay near their homes. When the boys roamed they foraged in the forest for wild foods, ate their fill, and brought home what remained for the other family members. Also, one man recalled visiting his relatives when he roamed the community as a boy, who invariably fed him a snack or a meal when he visited them. Thus, there were differences in behavior at meal time (boys' aggressive versus girls' passive food-getting behavior) and differences in the socialization of girls and boys which allowed boys greater opportunity to eat during and between meals.

Although single women with children were among the groups that had the most difficulty providing for the financial needs of their families, malnutrition rates for children within single female-headed households were mixed. Of eight single female-headed households with children, three had children who all had normal weights for their ages and two had only first degree malnourished children. Three had children who were first, second, or third degree malnourished. The children of the single male-headed household had normal weights. The normal and near normal weights of children in 63 percent of the single female-headed households may possibly be explained by women's higher status within their households and their sole control over family resources and thus greater ability to provide for the nutritional needs of their children. This argument would have to be studied in greater depth to be confirmed.

PHOTO 6.3 Young Ifugao children regularly cared for their younger siblings while their parents worked. Boys began participating in child care at a young age, and continued to do so as adults, although less often than women.

Still, single women saw a relationship between the difficulties posed by their single status and gender and their children's malnutrition. When I asked a lower class, single peasant woman, the mother of three children, why she thought her children were malnourished, she quickly responded:

> Because of lack of food; because no one helps me to support them and my wages are not enough for them. Because if you don't have enough money or food you cannot give them complete foods, like different foods for each meal throughout the

day. They mostly eat the same food throughout the day; but sometimes it will be varied.

Large family size also was often cited as a cause of malnutrition, and it was one factor which certainly exacerbated the problem of malnutrition in families. However, among the twenty-two households that had the most cases of second degree malnutrition in my sample, almost one-half, or ten, of these households had only three or less children living in the household. Of the six households with children who had third degree malnutrition, one had three children and another had four children living in the household. It appeared that large family size was not the most significant factor causing malnutrition in Ifugao.

Adult Malnutrition. The majority of women and men weighed in my sample had normal weights in 1992 (a total of 149 adults eighteen years old and older, seventy men and seventy-nine women, were weighed at least once).[25] Only 12 percent (eighteen) of adults weighed had weights below normal for their heights, and some of those who were underweight for one weighing had normal weights at least for one of the other three weighings. Forty percent (six) of fifteen underweight women were pregnant at the time they were underweight, which would likely have had an impact on both their own and their developing fetus' health. (All pregnant women in Ifugao did not tend to become underweight, however, as one pregnant woman had normal weight and seven other pregnant women were overweight during their pregnancies.)[26] Another 33 percent (five) of the underweight women were elderly women. Only three men were underweight for their height, two of whom had a chronic illness; another was an elderly man. Although the numbers of persons weighed was low, this data suggested that pregnant women and elderly and chronically ill adults in Ifugao were more susceptible to undernutrition than other adults. The Ifugao Department of Health provided a program that monitored pregnant women, measuring their weights regularly and offering them free vitamin, iron, and food supplements during prenatal clinical visits, when these supplements were available from the central government office.

Twenty-two percent (thirty-three) of all adults weighed in my sample were overweight for their age for at least one weighing, seven of whom were pregnant women. These adults were from all social class groups, but the highest percentages of overweight adults were from the middle and upper classes, many of whom no longer engaged in physical labor for their regular livelihood and had access to a wide variety of food.

The diet of upper class adults influenced an increase in diseases often associated with industrialized countries. A daily diet for upper class adults high in animal fat, salt, and sugar was one factor influencing an increase in cases of hypertension and heart disease in Ifugao. Lower class adults were less likely to eat meat and fats every day due to their high cost.

The incidence, or at least detection, of cancer occurring among Ifugao adults was also reported to be on the increase in the past decade. Ifugao people said this was due to the recent increase in use of chemical pesticides and fertilizers by Ifugao farmers on their crops and the feeding of hybrid animals with chemical feeds. The use of each of these was encouraged by both government agricultural technicians and international development agents, especially for hybrid animals, cash crops such as vegetables and fruit trees, and high yielding rice varieties where they could be grown in Ifugao. The agents also taught Ifugao farmers about natural pesticides and fertilizers. Ifugao people in one barrio believed that pesticide ingestion may have led to the death of one of their community members, an eighteen-year-old Ifugao man who died in the early 1990s after returning home from spraying pesticides in a field in the lowlands.

Women's Malnutrition. Women have two nutrient deficiencies at higher rates than men, specifically iron deficiency anemia and iodine deficiency, causing goiter. In 1989, 68 percent of all Ifugao women had goiter (Department of Health, Ifugao 1989). Although there were no statistics available for rates of goiter among adult men in Ifugao Province, among the seventy men in my 1992 sample, only 10 percent (seven) had goiter, six of whom had only first degree goiter. In contrast, among the seventy-nine women in my 1992 sample, 61 percent (forty-eight) had first, second, or third degree goiter.

In 1989, 33.79 percent of pregnant and lactating women in Ifugao Province were found to have iron deficiency anemia (Department of Health, Ifugao 1989). Some causes of the higher rates of anemia and goiter among women were physical, such as menstruation, pregnancy, and childbirth. In addition, poor Ifugao women, as well as men and children, did not always have access to adequate amounts of vegetables rich in iron and vitamin C (green leafy and yellow fruit and vegetables).[27] They could not always cultivate these vegetables, nor could they always afford to purchase them if they were available for sale. The Philippine government's Department of Health attempted to provide women with free vitamin and iron supplements. But these were mainly given to pregnant and lactating women, and only given to other women on an irregular basis.

The Department of Health also, over many years, tried to provide free packages of iodized salt to families, but this supply was also sporadic. Iodized salt was sometimes available for sale in local stores; but, since it was more expensive than non-iodized salt, lower class families rarely viewed spending their limited cash resources on iodized salt as a priority. This depicted the low priority that costly preventive health measures received among lower class Ifugao families who lived only on a subsistence level income. It also depicted the lower priority women received, and even conceived of for themselves, in relation to other family members, regarding women's personal nutritional needs. Ifugao women tended to sacrifice their personal needs for their family, although Ifugao men sacrificed their needs for their family as well. Many women, including health workers, perceived women's undernutrition to be due, in part, to women's continuous engagement in hard work, work that seemed to them to be never ending.

PHOTO 6.4 While her grandparent guardians work in their rice fields, this preschool girl fends for herself at lunchtime. She often found only cold, cooked rice to eat. Preschool children, and school children during summer break, often stayed home alone while their parents worked.

Occasional medical surgical missions provided surgery to Ifugao people within Ifugao hospitals to remove large goiters. Through a UNICEF funded program, almost all Ifugao people had been given free lipiodol tablets or injections to prevent or alleviate goiter in the early 1990s. Additionally, to improve these nutritional deficiencies, the Ifugao Department of Health recommended that the agricultural sector intensify its effort to encourage and teach families about "Bio-intensive Gardening," and that "efforts should likewise be exerted to allow the efficient distribution of the available food supply to a majority of the population" (Department of Health, Ifugao 1989).

Malnutrition and Religion

Biomedical health personnel and Ifugao Christian proselytizers often blamed the local Ifugao religion for poverty and malnutrition. Biomedical personnel suggested that *baki* proscription of vegetables and fish during specific periods of the year was a significant cause of malnutrition among Ifugao children. Some Ifugao Christian proselytizers often criticized Ifugao families for sacrificing many animals for rituals, claiming that this was one of the "root causes" of poverty in Ifugao and was related to malnutrition among the poor. However, through my interviews I found that of fifty-eight respondents, only 12 percent (seven) reported that they strictly followed *baki* food restrictions. These included the long period of restriction on vegetables and fish during the two or three harvest season months, and during and sometimes following ritual periods. Sixty percent (thirty-five) of respondents reported that they minimally followed food restrictions. This included not eating vegetables or fish during a *baki* ritual, with ritual meat taken home, or for a few days following a funeral or *baki* for illness. These minimal food restrictions lasted from one meal to a few days, intermittently throughout the year, and, more rarely, up to one week. Some people reported their families just excluded fish during the harvest season, eating everything else available. Twenty-eight percent (sixteen) of respondents reported that they did not follow any food restrictions. In sum, a total of 88 percent (fifty-one) of respondents had no or minimal food restrictions, making it unlikely that the food restrictions prescribed by the Ifugao religion were a significant cause of malnutrition among Ifugao children in the early 1990s. Furthermore, Barrio C, whose residents were predominantly Christian, had a higher rate of malnutrition among children under six years old in the first quarter of 1992 than either Barrio A or B, each of which had a higher number of followers of the Ifugao religion residing in them. The argument that Ifugao religious food restrictions were a significant cause of malnutrition among Ifugao children did not appear to be valid. The argument served only to mystify the problems of social class, ethnic, and gender inequality, which had a greater impact on Ifugao children's and women's nutritional status.

Women's Understandings and Perceptions of Malnutrition

The biomedical concept of malnutrition was introduced in Ifugao only with the introduction of biomedicine in the early 1900s. Prior to that time, and during most of this century for the majority of Ifugao people, thinness was conceived of as *na-ong-ong*.[28] It has been only since the 1970s, with the prioritization of nutritional programs nationwide to alleviate malnutrition by President Marcos and with the institution of the weighing surveillance program, called Operation Timbang, and volunteer BNSs in Ifugao in 1983, that the concept of malnutrition became more widely known among Ifugao people.

Most women whom I interviewed had a basic understanding of the biomedical concept of "malnourished."[29] Most women interviewed understood the term "malnourished" to be a lack of food (fourteen responses), lack of nutritious foods (seven), people whose "weight is lacking" (ten), and or a lack of vitamins (eleven).[30] Four women said that the term malnourished was a lack of proper combination of food or lack of "complete" food (the term used for balanced diet), and one said it was the lack of six basic foods. Other women said that it was a lack of vegetables (one), it affected children's growth (one), and it was those people who will not eat (three) or who were very thin (two); and one thought it was having "low blood." Quite a few said it was when a person was sickly or not healthy (ten). Sixteen said they did not know what malnourished meant; but of those women, twelve respondents were elderly and never had their children weighed since there was no weighing program when their children were young, or they had no small children living in their households.

When women who, at some time, had malnourished children were asked why they thought their children may have become malnourished, the two most frequently given responses were, first, because their children did not like to eat much, especially vegetables, and particularly when they were ill (which was regularly for most Ifugao children) (fourteen), and second, because of a lack of food or viand (nine). Some specified that it was usually due to frequent illnesses, especially diarrhea. Other women said their children were malnourished because of a lack of their own breastmilk (four), a lack of vitamins (two), and thinness was inherited from their father (one). One woman said her children were malnourished because she did not know what to feed her child. Another woman said that her child was malnourished because he needed to have *baki* performed (*lawit*) since a spirit was holding her child.[31] Some mothers had no clear idea why their children were malnourished (six).

The majority of Ifugao women interviewed who had malnourished children—71 percent (twenty-five) of thirty-five respondents—said that they had no knowledge that their children were malnourished prior to being informed by a BNS, following the weighing of their children. From their observations, their children's body size appeared normal. Only 31 percent (six) said that they could see their child was malnourished prior to the weighing because they were *na-ong-ong* (thin), they were not eating well, or, as one woman said, she knew that her children did "not have good food to eat." This lack of detection of malnutrition of their chronically malnourished children created confusion among women about why their children were malnourished when they appeared to have normal weights and body sizes. Eleven women said that after being told their children were malnourished they could not understand why, since they thought they had been feeding their children well. Some women, but not the majority, denied their children were malnourished because it was shameful. One woman, who had been told her children were malnourished, said:

> Those [who are malnourished are] the ones who have a big head and stomach, and very thin arms. My children do not look like that, so I don't think that they are malnourished. That's the way I think because I don't like to think that my children are malnourished. So that's the way I think. They keep on saying that my children are malnourished but I say they are not.

This woman's mother expressed the shame and stigma felt by Ifugao parents of malnourished children when she said, "My grandchildren are malnourished. They say, 'they are all malnourished,' but that's not true! It's shameful, as if we have no food! Really! When they say you have no food, as if we don't have anything; it is like it shows that you are not working for the children, earning for them."

Others felt worried upon being told that their children were malnourished because they thought their child would die or become more ill. Some women felt sad, and others asked either the BNS or simply themselves, "What will I do then, since I have no money to buy food?" One said she thought that the devil had caused her child's malnutrition because she had delivered her child in the swidden field. One said she just accepted it, while another, feeling blamed, told the BNS, "It's not my fault." One woman misunderstood the meaning of malnourished and said that she felt "good upon (hearing that her child was malnourished), because at least they are in good health."

Part of the problem regarding their lack of understanding of why their children were malnourished was that the concepts of "malnourished" and "nutrition" did not coincide directly with their local understanding of the causes and symptoms of *na-ong-ong*, or extreme thinness. Also, apart from health care volunteers, who numbered about ten per barrio in those barrios that had volunteers, most women (and less men) either did not receive much nutrition education from health programs or they did not fully grasp what they were being taught. Most of the women interviewed remembered being commonly told, upon having their children weighed or receiving food supplements, to "feed your children good food," to "feed your children more vegetables," or that "your children need more vitamins." Returning to their homes after having their children weighed, many of these women attempted to feed their children what they believed to be good food, or more vegetables, and then faulted themselves if their child's nutritional status did not improve by the next month's weighing.

I found that of fifty-five female respondents, 71 percent (thirty-nine) did not have a clear understanding of how to construct a meal providing most of the necessary nutrients for proper growth and development, or of the nutritional importance of this. As stated earlier, a common method of constructing a meal among lower class members was to serve rice or sweet potatoes and one viand (vegetables or a protein), usually "whatever we plant" and was ripe, or "whatever we can find to eat" (i.e., wild vegetables, fruit, fish, etc.). In addition, many women said that on some days, "When there is nothing, there is nothing" to eat with rice or sweet potato. The majority of Ifugao women did not engage in meal planning.

When asked what could be done to improve a malnourished person's nutritional status, 35 percent (eighteen) of fifty-one female respondents said that they did not know. Thirteen said the malnourished person should eat the right or nutritious foods, while some said to feed them vegetables and fruit (five) or give them vitamin tablets (four). A number of women said malnourished persons should eat anything that they like to eat (nine). One person each responded: performing *baki*; cleaning children and washing their hands before eating; having parents care for their children rather than other children caring for them during the day; giving them purgatives for worms; and obtaining instructions from a doctor or bringing them to a hospital; feeding them corn; and "feed them rice, sugar, salt, and rice gruel, because only if we are rich we will buy milk."[32] Two respondents each said: curing them of an illness; gardening and raising animals; and giving them milk. Interestingly, only two women said to feed malnourished persons food supplements, although more than two had received them. This reflected Ifugao women's view that food supplements do not actually improve their malnourished children's nutritional status and, as will be discussed in the next chapter, reflected the inappropriateness of the food supplement program as it was operating in Ifugao during the early 1990s.

The lack of adequate nutritional education for Ifugao women and men created a situation of extreme frustration for women who attempted to provide nutritious food to all of their children, and to their malnourished children in particular. A second, and probably more common, frustration among Ifugao women was, as stated above, that even when they did have knowledge of the importance of a well-balanced diet, they could not always provide one for their families due to poverty. A third frustration for women was their children's lack of appetite to eat nutritious food, as one woman exclaimed once in exasperation: "Even if you try (to give them nutritious food), they still won't eat." The children's lack of appetite might have resulted from their undernutrition or their frequent episodes of illness. A fourth frustration Ifugao women experienced was caused by the fact that their local notion of *na-ong-ong*, which was usually exhibited as extreme or severe thinness in people, did not correspond with the physical characteristics of first degree and sometimes second degree malnutrition. These were more commonly exhibited as thinness (not severe), small size, short stature, light hair color, and thin, sparse hair; and it was commonly accompanied by frequent illnesses. Due to this inconsistency between physical characteristics of the local notion of *na-ong-ong* and the biomedical notion of moderate and marginal undernutrition, Ifugao women had difficulty understanding why their children were identified as being malnourished, when they did not appear to be so to the women.

Most Ifugao women breastfed their infants, later feeding them rice gruel, usually with sugar or rice, to supplement their breast milk. Some women, even among the lower class, supplemented their breastmilk with bottled milk, but only a few used infant formula. A common practice of other lower class Ifugao women was to mix condensed milk with water to feed their infants. Some women fed their infants evaporated or dry milk.

A high percentage of the female respondents—62 percent (thirty-four of a total of fifty-five)—held the view that pregnant and lactating women have special health needs. They perceived these needs to include: taking iron and vitamin pills; eating nutritious food; drinking extra milk; eating more food since the fetus is feeding off its mother; getting anti-tetanus injections; eating ginger and *mongo* beans and drinking vegetable "soup" (broth) to increase the production of breastmilk; eating sour fruits; getting checkups at a clinic or hospital; exercising; sleeping well; and performing *baki* to aid in the delivery of the baby. Thirty-eight percent (twenty-one), however, said either that they did not know if pregnant and lactating women have special health needs (eleven), or that pregnant and lactating women do not have special health needs (ten). Most of the women giving the last responses lived in the same barrio, so it appeared that this information was shared among women living in the same community.

Everyday Practices to Combat Malnutrition and Poverty

When I asked women if they had done anything differently upon being informed that their children were malnourished, 41 percent (fourteen) of thirty-four women reported that they did nothing different. Many added that the reason was that they had no resources to improve their families' eating patterns. Only one woman said she gave her child food supplements, despite the fact that more than one woman had actually received the food supplements. Other women (seven) said they tried to give their children more nutritious food when they could, such as vegetables, meat, fish, and eggs; and six said that they gave their children vitamin tablets. Three women brought their children to the hospital, while one performed *baki* for her malnourished child. Other food given to the children were milk (four), corn (one), and margarine and oil (one). One woman expressed in frustration that she tried to give her children more vegetables, but the children preferred to eat sugar with their rice.

Many of the women answering this question during their interview with me, however, were not considering their everyday practices that aid their families in combatting hunger and malnutrition. Since many of the poor families did not always have enough to eat, there was a strong pattern of food sharing among Ifugao people. Traditionally, rituals were a means of sharing food according to a family's resources. The wealthy were required to sponsor many more rituals than the poor and to provide much more food for the attendees to maintain their honor, respect, and prestige in the community. Although all wealthy people held some degree of social status, they were not all respected unless they fulfilled the cultural responsibilities of the wealthy. Respect in Ifugao was generated by one's actions, in the forms of generosity, kindness, and honesty, and by following cultural norms. Each family was expected to share their food resources at social gatherings they hosted (i.e., for *baki* rituals, church related events, births, funerals, etc.), at which time rice and meat were almost always served. This cultural prescription provided the poor with greater opportunities to eat meat, as a source of protein, and rice, thereby providing a degree of nutritional support for the poor. In recent years, with the penetration of Christianity and its focus on the western concept of individualism and the progress of the nuclear family, this cultural prescription had been eroded through the reduction of the number of *baki* rituals being sponsored and animals being butchered and served at social gatherings, though the practice had not been abandoned.

When Ifugao families had no more harvested rice to eat and no money to purchase rice, they usually requested to borrow rice or money to purchase rice from people who had rice or cash available to lend. First, an Ifugao person asked their relatives for a loan, who would not charge interest. If she could not locate a relative who could loan food or money, she asked a friend or someone she knew well, who would not charge interest or charge only a very small interest. Last, if there was no friend available to give a loan, she asked for a loan of food or cash from upper class families. The reliance on wealthy families for food during the "hungry time" (before harvest) each year was common historically as well (Barton 1919:3). Rice or cash borrowed from upper class families was usually repaid in kind with interest, in cash with interest (often at about 10 to 15 percent), or through future labor. It was also a common practice to buy food in stores on credit (*utang*). Since most poor families needed to borrow food or cash for food at certain times throughout the year, especially the months prior to the next harvest season, the maintenance of good relationships with the upper and middle class members of society, or patrons, was very important as a strategy to avoid hunger or starvation. The upper class practice of charging interest with loans of food or cash was viewed by the poor not as a form of "help" but rather as a business transaction benefitting the wealthy.

In addition to this practice, lower class families built networks of social interaction and assistance, especially among relatives and close friends, as a tactic of survival. This form of assistance was viewed more in terms of "helping" each other, an intensely strong social value held among Ifugao kin. Sharing food with one another was an everyday practice for both wealthy and poor families. It was considered proper hospitality to ask a visitor if they would like to eat something. Partaking of the food offered by another person displayed friendship or, at the very least, courtesy. If an Ifugao person was traveling to another barrio or municipality where their relatives or friends resided, they usually were confident they would be served food. People even entered the homes of close relatives and ate their food if they were not at home. Families usually cooked more rice at each meal than could be eaten by household members, in order to have enough rice left over to offer unexpected visitors. If a person discovered he had no rice or vegetables before a meal, it was common for him to ask a neighbor or relative if he could borrow food for that meal. Or, if a person had no vegetables to cook for her family, she commonly asked her neighbor who had a garden if she could gather some vegetables. It was also normal practice for relatives to gather sweet potatoes from each others' swidden fields, if one relative had no swidden field or their sweet potatoes had not yet matured. On numerous occasions I also observed visitors arriving at a friend's home to find a fruit tree brimming with ripened fruit, and asking the owner if they could take some fruit home with them. They were invariably given permission to do so. Ifugao people commonly used the English term "beg" to describe their asking for food from other people, when speaking English. A significant aspect of this everyday practice of food sharing was the general understanding that the sharing was reciprocal. Someday, when the person giving would be in need, he would be provided for in turn.

This system of reciprocal food sharing was only intermittent between the same families, however. Also, while financial assistance was readily given for an ill person in need of expensive biomedical treatment, long-term food sharing or financial assistance for recovery from long-term malnutrition was not practiced among families. For example, one Ifugao family had two children who were malnourished in 1992, one second degree and one third degree. Their malnutrition was known publicly in the community. That family was not given continuous food or financial assistance by relatives or friends until the children's weights became normalized. By 1993, when I visited them again, the children were still malnourished but to a lesser degree. One reason offered by an Ifugao woman for this difference in sharing practices for the ill and the malnourished was that while poor relatives and friends could offer assistance to a family with an ill member once or twice, they may not be able to offer them long-term assistance due to their own financial insecurity. Or they may not wish to give assistance if they perceived the parents to be "lazy," in their judgment, or not providing as well as they could for their family. Many felt it was the parents' responsibility to improve their children's nutritional status. Another reason may have been parents' unclear understanding of the concept of malnutrition and how to improve their children's nutritional status. Many Ifugao parents did not view malnutrition under the same rubric as a state of illness, and therefore may not have viewed the practice of family assistance for illness as applicable to malnutrition. Since so many families had at least one malnourished child within their family, each was likely concerned with their own malnourished child and thus was unable to extend their concern to the malnourished children of others.

Nevertheless, sharing food at rituals and social events, borrowing food from relatives, friends, and the upper classes, and the everyday practice of sharing food among Ifugao families were important cultural forms of social interaction providing, although to a limited degree, a safety net from starvation. Cadelina wrote that economic crises represented resource scarcities. Social networks were an adaptive response to these problems, as they redistributed resources and reduced scarcity (Cadelina 1985). While social networks in Ifugao did not actually reduce scarcity, since they could create deeper economic burdens for poor families who borrowed food or money at high rates of interest from wealthy people, they did provide a safety net from starvation. National and international health organizations had not considered the relevance and importance of these already established everyday networks of assistance in their nutrition programs. They even discouraged the practice of ritual butchering of animals which aided in the nutrition of the poor, citing the expense it brought to families sponsoring rituals, while promoting a more individualistic form of family management of resources. With changes and reductions in food sharing at rituals and social gatherings, the poorest families lost the most nutritionally, while the wealthy families gained the most by retaining their surplus resources.

Although limited, adult dependence on each other (usually among female relatives) to provide child care whenever possible was a practice that aided in the proper feeding and general care of young children while their parents were working or away. Unfortunately, this was not always possible, resulting in children caring for children or children staying home alone during the daytime. Also, poor women became involved in volunteer health work, both governmental and NGO, in an attempt to address the health care needs of their communities which had not been met by free government programs and which could not be acquired from expensive private health facilities.

Other everyday practices in which both women and men engaged to alleviate their children's malnutrition and their family's poverty included: participation in development projects and seeking aid from any source in a desperate attempt to improve their lives; participation in income generating projects, such as community cooperatives, weaving, etc.; seeking any paying labor they could locate; engaging in animal husbandry, especially new hybrid pig projects; using contraception (by a few couples) to limit the number of children they conceived and to space the timing of the births of their children; using biomedical services, Christian healing rituals, and/or *baki* to heal the malnourished and the ill; using high yielding rice varieties where they were viable in warmer climate areas; cash cropping on a small scale; cultivating bio-intensive gardening to provide vegetables for their household use; migrating to obtain employment; seeking personal education regarding agriculture and their family's health and welfare (especially health workers); and participating in food supplementation programs, with some parents using the strategy of arguing that their children were malnourished even if they were not in order to obtain supplemental food (this practice contrasted with the notion of shame related to child malnutrition).

A percentage of Ifugao people were rumored by others to have engaged in corruption of government funds as a strategy to pull their families out of the strictures of poverty. This was one of the most common forms of exploitation experienced by Ifugao people, identified by many as a regularized, almost expected (although not respected), activity of persons dealing with government or other institutional funds. Not all of those dealing with government funds were accused of participating in corrupt activities, but many were criticized regularly for being corrupt. For example, some were accused of using less funds than allocated to construct government infrastructure projects, and then pocketing the remainder or sharing it with others involved. Others were accused of never having built projects for which they received government funds. The majority of those accused of corruption were men, especially since most persons who held government political and professional positions and who contracted infrastructure projects were men. While corruption could be viewed as a strategy to escape poverty, it was also one of the most prevalent forms of exploitation identified by Ifugao people as having occurred in Ifugao, wherein funds allocated by the government to benefit a large number of Ifugao people benefitted only very few.

Regarding initiatives that would improve women's, and relatedly children's, economic, health, and nutritional status, a small minority of women began arguing for general equality between men and women, equal pay for women and men in agricultural and other labor, equal sharing of household and child care duties with men, and the election of women into political office. Some of these activities usually were initiated in Ifugao by members of women's groups from nearby urban areas, female government workers, international development agents, and NGO women's and health organizations operating in Ifugao. By the early 1990s, a minority of Ifugao women had slowly begun to argue for these changes themselves.

Regarding political economy and struggles related to the ethnic identity of Ifugao people, there were political divisions among Ifugao people, and among people within the Cordillera mountain region generally, about the tactics and strategies that should be undertaken to achieve good nutrition among the people of the region, to reduce poverty, and to maintain the rights of "indigenous people" of the region. Most Ifugao people, of all social classes, took a position of full engagement in national policy and international development activities. Others, mostly lower class persons, took a more leftist or progressive political stance, such as those organizing and arguing for genuine regional autonomy, demilitarization of the Cordillera region, and respect of ancestral land rights. A smaller number, again mostly lower class members, committed themselves to the revolutionary movement as members of the NPA in an attempt to create social change that would alter the Philippine political system and social structure from a capitalist to a communist system. Many changed their political orientation and activities as political and social circumstances and their personal lives changed, such as revolutionaries who accepted government amnesty and rehabilitation programs under Presidents Aquino and Ramos, and then returned to live openly within the Philippine government system.

These variable tactics and strategies undertaken by Ifugao people in an attempt to improve their lives demonstrated the variable, dynamic, and always contested quality of the everyday lives and practices of Ifugao people. It also depicted some of the social class tensions played out in Ifugao between members of the upper and middle classes, on the one hand, and some members of the lower class, on the other, who struggled for greater economic and political equality and respect of their human rights.

The importation of the western biomedical concept of malnutrition aided in the identification of children who had nutritional deficiencies. Yet, it also led to both confusion and frustration on the part of Ifugao women who did not always clearly understand the biomedical concept of "malnourished" or how they were to help their malnourished children. Ifugao parents, especially women, sometimes felt blamed for their children's poor nutritional status. Many women found that they were not able to raise their children's nutritional status, despite the fact that they were trying their best, in the face of numerous impediments such as limitations on their cultural understanding of the biomedical concept of "malnutrition"; financial, employment, and educational limitations; and women's heavy workloads. There were some cases of malnourished children who recovered and acquired a normal weight, in spite of these limitations. But the nutritional status of most children, as reported by a public health nurse and other health workers, usually moved back and forth from malnourished to well nourished, or among different degrees of malnutrition.

Malnutrition in Ifugao was a complex problem of social class, gender, religious, ethnic, and international relations. Yet many Ifugao women internalized the cultural construct of women being primarily responsible for child care and the health and nutrition of their children. This was reinforced through biomedical and development practices, as briefly described here and explored more extensively in the next chapter. Women's low social position in significant areas of their lives (particularly economic and domestic) had an influence on their children's poor nutritional status. Their social class level and the problems they experienced related to their ethnicity interacted with their gender position to create specific nutritional problems for families of differing social class levels.

Notes

1. Martin 1994, 1987; and Scheper-Hughes and Lock 1986.
2. Foucault 1994; Martin 1994, 1987; Lock and Scheper-Hughes 1990; Rhodes 1990; and Scheper-Hughes and Lock 1987, 1986.
3. Foucault 1994 and Rhodes 1990.
4. Waitzkin 1983; Frankenberg 1980; and Taussig 1978.
5. Baer and Singer 1995; Morsy 1990, 1979; Rhodes 1990; Navarro 1986, 1985; and Virchow, cited in Waitzkin 1981.

6. Rhodes 1990; Martin 1987; Young 1982; and Taussig 1980.

7. See Food Tables at the end of this chapter: Table 1 lists the most commonly eaten foods in Ifugao; Table 2 lists other available food in Ifugao, eaten less often by the poor in Ifugao; and Table 3 lists food supplements irregularly offered by government and private organizations to second and third degree malnourished children under six years old and pregnant women in Ifugao during the early 1990s.

8. See Weismantel 1988; Kahn 1986; Harris 1985; Laderman 1981; Lindenbaum 1977; Vogt 1976; Douglas 1966; Leach 1964; and Levi-Strauss 1964.

9. See Scheper-Hughes and Lock 1987:18-19; Turner 1984; and Douglas 1970.

10. Protein energy malnutrition is defined biomedically as a lack of adequate amounts of proteins, nutrients, and calories, and is characterized by underweight status, muscle wasting, and less fatty tissues under the skin.

11. In analyzing children's weight-for-age in 1992, BNSs used the 1992 FNRI-PPS (Food and Nutrition Research Institute-Philippine Pediatric Society) Anthropometric Tables and Charts for Filipino Children, prepared by Rodolfo F. Florentino, M.D., Ph.D., Perla Santos-Ocampo, M.D., Josefina A. Magbitang, M.S.P.H., Teresa S. Mendoza, M.S.P.H., Emilie G. Flores, M.D., M.P.H., and Bernadette J. Madrid, M.D. The anthropometric tables and charts were published in cooperation with Nestle Philippines, Inc. These were the most current anthropometric standards for Filipino children, distributed to local government hospitals and Rural Health Units in 1992. They were based on data collected in 1985 in a nationwide survey among more than 23,660 clinically and physically healthy Filipino children (Florentino et al. 1992:2).

12. The charts used by health workers in analyzing Filipino children's nutritional status were organized by arranging weights and heights in percentile groups, representing the positional values of a given child compared to the reference population of healthy Filipino children of the representative sample. The charts included -3D (standard deviations), 5th, 10th, 25th, 50th, 75th, 90th, and 95th percentiles and +3D. Children whose weights or heights fell below -3D were considered to be severely underweight or underheight, or third degree malnourished. The 25th percentile was the suggested cut-off point for marginally underweight or underheight, or first degree malnourished. Still, children whose weights or heights fell between the 5th and 95th percentile values were considered to have normal weights and heights. Those children whose weights fell above the 95th percentile are considered to be overweight or tall.

13. Philippine government statistics on malnutrition did not include first degree malnutrition. The numbers of malnourished children reported in their statistics reflected only second and third degree malnutrition among children. This was done because, according to one high level professional working in a government office affiliated with the FNRI, while first degree malnutrition was considered to be a borderline, or marginal form of malnutrition, it was still considered to be a "normal" nutritional status. However, this became problematic for and confusing to Ifugao parents of first degree or marginally malnourished children who were told by health workers that their children were "malnourished," hence, not having a normal nutritional status. I will expand on this issue in greater depth in the following chapter.

14. Goiter is the enlargement of the thyroid gland due to absence or lack of sufficient iodine intake.

15. The malnutrition rates for Ifugao that I am using here are meant primarily to give the reader an indication of the character and extent of malnutrition in Ifugao. I maintain no strict adherence to these figures.

16. This figure was obtained from the municipal government RHU. It was a survey, taken by a BNS, of all children zero to six years old for the first quarter (January to March) of 1992 in that barrio, as part of "Operation Timbang," the government health department's nutrition/weighing surveillance program.

17. This figure was obtained from the same RHU records, stemming from charts described in endnote three, also for the first quarter of 1992.

18. This figure was also obtained from the local RHU's records, also for the first quarter of 1992.

19. Since I chose households based on my knowledge of some of the previous nutritional statuses of the children under six years old, my anthropometric measures cannot be used to represent rates of malnutrition within the three barrios, or within Ifugao Province as a whole. They can be used, nevertheless, to better understand the life circumstances of those families in my sample whose children were malnourished, and of those whose children had normal weights.

20. My sample included 16 percent female-headed households of all households in my sample, which was close to the Ifugao Province percentage of 15 percent of all households in the province being female-headed (National Statistics Office, Republic of the Philippines 1990:41).

21. Although this ratio was not exactly equal to the actual social class ratio among the entire Ifugao population, it was a close approximation. My sample ratio for social class was 8 percent upper class, 11 percent middle class, and 81 percent lower class. The Ifugao population social class ratio from a 1990 census report of the 1988 Ifugao population was approximately 4 percent upper class, 21 percent middle class, and 75 percent lower class (National Statistics Office, Republic of the Philippines 1990:60). A UNICEF document set the number of Ifugao families with incomes below the poverty line in 1988 to be 74.58 percent (1988 FIES; UNICEF 1992a:2).

22. More explicitly, seven women and nine men had no formal education at all; fifteen women and eleven men had attended some elementary school, while seventeen women and ten men had completed elementary school; six women and seven men had attended some high school, while eight women and five men had completed high school; and five women and five men had attended some college, while five women and six men had completed college.

23. One hectare is equivalent to 2.47 acres.

24. In analyzing children's weights and heights that I collected, I used the FNRI-PPS Anthropometric Tables and Charts for Filipino Children, 1992. (See endnote 11).

25. These were the only weight reports I could acquire for adults, since there were no regular weighings of adults in Ifugao by any health organization. To analyze the weights and heights of adults that I collected, I used the most current Weight-for-Height for Filipinos (25-65 Years) chart, published by the Biomedical Nutrition Division, of the Philippine Food and Nutrition Research Institute, Department of Science and Technology, Manila. For pregnant adult women, I used the most current Weight-for-Height Table at Given Weeks/Months of Pregnancy Chart, also published by the Biomedical Nutrition Division, of the Philippine Food and Nutrition Research Institute, Department of Science and Technology, Manila, May 1988.

26. Among fifteen underweight women, one was severely anemic, five were elderly, four were underweight for only one of three weighings (including two of the elderly women), and one upper class woman was consistently underweight for her height.

27. Vitamin C can aid in the absorption of iron into the body.

28. See chapter five for more details about the concept of *na-ong-ong*.

29. Many women were more familiar with the term "malnourished" than the term "malnutrition," most likely because they had heard the phrase "malnourished children" or were told that their "child is malnourished" more often than the term "malnutrition."

30. Many women offered more than one response.

31. Another woman interviewed had *baki* previously performed for her own malnour- ished child, and another woman interviewed had witnessed *baki* performed for a malnourished child.

32. Some Ifugao women had been instructed by biomedical personnel that corn had more nutrients than rice or sweet potatoes.

TABLE 6.1 Most Commonly Eaten Food in Ifugao[a]

Carbohydrates	Vegetables	Fruit	Proteins	Beverages	Condiments
Camoting kahoy	Ampalaya	Banana	Breastmilk	Beer	Honey
(tuber)	Avocado	Calamansi (citrus)	Brown peas	Coffee with sugar	Patis (salted fish
Corn	Cabbage	Coconut	Chicken	Gin	sauce)
Gabi roots	Cucumber	Guava	Eggs	Rice wine	Pepper
Potatoes	Gabi leaves	Mango	Insects	Soft drinks (soda)	Refined sugar
Rice	Garlic	Papaya	Legumes	Water	Salt
Rice cakes	Ginger	Pomelo (grapefruit)	Mung beans		Soy sauce
Sugar	Eggplant	Rattan fruit (sour	Pork		Sugar cane
Sweet potato	Okra	fruit)	Salted dried fish		Tamarind
	Onions	Star apple	Sardines		Vinegar
	Pechay	Wild berries	Shell fish		
	Sayote		Small fish		
	Sayote leaves		Soy beans		
	Squash		Tilapia (fish)		
	String beans				
	Sweet potato leaves				
	Tomatoes				
	Watercress				
	Wild vegetables				
	Wombok				

[a]Although the food, beverages, and condiments listed above were "commonly" eaten by most Ifugao people of all social classes, they were not always seasonably available, nor were they all available to all Ifugao people. It depended on their access to land, a cash income, and a market; their health status; and the character of the environment in which they lived. The climate and land area varied among different Ifugao barrios; as a result, not all of the foods listed could be cultivated in all Ifugao barrios.

TABLE 6.2 A Sample of Other Available Food in Ifugao, Eaten Less Often by the Poor

Carbohydrates	Fruit	Proteins	Beverages	Condiments	Snacks
Bread	Jackfruit	Bangus (fish)	Milk	*Bago-ong* (fish paste)	Baked desserts
Lugao (rice gruel)	Mandarin oranges	Beef	Milo (sweetened chocolate powder)	Coconut milk	Cakes
Pancakes	Pineapple	Canned fish	with milk	Jelly	Candy
Pancit noodles	Santol	Processed cheese	Soft drinks (soda)	Monosodium gluta-mate (MSG)	Chips
Spaghetti		Corned beef	Sweetened juice		Cookies
		Dog			Crackers
		Duck			Ice cream
		Eel			Sweet breads
		Goat			
		Infant formula			
		Milk			
		Peanut butter			
		Peanuts			
		Smoked fish			
		Toyo (fish)			
		Turkey			
		Water buffalo			

TABLE 6.3 Food Supplements Offered by Government and Private Organizations on an Irregular Basis During 1992 to Second and Third Degree Malnourished Children Under Six Years Old, and to Pregnant Women

Most Commonly Offered	Offered Less Regularly
Bulgar	Dried fish
Cornmeal	Dried milk
Green peas	Oil

7

Maintaining Inequality

Joint government and international development programs (UNICEF and EC) operating in Ifugao neglected to address seriously large-scale and local social structural inequalities and cultural relations influencing and operating in the communities in which they maintained their operations. These inequalities and cultural relations included socioeconomic and gender relations, food sharing ideologies and practices, and ideologies of assistance, each of which significantly influenced the incidence of hunger in Ifugao. The neglect of international development programs to address unequal social relations helped to maintain the inequalities. Many Ifugao people with whom I spoke perceived the UNICEF program to be ineffective in establishing substantial changes in Ifugao people's lives by 1993, approximately five years after the program had first been implemented in the province.

Neglecting Existing Social Inequality

Human relations, Michael Taussig argued, are embodied in signs and symptoms of disease. The biomedical designation of illness and disease (including malnutrition) as objective "things" of the body, however, conceals the social relations behind them (Taussig 1980). While trying to achieve good health for Filipino people, the biomedical Philippine government health program constructed the problem of malnutrition as primarily an objective problem of the individual, the family (i.e., a result of family poverty, lack of family vegetable gardens, etc.), and of the community (i.e., in terms of poor sanitation, lack of infrastructure, etc.). This construction mystified the social structural relations operating to bring about the problems of widespread poverty and unequal access to food resources among Ifugao and other Filipino people.

In Ifugao, malnutrition was discussed by most Philippine government health personnel as a problem of the individual. In other words, on a day-to-day basis, malnourished Ifugao people were viewed and treated by personnel of the government's biomedical program as individuals who had an objective medical problem—malnutrition. It was to be managed and, it was hoped, alleviated through programs for individuals and families, such as regular weighing surveillance of individuals, food supplementation, education primarily for women in their role of "mother," and other project-focused programs for families. Also, despite the apparent neutrality of development discourse, a gender bias was evident. In certain components of the joint UNICEF/Philippine government health and nutrition program—as part of the joint UNICEF/Philippine government ABCSD program or the Ifugao Child Survival and Women Development Programme—operating in Ifugao, women were held primarily responsible for the nutritional needs of their family members.

It should be noted that in discussing these concerns regarding international development and national programs, my criticisms are not directed against individual health or development employees on the international, national, or local level. Instead, they are directed at structural problems within development models, which at times exhibit biases and foster approaches to planned community change that do not consider the needs of specific local groups within larger populations, such as women (Justice 1986).

In 1992, family poverty was often identified as a primary cause of malnutrition by international development and Ifugao biomedical personnel, as well as by some Ifugao people themselves. However, the identification of family poverty by biomedical and other government and international development personnel rarely extended beyond the objective fact of poverty. The government and international development personnel did not provide an analysis or discussion of the social causes of poverty, nor were they expected to so in their daily work. Such an analysis might have included a discussion of unequal social class relations, imbalanced international lending and trade relations between the Philippines and industrialized countries, or the lack of implementation of a genuine agrarian reform program.

Instead, poverty was presented by the program personnel as an objective, ahistorical fact. While there was no discussion of how widespread poverty developed historically in the Philippines, government and international development personnel asserted that families could escape poverty through hard work and participation in income generating and other projects. The problem of poverty and its solution had been depoliticized by the international development programs; actions which potentially could lead toward social structural change as one part of a solution to poverty were submerged under everyday project oriented development activities (Green 1989). Unfortunately, as an Ifugao woman said, despite many years of development agents and researchers working in Ifugao, the majority of the people's socioeconomic status had essentially remained the same by 1993, that is, below the poverty level. In a discussion I had with another Ifugao woman, who was a health volunteer, I commented that there were many development programs operating in her barrio (there were at least six operating there simultaneously). She replied, "Yes, there are many government and non-government agencies working here, but there is no change."

By 1993 the National Nutrition Council was beginning to acknowledge within its publications that macro-level economic factors had an impact on nutrition (National Nutrition Council 1993:73-83). Also, a UNICEF report published in 1987 and 1988, entitled "Adjustment With a Human Face," documented that increases in malnutrition of children, deterioration in health services, and decline in educational services and household income in the Philippines were direct results of structural "adjustment programs" of the IMF and World Bank (Hildebrand 1991:12). Despite these statements, the joint UNICEF/Philippine government development program operating within Ifugao in 1992–1993 had no component which addressed the relationship between structural adjustment programs and increasing malnutrition with the Ifugao people who participated in their program. Instead, women were encouraged to attend "Mothers' Classes," parents were encouraged to plant "backyard gardens," and children's growth was monitored. These programs were presented as some of the primary solutions to their children's and their own malnutrition.

The UNICEF/Philippine government program did not train health professionals to discuss with Ifugao people the historical, social development of poverty and malnutrition in the Philippines. Instead, working from a biomedical model of primary health care, families were instructed by UNICEF/Philippine government program health professionals that the primary solution to their poverty and malnutrition was one which was depoliticized. The 1992 UNICEF/Philippine government plan for Ifugao specified: "Nutrition activities will focus on community-based growth monitoring, iodine and iron deficiency disease control, family food gardening and income generating projects" (UNICEF 1992b:18). Other activities included in the broader UNICEF/Philippine government Child Survival and Maternal Care program included "the expanded programme of immunization, (health care for children) under-six clinics, growth monitoring, advocacy for breastfeeding, pre- and post-natal care, food production, water and sanitation, and livelihood" (UNICEF 1992b:14). The UNICEF/Philippine government program in Ifugao also included child minding centers; infrastructure development, especially water system projects; education services through mobile teaching, including literacy programs for women; and the creation of women's organizations (UNICEF 1992a).

Ifugao people noticed that one problem faced by UNICEF personnel in the implementation of a comprehensive approach to health care at the community level was that in many barrios only one or two elements of the planned comprehensive program had been established (though, as noted earlier, a few barrios were almost overwhelmed with numerous different development projects working simultaneously in their community). Many people perceived UNICEF to focus primarily on infrastructure projects, such as installing water systems and toilets. This problem may have been due to limitations of funding and personnel, which made the program less comprehensive than intended within individual communities. Another perception held by numerous Ifugao people, including volunteer health workers, was that "UNICEF is not as successful in Ifugao as they had planned because the program funding was channeled through Philippine government agencies." Health workers heard this procedure did not work well, and that, because of this, UNICEF began to channel money and programs through NGOs instead. Each of these perceptions led people to have different views of the UNICEF program, which further complicated the intended development process.

Regarding the approach of the development programs, the UNICEF/Philippine government plan did discuss "inequity among income groups and unequal access to service delivery" among the "Overall Structural and Social Problems" faced by Ifugao people (UNICEF 1992b:3), as well as "insurgency problems" (UNICEF/ Ifugao ABCSD Programme 1990:3). But the program's personnel did not analyze, with the Ifugao people with whom they were working, why those problems existed. Nor did the plan relate the problems to political and economic linkages between the Ifugao community, the state, and other nations. UNICEF literature on the "The Situation of Children and Women in the Philippines" and in the Ifugao Child Survival and Women Development Programme plan and other UNICEF documents, did acknowledge repeatedly that poverty was a primary cause of malnutrition, as well as of the numerous other problems faced by women and children in the Philippines generally and in Ifugao specifically (UNICEF 1990a; 1990b). Yet, again, the UNICEF texts did not analyze the historical social, political, cultural, and economic reasons for poverty or malnutrition. Both the texts and the personnel neglected to discuss the significant influence of social, political, and economic relations on the nutritional status of Filipino people. This reflected not so much disregard of these issues by health personnel or the government health system, but rather a biomedical approach to health care and development models that did not adequately address social, cultural, and political forces influencing health, specifically nutrition. It was also a result of political conditions within the Philippines that led to the labeling of such discussions as subversive.

Exemplifying this practice in Ifugao were annual National Nutrition Day programs and seminars, which I attended in 1992 and 1993, that were a part of the Philippine Department of Health's July National Nutrition Month's activities. At one of these nutrition programs, local state agency professionals provided education seminars for volunteer health workers. Approximately thirty-five female and two male community volunteer health workers attended the seminar. It included instruction on diet and nutrition; agricultural techniques for improved food production; leadership training; "moral values on nutrition"; the plans of the National Government under President Ramos, specifically the "Philippines 2000" plan for national economic development; and instruction on Christian values. Land reform was briefly mentioned during the discussion of the National Government plans, as being part of the government's current program. Although the government professionals provided admirable and useful instruction on these topics, most of the instruction and discussion focused on personal, familial, and community responsibility for the health and nutrition of the volunteer health workers' families and communities. The assumption was that better nutrition would be attained through education and improved and increased agricultural production. This focus was not provided because of a bias on the part of the individual instructors. Instead, it was a result of their having been trained by a biomedically oriented health program that emphasized apolitical solutions to malnutrition among local people.

An article printed in a local UNICEF/Philippine government newsletter, produced and circulated within Ifugao, depicted a biomedical and community level approach to alleviating malnutrition. The article did acknowledge the problems of poverty and shortage of farming land as influencing malnutrition by stating:

> Malnutrition cannot be cured simply by medicine or a food supplement. It is a far more intractable condition, tied to the many deprivations connected to poverty which families in the developing world are struggling to shake off: ignorance, shortage of farming land, lack of economic opportunity, vulnerability to disease, absence of regular health check-ups, unclean water and unsanitary conditions (Mountain Movers 1992).

Despite this awareness, the article also depicted the UNICEF/Philippine government emphasis on implementing individual, family, and community projects to achieve its goals to "halve the malnutrition rate by the year 2000, to save 100 million children from malnourishment during the decade." Another article in the same UNICEF/Philippine government newsletter, entitled "BIG (Bio-intensive Gardening): A Solution to Malnutrition," also promoted this limited approach (Bango 1992:8).

Gender and International/National Development Programs

People's concern for women's position in the international development process, involving conceptions of their status and roles in societies, emerged during the 1960s. Since at least the 1970s, international development programs have engaged in activities which explicitly attempt to raise the social status of women in Third World societies. During this process, gender ideologies have been introduced by western international development agents, primarily promoting women's equality with men. In Ifugao, international development agents made a conscious attempt to raise Ifugao women's gender status in the early 1990s. For example, a UNICEF program goal in Ifugao was to "ensure the survival and enhance the total development of Ifugao children and women" (UNICEF 1992a). Unfortunately, these projects maintained local gendered power relations which inhibited women from attaining prestige or power. International development institutions operating in Ifugao, specifically the joint UNICEF/Philippine government program and an EC development program, participated in the process of the social construction of Ifugao women's social roles and value.

As noted earlier, scholars, feminist organizations, and international development organizations have proposed a relationship between women's lesser prestige and power at the family and community levels, and women and their children's poor nutritional and health status (Senauer 1990; Schoepf 1987; Vaughan 1987). Some scholars have further proposed that social programs geared toward the raising of women's social position (such as women engaging in work programs [i.e., income generating projects or cooperatives] or programs providing child care) would enhance the health and nutritional well-being of both women and their children (Women Development and Technology, Inc. 1992; UNICEF 1993). This position sparked the recent generation of "women in development" and other programs oriented toward the enhancement of women's social position with the objective of alleviating malnutrition and other health problems of women and children.

But in Ifugao, even with the inclusion of women in national and international development programs, the international development and government personnel's practices on the local level effected the maintenance rather than the enhancement of Ifugao women's subordination to men. This resulted mainly because the larger development institutions operating in the early 1990s (UNICEF and the EC) neglected to grapple with the multiple power relationships operating within Ifugao. These included gendered social practices that disadvantaged women, social class relations, and state and military exertion of power, each forms of power relations that Ifugao people themselves identified as being problematic. As earlier discussed, power held by individuals within Ifugao society was derived mainly from wealth, ownership of irrigated rice fields, the ability to garner support and a following of community members, political office holding, and control over private or public armies. Power could also be gained through formal education, strong oratory skills, travel, experience in the wider community, spiritual potency and knowledge, male gender position, and seniority based on age. Many of these positions and practices culturally associated with power and prestige in Ifugao have been found in other Southeast Asian societies (Tsing 1993; Atkinson and Errington 1990).

In regard to the social construction of gender roles, the UNICEF/Philippine government development program constructed women primarily in the role of "mother." According to a 1992 UNICEF/Philippine government "Ifugao Provincial Plan Of Operations" for the "Ifugao Child Survival and Women Development Programme" one of the "General Objectives" was "to enhance the capacity of Ifugao women to participate in family and community activities for child survival and development and for socio-economic development of their communities" (UNICEF 1992b:8). Under the subheading, "Specific problems confronting Ifugao women," the plan argued:

> On the Ifugao women, the effects of structural and social problems are manifested in low female literacy rate, high maternal mortality rate and heavy family burden that

is lodged in Ifugao mothers. The female literacy rate of 53.76 percent in 1980 is well below the national average of 83.0 percent. The low appreciation on pre-and-post natal care is due to the illiteracy of women alongside cultural practices that are risk factors in maternal deliveries. Together with iron deficiency anemia and goiter, these may explain the high maternal mortality rate of 1.39 deaths per 1,000 livebirths. The low status of women in Ifugao culture constrains the Ifugao woman to see her role in the family and community. In addition to their motherly responsibilities, they are usually tied down to such farming activities as weeding, caring of farm animals and harvesting. (UNICEF 1992b:7)

In this discourse, written mainly by professional Ifugao government and UNICEF/Philippine government employees, women were perceived to have low social status. This was acknowledged as an important factor contributing to the poor health and nutrition of both Ifugao women and their children. Despite this perception and the goal of raising women's social status, clearly expressed in this document and in other UNICEF/Philippine government programs, women were still portrayed by the UNICEF/Philippine government personnel primarily in the role of "mother," despite the numerous roles Ifugao women played in their daily lives. This construction was also displayed in a 1990 UNICEF/Philippine government document on the "Situation of Women and Children in the Philippines," circulated in Ifugao government offices in 1992. Of fourteen drawings contained in the document, ten depicted women in the role of mother—pregnant, or holding or positioned near a child—while only four depicted women without children. None of the pictures portrayed women engaged in labor outside of the home. Nor did the documents depict men caring for children, which may have supported Ifugao men's practice of caring for their children (UNICEF 1990b).

This kind of document represented women in a very limited manner, neglecting an Ifugao cultural ideal of women occupying many social positions during their lifetimes. Portraying women in a variety of roles would not in itself provide women with greater prestige or power, as depicted by Ifugao women's low agricultural pay rates. Yet, it may have provided women with a representation of a wider range of choices for themselves, and a richer, more varied life experience. The representation of women as primarily providers of child care continued the existing ideology in Ifugao culture, thereby perpetuating a gendered practice that diminished women's opportunities to acquire prestige or power, such as by traveling or becoming community leaders.

In another case, one Ifugao woman said that when she was told by RHU personnel that her child, after being weighed, was malnourished, the RHU personnel suggested she attend a "Mothers' Class." No suggestion was made to her that her husband attend as well. The majority of health classes provided by the Philippine government were called "Mothers' Classes," thereby subtly discouraging males from joining the sessions. This title evoked the message that health and child care were primarily the responsibility of women, and it disregarded the traditional Ifugao practice of men significantly contributing to child care. That this view was held by many Ifugao people was exemplified by the perspective of a thirty-year-old man, who said he had seen some children die of malnutrition. He observed a neighbor's child die soon after the child was diagnosed as malnourished by the local RHU midwife. He felt that the cause of child malnutrition and associated child death was that "many mothers did not know how to feed their children." He made no mention of fathers' role in ensuring good health and nutrition of children.

The UNICEF/Philippine government newsletter, produced and circulated within Ifugao, also focused on women's role as mother and as the primary provider of health care within the family and community in discussing approaches to alleviating malnutrition. For example, one paragraph in the newsletter read:

> To achieve this target [halving the malnutrition rate by the year 2000] emphasis is being placed on the prolongation of breastfeeding, and adequate diet including breastfeeding, and improved health-care practices, including the provision of clean water, better sanitation and increased access to medical treatment. . . . The key is to diagnose malnutrition problems early and help mothers reverse them through action programmes undertaken by individual communities (Mountain Movers 1992:5).

Women, as "mothers," were expected to take on primary responsibility for their children's poor nutritional status. Also, the programs focused on small, local communities. No mention was made of attempting to change political and economic conditions, nor of encouraging men to be responsible for achieving improved nutritional status of their children. The ideology of women being primarily responsible for child and health care within their families and communities was reinforced by the UNICEF program's practices, despite their intention to the contrary.

In contrast, Ifugao women's discourse depicted how Ifugao women viewed themselves as performing multiple significant roles. Ifugao women viewed their roles as workers outside of their homes as being of primary importance to themselves and their families. A development model that constructed women primarily as "mothers" was inappropriate for Ifugao women, particularly in light of how Ifugao women conceived of their own lives and the importance they attributed to their multiple roles in society.

As I discussed briefly in the last chapter, women were often indirectly blamed for their children's malnutrition and poor health. For example, a 1987 report on the situation of women and children in the Philippines stated, "To a large extent, the quality of life of the Filipino child is influenced by his mother's conditions through pregnancy and birth, her education and child-rearing practice" (UNICEF 1987:81). Likewise, in a 1989 UNICEF/Philippine government sponsored report on a survey of "High Risk Families" (families "at high risk" or "at risk" for malnutrition among their family members), the Masterlist of High Risk and at Risk Families: Province of Ifugao, distributed to local government hospitals and clinics in Ifugao, described conditions for high risk for malnutrition as being: if the families already had second and or third degree malnourished preschool children, plus two of the following—a chronic illness in the family; an illiterate mother; a working mother; and underemployed parents (UNICEF 1991:17).[1]

While the father was assumed to be included in the categories "underemployed parents" and "chronic illness," and was thereby viewed as having some influence on the nutritional status of household members, women's influence as "mother" on the nutritional status of their children was stressed. This view not only de-emphasized the father's role in influencing the nutritional status of the family members, thereby placing greater responsibility—and blame—on "mothers" for their children's nutritional status, it also disregarded political, economic, and cultural influences on nutritional status. This model of risk for malnutrition, which focused on the family—and primarily on women as "mothers"—tended to assign blame on the individual (especially women) and the family for malnutrition, or at the very least identified these as the targets of intervention while ignoring other cultural and social factors which influenced malnutrition. It also stigmatized women for working ("working mothers"), thereby countering the high Ifugao cultural value placed on women working outside of the home (such as the woman in Chapter 6 who was chastised by a BNS for working as a sander of wood carvings rather than caring for her children). It additionally ignored the fact that the majority of Ifugao women needed to work regularly outside of the home to survive. And it created a new cultural value for women, that of staying at home to mother their children's nutritional and health needs, thereby ignoring their own needs and personal development that may have differed from this value. In this model of risk assessment, fathers were not expected to stop working outside of their homes. This model placed poverty stricken women in a double bind. While they were told that their work outside of the home had a detrimental effect on their children's nutrition, the loss of women's income for the family, primarily in the form of food, also would have a detrimental effect on their children's nutrition.

This case presented an example of a modern international health program which sought the advancement of women's social position, yet simultaneously restricted women's potential and confused and created anxiety for women by sending them mixed messages. The program model of risk stressed women's role as mother over their role as worker outside of the home, and it further stressed their greater responsibility than men to meet the nutritional needs of their children. Women's self-esteem may have been lowered rather than enhanced by this model of risk, as it created confusion among women, a sense of being at fault for their children's malnutrition, and a feeling of being trapped in a no-win situation in regard to how to best help their malnourished children.

Considering the substantial proportion of men sharing some health and nutrition responsibilities with their wives, and participating in child care intermittently, government and international development agencies' focus only on women for nutrition education in "Mothers' Classes" and their identification of "illiterate mothers" as placing their families at high risk for malnutrition appeared to be inappropriate in Ifugao.[2] I spoke with an Ifugao government social worker and a midwife who said that men should also be trained in maternal health and child care since these were men's responsibilities as well as women's.

It would seem that if development agencies continue to emphasize nutrition education, there should be greater consideration given to the father's role in the nutrition and health of their children in each particular culture and society in which the programs are operating. There should also be greater encouragement and inclusion of men in child and health care programs (for example, renaming "Mothers' Classes"), education of both fathers and mothers in health and child care matters, and elimination of an ideology purporting that only a mother's illiteracy and work outside of the home place children at risk for malnutrition.

UNICEF is a program focusing on women in the maternal role, as the program attempts to aid children. Other United Nations programs may take a more balanced perspective of women's lives, such as the United Nations Development Fund for Women (UNIFEM) and the United Nations Educational, Scientific, and Cultural Organization (UNESCO). However, in looking at the possible influences of the program on gender ideology, the UNICEF/Philippine government program of the late 1980s and early 1990s operating in Ifugao had the unintended effect of emphasizing the maternal role for women while discouraging men from being active participants in child care. At the same time, however, the UNICEF/ Philippine government program in Ifugao did have as one of its stated goals the raising of women's social status, which development agents hoped would lead to an improved health and nutritional status for women and children.

As previously argued, international development program personnel reinforced existing unequal gender relations. For example, both UNICEF and Philippine government literature acknowledged the negative impact on women's social status of the traditional practice of paying women less than men for labor (UNICEF 1990b:62; National Commission on the Role of Filipino Women 1989:10). However, the UNICEF/Philippine government program and other development programs neglected to address seriously this problem with Ifugao women and men.

Personnel of another international development program operating in Ifugao, the EC's CECAP, did not seriously consider women's low pay rates during a 1992 community development meeting. This meeting was intended to evoke the problems community members faced. When the issue of women's and men's differential pay rates for agricultural work was raised by an Ifugao man during this meeting, a heated discussion ensued for approximately one hour. Some women and men advocated equal pay, while others advocated the retention of the traditional differential pay system. Much later in the meeting, when the problem of women's low pay rate was brought up again, the CECAP development agent facilitating the meeting, who was a Filipino man of another ethnicity, stated:

> We have to leave this problem of women's low pay, because we cannot do this in three years [the projected time period of the EC program's operation in Ifugao]. . . .

We only have to leave out women's wage increase; leave this to another group who will advocate for wage increases for women of the Cordillera.

Although this meeting was explicitly intended to evoke the problems and concerns of the people residing in the barrio and later develop solutions to resolve them, the one concern which may have had a significant impact on women's lives was not fully addressed or resolved.

It is not only through the efforts of international development institutions that social changes which may benefit women can be achieved. Still, in this case the development agent could have better facilitated the pay rate problem set before him by some Ifugao women and men, since it was a stated goal of the development organization to enhance Ifugao women's social and economic status. The development agents in Ifugao often neglected to analyze and grapple with existing power relations, including those embedded in gender relations and practices operating at the local level, despite their intention to do so. A project orientation of development models and a decontextualization of community problems led to this practice.

In lieu of addressing women's low pay rates in Ifugao, the UNICEF/Philippine government and the EC programs focused mainly on income generating projects and women's cooperatives to raise women's incomes. Many participants in this program were female farmers. With this international development practice, women were placed in the position of having to take on even more work to raise their incomes; alternatively, the development agents could have attempted to raise women's incomes by altering the system of differential pay scales for male and female agricultural labor. Women's participation in development programs that added additional work to their already heavy workloads was identified in one 1993 UNICEF report as a problem inhibiting some women's participation in income generating activities (UNICEF 1993:189). The UNICEF report cited an earlier study by Cristina Montiel and Mary Racelis Hollnsteiner which found that one of the causes of Filipino women's limited participation in labor organizations was that women's family responsibilities and domestic tasks occupied so much of their time that they had little time left for participation in other activities (Hollnsteiner and Monteil 1976, cited in UNICEF 1993:189). Also, as discussed earlier, numerous Ifugao women expressed to me their feelings of being overburdened by their work inside and outside of their homes. With the UNICEF and EC programs' focus on raising women's incomes by increasing their work load through income generating projects, the local gendered power relations represented by differential agricultural pay rates between the sexes was maintained. This practice sustained traditional, and sometimes traditional western, ideologies of men legitimately earning a higher pay than women for comparable labor and of husbands being the main "bread winners" of a family.

Although the discourse of the UNICEF and Philippine government documents acknowledged the need to raise the status and the pay rates of women in low paying work, their programs did not always do so in practice. This was exemplified by the UNICEF/Philippine government sponsored Child Minding Centers program. The UNICEF/Philippine government plan specified that the UNICEF/Philippine government nutrition activities would include Child Minding Centers (CMCs) and Day Care Centers, since young children often remained alone in their homes during the day while both parents worked outside of the home. The problem of children caring for children while both parents worked was cited numerous times by both health workers and Ifugao women as one cause of child malnutrition in Ifugao. With good intentions, the UNICEF/Philippine government program instituted CMCs that children could attend during the daytime while their parents were occupied with other matters. Ifugao women did not entirely benefit from the program, however.

In practice, only women were sought to fill the positions of CMC custodians, reinforcing the Ifugao, and again sometimes traditional western, naturalization of women as the best providers of child care. Although at least two men attempted to work as CMC custodians, one female government social worker told me that men were discouraged from working in this job since, in her view, women are "naturally" better providers of child care. In fact, this social worker said that one man had applied for the position but was discouraged from taking it by the program organizers in the area in which he applied. The ideology of women being better child care providers than men was viewed as a biological fact by some development and government personnel, rather than a cultural construction.

While the female custodians were expected to work forty hours each week, they were designated by the joint UNICEF/Philippine government program as being volunteers and were only paid an "honorarium" by the program.[3] They were paid 700 pesos per month, approximately thirty-five pesos per day, at a time when the daily minimum wage was approximately eighty-five pesos per day in the Ifugao region. After a center became accredited, which could take up to one year or more, a custodian could be paid more money. A Philippine municipal government Day Care Center program paid women only 500 pesos per month, which was only twenty-five pesos per day, "because that's what is budgeted by the Municipal (government)," according to a female government social worker. In one municipality, provincially paid Day Care custodians received 600 pesos per month.

During one interagency meeting in an Ifugao municipality that focused on the UNICEF ABCSD program, a female government social worker discussed the low honorarium of full-time Day Care custodians. She said, "It is a sacrifice for Day Caretakers." She noted that when UNICEF phased out from Ifugao in the next few years, the CMC program would be turned over to the government Day Care program. At that time, the 700 pesos the CMC custodians received as an honorarium would most likely be lowered to 500 pesos per month, the amount the government Day Care custodians were then paid. Another member of the meeting asked, "Can't the government work out other benefits for Child Caretakers, like Medicare?" The social worker stated, "Not UNICEF, but maybe the local government can do something about this now, now that we see the problem." Thus, in her view, the UNICEF program did not seem to be amenable to increasing the pay or benefits of the child custodians.

Some of the local government social workers implementing this program made special efforts to find additional sources of funding for the female custodians, since they could clearly see that thirty-five pesos per day was not an adequate salary for the women to support their families. This compared unfavorably to typically male designated government labor engaged in by men on a regular basis, such as long-term manual labor on infrastructure projects, which was usually paid at least a minimum daily wage.

The UNICEF/Philippine government's low "honorarium" for women working in the CMC program devalued symbolically women's labor. Child care labor, specifically, was represented as not being valued highly enough to generate even minimum pay through this program. Additionally, the female custodians were being exploited for their labor, since women who were in desperate conditions of poverty would often work at low paying jobs just to earn some amount of income. Also, women were once again naturalized as being the best providers of child care through the practice of hiring mainly female custodians.

Locally inspired gender differentiation is never completely maintained, though, since creative resistance to the imposition of unfair and unreasonable gendered practices is often part of an ongoing process in the historical construction of gender identities. In this case, there was some resistance to the treatment of women. Many Ifugao women refused to apply for the child minding custodian job since they could not afford to earn such low pay. Other women quit the position after serving in it for a time, also due to the low pay. Social workers listened to women's complaints about their low pay, prompting the social workers to seek additional sources of funds or other compensation.

Two women who were community health workers also criticized the CMC program, saying that the "CMCs were visioned by UNICEF (officials), not by community members." One woman said, "[One barrio] was supposed to have a CMC but there is none there. In Ifugao this would not work because a mother would rather bring her children to the field with her or leave them with a neighbor or relative, not leave them in one center. The CMC was supposed to have books and toys, but there were none. It's not that there is no need for child care, but maybe there could be another system."

As Dorinne Kondo (1990) has discussed in her work, individuals craft their own identities in the context of power relations and historical cultural and social realities. Each individual constructs multiple identities, as a creative life-long process, elements of which sometimes contradict each other (Kondo 1990). In the Ifugao case, the creation of gendered identities may be viewed as a process occurring in the context of local gendered, class, and religious power relations within Ifugao communities, as well as in the context of the power of international development and national and local governmental forces.

Ifugao Ideologies of Assistance, Volunteer Labor
for Development, and Gender

Development agents working within Ifugao viewed the provision of volunteer labor by lower class Ifugao people for program activities as being a reasonable and important expectation. This was due in part to the prevailing development ideology that a "community counterpart" was necessary for the success of development projects. Ifugao people were often told by development agents that they must "sacrifice" themselves for the good of their communities. It was invariably lower class people, rather than people of higher socioeconomic classes, who were asked to make this "sacrifice" of time and energy in development projects for their communities.

I often observed resistance to this demand for unpaid labor for development programs among poor Ifugao people, including programs to aid malnourished children. One important reason for resistance to this demand was the perception that the poor were struggling each day just to produce enough food to eat or to earn enough money to both eat and send their children to school. The poor felt they had little free time remaining for additional work. They would become anxious when faced with the prospect of engaging in long- or short-term unpaid volunteer labor. There was also an important cultural reason for poor Ifugao people's resistance to engaging in unpaid volunteer labor organized by government and international development agencies. This was their cultural ideology surrounding the provision of assistance to other individuals or to their community.

Ifugao people regularly engaged in different forms of reciprocal assistance as a cultural practice. For example, the Ifugao term *baddang* essentially meant to help or to provide assistance that was unpaid. Usually this assistance was understood to be reciprocal, that is, comparable assistance returned at some unspecified date in the future. One form of *baddang* that I participated in was rice harvesting, provided by the family of the husband of a newly married couple for their first harvest on the rice field inherited by his wife upon their marriage. After the rice harvest *baddang* was completed, the family of the wife provided a feast of pork and rice for the husband's family. The aim of this *baddang* was primarily to develop a bond between the families of the newly married couple. Approximately fifty of the husband's relatives traveled from distant barrios to attend this joyous occasion. Both men and women harvested the rice together.[4] They talked, joked, and sang songs while they bent over in the muddy paddy, cutting the rice stalks.

Another form of *baddang* that I observed was the construction of a nipa palm roof for a family's "native house." Throughout the week prior to the actual construction day, men and women gathered nipa palm from the area surrounding their homes and fields. On the day of construction, men in the barrio gathered together to help the male owner of the house construct the roof. The family who owned the house provided a feast of pork, rice, and rice wine to the men constructing the roof and anyone else in the barrio who wished to attend. Women watched the men work, or worked in their fields until it was lunchtime and then joined in the feast. This *baddang* was a festive occasion as well.

A third form of *baddang* that I participated in was another rice harvest for a woman who had recently had an accident and was too ill to work in her fields. She had fallen on her curved harvesting knife while walking on a slippery rice dike. The knife penetrated her back, and she had feared dying from the wound. Her friends pitied her and wished to help her. After her friends finished harvesting her field and had carried the rice to her home, her family fed them. She tearfully thanked all of her friends for their gracious assistance to her and her family in their time of need.

In each of these cases, *baddang* was provided as a means of creating or reinforcing social relationships, such as bonding two families of a newly wedded couple, aiding a family who was perceived to be too poor to be able to pay the laborers required to construct a roof, and expressing sympathy for an ill friend. Poverty stricken families especially benefitted from *baddang*. Members of the families who received the assistance may have already assisted those who helped them through *baddang*, or would do so in the future. These families provided a meal to all those who assisted them as an expression of their appreciation for the aid of their friends and relatives.

International development organizations whose personnel asked for unpaid labor from lower class people, on the other hand, were commonly perceived to be capable of paying for the labor. For example, many Ifugao people in one municipality regularly commented upon the expensive trucks purchased by the EC program, which occasionally transported the development program employees through their barrio roads. People questioned why the money spent on the trucks for transportation of the employees could not have been spent on community projects instead. Some people were also aware of the salaries paid to the full- or part-time employees of the programs, most of whom were Ifugao professionals. Rumors had spread about the high cost of the rooms that foreign officials rented during their stay in Ifugao.

Although these may not appear to be significant or unusual ways of spending development funds, to the lower class Ifugao people, some of whom were continually being asked to contribute unpaid volunteer labor for community projects, these expenditures and salaries were symbolic of the programs' wealth and access to money. The expenditures also highlighted for the poor Ifugao people their lower class position in relation to the development program funders. Some Ifugao people were being asked to provide free labor for community projects they may not have needed or desired. An international development program policy requiring poor people to perform unpaid labor, while the personnel were perceived to be paid high salaries and spending a great deal of money on themselves and materials, generated resentment and resistance to this policy among the poor.[5] Also, the international development policy requiring unpaid volunteer labor for projects by organizations which poor people perceived to be wealthy and capable of paying them did not correspond with the Ifugao cultural notion of *baddang,* or reciprocal assistance according to one's means, and thus often was resented.

Further, I found that poor women were expected to volunteer more long-term, unpaid labor than men were, especially in such areas as community health volunteers or child care providers. I am specifying long-term, unpaid labor here, since when men were asked to provide unpaid volunteer labor it was usually for specific, time-limited projects (such as footpath construction or latrine building projects). Some men also worked as community health volunteers, but much fewer than women; and, as has been seen, men were discouraged from working as child care providers.

The notion of women retaining the primary responsibility for providing unpaid child and health care within their families and communities was reinforced by the UNICEF/Philippine government program personnel by their encouraging women to provide volunteer work in these areas. Through observations of development practices in Ifugao, a strong connection can be made between their ideological devaluation of women's labor and low earning power, and the expectation that women can readily provide unpaid or underpaid, long-term volunteer labor for development programs. The development programs' practices of undervaluing and underpaying women's health and child care labor in the community also indirectly encouraged the idea that since men of households could earn greater amounts of cash than women, women should spend more of their time providing unpaid labor for their families, such as child and health care.

One lower class woman, who had volunteered regularly for long-term volunteer health and government work in her community for a number of years, said she thought Ifugao women had a lower position than men. She pointed out that development projects operating in Ifugao which involved women rarely benefitted women themselves. Instead, women's involvement in development projects benefitted their families or their communities. She also offered her view that the solution to raising women's position relative to men was enhancing women's ability to earn cash. She stated that while there were some cash-generating projects offered by development programs for families, most of them were joint projects involving both husband and wife (such as raising hybrid animals). She expressed in dismay:

> But the woman is striving on how to help her family. Even if we are going to the fields, we are helping; it is worth a fortune. But, what can women do so that they can have more privilege, opportunity? That's why we are always laughing, because we have so many development works—health workers, health monitors [all unpaid work]—but what is our improvement? It is like we are always volunteers, but our life is the same. It is always good for the whole community. It is as if you cannot plan something for your own life.

PHOTO 7.1 A UNICEF/Philippine government-sponsored Nutrition Day seminar, teaching Ifugao women how to cook nutritious meals. This was part of a number of Nutrition Day events in an Ifugao municipality.

Women resented not being paid for their labor in government or development health programs when they perceived the program was capable of paying them. As the woman above noted, women had many types of volunteer work but could find no "improvement" for themselves since they were not paid or were underpaid for their work. Some women did assert themselves in this situation. As noted earlier, some of the CMC custodians quit the child custodian position because the pay was so low. I was told by the above woman that at one 1992 meeting with local UNICEF/Philippine government and an NGO organization's officials, a few female volunteer health workers requested that their "honorarium" and benefits for their health labor be increased, since they felt they were being exploited by being underpaid for their labor. The health worker explained to the officials that other health workers had not conducted their health survey for the last quarter because they felt they were not being compensated for their efforts. They were requesting at least a small per diem of 50 pesos per quarter for their work. She said the officials laughed at their request, with one asking her, "What is the meaning of volunteer?" They refused to meet the workers' request. This problem resulted in struggles between community members and development agents, as women demanded that they receive a small per diem or salary for their work and sometimes did not complete their work if they were not paid, while development agents retained a high expectation of community members' provision of free labor and time.

The lack of payment for women's community health, development, and other volunteer work led to conflicts between some wives and husbands, particularly when women desired to continue volunteering their time and work to the community. A female volunteer for four community organizations said that one problem for women was that they were sometimes criticized by their husbands for attending community meetings. She said their husbands would say to them, "Why do you always go to meetings? What do you bring home at the end of the day after your meeting?" She also said that she sometimes felt criticized by others in her community for not focusing her energy on her family and instead engaging in community health and other development work. Unfortunately, women's unpaid labor for their community, provided through government, international development, and NGO programs, was undervalued by their families, their communities, and the development organizations themselves. Ironically, husbands sometimes competed with various organizations for women's unpaid labor.

One health worker said that problems she experienced from her volunteer health work included:

> [having] no time, encountering negative reactions from others in the barrio, and no pay. It is so hard to take time away from my own work, taking care of my own babies, so even though you have in mind that you would like to help, you cannot. And lack of medicines, and even if you'd like to help with herbal medicines, you cannot because you have to buy some things; like for [medicinal] syrups, you need sugar.

One of the significant points of this discussion is that although the development programs intended to raise women's social status, the programs' practices of not paying or underpaying women for different types of long-term volunteer labor and of reinforcing women's roles of mother and primary provider of health care actually undermined the programs' objective. In many ways, the practices of the programs reinforced women's low prestige and power in relation to men.

The UNICEF/Philippine government program did have a "women's organization" component, which was implemented by the government social work agency. Its overall purposes were the enhancement of women's role in social development and to "enhance the capacity of Ifugao women to participate in family and community activities for child survival and development and for socio-economic development of their communities" (UNICEF 1993:2). This component involved, as one social worker described it in the interagency meeting for the UNICEF/

Philippine government ABCSD program described above, "income generating projects [for women], to give them training to organize the women, and education on sanitation and self care for women." It also involved the provision of literacy and social communication skills and development opportunities; the promotion of the "total development of children and women through child rearing"; the organization of "women's groups as a venue for consciousness raising and mobilization for child survival and women development activities"; and the training of "four provincial staff who will, in turn, train service workers in women organizing" (UNICEF 1993:42-43). The seminars also could include training in leadership and community participation, responsible parenthood, parent effectiveness, nutrition training, early childhood ailments, business management skills and development, herbal medicine training, and soap and floor wax making, among other topics (UNICEF 1993:98).

This was the component of the UNICEF/Philippine government Ifugao ABCSD program that most directly drew a specific relationship between the enhancement of women's social position and the subsequent improvement in their children's nutritional status. As one UNICEF report on the progress of the women's organizations program stated, "one of the major criteria for selection of areas targeted for the ABCSD program was the presence of high prevalence of malnutrition and the presence of disadvantaged women . . . malnutrition is one of the key issues being addressed by the ABCSD Programme" (UNICEF 1993:175).

In selecting women to participate in the women's organizations, mothers with malnourished preschool children were considered to be the priority target beneficiaries (UNICEF 1993:175). In actuality, many of the women involved in the women's organizations did not have malnourished children, and some had no children at all. By 1991, after three and one-half years of the program, 160 women's organizations had been organized in Ifugao and seventy-seven had been provided with money for income generating projects. Some were successful, in terms of having a strong organization and profit making projects, while others were less successful (UNICEF 1993). A UNICEF report stated that the most important outcome desired from the women's organizations was the "reduction of malnutrition and enhancement of child survival and women development in the community" (UNICEF 1993:180). However, according to this report, which was based on a study of three Ifugao women's organizations in 1993, women involved in the women's organizations were not conscious of the fact that the reduction of child malnutrition in their families was a priority goal of the organizations (UNICEF 1993:183, 199). As noted earlier, many people associated UNICEF programs with infrastructure projects.

Unfortunately, the consciousness raising aspect of these groups—that is, efforts regarding women's value and their equality with men (UNICEF 1993:202)—was not very effective. This was exemplified in part by a social worker's comments, made during the UNICEF/Philippine government ABCSD meeting described above, that the "self care" education for women in the women's organizations was needed because, "Wives should fix themselves [beautify themselves] so there would be no reason for husbands to go look for someone else [another woman]." This social worker implied that women were not adequate as they were, and that if their husbands went "to look for someone else" it would be the fault of the women, not their husbands.

A female member of one of the UNICEF/Philippine government women's organizations said she attended a week-long seminar for the women's organization during 1992–1993. She recalled that the discussions during this seminar included family planning, support for their children, child care, money management, and women's cooperatives. She belonged to a wood finishing and weaving women's cooperative, for which the UNICEF/Philippine government program gave the women loans that they could pay back with no interest. Other seminars were also held, sometimes quarterly. When I asked her about certain issues that may have been raised at the seminar, she said that she did not recall any discussions about women's equality with men or the low pay rates of women in Ifugao. She did recall that the social worker taught them the following:

> If you have children and a family, you wash their clothes very well when they go to school, and so for your husband, you prepare well for him too. Because sometimes the women don't know what to do, so it will cause problems in the family. And you have to care for them, especially your husband; when he gets tired you could serve him. When the husband comes home he should rest because he is tired. Sometimes, when the wife is also working, it is the same. It is the same with the husband and wife, they could help one another. And she [the social worker] talks about the Bible . . . but the majority of Ifugao men don't like to do work inside the house. It is mainly the responsibility of women.

In this case, although a message of equality between women and men, or wives and husbands, had been offered, the messages this woman remembered were mixed. She had said women's equality with men had not been raised during the meeting. She remembered from the seminar discussions the ideas that women have a duty to serve their husbands and that women sometimes "don't know what to do," resulting in women creating problems in the family. This blaming of women for their family problems was similar to the blaming of women for their children's malnutrition. Few men attended such meetings, and the men were not provided with a message that they should help their wives when they were working.

There have been attempts by government employees working within the UNICEF/Philippine government program to raise women's consciousness about their equality with men, usually by female government employees. However, the actual messages given to women in seminars again were usually mixed. One afternoon in 1992, I attended a UNICEF/Philippine government seminar entitled "Family Life Development Module." Fourteen women, a few of their children, and only one man attended the seminar. All sat on wooden benches in a small Catholic church. Some of the comments the female Ifugao facilitator made during her lecture included the following paraphrase:

> Facilitator: Acceptance of each other. Before, when men were discussing, men would say, "You are only a woman. So, you do not know anything." Women were thought of as having lower status than men. Today, when there is a decision to be made, there must be sharing. Now, women must be a complement of her husband, or they are a complement of each other. In labor, men are stronger than women, but in their mind women are stronger than men.
> Women in the audience: Yes.
> Facilitator: What do you think?
> Women in the audience: Yes.
> Facilitator: Men get drunk. Women's kindness is very strong. Not a master and slave relationship, but instead it should be equal and they should help each other. The Bible says, "Love is not indecent or immoral. Love does not look for its own interest." If you love your spouse, you want them to be happy. Patience. Give your husband moral and social support. Don't compare your husband to other husbands. Openness in communication. Especially if there is a problem. We are not perfect, we have weaknesses, so what shall we do? Talk together. Solve immediate problems through discussion. Don't bring up all the old problems from one month or one year ago. Don't use sex as punishment of your husband if you are talking about your problems before you sleep. Ask about your feelings. Don't condemn your husbands. Instead, let your feelings be known to your husband. You communicate your feelings. You may have mixed feelings. Don't yell at your husband in front of the children if he makes a mistake.

Overall, this discussion was positive for women, promoting women's equality with men, and the idea that women should feel free to express their feelings to their husbands. Yet, the message was mixed since much of the discussion centered around what women should not do to their husband to make him feel badly (i.e., compare them to other husbands; bring up old problems; use sex as punishment; condemn them; yell at them in front of the children). Essentially, in learning how to interact with their husbands, the women were taught that they needed to cater to their husbands' feelings, while there were no suggestions given to the man attending the session how he and other men may cater to their wives' feelings. This seminar was formatted as a lecture, and there was little discussion and no contestation among the attendees about the issues raised.

There were government workers who advocated women's equality with men in discussions with Ifugao community members. During the discussion of women's and men's differential pay rates at the EC sponsored community development meeting described above, a government social worker and a government agricultural technician, both of whom were women, advocated equal pay for men and women. Also, Ifugao women were being influenced by local NGO workers, of both health NGOs and broader development NGOs. As one female Ifugao health volunteer explained:

It's only from the local health NGO that they remind us how women should be aware, to fight for their rights. Those women for the UNICEF village monitor didn't talk about women's wages. For the local health NGO, in leadership training we touched on the idea that even if you are a woman and you are a leader, you must have to develop your skills in leadership. The trainers of the local health NGO said women should have a part in the decision making, not only the man is concerned in the decision making; and women should develop their skills in order that they will help their husband in order to make a living; and for child care that men and women should be equal in the child caring with their presence when both are at home. If the man is not present, it is the responsibility of the woman. If the man is the one present at the home, that is his responsibility also.

By 1993, the UNICEF report on their women's organizations stated: "The impact of the women's organizations on the program level objectives, specifically on the attainment of better health and nutrition for mothers and children, as reflected in certain indicators such as reduction of malnutrition rate among pre-school children, decrease in infant mortality and morbidity rates, is imperceptible" (UNICEF 1993:194).

In sum, the UNICEF/Philippine government program in Ifugao implemented many community programs, developed community organizations and cooperatives, established a number of water systems throughout Ifugao province, and was very active in evaluating its program's successes—as well as its problem areas—in an attempt to seek ways of improving its program (UNICEF 1993; Women Development and Technology, Inc 1992).[6] There were always changes slowly occurring within Ifugao regarding how women and men perceived gender roles and relations, in part due to the influence of the many health and development organizations operating within Ifugao. Yet, international development agencies' neglect of existing unequal gendered power relations operating in Ifugao (such as differential pay rates) hindered progress toward enhancing women's social position. The UNICEF/Philippine government project-oriented, educational, and biomedical approaches were implemented only at the individual, family, and community levels as the primary approaches to alleviating malnutrition. They were also coupled with devaluation of women's work and promotion of women's roles as mother and primary provider of child and health care. Consequently, they were not likely to result in substantial improvement in women's social position or in sustained improvement in the nutritional status of Ifugao people.

Maintaining Unequal Gender Relations

As Ifugao people gradually became embedded in a modern capitalist market system through colonialism, Christian missionary activities, the movement of transnational capital, and international development practices, traditional western gender ideologies impinged upon local gender ideologies. In the Philippines generally, and in Ifugao as well, the Catholic church was an important historical force influencing gender roles. The process of missionary influence on gender roles continued with both Catholic and Protestant religious leaders and missionaries working in Ifugao, many of whom were Ifugao people. International development was another force having some influence on gender ideologies, but often in ways that were unintended. These include gendered ideologies regarding motherhood, child care, labor, and income contributions within families.

By emphasizing a role for women as mothers and as primary providers of child care within the family and the community, women were ideologically marginalized to roles not generally associated with a high level of prestige. Women were restrained from travel, through which they could potentially gain power and prestige within the community. Also, women with young children often had less opportunity to acquire spiritual potency and secular power, because they attended rituals and political meetings less frequently due to their responsibility to care for their children.

In addition, one of the main reasons men rather than women traveled more frequently to other villages or cities to locate wage labor was the differential pay rates for men and women's labor, even outside of Ifugao. With the introduction of a capitalist market economy, cash earnings became more highly valued than other types of household income. If the tradition of men earning more cash and other types of income than women for comparable work is accepted by development agents and never fully addressed by them, as occurred in Ifugao, then women will continue to earn less cash than their husbands, according greater prestige and power to men within their families and communities, while women will be viewed mainly as volunteers for development projects. Also, men will continue to have greater legitimation for their travel and more opportunities to gain experience, knowledge, and power, thereby enhancing their potential for leadership. These benefits will not be as readily available to most women, who remain behind caring for their children and farm or business. Women's greater participation in unpaid volunteer labor within their communities will keep their contribution to family incomes at a level lower than that of their husbands', thereby maintaining the edge he has on prestige in making the major contribution to the family's income. Unfortunately, an increase in women's cash earnings may not alone guarantee an increase in their power and prestige within families and communities.

As Kondo (1990) argued, people do resist and exceed the culturally specific forms and metaphors that shape their lives. There have been different ways in which these gender ideologies have been reappropriated and subverted by Ifugao women and men. One example already given was women arguing for equal pay with men in development meetings. Another practice engaged in by some married and unmarried women was to leave Ifugao to seek jobs offering higher wages, particularly international migrant labor. These married female migrant laborers left their husbands to raise their children, undermining the notion that women should be primary child care providers for their children. They also subverted the notion that men should be the "breadwinner" of the family, since many female migrant workers earned higher wages than their husbands.

In another example, despite the low honorarium, some men attempted to work as CMC custodians, in the face of the persistent view held by some professionals that women were naturally better providers of child care. Some women left their minimally compensated CMC work, and some women health care workers demanded pay from government and development officials for their labor provided to national and international development programs. At the same time, however, Ifugao women and men simultaneously created gendered identities which entailed contradictory elements. These contradictions were influenced by other forces as well, including the Ifugao culture, Christian churches, and feminist movements.

Government Food Supplementation Programs

Policies of food supplementation programs also disregarded cultural values and social relations operating within Ifugao. The nutritional importance of these for Ifugao people were not recognized by most program personnel. Food supplementation programs in Ifugao were mainly based on western, individualistic, biomedical modes of thinking. One of the basic premises of the programs was that malnourished individuals and, for some programs, pregnant and lactating mothers needed an immediate source of food to alleviate their existing state of malnutrition, in addition to other program services, education, and projects.[7] Working from this premise, parents receiving food supplements were instructed to give the food supplements solely to the designated malnourished child or pregnant or lactating mother. The types of food offered through different programs included dry milk, green peas, bulgar, corn meal, dried fish, and oil. The amounts and combinations of food given varied over time, as well as the schedule for distribution, since they were not provided regularly.

For Ifugao people, the sharing of food was a highly valued cultural practice. Sharing food in various social settings such as in the home, in agricultural fields, or at social occasions such as rituals, community events, or celebrations, created social bonds, accorded honor and prestige, and indicated respect, friendship, and hospitality. Within a family, all food was regularly shared among all family members, although not necessarily equally. Given this cultural ideology, parents most commonly gave each of their children, and sometimes the adults, in the household a share of the food supplements. For Ifugao parents, this was the culturally appropriate way to act, particularly in a lower class family wherein food was not plentiful. People were criticized by others if they were thought to save the best foods for themselves.

The food supplementation program become a constant source of frustration and conflict between the program workers and parents. The program workers constantly criticized parents for sharing food supplements intended for one malnourished person with all family members. Yet, parents were, and perceived themselves to be, acting in a culturally appropriate manner by doing so. Ifugao people were embedded in a different moral economy from that of the western societies that created the food supplement programs. In lower class families, where most members experienced hunger though at differing levels, all hungry family members ate the food supplements.

Parents were also criticized by program personnel for being just "interested in getting the [food] supply," instead of desiring nutrition education as well (Fieldwork Interviews 1992; UNICEF 1993:197). This was confusing for parents, who did not understand why they should not be interested in obtaining food supplements if the supplements were being offered to them. The UNICEF/ Philippine government program policy of providing food supplements only to second and third degree malnourished children, and not to first degree malnourished children, further confused parents. Those with first degree malnourished children had difficulty understanding why, after being told by a health provider that their child was malnourished, they were not offered food supplements. At the same time, they were being instructed that food supplements would facilitate a child's recovery from malnutrition. Some women thought that their children could not really be malnourished. Others resented that their children were not being treated for malnutrition when they were found to be malnourished, but still being asked to submit to a growth monitoring weighing each month. As one BNS said:

> Some parents are always asking me questions and say, "You are always weighing [my children] and you do not give something [i.e., food supplements or vitamins]." They say, "Oh, my child is normal." I tell them I just want to see the weight of their child. Mothers seem to be most interested in getting the food supply. One woman said what she wants is to be prescribed vitamins that she can buy for her child. I tell them I am only a BNS; they should go to the doctor if they want a prescription. It is those illiterates who are always asking questions; and they go to the weighings to get food supplies. I tell the midwife; and she is the one to explain to them. . . . The educated are also asking questions. . . . Some children do not like to be weighed.

In this discourse we find an Ifugao woman who had been strongly influenced by one biomedical approach to healing, that of providing pills (vitamins) to individuals for sickness, even when the "sickness" was socially produced malnutrition. This woman believed that medication, rather than food, could cure hunger, a belief found in other developing countries such as Brazil (Scheper-Hughes 1992).

Essentially, the individualistic, biomedical approach of the food supplement program was culturally inappropriate among Ifugao people, who placed a high value on sharing food. Parents were criticized for desiring food supplements for their families when it was being offered to them and when they were hungry. This created conflict, hostility, and misunderstanding on the part of health and development personnel and the Ifugao people. The policy of some programs to provide food supplements only to second and third degree malnourished children further confused parents of first degree malnourished children, who then questioned the meaning of malnutrition and their role in helping their malnourished children, since they were told the food supplements would help their children recover from malnutrition.[8]

Assertion of Identity:
Non-governmental Community-based Health Organization

In one barrio, women were active in all health programs offered there (government, international development, local NGO, and Christian).[9] One of the goals of the women was the alleviation of malnutrition among the members of their community. This was not a self-identified goal, since malnutrition was a concept introduced to them by these organizations. However, the alleviation of hunger and greater access to food were self-identified goals, as these were problems they experienced.

In this barrio, women participated in the local health NGO discussed in Chapter 4, which had been operating for almost three years by 1992. The facilitators of the NGO health program were members of a nearby upland ethnic group, located in a province bordering Ifugao. The common language spoken between the facilitators and the Ifugao health volunteers was Ilocano, the regionally spoken dialect. As discussed, this health NGO approached health, illness, and health care from a broad perspective that considered political, economic, socio-cultural, and biological (or organic) factors as influencing health and illness. Some of the international development/government seminars that I attended in Ifugao also discussed some of these issues with Ifugao peoples. The main difference between the approaches of the international development/government programs and the health NGO was that the facilitators of the health NGO tried, during their orientation sessions with Ifugao people, to develop an interpretation of the causes of poverty while asserting that poverty was a factor influencing malnutrition and other illnesses in Ifugao, as well as in the Philippines at large. The international development and government agency personnel, on the other hand, seemed to view poverty as a given fact of life, and thus usually did not discuss the causes of poverty.[10] The approach of the health NGO was to facilitate the development of a critical consciousness among community members about the social, economic, political, and biological reasons for and solutions to their conditions of health and illness.

The primary health care orientation of the health NGO posited that health was a social phenomenon and only part of a larger societal system. The health NGO facilitators tried to use a "wholistic approach to health problems," assessing health problems with community members on local, regional (Cordillera region), and national levels. They argued that the local and Cordillera health situation should not be viewed in isolation from the national health situation. According to the health NGO's orientation handbook:

> Health is seen as part of a whole. It is related to existing social structures [economic, political, cultural]. The health care system is only a portion of a whole social system. Hence, health problems arise from and contribute to structural problems. A wholistic approach is inevitable. Solutions to health problems are necessarily linked with solutions to prevailing economic, political, [and] cultural problems of the people. Since health problems are not isolated from other existing economic political and cultural problems of the community, the struggle to find solutions to these should be in partnership with the different partnerships, disciplines and sectors of society. Only [if] we join hands with them . . . can we effect progressive improvements in the living conditions and in the quality of life enjoyed by the society and shared by its members (Health NGO 1989).

In addition to micro-level problems, macro-level problems influencing hunger and sickness depicted in the NGO handbook were, economically: low wages, unemployment, underemployment; and, politically: landlessness, maldistribution of facilities, graft and corruption, state neglect, drug industries being dominated by multinational corporations, decline in the quality of medical education, deficient response mechanisms to health problems by the government, either local or national, as evidenced by scarce facilities (health centers, hospitals, water, or sanitary facilities), maldistribution of facilities and manpower, and minimal services. The NGO asserted that it was only through improvements in the economic, political, cultural, and physical situation that improvements could be made in health and malnutrition (Health NGO 1989: 6-8, 13, 15-16). One of the health NGO facilitators said that malnutrition was primarily due to a lack of food, and

> food is back to economics. Since malnutrition is an indicator of health, and they know that so many people in the Philippines are malnourished, so going deeper into malnutrition goes back to lack of food. Usually we let them analyze it. Why, why, why; it goes down to economy, or maybe she didn't know about a balanced diet, but even if she did, maybe she couldn't afford to buy food, so it goes back to a poor economy. Our stress is preventative rather than curative.

Some of the techniques the NGO facilitators used in their orientation sessions were drama, radio drama, slide shows of actual cases, small group discussions or workshops, evocative discussions, and use of visual aids. Health problems, their causes, and means to their solution were elicited from people who attended the health training sessions.

This was the only program I observed within Ifugao that was really "community based." The Ifugao people within the training sessions planned their activities themselves. In contrast, the UNICEF/Philippine government and other develop-

ment agencies' personnel either planned the program activities outright through a
top-down approach, or had people in communities participate in planning sessions
but then ultimately left the final decisions to program facilitators who decided what
projects and programs the agency would implement.

One Ifugao community health volunteer of the health NGO, who had also
worked with the UNICEF/Philippine government program and other development
programs, commented:

> It is different from the government because the health NGO is community based,
> whereas the government is hospital based. In the government health program
> *Barangay* Health Workers are chosen by the midwife or barrio captain. A new
> structure is chosen for us. But the health NGO works with an organized group already
> existing in the community. . . . The health NGO philosophy is holistic; health is
> everything, politics, economics, as well as disease. We cannot tackle disease itself,
> but all of the reasons . . . .
>
> The child minding centers were visioned by the UNICEF, not the members of our
> community. But for the health NGO program our community comes up with our own
> health plans, the trainings we need, when and how to go about it based on our own
> health needs. We heard that UNICEF was not as successful in Ifugao as they had
> planned because the money was channeled through government agencies. That didn't
> work well . . . .
>
> We work with the health NGO because the government cannot cope with the
> health needs of remote areas. [We teach] their communities [to be] self reliant, not
> reliant on the midwife. Health workers of the health NGO are given medicines to give
> out. The government midwife would not do that. The health NGO philosophy is that
> they believe that people can learn to do things for themselves, transfer of skills
> through nonformal education. We are even given medicines that the midwife can't
> disperse. But we must stick to primary health care, dressing wounds, we can give
> injections, and dental extractions. A government health worker usually assists the
> midwife. A sick person goes to the health worker, then she takes them to the midwife.

The health NGO trainings resulted in the health workers' feeling that they had
more control and authority in conducting their health work than they had when
working through the top-down approaches of the government, UNICEF, and EC
health and development programs, each of which directed the health workers in
their activities.

Although the approach of the health NGO was to address larger economic and
political problems in its orientation seminars, the facilitators were reluctant to
confront these issues in actual practice. The NGO facilitators were effective in
"conscientizing" people, enabling them to understand the NGO's interpretation of
how their health problems, including malnutrition, developed from historical
political and economic conditions. But the facilitators did not move beyond that
process to facilitate organizing and action among Ifugao people to change and
improve these social problems. One facilitator of the health NGO explained, "We
believe that people will organize themselves once they are organized on an issue."

After the orientation session, the health NGO facilitators relied mainly on a biomedical model of primary health care. A major project of the Ifugao community was the building of a barrio health clinic, with the help of the health NGO and foreign funding. The facilitators held numerous health training sessions with volunteer health workers, all of whom were women. The facilitators also provided direct primary health care services to ill people within the community, guided the health workers in their community health services and health surveys, and helped to develop an herbal medicine program. The NGO facilitators also began their seminars with Christian prayers, as government and international development programs had.

Despite their reluctance to directly act toward resolving macro- and micro-level economic and political problems, it was likely because of this socially oriented health philosophy and the facilitators' critique of government services and operations, that the health NGO was branded by the government military as being a communist front organization. Neither the UNICEF nor the EC development programs were accused of being communist fronts, in large part because they worked through government agencies. One health NGO volunteer worker thought that the government military's living in the local school near the NGO health clinic was a reflection of the "domination of government structure" over health care practices.

With the military groups camped within their barrio intermittently over the course of many years, it would have been difficult for the health volunteers to take social action that might antagonize the government soldiers, if they had any desire to do so. Health volunteers in other municipalities had been harassed or murdered by military or CAFGU personnel (HAIN 1992:304; Estrada-Claudio 1988:21-23; Palpal-Latoc 1988:22). This may also help explain why the health NGO facilitators hesitated to act upon their ideological beliefs, and why UNICEF, EC, and other international development programs remained silent on the issue of political and economic causes of poverty, poor health, and malnutrition. Despite the pressure, the local NGO volunteer workers persisted in providing health services to their community through the NGO, as well as through government and international development agencies, as seen in Chapter 4.

While the intentions of the UNICEF/Philippine government and EC development programs' personnel were admirable and their commitment to the programs commendable, the approaches of the programs were inadequate to resolve hunger in Ifugao. They did not act upon larger social processes that influenced hunger, such as social class relations, land reform, militarization, and unbalanced international economic relations. Through their model of health care and development, the problem of malnutrition was to be solved at the individual, family, and community levels through changes in individual practices, family income, environmental conditions, new technology, and biomedicine. They did not engage in fundamental social change with Ifugao people and, in many Ifugao people's perception, did not effect many substantially beneficial changes in their lives. When local health NGOs tried to effect meaningful change by addressing economic and political problems faced by the Ifugao and Filipino people, the state military repressed local action which may have been taken to solve these problems. This state repression took the form of aggressive force, continuous surveillance, and a threatening presence.

By 1993, despite almost five years of UNICEF/Philippine government and EC international development program operations in Ifugao, improvements in the nutritional status of women and children were minimal, as stated by UNICEF/ Philippine government program personnel (UNICEF 1993:194). However, credit should be accorded to UNICEF/Philippine government personnel, since as seen by the 1993 UNICEF report on women's organizations, they did make efforts toward analyzing and improving their program.

Using a project orientation, and providing an imagined development of the community, joint international and national development programs may have diffused community action geared toward fundamental social change. Also, development practices that operated in a context of a low intensity conflict strategy of total war also dissipated potential community based or grassroots practices and social movements. This was sometimes enforced through state militarization and violence.

The naturalization and reinforcement of women's roles as mother and provider of health care, and the continued devaluation of women's labor through some international development practices, subverted the intended goals of development programs to alleviate health and nutritional problems through the enhancement of women's prestige and power. The development programs also neglected the problems voiced by some women at the local level (such as women's low pay), while simultaneously providing women and men with an image of the development of their communities through their discourse and programs. Close attention to the effects of the international development project on gender roles and identities allows us to rethink the viability of western development programs specifically geared toward raising the prestige and power of women in Third World societies.

Notes

1. UNICEF in Ifugao defined "High Risk Families" as families with second and third degree malnourished zero-to-six-year-old preschoolers plus any other factors cited above, and "Risk Families" as families with three or more risk factors (UNICEF 1991:17).

2. As seen earlier, 26 percent of married women with children interviewed reported that their husbands participated equally in child care within their families, 6 percent reported that their husbands were primarily responsible for child care, and all married women with children reported that their husbands babysat their children sometimes, while the women were working outside of their home. Also 45 percent of married women interviewed reported that they shared nutrition and health responsibilities equally with their husbands

within their families, and 4 percent reported that their husbands were primarily responsible for these concerns in their families.

3. The forty-hour work week of Child Minding Center custodians included working five days per week for six hours each day in the center, during the major portion of the day (from 8:00 to 11:00 a.m. and from 1:00 to 4:00 p.m.), plus visiting the homes of absent students and making toys for the children during the remaining two work hours of each day.

4. *Baddang* was one occasion wherein men joined women in harvesting rice.

5. There was at least one project, a road building project in Ifugao sponsored by the EC, that did pay workers in the early 1990s, since it was perceived to be such an extensive project. However, this was not the normal practice for the program.

6. Programs included immunization, oral rehydration, children under-five clinics, biointensive gardening, iron and iodine supplementation, food supplementation, and income generating.

7. Second and third degree malnourished children and pregnant and lactating women were eligible to receive food supplements from the UNICEF/Philippine government program.

8. There were many other problems associated with food supplementation programs, some of which I have discussed in Chapter 5, and others such as the political motivations of donating countries. But I have focused only on a few of the issues due to limitations of space.

9. Ironically, many of these organizations would only operate in barrios that already had established a community organization. This was viewed as facilitating the success of their programs. The result of this policy in Ifugao was that some barrios had three or four development organizations operating, while other barrios without previously established community organizations had no development organizations operating in their barrios. For example, one barrio that had a previously established community organization had two international development programs, two local NGO programs, Philippine government projects, and Christian aid programs operating simultaneously in the early 1990s. Other barrios had none. One woman from the former barrio sarcastically exclaimed during one community development meeting: "They (volunteers of development programs in her barrio) are overlearning!" She said this because of the high number of programs operating in her barrio. This barrio also was accessible by vehicles, making it easier for program personnel to travel to the barrio, which might have influenced their choice of working there.

10. An exception was the development meeting during which the Ifugao religion was blamed for Ifugao people's poverty.

8

Power and Contradiction: Unlikely Alliances

When considering problems of health and healing and the means used to alleviate poor health among Ifugao people, I found that there were numerous complicated alliances and disjunctures of power among different groups of people. These included Christians; followers of the local Ifugao religion; Ifugao, other Filipino, and foreign development agents; Ifugao government biomedical providers; and NGO workers. Many of the individuals comprising these groups simultaneously belonged to or aligned themselves with more than one group, thereby at times engendering contradictions on particular health issues and multiplying the complexity of the power relations operating around development practices. This often went unnoticed, however.

In this chapter, I continue to examine the manner in which religious beliefs and practices play an integral role in healing and can influence nutritional status. I explore the struggle among Christian groups and proponents of the Ifugao indigenous religion, and I examine these groups' relationships to a development program and biomedical programs operating in Ifugao. I consider what impact these power relations had on the processes geared toward improving the health and nutritional status of Ifugao people and on the meanings each group attributed to illness, undernutrition, and poverty. In the Ifugao context, Christianity in general, and particularly new fundamentalist Protestant religious movements that had proliferated throughout the Philippines in recent years (Tefft 1991:6; National Council of Churches in the Philippines 1989), facilitated the ongoing recreation of local ideologies and social structures. This chapter will explain three propositions regarding influences of Christianity on Ifugao culture, gender, and Ifugao people's nutritional status.

First, although ideologies and social structures advocated by Christian groups (such as an ideology of individualism to attain wealth and a reduction of the practice of the communal ritual feasting of the Ifugao religion, viewed as spiritually evil and a waste of resources) corresponded to recently developed capitalist market structures into which the Ifugao community had been incorporated, they did not necessarily benefit members of each economic class equally. Second, through religious instruction historically and in recent years, some Christian groups in Ifugao attempted to redirect Ifugao women's ideologies and practices, sometimes resulting in a reduction of women's social position in Ifugao society. Third, fundamentalist Protestant groups operating in Ifugao promised that Christianity would be an avenue to good health and prosperity.[1] Despite the good intentions of these Christian activists, this promise sometimes detracted from the exploration of broader analyses of social, political, and economic structures which historically have generated conditions of poor health and widespread poverty. In other cases, however, such as the example of liberation theology, Christianity could be a vehicle for this form of exploration.

Religious Tensions and Struggles

Religious tensions in Ifugao transpired mainly at the level of discourse during my research period. There was a struggle for authority between the leaders and some followers of the Ifugao religion and members of Christian groups. Alliances of power were discernable between Ifugao Christians and western oriented Ifugao and other Filipino development agents, including biomedical personnel, mainly as a result of a shared world view involving ideas of modernization, progress, prosperity, the benefits of technology, and so forth. These groups worked against the followers of the Ifugao religion, though not always consciously or intentionally. These alliances at times were ruptured, though, especially when issues such as the use of contraception or women's inequality with men were being considered.

For Ifugao fundamentalist Protestants in one Ifugao community, the Bible was used as the primary source of truth and instruction. The fundamentalists held a highly dichotomous view of the world (good-evil), in which Christians fell on one side while followers of the Ifugao religion fell on the other. There was little tolerance for Ifugao religious beliefs.

Regarding the position of women, Filipino scholar Marilen J. Danguilan found dualistic thinking and hierarchical patterns to have been prevalent historically among Catholic theologians and officials in the Philippines. She argued that this mode of thought continued in the modern Philippines, perpetuating the oppression of women. This mode of thought was characterized by the split between subject-object, superior-inferior, spirituality-carnality, mind-body, culture-nature, and men-women (Danguilan 1993:31). Likewise, some fundamentalist Protestants in Ifugao argued that men were the "stronger" sex, while women were the "weaker vessel." Dualistic thinking among fundamentalist Protestants in Ifugao was often overtly expressed, as depicted in the dialogue recorded in the next section from a community meeting sponsored by an international development organization operating in Ifugao.

Christianity, Development, and the Denigration
of the Ifugao Culture and Religion

There were a number of secular international development organizations operating in Ifugao in 1992. As noted earlier, during most community meetings organized by development agents or government workers, Christian prayers were recited at the beginning of each meeting. At one important meeting organized by development agents in an Ifugao barrio, the agents invited people whom they considered to be barrio leaders and others representative of the different sectors of the community. Significantly, when asked later if any of the local *mumbaki* were invited, development agents responded that none had been specifically invited to that meeting. The only religious leader invited was an Ifugao fundamentalist Protestant pastor, despite the fact that *mumbaki* usually were considered local religious leaders in the barrio. This was significant in light of this development agency's officially stated goal of maintaining cultural systems while promoting development activities. It also exposed the already predetermined nature of the view of development agents and some Ifugao people that followers of *baki* had a "negative attitude" toward development.

This meeting was the first of a three-day planning session, which was one component of a series of sessions held in that barrio to create a development plan for the community among the community members. When the sessions were completed, the development agency would then attempt to carry out as many aspects of the plan as they could.

Approximately fourteen women and eight men from the barrio attended this meeting, held in the community's concrete, four classroom elementary school building one sunny Friday morning. There were almost as many development agents present as community members, because this series of meetings also served as a training for new development agents. After a prayer was led by the Protestant pastor, the community members were requested by the facilitator, a Filipino man of another ethnic group, to participate in a planning process called "The Logical Framework." The facilitator also called the process "Objective Oriented Project Planning." Each of these were examples of imported western management frameworks. The community members were asked to write problems they perceived existed within their community on a card (if they were literate). The facilitator would then use these suggestions to create a "problem tree" on the blackboard for analysis by all present. Among thirty-six cards which identified problems perceived by community members, one card read, "Customs and Traditions, Example: Pagans." After the facilitator read this card aloud, he stated:

> Facilitator: The problem should not be stated in a negative way. We don't intend to hurt anyone. Because there are some traditions which are positive, no?
> Ifugao Fundamentalist Protestant Pastor: How about the *kanyao* [referring to *baki*]? That is negative, the *mumbaki*.

Ifugao Social Worker: Regarding health, like during harvest time, they do not eat vegetables.

Facilitator: The customs and traditions which affect the economies and health?

The facilitator wrote a new card, which read: "The Practice of Pagan Rituals." The local religion had now been solidly identified as a community problem.

On the second day of the meeting, a Christian prayer was again said to begin the meeting. The facilitator then instructed the same community members of the previous day to first work on improving and clarifying the problems they had identified on the first day. Later, they would develop the "objectives" of their plan. The following dialogue transpired at the second meeting:

Ifugao Fundamentalist Protestant Pastor: There is [the] practice of pagans, poor sanitation, and poor health. So there is "poor [Christian] spiritual growth," but I don't know where to put that. [He was referring to a chart that was being constructed by the facilitator identifying community problems.] Is that a problem?

Facilitator: Where would that lead to?

Ifugao Christian Man: A lack of education, negative attitudes.

Ifugao Fundamentalist Protestant Pastor: Why is there practice of paganism? Because they don't know the word of God. This leads to poor sanitation because when they are Christian we must practice outward cleanliness. So paganism leads to poor sanitation, even if there is high income, if pagan.

Facilitator: Maybe we can place it as a root cause. Because of low spiritual growth it can lead to all problems.

Ifugao Christian Man: I think that is the overall root of low income, massive poverty. It [Christian spiritual growth] will affect everything. For insufficient supply of water, you will exert good effort [if you have Christian spiritual growth].

A number of Christian Ifugao people, referring to paganism, said: Overall cause, the root cause of all those [community problems].

Facilitator: It contributes to low income, low [Christian] spiritual growth: "because I don't fear God, I will have low income?"

Ifugao Christian Man: "Because I am ignorant."

Ifugao Social Worker: If you have low spiritual growth you will not have the initiative to work well to feed your family.

Ifugao Woman: [low spiritual growth] Results to low development.

Ifugao Christian Man: There's a lack of knowledge in Christ, Christianity.

Ifugao Woman: If they are poor in spiritual growth they probably practice pagan rituals, and then they have negative attitudes and coupled with lack of knowledge. It relates to family planning.

Ifugao Fundamentalist Protestant Pastor: If we think of the Bible, it says go forth and multiply. But if we are a spiritual man, as head of the family, then we have to exert self-control, which leads to family planning. [This pastor is against the use of contraceptives, and is suggesting abstinence.]

Ifugao Social Worker: Responsible Parenthood!

The conversation then turned to another subject. Later in the discussion, when "The Practice of Pagan Rituals" was explicitly defined by the people in the room and the facilitator as being a community problem, the defined objective offered by the Protestant pastor to resolve this problem was "Pagan Rituals Abolished." He then asked, "Is that hurting," followed by a grin, referring to instructions not to make statements that may "hurt anyone." The community members finally settled on "Pagan Rituals Reduced" as their development objective, after a professional Ifugao woman argued that they write only "reduced" because "not all pagan rituals are bad."

This dialogue exemplified how through conversion to western Christianity, many fundamentalist Protestants came to perceive themselves to be modern, civilized, wealthy, and having good sanitation and good health through their observance of Bible instructions. Fundamentalist Protestants depicted the followers of the Ifugao religion, in contrast, as being backward, primitive, and having poor health and sanitation. Fundamentalist Protestants in this meeting viewed themselves as being good, moral, and having acquired the truth, while they viewed followers of the Ifugao religion as being evil, immoral, and ignorant. The Protestant pastor had at another time said, "Believers [in Christianity] are not often afflicted by illness, but more illness than demon possession."

Some fundamentalist Protestants proposed that wealth, good health, and development could be acquired through following the Christian religion, whereas those who followed the Ifugao religion were said to be poor primarily due to practices and ideologies associated with the Ifugao religion. Again, followers of the Ifugao religion were accused of having a "negative attitude" toward development programs. Paganism was also closely associated with dirtiness ("paganism leads to poor sanitation") in Ifugao by Christians. In another conversation with me, the Protestant pastor said, "You can see from their [followers of *baki*] life that they don't mind outward holiness. You can see by their clothes, by the way they live. That will affect their health. But Christians, we have to be clean."

This line of reasoning was inadvertently supported by the development agents, when they validated these claims by including them within the problem analysis. This was in keeping with the tendency of international development organizations in Ifugao to take an ahistorical, culturally and politically decontextualized approach to development activities.

Most significant in this conversation was the masking of larger social and political causes of poverty, poor health, nutritional status, and sanitation (such as social class relations, imbalanced international relations, local and national political corruption, inadequate land reform programs, etc.) by fundamentalist Protestants through their blaming of the Ifugao religion as the root cause of all social problems in the community. Pertierra has noted, in contrast, that in a lowland Philippine Ilocano society it was precisely the lack of money, or poverty, which sustained people's reliance on local healing rituals, if they were not able to pay monetarily for the services of a doctor (Pertierra 1988:129). This Ilocano group did not perceive their local healing rituals to cause poverty.

Significantly, I found that the fundamentalist Protestant assertion that the Ifugao religion was the root cause of poverty, poor health, and relatedly, malnutrition, was not valid. As noted in Chapter 6, of the three barrios in which I conducted my research, the barrio that had the highest rate of malnutrition was the barrio that had the highest percentage of Christians residing in it and the lowest percentage of people who believed in or practiced the Ifugao religion. In stating this finding I am not suggesting that Christianity causes malnutrition. Instead, I am pointing out that the Ifugao religion was not the root cause of poverty or malnutrition but that these were instead caused by other complex social factors. In fact, the Ifugao religion may have had some positive effects on the nutritional status of the poorest Ifugao people.

The arguments at this meeting facilitated the acceptance of both Christianity and international development programs as being progressive and leading to greater economic development, while they stigmatized and blamed followers of the Ifugao religion for the poverty of the community. Rather than viewing the *baki* as a dynamic and always changing process, which historically had been altered to correspond with contemporary social and economic changes, the development agent accepted the Christian argument that the practice of *baki* should be reduced. The development agent also took this argument at face value without inquiring among those who practiced *baki* how they felt about their religious beliefs, economic status, and lifestyles.

This particular meeting had few defenders of the Ifugao religion. The condemnation of their beliefs within development meetings, coupled with the emphasis on Christian prayer at development and government meetings, likely were important factors which discouraged followers of *baki* from attending these meetings or influenced their remaining silent within the sessions. Tensions did arise in another development meeting, however, when—following a similar discussion wherein Christians argued that the Ifugao culture was backward—an Ifugao woman proclaimed that the Ifugao *ugali*, or customs, were good and valid.

Biomedical providers also criticized *baki* for two main reasons. Regarding overall biomedical treatment, some biomedical personnel argued that practicing *baki* prior to visiting a biomedical institution delayed biomedical treatment, thus worsening the course of a disease. Secondly, regarding nutrition, *baki* was viewed as contributing to poor nutritional habits by biomedical providers since it restricted the eating of vegetables, fruit, and fish during certain periods. As noted in Chapter 7, I found in interviews that the majority of Ifugao families followed these food restrictions only during rituals and until the ritual meat was consumed. Most families no longer restricted their intake of the foods during the long harvest season, even if they were followers of the *baki* religion.

There were attempts by development agents in meetings and publications to promote "positive" aspects of the Ifugao culture. During these times, some Ifugao people defended their cultural practices, and a few defended the specific cultural practice of *baki*. However, a Christian bias on the part of many development agents was often displayed, generally resulting in their according low status to the Ifugao religion and viewing it in negative terms. For example, one development agent asked Ifugao people at a community meeting:

Development Agent: What cultures and traditions hinder your development in [your community]?
Ifugao Christian Man: Negative attitudes about CRs [comfort rooms], pigpens. If you call them to meetings they say, "you will go because you are the only ones they invited." Many *bakis*? Now we are becoming civilized with the coming of Christianity. Still, some have negative attitudes.
Ifugao Man: Many are still not Christian.
Development Agent: What do you consider to be the most important value here in [your community]?
Ifugao Woman: Traditional.
Development Agent: What do you want to say about what is traditionally important?
Ifugao Woman: The *ugali* [which can include *baki*] of the people is good.
Ifugao Christian Man: For others, Christians are good, and what they do is good.
Development Agent: So, there are differences here. What do you greatly value?
Ifugao Woman: Of course, what is good. If our *ugali* is good, our life will be good. If our *ugali* is bad, our life will be bad.

Following this, the development agent wrote on a large posted paper under the word "Traditional":

-*Canao* [this was referring to *baki*] - more are practicing than Christians;
-Traditional [an arrow leading to:] education, Christianity;
-Good Character/Good life.

In this scenario, when the formal topic of "Customs and Traditions" was raised by the development facilitator, the question first asked was negatively constructed: "What customs and traditions hinder your development in [your community]?" In the last example of the poster paper depiction, the implication of the arrow leading from "Traditional" to "education, Christianity" was that it was ultimately desirable to change tradition through education and Christianity. It also implied that with education and Christianity there would be development and progress ("Good Character/Good Life"), and that the Ifugao customs would only hinder development.

In this manner, development agents were seen to be spreading the notion of western development, western religion (Christianity), and modern education as being superior to traditional religions and customs. Local cultural practices and beliefs were often viewed as primitive and as impediments to the development plans. Although this was not overtly stated by development agents, it was the implication from the tone and discourse of the discussion. The facilitator also repeatedly asked how many people were Christian in their barrio now, implying that a goal might be for all people of the barrio to eventually become Christianized, thereby enhancing the "development" of the community. The community members were never asked by the development facilitator what modern technology and practices, or what Christian beliefs and practices, might hinder the "development" of their community.

In an attempt to validate valued aspects of Ifugao culture, the development agent in the end presented the Ifugao tradition as ultimately being transformed to Christianity through education, leading finally to "development." This discourse also depicted how development practices can create many social changes apart from the actual projects implemented: changes in ideology, views toward religion, ideas about the terms "civilization" and "uncivilized," and the breakdown of local cultures.

A *Mumbaki's* View of Christianity

The followers of the Ifugao religion usually took a defensive stance in regard to their religion, rather than an offensive position against Christians in their community. One *mumbaki*, who in his mid-thirties was still in the process of training to become a full-fledged *mumbaki*, expressed the following sentiments at a *baki* for the blessing of a new house:

> The new coming religions want to corrupt the *baki*. But for me there are still so many people performing *baki*. Like me, my two daughters, I spent so much on medicines, but they weren't cured until we did *baki*. The Christians are laughing at me because I'm still doing *baki*. They might call me dizzy or crazy because of their religion. But for me, that [*baki*] is the true religion in our place. My first son, he had lots of medicine. He was the only one cured with medicine. I feel bad because they might call me a stealer. Our religion, they call it satanous. *Maknongan* is the best because he made us. But for the other religions, *Maknongan* is satanous.
>
> But this occasion is very good for the people here and the owner because they are praying for this house and their family life; and the other religions are calling us satanous. But for us, we are not satan, we are just here to celebrate this house and the family that lives here. They understand, but they want to corrupt this *baki*. But for me I will not stop this *baki*, and the old people, they will not stop this *baki* until they die and the children and grandchildren will die. Even if the Christians call me satan, I am not a stealer man. Because if someone steals, even eggs here, that's a very big punishment.
>
> If we get a pig worth P10,000 and give for *baki*, the people of the other religious say, "Why do you do that? What is left for you?" But this is good because this is our old tradition.
>
> As for me, in my mind, it would be good if that religion didn't want to corrupt our old religion in our place, and those religions won't come from other places. That is

our sickness [or problem] because they want to corrupt our *baki*. I am only a pagan, not a religious [i.e., Christian], but I will follow the commands of god, I will not steal from other places. The Christians do bad things. . . . Like me, in the beginning of the coming of [Christian] religion, every night they came to my house to invite me to Bible study. When they finished their Bible class they got my wood without asking for it. I didn't attend the Bible class, but I would not get anything of theirs, even that had fallen on the ground.

During his narrative, this man appeared to be very distressed, sad, and anxious about his conflicts with fundamentalist Protestants who stigmatized him as being satanous and immoral, and as holding less worthy spiritual beliefs than their own. These accusations also seemed to wear on his self-image as he kept repeating that he was "only" a pagan. However, he did not view Christianity as being entirely superior to the Ifugao religion; he noticed contradictions between fundamentalist Protestant rules and ideology and the actual behavior of some Christians (stealing wood). He viewed the value of *baki*, in part, in terms of its ability to cure illness and its significance in the social life of community members.

Not all community members, including Christians, appreciated sermons delivered by some Christian religious leaders during community events. Some people, particularly men, would locate themselves at a distance from one Christian sermon deliverer, avoiding his chastisements against the Ifugao religion, drinking alcohol, and gambling. At one Christian dedication of a newborn baby, a large group of male attendees continued gambling while a pastor delivered his sermon nearby.

Other Ifugao people related stories to me about how they had been affected by Christian identifications of *baki* as satanous. A Christian woman related the following to me, when I asked:

> Lynn: Why don't you perform *baki* anymore?
> Woman: Because that prayer is no good—satan. Because satan is no good. The people say that we will not go in satan, we will go to God. Because with the *baki* we will not go to heaven.
> Lynn: Who told you that *baki* is satanous?
> Woman: The [Filipino Catholic] priest. Even my mother tells me: "I will not go to that man [*mumbaki*]. And he . . . [came] to my house and did a prayer." And when the man [*mumbaki*] prayed he took a chicken and he pointed it at her and blew on her. When the *mumbaki* did that she was young. She thought it was good. But when the Catholic priest comes, we don't need that [*baki*]. We will not remember *baki* today, we will remember God.

A former *mumbaki* stated that he no longer practiced *baki*, "because it no longer goes with the present society. It is primitive." He and other former *mumbaki* in the room related that they heard criticism from other people that *mumbaki* were backward and holding the society back.

On the other hand, a Christian woman, who was also a volunteer health worker, said that she had been criticized by *baki* practitioners for not following food proscriptions during a designated period. She said that she sometimes followed the *baki* food proscription because at times she was chastised by elders in the community who accused her of negatively affecting the whole community by eating prohibited food. In the face of this criticism, she sometimes pretended that she believed in *baki* and followed the food proscriptions only when she was in the presence of *baki* followers. She was ashamed to be criticized in front of others in the community. When not in their presence, though, she sometimes ate proscribed food.

Discrimination and Ethnic Identity

The degradation of the Ifugao religion, and culture generally, by fundamentalist Protestants, and sometimes by Ifugao development agents, contributed to the discrimination experienced by Ifugao people in other areas of the country. This degradation of ethnic upland groups by majority Filipino groups was not a new phenomenon, however. Numerous Ifugao people, particularly college-aged men and women who migrated to municipalities or cities outside of Ifugao where their colleges were located, or those who migrated for work, related stories to me of their experiences of harassment and discrimination based on their ethnic heritage. Ifugao students had to contend with jokes implying that Ifugao people had tails and that they continued headhunting practices.

Another example was found in a 1993 Manila-based newspaper, distributed throughout the country, which printed a cartoon under a section of the newspaper named "Inquirer Trivia." Under the subheading, "Word Watch," was the word and definition: "Booboisie (BOO bwah zee): a class of the general public composed of uneducated, uncultured persons." Depicted next to this definition was a cartoon drawing of three men dressed in the style of the Cordillera mountain ethnic groups (the men wore G-strings, headdresses and armbands, and two of the men held spears). This resulted in the printing of two critical articles reacting to the cartoon in the *Unibersidad ng Pilipinas* (University of the Philippines) collegian newspaper, in support of Cordillera ethnic groups (Birosel 1993:3).

In another case, an Ifugao human rights worker said that some Ifugao people avoided using the services of a hospital in a nearby lowland province, staffed by non-Ifugao personnel, due to rumors of poor service given to Ifugao patients compared to that given to the province's majority ethnic group. She said, "Some people have said 'We do not want to bring our patients to [the nearby lowland province] because we are being discriminated against or not treated too well.' They prefer to be treated in an Ifugao hospital."

Another example was found in a July 1993 edition of the monthly publication of the UNICEF Ifugao ABCSD. The publication displayed a cartoon depicting an evolutionary-like series of four men situated above an editorial captioned, "Why Education." At the left-hand side, located at the supposed beginning of the evolutionary development of humans, stood a short ape above the designated time period "1000?" Next in the evolutionary lineup was a boy dressed in traditional Ifugao garb (G-string and headdress, holding a spear), standing slightly taller than the ape, above the designated period "1800s." He was the first in the sequence of human beings, standing at the "primitive" end of the evolutionary scale, closest to the ape. Next, slightly taller than the boy resembling an Ifugao person, stood a boy dressed in western-style tee-shirt and shorts, holding a book. This boy was situated above the designated time period "1930s." The latter two boys had no facial features, their faces mere outlines. They appeared sad or serious, and looked straight ahead rather than at the reader. Finally, a boy dressed in modern western-style clothing (long pants, belt, shoes, and eyeglasses), holding numerous books and wearing a western-style canvas backpack, stood squarely at the destination point of the evolutionary scale. This boy looked directly at the reader with a great smile, evoking the message that this was the lifestyle to be aspired to. He was positioned above the designated period of "1990s" (Mountain Movers 1993:2).

A final example was an article printed in the *Baguio Cordillera Post* (newspaper) on January 19, 1992. The article reported that the regional office of the government agriculture department blamed low rice productivity in the Cordillera region primarily on the "indigenous sociocultural practices" of the Cordillera ethnic groups. The newspaper was distributed within Ifugao as well as throughout the Cordillera region. Entitled "Spirit Worship Hinders Cordillera Food Production Efforts: Unrelieved Poverty in the Highlands," the article read:

> Spirit worship and strict adherence to other tribal customs help explain inability of the Cordillera region to grow food crops at the self-sufficient level. . . . Another is lack of cost-efficient appropriate technology that would increase production of the upland farms, reports the regional office of the agriculture department based in this city. . . . The region is listed by the government as one of the more economically depressed areas of the nation. It rates priority in the government's efforts at poverty alleviation. Majority Cordillerans belong to ethnic minorities who cling fast to tribal customs and traditions which dictate their life-styles, especially in farming. . . . The department's report laments persistence of what it describes as 'indigenous sociocultural practices' of the region's farmers. The description refers to spirit and the various rituals involved in paying homage. In worshipping the spirits which the region's farmers believe influence success or failure of the crops they sow, animals are slaughtered as sacrifices and such ritual necessarily eats time or delays the planting season. More delays are suffered if entrails of the sacrificed animals read wrong or portend a bad crop. The worshipping and sacrificing are repeated to enable a more favorable reading from the entrails. . . . Another reason behind the low farm productivity is that the small farmers are seldom reached by government farm extension services. Such a lack also explains why the planters refuse to adopt government recommended farming practices. But the extension workers cannot be entirely blamed since majority of farming villages in the Cordilleras do not have

modern roads and can only be reached through footpaths, a good number of them steep and winding (*Baguio Cordillera Post* 1992:17).

In placing primary blame on "indigenous sociocultural practices" (such as waiting for the village *tomona*, or *kadangyan* family, to begin planting or harvesting) for low rice yields (which were one-quarter of the national average), the government report ignored current concerns among Cordillera peasants about decreasing fertility of the soil and the drying up of irrigation sources in the upland areas, mainly due to widespread deforestation and the use of chemical fertilizers and pesticides. It also neglected to note that high yielding rice varieties cannot be used in most of the upland areas due to the climate (in some lower areas of the region high yielding varieties could be grown) and that, also due to the climate, only one crop of rice could be planted annually in most areas of Ifugao. Additionally, in apologizing for the extension workers who could not visit the farming villages due to lack of modern roads, it neglected to point out that the government was responsible for building roads and that the government did not hire an adequate number of extension agents to cover all of the Cordillera region. Nor did the report note that the Cordillera people themselves hiked these footpaths on a daily basis.

This assault on Ifugao peoples' ethnic identity was worsened by fundamentalist Protestant accusations that the Ifugao local religion and practices were evil, satanous, ignorant, and backward. An Ifugao Christian woman once stated: "Becoming a Christian is a blessing. *Baki* is a worship to the evil spirits; adoring the evil spirits and they have their other gods." In the face of discrimination, conversion to Christianity for Ifugao people thus provided an avenue to acquiring an identity and status equal to that of other majority ethnic groups within the Philippines. Conversion to Christianity also became symbolic of Ifugao peoples' acquiring modern, "progressive," western ideologies and practices.

Additionally, conversion to Christianity offered increased access to information and resources provided by national and international development agencies. This was due to the agencies' affiliation with Christianity and Christian leadership in local communities and, in some instances, their own denigration of "indigenous sociocultural practices." Hefner noted that religious conversion and the reformulation of traditional religions often are expedited during a period when people are experiencing tensions and conflicts due to incorporation into a new, larger social order. This, as seen in the Ifugao case, can create a crisis of identity, and sometimes a crisis of authority. Relatedly, religious conversion minimally requires the acceptance of a new locus of self-definition and a new reference point for one's identity (Hefner 1993). This explanation is particularly apt for the earlier periods of foreign expansion during Spanish and U.S. colonization and missionization of Ifugao, as well as for the contemporary period involving western expansion through development and missionary discourse and practices. Both were periods of fundamental political, economic, and institutional change which affected

Philippine ethnic groups' sense of self-worth and community, change which also created conflicts related to dignity and self-identification (Hefner 1993).

Pride in Ifugao Heritage

There were many Cordillera leaders and people, including Ifugao, involved in organizations and movements which countered the valorization of international development activities and westernization by promoting Cordillera ethnic groups' cultural beliefs, practices, and rights. One example was the Cordillera Peoples Alliance (CPA), an organization of people from the many ethnic groups comprising the Cordillera region. As previously mentioned, the CPA worked toward the regional autonomy of the Cordillera region from the national government, as provided for in the 1987 Philippine Constitution (Dizon 1993b). Another organization was the Cordillera Resource Center for Indigenous Peoples Rights, which was involved in numerous issues facing the Cordillera people, including ancestral land rights, protection of the Cordillera region's resources for the Cordillera people, and human rights abuses by the military (Loste 1993).

There were numerous other organizations in the Cordillera region that promoted the culture and rights of local ethnic groups. A sense of regional ethnic pride emerged, despite the discrimination experienced within and outside of the Cordillera region and the marginalization of local ethnic groups within the Philippine nation. There was also a small movement in the country at-large, in the arts and within the universities particularly, to promote Filipino minority ethnic groups.

Alterations in Ideology and the
Cultural Practice of Food Distribution

There were a number of reasons given by Ifugao people for the relatively recent conversion of high numbers of their ethnic group to Christianity.[2] One reason was that through conversion people were no longer afraid of spirits affecting their lives; they felt protected by their new faith in God or Jesus Christ to ward off these spirits. One Ifugao woman said, "Whenever we dreamed bad dreams which had bad interpretations, we had *baki* to save our lives. After that, when we were Christians, He [God] gave us peace of mind, courage. We don't do *baki* because we believe God is the most powerful." As previously stated, promises of good health and prosperity also facilitated conversion to Christianity. The same Christian woman further said, "If you follow God you will progress on the physical and spiritual. . . . Strength, nice feeling to go and work, peace of mind, because you are interested in going to work. God will give you more blessings on your daily life. She will give you more blessings on the food of your physical strength, what you have to plant all around."

Access to resources also may have influenced some Ifugao people to convert. For example, as seen in Chapter 5, many Christian organizations offered some form of aid or development programs to Ifugao members. The Methodist church described earlier facilitated the development of a cooperative egg production organization among members of the church, using a loan granted by an international development agency. Other institutions offered direct resources. Also, social networks established among church members could, in come cases, provide some access to resources or employment. Faith also was an important factor in maintaining Christian allegiance. Faced with numerous hardships, faith in an all-loving and all-powerful God alleviated some of the lower class Ifugao people's emotional distress.

Of all the reasons given by Ifugao people for Christian conversion, the one reason offered most often was that it had become too expensive to provide the prescribed number of animals to be sacrificed at *baki*, including *baki* for illness. One Christian woman said: "It is expensive to sacrifice all of those animals. Even if he has no money, he will mortgage all of his fields in order to save the life on the day of the ritual. The pagan priest is very happy because he has meat. But sickness could have been cured without *baki* because you could have cured it at a hospital. Very expensive; it makes you poorer, you have no progress." An older Christian woman, in her late sixties or early seventies, said: "When we were still just married we went to the [Christian] religion, and stopped *baki* because we had to kill so many pigs, chickens, eat rice. Without *baki*, they only butcher one pig or one chicken. They don't believe in spirits anymore."

There were two stated reasons for not sacrificing animals in Christian prayer rituals. A Christian pastor related:

> [First, the followers of *baki*] are on the old belief that they have to offer chickens, pigs and *baki*. But now we can worship God without those things. . . . In the Old Testament, that's the way they worshipped God. But when Jesus was born, he fulfilled that instead of animals it was Jesus Christ who was offered. Those animals were given to men to use and not to offer animals to God, because God gave those animals to use.
>
> [Second], we can see that is the reason there is no improvement of life. The reason is on their belief. When there is offering they will use them [animals] instead of selling for a good house, educating. That is the main reason that they're still not yet educated. They need education. Because in every situation, they have to offer. Example: in harvest time, they offer. Then they bring their rice, offer again. And before bringing it out again, they play *baki* again, plant rice again, *hardchang baki* again. So, there is a cycle for playing *baki*, while they are working. So how do they expect material progress? And when they have sickness and they bring to hospital, they still practice *baki*. This affects the life of people, most especially their education.

PHOTO 8.1 Ifugao people sharing food during a house-blessing *baki* ritual. With a reduction in the performance of *baki* rituals, poor people had fewer opportunities to benefit from food served during these rituals.

In the past, animals were not as costly—relative to Ifugao people's total income—as they were in the early 1990s. As Ifugao people became incorporated into the state and drawn into the national market economy, they experienced an increased need for cash to purchase their new daily needs in the market, clothing, and costly medicines, to send their children to schools, and so forth. They often made the decision to sell food that they used to eat (particularly animals) for cash, due in large part to these new needs which developed since the American occupation. This process also was found in lowland areas of the Philippines (Pertierra 1988).

This change—coupled with the lack of the requirement to provide sacrificial animals during Christian prayer services and Christian promises of prosperity, modernization, and development—encouraged Ifugao people to convert to Christianity. The Christian restriction on the necessity for feasting was found to be a highly significant factor in facilitating conversion to Christianity in other areas of the Philippines as well, such as among some poor Ilocano people of Zamora, Ilocos Sur (Pertierra 1988:168). One problem with the argument of the Ifugao Christian pastor cited above, however, was that he claimed the main reason for poverty and lack of education was the sacrificing of numerous animals during *baki*. In this construction, he ignored larger social and political factors (again, such as local and national social class relations, international economic relations, etc.) which contributed to the development of widespread poverty in the Philippines and related problems in the Philippine educational system.

Body maintenance, particularly in times of illness, creates social bonds, expresses social relations, and reaffirms or denies them (Turner 1984:191). Historically, a system of sharing and displaying wealth was developed in the form of the Ifugao culture and religion, as the *baki* ritual. As discussed earlier, wealth in Ifugao historically was perceived to be mainly based on the ability to continuously consume rice and meat products. In this system, the *kadangyan* were expected to provide more sacrificial animals, rice, and rice wine at *baki* than the poor, which would be eaten and drunk by all community members. The more affluent were also expected to provide more *baki* throughout the year than the poor. Through this process, *baki* provided some redistribution of resources among the social class groups, particularly benefitting the poorest families who were lacking rice and meat products.

The numbers of animals prescribed by *baki* in some cases created hardship and indebtedness for lower class families in recent years, especially due to the relative increase in the price of sacrificial animals such as chickens, pigs, and water buffalo. A number of Ifugao people complained of having to mortgage rice fields to practice *baki*, which were sometimes regained in the future, but not always.

However, this difficulty must be viewed not only in terms of the Ifugao people's need for cash in the new market economy, but also in terms of new western ideologies of individualism and personal financial progress, or financial progress of the nuclear family. This ideology was furthered by fundamentalist Protestants in the early 1990s, who encouraged the retention of a family's animals, or the sale of them, to provide for the needs of family members. The fundamentalist Protestant pastor quoted above used a specific western understanding of progress: material progress of the nuclear family. This contrasted with the social and religious progress of the entire community, which was a value held more strongly by Ifugao people prior to the influence of western ideologies of individualism. The propagation of an ideology of individualism by Christians has occurred in other ethnic communities where Christianity has been incorporated as well, such as among the Ga of Ghana (Mullings 1984:36). Fundamentalist Protestants encouraged Ifugao people to develop a more individualistic, western notion of family resources, wherein the nuclear or limited extended family retained their resources by not performing *baki*. The fundamentalist Protestants believed they would ultimately become more wealthy through this practice, as families saved their resources to provide for the education of their children. This argument supported the Christian objective of converting non-Christians to Christianity.

The argument is also in-line with contemporary discourse among American fundamentalist Christians who propose that faith in Christianity, or participation in Christian networks, can provide wealth and good health (Barron 1987; Goelz 1983). This can be accurate, to some degree, if the church is wealthy and offers access to resources or employment through social networks. However, in a social context of high unemployment and underemployment, acquiring an education does not guarantee upward mobility. The continuation of *baki* and sharing food at some Christian events reflected, in part, the continued need for the sharing of resources in the face of financial insecurity. Further, the penetrating ideology of individualism was breaking down a system of redistribution of community resources that still operated in the contemporary economic system of Ifugao.

Additionally, numerous persons stated that biomedicine was very expensive in the Philippines— as was *baki* for healing—since there were many costs involved in biomedical care, despite the free services of medical personnel at government hospitals. The medical expenses caused hardship for both the middle class and the poorest families in cases of serious illness. Similar to those practicing *baki*, families at times mortgaged or sold their rice fields, and sometimes borrowed money from their relatives or upper class families at high interest rates, in order to acquire medicines or biomedical services at private medical institutions. Relatives usually offered any assistance they could as well.

As noted above, although many Christian rituals did include the serving of food, in a similar fashion as *baki*, it was not required. I attended many Christian prayer services during which no food was provided. Although Christian leaders instructed families to discontinue butchering many animals, numerous Christian families continued the practice, as well as serving rice and other foods at funerals, fiestas, marriages, house blessings, baptisms or Protestant dedication of babies, birthday parties, graduations, and holidays such as Christmas, New Year, and Easter. At these Christian and secular events, the act of sharing food was a retention of the traditional *baki* practice of sacrificing and sharing food. However, food was not *always* provided at these events, nor at Christian healing rituals, and Christians no longer sponsored *baki* for agriculture or met obligations to their ancestors. Thus, although Christian sponsored community events often did include serving food, the practice was much reduced in recent years.

This change in the Ifugao social structure may have had a significant nutritional impact, particularly on the poorest families in Ifugao, since *bacnang* and *kadangyan* families practiced rituals sharing animal and rice resources with community members much less often than they had in the past. *Baki* used to be performed on a regular basis. Sometimes a number of *baki* were performed each week in communities when most Ifugao people were practitioners. Through the practice of *baki*, the poorest families, who could not afford to eat rice or meat regularly, could still share in the food resources of other community members, with the greatest share coming from the wealthy. Since meat products were not eaten on a regular basis by most poor people in Ifugao and poor families could not always afford to purchase oil for their cooking, meat served at rituals was a good source of protein and fat for lower class persons who were lacking in each of these foods in their diets. Also, while members of the lower class continued to eat more sweet potatoes than the upper class (although the poor did have greater access to rice than in the past due to the importation of lowland rice into Ifugao markets), the poor were able to eat more rice during *baki*. Without *baki*, the upper class retained more of their food resources than they had with the regular practice of *baki*, and the poorest families had fewer opportunities to partake of the upper class families' resources. Although food was still shared at Christian gatherings, in some instances for reasons of prestige and rank, the number of occasions at which it was shared was reduced. An important cultural practice that provided, to some degree, a safety net for the nutritional welfare of the nutritionally and economically vulnerable—the poorest members of the community—was thus being diminished.[3]

Women and Christianity

Conflicts sometimes arose between Christians and community health workers. Personnel of NGOs, and sometimes of government and international development organizations, instructed women health workers from one community that they were equal to men and taught women about the use of contraceptives in family planning. Some of these same women belonged to Protestant churches, where they learned they should be subservient to their husbands, to accept lower pay than men for their agricultural labor, and to reject all artificial methods of contraception. For example, a "Message From Pastor" (a Methodist pastor), read:

> How to live a happy home. A) Seek first whom you feel happy. Proverb 18. B) Seek the obligation of a family. Genesis 2:24. C) Leave the house of your parents. Romans 7:2. 1Con. 7:13-14. Eph. 3:23 D) Right of husband. Responsibility of a husband as a head (of household). 1. Gen. 2: Guide his family. 2. Decide everything in the family. 3. Husband love your wife. V.25. 1 Cor. 13:4-7 Love Chapter Eph. 3:22 E) Wife submission to her husband.

In another example, at the EC development meeting described previously, one problem identified was, "Low Salary Rate For Women." The objective defined was, "Wage for Women Increased." One women protested that the objective should read: "equal to men's wages, not only increased!" A number of women supported her protest. A Christian man then countered their declaration with, "You are against the commandments! It (equal wages among men and women) is against the commands of Moses!"

At another gathering for a Christian dedication of a newborn child, the same Methodist pastor gave the following message (paraphrased) to the attendees:

> [For women:] Submit yourselves to your husband, always stay in the home to care for your children, and provide for your husband. If your husband is doing something wrong, like being an alcoholic, never go out into the community and say bad things against your husband to other people. Instead, you should praise him by saying he is very strong, and he does a lot of work. You should always sleep together, always in the same bed; do not sleep in separate beds even in the same room because that is like separating from your husband. [At this comment, a few women chuckled and said, "But what if you are very old and you prefer to sleep in separate beds? There are exceptions." At this the pastor stated flatly, "Do not ask questions now."]
>
> [Then he continued for men:] Because women are the weaker vessel you must always teach them what to do. If your wife does not know how to wash the clothes, you should teach her how to wash them instead of going around complaining that she does not know how to wash. You always have to teach your wife how to do things. If she is not doing her work, like washing the clothes, instead of creating a rift in your marriage by telling her directly that she should wash the clothes, you should wash them yourself in front of other people in the community so they will say negative things about her and shame her into washing the clothes. The same with sewing.

Women here were viewed as being weaker, both physically and intellectually, than men. Women were to be publicly shamed into doing family work, while men were never to be shamed in public. Some women heard these Christian instructions and followed them in practice. One recently converted Christian woman, who was also a community health worker, said:

> As it says in the Bible, "be submissive to your husband" because you cannot overpower him, because he is a man. The meaning here is in family decision; you suggest what you want and your husband will see if it is nice. If it is nice, then you are two making the decision. If he thinks it wrong, you will accept that and see that it is also wrong. Like if you say that you need a big dresser but he has no money and you have none because you are only a babysitter. Then you talk it over, you decide. If he says wait, you wait because we have no money. You will submit to him. Even if you disagree with his decision you must accept because you cannot overpower the head of the family and wait for him to see your side. That's what I experience in my family.

As noted in Chapter 3, there was a common perception among Ifugao women, and some Ifugao men, that women work more in Ifugao than men in terms of hours spent working and number of duties to be accomplished daily. This same Christian woman found an explanation in Christian ideology to support this perceived inequality. During one of our conversations, we discussed the following:

Woman: God said, "You, Eve, you are already cursed. And when you bear a child you will suffer the pain." And this is also connected to our work. We will work more [than men] because of that sin.

Lynn: What did you think was the reason women worked more than men before you became a Christian?

Woman: That's just the way because that's the work of the woman. That's a part of life. Women have continuous work. The only time they can rest is at lunchtime. Men will go out and drink there. If there's a *baki*, the men will just sit there and drink wine and gambling. But for women, how can you just go there? You have to take care of the babies, so how can you go to that meeting? And you have to do all of the wash. The only time you have is in the night time. Then, early in the morning you have to cook again. So we have no rest. But for me, since my children have become older, I have more time, like for going to meetings. They can help with some of the work.

Other Christian women listened to Christian teachings and, while they sometimes publicly acknowledged their validity, they did not always adhere to them in practice. As an example, the Christian woman who was the wife of the Christian man who pronounced that women receiving wages equal with men for agricultural work was going against the commands of Moses was also in attendance at that meeting. In the meeting's discussion about the low agricultural pay for women, another woman argued, "There is no equal payment between boys [men] and girls [women] because the boys [men] exert more effort." At this, the Christian wife stood up and proclaimed loudly, "If it is more effort, then I will exert more effort just to catch up with the pay of the men!" She objected to the unequal agricultural pay rate in Ifugao based on sex, and she was not afraid to state this publicly in front of her disagreeing Christian husband.

Some Christian churches objected to the use of artificial methods of contraception (including the Philippine Catholic Church and a Methodist church in Ifugao). However, the majority of women that I interviewed stated that their decision to use or not use contraception was not strongly influenced by their religious beliefs. Instead, their decisions were based on considerations such as their perceptions of, and folklore related to, the physical risk to their bodies posed by contraceptive methods available to them; their related fears of being unable to work hard following use of contraception or tubal ligation surgery; the cultural value of having, and their desire to have, many children; and pressure from their husbands. Likewise, a 1991 survey commissioned by the Philippine Legislators' Committee on Population and Development investigated the attitudes of 1,200 respondents (said to be a "statistically representative sample of all adult Filipinos, male and female, singles and marrieds [and] reflects the national situation, with 84 percent Roman Catholics") regarding institutional influences (religion, physicians, schools, and political officials) on their attitudes toward family planning. A reporter of the *Philippine Daily Inquirer* newspaper wrote that the majority of respondents did not feel strongly restricted from using family planning methods, whether by the rules of their religion, education received, or advice of physicians. The majority supported the freedom of couples to choose family planning methods (David 1992a:5).

Nevertheless, by July 1993, the Philippine Government health department was fighting an ideological battle with the outspoken Catholic Church and some Filipino national Senators over the use of artificial contraceptives to address population growth, to allow women control of their own bodies and reproduction, and to aid in preventing AIDS (Acquired Immunodeficiency Syndrome) (*Philippine Daily Inquirer* 1993c:1, 8).[4] President Ramos and Health Secretary Juan Flavier developed a campaign on population control which encouraged education on artificial and natural birth control methods, family planning for small family size, and informed choice of use or non-use of contraception. The program included distribution of free condoms to poor families. Abortion was illegal in the Philippines.

President Ramos' stated objectives of the family planning program were to cut the country's 2.3 percent (also reported as 2.48 percent) population growth rate to under 2 percent by 1998 as part of a plan to reduce poverty from 50 percent to 30 percent (President Ramos was the country's first Protestant president) (*Philippine Daily Inquirer* 1993a:1; *Philippine Daily Inquirer* 1993c:8). Health Secretary Juan Flavier stated during a radio report, "The most important factor (in the program) are the women themselves so they can have responsibility over their own bodies" (*Philippine Daily Inquirer* 1993b:6). Other government objectives were to deter the spread of the AIDS virus through the use of condoms, "reduce and eventually reverse" migration into the cities and uplands, check environmental degradation in the upland areas, and improve the quality of life (*Philippine Daily Inquirer* 1993a:12).

The Philippine population in 1992 was sixty-four million, up from 60.7 million in 1990 (Puno, Jr. 1992:11). The Philippine population was expected to double to 120 million people by 2020 (Puno, Jr. 1992:11).[5] The Philippine government family planning program's information campaign was funded by USAID, which provided a grant for the program to Johns Hopkins University, in Baltimore, Maryland, for US$70 million. Additionally, US$25 million was allotted from the United Nations Population Fund program to the Philippine government (Lacson 1992:1). The Asian Development Bank also reported in its 1992 annual report that it planned to provide loans in the Asian and Pacific region for family planning, as part of its strategy to increase economic development and lessen poverty rates (*Philippine Daily Inquirer* 1992e:10). In 1992 the Philippine government was also seeking US$200 million in foreign loans for the family planning program (*Asiaweek* 1992:26) and requesting local government agencies to support the program financially.

The family planning program threatened the power and control the Philippine Catholic Church attempted to exert over its parishioners, as well as over its priests, to oppose extramarital sex and artificial birth control. The Church claimed to have the allegiance of 85 percent of the Filipino population. The Catholic Church stated that only natural family planning methods were allowed (*Philippine Daily Inquirer* 1993a:1). Archbishop Jaime Cardinal Sin, who aided Cory Aquino in the 1986 "EDSA Revolution" to overthrow President Marcos, was outspoken in his opposition to the government family planning program. He asked the Catholics in the country to "obey" the Church's instruction on family planning, provided by Pope John Paul II, rather than listen to the government because the church has more "wisdom" than the government (Tampus 1993:1).

Officials of the Philippine Catholic Church stated in the media that artificial methods of family planning were "evil" and "against the will of God." The archbishop said that he received his position on family planning by consulting economists, doctors, social scientists, and politicians. He further stated, "But over and above the professional help of these advisers, the bishops prayed together and went over revealed truths in Scriptures and the magisterium of the Church. . . . If what they [government officials] say has nothing to do with what the Lord says, their smartness has betrayed their foolishness, their intelligent argumentation has betrayed their stupidity" (Tampus 1993:6). The archbishop argued that the Philippine government was not promoting natural family planning methods as aggressively as artificial methods and that the latter methods could induce abortions (*Asiaweek* 1992:26).

Media campaigns were deployed in 1993 from each side of the battle. The Catholic Human Life Foundation purchased a full-page advertisement in the *Philippine Daily Inquirer* on July 25, 1993, to celebrate the twenty-fifth anniversary of the *Humanae Vitae*, the encyclical letter written by Pope Paul VI in 1968, which Pope John Paul II referred to in his arguments against artificial methods of contraception. The advertisement included a supportive message by Archbishop Jaime Cardinal Sin. In support of the Philippine Catholic Church's institutional objections to artificial contraception, Pope Paul VI was cited in the advertisement to have made four general "prophesies" of the consequences of using artificial contraception:

> First, the widespread use of contraception, he noted, would "lead to conjugal infidelity and the general lowering of morality." . . . Second, men will lose respect for women, Paul VI also argued, would "no longer care for her physical and psychological equilibrium" and will come to "the point of considering her as a mere instrument of selfish enjoyment, and no longer as his respected and beloved companion." . . . Third, the widespread acceptance of contraception, the Pope observed would place a "dangerous weapon . . . in the hands of those in public authorities who take no heed of moral exigencies." . . . Finally, Paul VI warned that a contraceptive mentality (sex willfuly [sic] denied of procreation) would lead man to think that he had unlimited dominion over his own body (Human Life Foundation 1993:14).

Eight days later, the government's Philippine Family Planning Program purchased a four-page advertisement in the same newspaper, listing names of hundreds of families, politicians, businesses, and organizations which endorsed the family planning program. The heading of the advertisement read: "More than 60,000 women and children will die this year because of unplanned pregnancies and birth complications." The endorsers were said to be helping to save those lives (Philippine Family Planning Program 1993:24-27).

The Catholic Church-based National Media Council vowed to "sabotage" the family planning program (*Philippine Daily Inquirer* 1993a:12). The Catholic Bishops' Conference of the Philippines issued a pastoral letter calling on health workers to defy the government's policy of informing couples about artificial and natural methods of birth control (Tampus 1993:6). President Ramos then advised that government workers who felt the government program violated their religious beliefs were free to resign from their jobs. Although the Catholic Church railed against this proposition, two women's organizations—Women's Health Care Foundation and the Alliance for Women's Health—supported President Ramos' position (Tadiar 1993:5).

Despite the proclamations by leading officials within the Catholic Church, a newspaper editorial claimed that "there has been growing acceptance in the hierarchy [of the Catholic Church] of extreme population rise as a problem, a far cry from the staunch traditionalist view that the matter is a non-problem" (*Manila Chronicle* 1993:4). Many dioceses set up pastoral health centers promoting responsible parenthood and natural birth control methods (*Manila Chronicle* 1993:4). The chairman of the Episcopal Commission on Family Life found it necessary to discipline priests by informing those who personally found nothing wrong with the use of artificial contraceptives that only the Pope and the bishops were the "official teachers" of the Catholic Church (Gonzales 1992:7).

Some Catholic women resisted the Church's stance on family planning. At a roundtable breakfast forum in Manila in 1992, which focused on a movement called "The Women's Vote for Health and Family Planning," a Catholic nun at the forum was quoted as saying:

> First, said Sr. Christine, people should define what they mean by "Church" in this context, because the teaching against artificial contraception does not necessarily reflect the thinking or conviction of the entire Church.
> So when we say that the "Church is against artificial contraception," she said, we really mean the "institutional Church," the bishops.
> "And who are the bishops?," Sr. Christine asked rhetorically, "They are males. They have not borne a child. They do not know poverty, not having lived among the poor. They have not seen how the children of the poor die because they do not have enough to eat." Her voice low but set on edge by an anger so deep it is beyond expression, Sr. Christine declared: "Only a nincompoop would not support a family planning program."
> . . . In an article entitled "Angry—Yet Faithful: How Women Cope with their Non-Responsive Church" *(The Catholic World*, Nov./Dec. 1991), Chinnici [a theology professor] relates: "Listen to any Church woman's group for very long and you will hear evidence of anger." (David 1992b:5).

Among groups outside of the Catholic Church and government, national women's organizations—KALAYAAN (*Katipunan ng Kababaihan Para sa Kalayaan*), GABRIELA (General Assembly Binding Women for Reform, Integrity, Equality, Leadership, and Action), and later Womanhealth, among others —supported and promoted women's reproductive rights as human rights since at least 1985. In 1986 many women's groups in Metro Manila fought against the Catholic Church in its recommendation to the new Constitutional Commission to make no provision for family planning or population programs. They also forestalled the signing of a Presidential Executive Order by President Aquino, which Church officials drafted to prohibit government funds to be used to discuss any reproductive contraception except natural methods. Only a minority of women and women's groups were pro-abortion at that time, so women's ability to choose an abortion was not stressed by women's groups during the construction of the 1986 Constitution.

In contrast, groups within the Philippine NDF made statements in the media against the government discourse on population regulation, though for different reasons than those of the Catholic Church. The Cebu MAKIBAKA, a women's group and affiliate of the NDF, criticized the government program by stating that the problem "lies not in uncontrolled population growth but unjust disbursement of government funds for the same population from the World Bank-IMF and foreign capitalists" (J. Y. G. 1992:19). Another NDF affiliate, a "clandestine church group," urged President Ramos to "stop fooling the churches" and to talk about the basic problems of the people rather than superficial issues (*Philippine Daily Inquirer* 1992b:6).

Other Philippine churches, on the other hand, supported the government's family planning program. Both the *Iglesia ni Cristo* (Church of Christ), the largest independent church in the Philippines, and the United Church of Christ, a Protestant church, openly supported the government program (*Asiaweek* 1992:27).

Through this battle between Church and State, Ifugao government health workers, volunteer health workers, and women generally, were faced with conflicting ideologies and identities: parent, health worker, or church member? The disparate ideas and instructions given by NGOs, government agencies, professional groups, development organizations, and Christian leaders created intellectual and moral contradictions for women health workers and other women. These contradictions did not appear to be fully resolved in their minds, since some women's discourse supported each perspective during different conversations or both perspectives were rationalized simultaneously.[6] Although most women stated that their choice of contraception use was not strongly influenced by their church, their access to contraception and education could be greatly influenced by the Catholic Church if the state compromises its family planning program and its services to Filipino women to accommodate the power exerted by the Church, as President Aquino had done.

For these reasons, state, religious, and women's power struggles surrounding contraception had an important influence on women and children's health and nutritional status, especially lower class women and children, as it influenced their access to contraceptive methods and both the number of children conceived and the spacing of women's pregnancies.

Some Ifugao women had been influenced by church instructions on contraception. The Ifugao Christian woman described above, who advocated equal pay for women and men, was both a member of the Methodist church and a volunteer NGO health worker. This local Methodist church denounced any form of family planning since, in the leaders' views, God wants to populate heaven with as many souls as possible. This woman related that a male American missionary visited their church in 1992 and expressed opposition to family planning. He supported his view by stating that there was no population problem since it was obvious to him that there was still a great deal of land for people to occupy, as exemplified by the Ifugao mountains around him. I asked her how she accommodated the conflicting messages she received regarding family planning through her health worker training and her Christian instruction. She stated without hesitation that she simply would continue her health work but offer no instruction regarding family planning or contraception to adults in her barrio.

Bryan Turner (1984) draws relationships between religion and medicine, as well as law, in western culture, contending that each regulates and manages human embodiment. Religious ritual practices regulate and constrain the human body with the aim of developing spiritual existence. Medicine, too, regulates and restrains the body (Turner 1984). This theoretical perspective is especially applicable to the control of women's minds and bodies. The rise of fundamentalist Protestant teachings of women's submission to men, and Protestant and Catholic males' imposition of their own constructions of women's sexuality and reproduction in Ifugao, may lead to a decrease in the already low position of Ifugao women in relation to men (although I did observe Ifugao women resisting male domination). These factors may also lead to a decrease in women's control over their own bodies and, relatedly, to poorer health and nutritional status among women and children, especially if women's social position is lowered, spacing of children is not practiced, and average family size remains large or increases.

The impact of Christian teachings on women's social position and their perceptions of themselves relate to nutrition, as seen in earlier studies cited, which drew a relationship between women's social position within their households and their communities and the health and nutritional status of themselves and that of their children. The impact of fundamentalist Christian teachings promoting women's submission to males in the household and the community counteracted attempts by Ifugao women, government and development agencies, health NGOs, and Filipino women's organizations to raise the social position of women in Ifugao, as well as in Philippine society at large. These teachings may have worked to reduce the potential for women's improved health and nutritional status as well.

Interestingly, although the objectives of government and international development organizations and Christian groups contradicted each other at times, agents of international development organizations continued to create alliances with leaders of Christian groups. Through the interactions of these different groups in their development and conversion endeavors, there were shifting and unstable alliances and relations of power, creating some confusion for community members who desired to be aligned with more than one group simultaneously. At times the alignments appeared to be solid, such as at the development meetings described above, and at other times the alignments were fractured due to variant ideologies, such as the cases of artificial contraception and equal pay. These shifting and contradicting power relations and ideologies often result in conflicting paradigms operating simultaneously, rendering "development practices" less effective.

Christianity and Social Reformation

Weber and others argued that world religions, including Christianity, had tremendous potential for facilitating revolutionary social change and reformation (Lancaster 1988; Weber 1956). Weber was convinced that belief in and practice of world religions could lead to a reassessment of the social order in light of a far superior transcendental realm, and hence to social transformation. There are numerous examples, even within the Philippines, to support this argument, such as Philippine Base Christian Communities and Liberation Theology among Catholic priests and nuns working against the Marcos and Aquino regimes; the Philippine Catholic Church's involvement in overturning the Marcos regime; and clandestine Philippine Christian groups operating within the National Democratic Front (Gaspar 1990; de la Torre 1986). Also, some Philippine Catholic groups called for large-scale social and economic restructuring and espoused the violent politics of communist insurgents (Tefft 1991:6).

Yet, in addition to this process of social transformation, Christian discourse and practice can in other instances, places, and historical periods lead to passivity and the sanctioning and acceptance of the existing social order, no matter how unjust. For example, the fundamentalist Protestants' blaming of the Ifugao religion as being the overall root cause of low income—and related poor health, malnutrition, and low level of education—among Ifugao people masked the broader social structural, national, and international forces that generate structures of social inequality. The Protestant fundamentalist Christian position in Ifugao led to a more passive political stance among some Ifugao people toward resolving these social problems. Relatedly, missionary aid can result in a kind of pacification of people, since missionary aid organizations, particularly foreign, have not historically questioned the sociopolitical causes of poverty—although there have been exceptions.

In addition, the fundamentalist Protestant group cited above was aligned with an international development organization which sanctioned the existing sociopolitical order and operated in Ifugao as guest of the state. An examination of the political and economic social order that resulted in mass poverty for almost 45 percent of the Philippine population and widespread nutritional deficiencies was neglected by fundamentalist Protestant proselytizers in Ifugao in their attempts to help resolve the problem of malnutrition. Instead, both development agents and fundamentalist Protestants linked poverty to local Ifugao cultures and practices (although not all Christian groups in Ifugao did this). In this case, the fundamentalist Protestant discourse and practices were not politically transformative on a local or national level. Rather, they masked macro-level causes of illness and poverty and subverted the potential to alter political and social relations on local, national, and international levels to resolve socially produced problems such as poverty and malnutrition.

As of the early 1990s, the continuous process of the breakdown of the Ifugao culture and its ritual ceremonies through the spread of Christianity and a modern, western oriented ideological, economic, and political system had not fully altered the meanings Ifugao people attributed to prayer, illness, or health. Instead, Christianity in Ifugao had been incorporated into local social forms of religious practice. However, there were changes in ideologies of assistance and distribution of wealth through the distribution of food products with the introduction of Christianity, which particularly influenced the nutritional intake of the poor. The encouragement, by some Christian sects, of women to act in submission to men, as well as Christian restrictions on women's control over their own bodies through use of artificial methods of contraception, could have a long-term negative impact on women's and children's health and nutritional status. In addition, the construction of a form of self-blame for poverty among Ifugao people, through some fundamentalist Protestant instructions, served to support other efforts to westernize, modernize, and develop the Ifugao community within the existing sociopolitical order.

Through the discourses and practices of government institutions, international development organizations, NGOs, and religious groups, Ifugao people were placed in the position of struggling with many conflicting influences and powers imposed upon them from without. The struggle was varied among different groups within Ifugao, such as gendered, social class, and religious. The changes effected in ideologies, social structures, cultural practices, and social positions within the Ifugao community—coming about with the Ifugao people's insertion into a national market economy and their exposure to national government, international, and religious influences on social power relations in their society—often had a negative impact on the nutritional status of lower class Ifugao people, as well as on Ifugao women and children of all classes.

Notes

1. The emphasis on improved health and increased wealth through Christian faith, morality, and rules for living is commonly found among contemporary American fundamentalist Christian evangelical and charismatic organizations (see Barron 1987; Goelz 1983; and Hexham 1982).

2. The greatest conversion period was the late 1950s and the 1960s.

3. Although the everyday sharing of food among kin and neighbors remained an integral aspect of Ifugao social relations, meat was rarely shared among people (only rice, sweet potato, and vegetables were regularly shared). Reasons offered for this practice were that meat was rarer, more highly valued, and expensive.

4. See also *Philippine Star* 1993:1-2; Tampus 1993:1, 6; Olivares 1993:4; and Esplanada 1993a:1, 13.

5. This figure was reported in a document entitled "Population and Development Profile: Philippines, Selected Indicators," prepared by the United Nations Population Fund, the National Economic and Development Authority, and the University of the Philippines Population Institute (Puno, Jr. 1992:11).

6. This problem is illustrative of "reference group theory," which holds that a person's identities and sense of self are usually experienced in reference to a particular group and its ideology, and that people usually have more than one reference group toward which they hold allegiance, particularly in a plural society. These may conflict with one another at times, requiring reflection and decision making about one's values and commitments (Hefner 1993).

9

Conclusion

In a distant barrio of a remote Ifugao municipality lived a poverty stricken extended family who grappled with hunger and malnutrition. While their household composition shifted over time, their family consisted of two grandparents in their seventies, one daughter in her twenties, another daughter who was separated from her husband, and her four young female children. They all lived in a small one-room "native house," while they incrementally built another small modern-styled home to accommodate all of their family members. During much of the early 1990s, the children's mother was working in a province approximately fourteen hours travel time away, leaving her four children under the care of their grandparents and aunt. All four children had been malnourished in recent months, and each had some periods during which their weights were normal. The youngest child, an infant, was severely malnourished during 1992. The family was very poor, and the elderly grandparents continued to farm their small area of rice fields and garden because they were in desperate need of food and income. The children were dressed in old, tattered clothing, and their appearance was unkempt. They were quiet and gentle, and very curious about my and my research assistant's visit to their home in September 1992.

The grandfather told us that one day, nine months earlier, after the children's father had drunk a good amount of beer, his face and back became very painful. So the grandfather and grandmother helped to bring him to the hospital. After that day, the children's father never returned home. He informally married another woman and had a then, three-month-old infant with her. The father gave his ex-wife only a little more than half of a traditionally negotiated marital separation settlement, and the grandfather suspected the mediator involved in the settlement kept the remaining half for himself and his friends. The father provided money for his children only once during a nine-month period, when his malnourished infant was placed in a hospital and money was needed to pay for medical expenses and canned infant milk. During that same time, the father also paid a remaining debt owed for a rice field he and his ex-wife had purchased. Both the father and mother planned to farm the field to provide food for their children, despite their permanent separation. The grandfather relayed the following to us about his family during our visit:

> We bought five cans of Bonna [infant] milk for the baby, for 325 pesos. One can lasts more than one week. We are taking care of the children because they [their parents] left. Their mother went to Baguio city three to four months ago, to work as a domestic helper. She went to work and to forget her problems.
>
> The doctor said that the baby is malnourished. She told me to buy Bonna milk, not just any milk, only Bonna, so that her body would become strong. We also mix the milk with rice gruel. The doctor told us not to include sugar, just add boiled water. We see that the baby is getting better. We are not adding sugar to the rice gruel anymore.
>
> The children's mother has sent 100 pesos to help buy Bonna milk, and she sent some toys for the children. When my wife went to the center of town, she only received the toys and 100 pesos, and a message from our daughter telling us to use it to buy Bonna milk. But I had already bought the Bonna, so we used it to buy petroleum for the light and some bread; but we saved some to buy something else.
>
> When we brought the baby to the hospital, some of the nurses told me that we didn't have to pay the full cost of dextrose given to the baby. Instead of paying 240 pesos we only paid 100 pesos. They used two viles, although one quarter was not used. They gave this to her because of her malnutrition, third degree. Last week she had a bad cough, so we bought medicine for her. Breastfeeding for the baby stopped when her mother went to Baguio. During May and August the baby had a cough and cold. We gave her vitamin A. In July she had pneumonia. We did not complete her vaccinations yet [and a number are still required]. . . . We will try to buy more Bonna after the last can is finished.
>
> I don't feel anything [about having to take care of my grandchildren], only that I have to be patient. I am trying hard. The second child has now gone with her father. She left two months ago. The parents of the child's father came to get her because she was sick with a cough. Now they are two [children] with the father, that girl and his new child.
>
> I expect that my daughter will send us money from Baguio, if some people will come here from Baguio, and she will send at least 100 pesos with them. I think she will be back for Christmas. It is not difficult to raise them; the only problem is when they cry. And, there is a problem for money. We have to sell something to get money.

This family experienced problems shared by many other poor Ifugao families, who continually faced malnutrition and illness of their young children; pressure to continue working at even a very old age for survival; labor migration of adult children within the Philippines, who intermittently sent small sums of money and goods to their families to assist them; the problem of earning money to purchase expensive medicines and canned infant milk products to aid their malnourished children in their process of recovery; and difficulty finding the patience to bear the burden of their families' health, emotional, and economic concerns. This family bore the added problem of single motherhood following marital separation. The single mother had to seek a higher income than most married Ifugao women due to a lack of adequate or consistent child support from her ex-husband, low pay rates for female agricultural laborers in Ifugao, and few other employment opportunities within Ifugao. She also needed to rely extensively on her natal family for child care and emotional and financial support. This woman's experience was commonly shared by single mothers.

In this case, local hospital personnel were able to provide some support for the family, support they extended to poor families as often as possible with their limited social service funds. The mother's absence and termination of breastfeeding upon her labor migration, in the face of marital separation and increased poverty, likely led to her infant's state of severe malnutrition and continued malnutrition and illness of her older children. While international development projects tried to rectify poverty and malnutrition in Ifugao for a number of years, the experience of this family was still all too common in the early 1990s.

Continuing Inequality

National and international development programs operating in Ifugao during the early 1990s made great efforts to incorporate women into their overall development efforts, in a sincere attempt to raise the social, nutritional, general health, and economic positions of women in Ifugao. Scholars have argued that an increase in women's social position will likely lead to an improvement in their nutritional status (Senauer 1990; Schoepf 1987:73, 94-95). National and international development ment agents and scholars have proposed that the enhanced social, nutritional, health, and economic status of women will likewise improve the nutritional and health status of their children both during pregnancy and lactation, and throughout their developmental years (Senauer 1990).

This ethnography, though, questions the recent call by feminists, scholars, and development organizations for the increased inclusion of women in western development programs as they currently operate in non-industrialized societies. This position is taken in light of the larger detrimental, or at best non-beneficial, impact of western development programs on people of non-western societies as a whole (such as macro-level economic development programs, involving structural adjustment programs; former "green revolution" agricultural programs of the World Bank; and programs that focus primarily on the micro-level, such as the UNICEF program in Ifugao). An example of the negative impact of aid and development programs was the decline in the already low income shares of the lowest 30 percent of Filipino families from 1988 to 1991, from 9.3 percent to 8.4 percent respectively, as well as of families in the fourth to eighth decile, whose income shares decreased from 38.9 percent in 1988 to 37.1 percent in 1991. During the same period, the most wealthy Filipino families in the highest decile increased their share of national income by 2.8 percent from 1988 to 1991 (National Statistics Office, Republic of the Philippines 1992a:3).

PHOTO 9.1 These children, held by their sister and mother, are twins. The child on the left is severely malnourished and the child on the right is second degree malnourished. Their father's long-term illness was one factor leading to their family's poverty and the twins' malnutrition.

In analyzing the economic policies of the Philippine government and of international lending and development organizations (which the Philippine government came increasingly to rely on) we find that in the late 1990s, after more than twenty years of both IMF/World Bank international development programs on the local level and structural adjustment programs recommended by USAID, UNICEF, EC, WHO, the Japanese government, the Asian Development Bank, and others, a high percentage of Filipino people, especially rural peasants nationally (47 percent)—including the majority of Ifugao people—still had annual incomes that fell below the poverty level (Racelis 1997). Also, a conservative estimate identifies almost one-third of all Filipino children under five years old underweight for their age by 1997 (UNICEF 1997).[1] Numerous studies have documented the detrimental effects on the lower class of World Bank development programs, international lending programs, and IMF/World Bank structural adjustment programs in the

Philippines. These included the generation of a massive national debt ($34 billion in 1996 [Lindio-McGovern 1997]) from loans with high interest payments for which almost 40 percent of the national budget has at times been allocated (38.6 percent in 1992); a concomitant decrease in the real amount of the national budget spent on domestic social programs such as education and health; increasing export-oriented industrialization, including export cash crop production; increasing underemployment and unemployment; increasing prices of food, other commodities, and services with price decontrol; liberalization and promotion of trade and foreign investment, to the detriment of small Filipino businesses; restrictions on union organizing; and lowered real wage rates.[2]

From 1988 to 1991, with increasing costs of commodities and services, there was a nationwide decrease in the percentage of family income spent on food, from 50.7 percent in 1988 to 47.6 percent in 1991, while there was a corresponding increase in the percentage of family income spent on housing, education, transportation, communication, fuel light, water, and other expenses (National Statistics Office, Republic of the Philippines 1992a:4-5). In rural areas such as Ifugao the percentage of income spent on food decreased from 58.8 percent in 1988 to 53.6 percent in 1991 (National Statistics Office, Republic of the Philippines 1992a:14). Increasing prices, related to structural adjustment programs, affected the percentage of income families could spend on their nutritional needs. In 1987, the Philippine DOH reported that the nutritional energy intake of children of all ages was only 87 percent of the required level, which was a drop from 89 percent in 1978; preschool children were found to obtain only 65 percent of their daily dietary requirements. With less family income being spent on food in 1991, the percentage of daily dietary requirements met by Filipino children had likely lowered even more.

The regional minimum wage rates, which structural adjustment programs dictated the Philippine government should keep low, were not really adequate for Filipino families to survive (HAIN 1994:7).[3] One research organization estimated that in 1992, in order for a family of six to meet all of their basic needs, an income of at least 228 pesos per day would be needed (Madew 1992:5). In Ifugao, with the daily minimum wage rates having been set at only approximately 85 pesos per day—and women's agricultural pay rates having been paid at approximately 40 pesos per day—the income of a family of six (whose principal adults' incomes were mainly derived from wage labor) would fall well below the minimum needed for an adequate standard of living. Low wage rates had an impact on most Ifugao peasant families who relied mainly on agricultural production for their income as well, particularly during the dry and monsoon seasons when many foods could not be cultivated or collected due to the weather. Obtaining rice was also difficult during the months prior to the rice harvest, when rice supplies were low and families relied heavily on earned wages for their subsistence needs.

Interrelated with the failure of economic development programs to improve the economic situation was the perpetuation of an unequal social class system in the

Philippines. The Philippine government historically has failed to implement an agrarian reform program to redistribute agricultural lands to benefit a major proportion of the landless (Lindio-McGovern 1997; Kulkarni and Tasker 1996). In fairness, much more land was redistributed during the Ramos administration than in the past (Habito 1997; Racelis 1997). Yet, even during his administration, over half of more than three million farmers were still waiting for their share of land and agricultural resources. Landlord resistance remained a constraint to land reform. Recent land conversion, from agricultural to other types for new purposes (factories, golf courses, and other leisure activities), threatened food supplies and the land reform process and displaced local farmers, who may not have had other skills to apply to new jobs. Upland farmers, such as those in Ifugao, were concerned about obtaining tenure security and maintaining and protecting their resources (Racelis 1997).

In addition, the distorting of the Philippine economy through corruption by some government officials historically and currently exacerbated the problems of social inequality and poverty (Aquino 1987). By 1991, after almost twenty years of numerous western development programs and structural adjustment programs focusing on economic growth as the path to development—coupled with the ineffective implementation of agrarian reform—the national income share of 70 percent of Filipino families was only 34.2 percent, while the national income share of the most wealthy 10 percent of Filipino families was 38.6 percent (National Statistics Office, Republic of the Philippines 1992a:12).

In more recent years, President Ramos promoted a program of national growth and development through a Philippines 2000 plan, focusing on four broad areas: domestic political stability, social reforms, promotion of foreign investment and trade, and regional political stability. Also promoted were Ramos' "Five Ds of Philippine people power": devolution of the central government, decentralization of development, democratization, deregulation of industry, and development on a sustainable basis (Habito 1997; Kulkarni, Tasker, and Tiglao 1996). The Ramos government asserted that the Philippine poverty level had been reduced to 35 percent in 1995, from 45 percent in the early 1990s (Ramos 1997).

Yet, when looking at more specific rates of poverty which vary by locale for the late 1990s, we find that 47 percent of Filipino people lived below the poverty level in rural areas and 34 percent lived below the poverty level in urban areas. These figures indicated that a substantial number of people still suffered from poverty in the Philippines by the late 1990s (Racelis 1997; Hernandez 1997; Kulkarni and Tasker 1996). Some observers cautioned that despite indications of economic growth in the Philippines, the fruits of this growth had not been widely distributed among the population. The growing economy was thus perceived by many as doing little to help the poor within a reasonable time period, while it benefitted the middle and upper classes (Racelis 1997).

President Ramos created a Social Reform Council to aid in the process of distributing the benefits of economic growth more evenly throughout the Philippine population. Still, deprived sectors of the population (i.e., women, children, poor farmers, fisherfolk, and elderly) retained needs not met. These included broadened access to quality social services, asset reform, improvement of government services, and sustainable development which promoted environmental concerns as well as economic growth (Racelis 1997).

Deles argued that President Ramos' promise of social reforms had not been fulfilled due to poor social reform legislation, limited and delayed executive action, and nominal and slow releases of government allocation of resources for reform processes. One result of Ramos' policies was that deprived sectors of the population were losing out to market reforms (Deles 1997).

Government officials sought to achieve the status of NIC for the Philippines in the near future and to increase agricultural, industrial, and service productivity. The government attempted to increase production of goods for export, including agricultural exports (Bautista 1997). Thus, the emphasis on producing agricultural products to generate foreign currency and profits through export, rather than to provide low cost food for national consumption, continued through the late 1990s. Racelis commented that agriculture, as it was organized in the late 1990s, offered little hope to small farmers and their families, leading to urban migration and increased numbers of squatters who are stigmatized (Racelis 1997).

During the Ramos administration, the IMF still exerted a powerful influence over government decision making, policies, and practices; and the structural adjustment measures under the Philippines 2000 plan reflected IMF policies (Lindio-McGovern 1997). While economic growth and development was promoted by international and national agencies, almost half of the peasant population still found it difficult to raise adequate quantities of food on small areas of land. Also, both small landowning and landless peasants struggled to purchase food with rising costs food (Kulkarni and Tasker 1996). Children continued to be drawn into agricultural and other forms of labor as a means of survival in the face of stark poverty, affecting their health, nutritional well-being, and their education.[4]

Power, Conflict, and "Development"

Over the last few decades, the practices of international development programs operating in the Philippines essentially maintained the unequal social class structure, as shown by the figures above. At the same time, the macro- and micro-level development strategies of industrialized countries in the Philippines benefitted the industrialized donor countries through the liberalization of trade; the maintenance of low wage rates paid to workers of transnational corporations operating in the Philippines; restrictions on labor union organizing; the creation of markets for commodity goods of industrialized countries; the generation of profit from interest paid on money lent to the Philippine government; and the sublimation of resistance movements that would threaten existing social structures (which allow for these benefits) through development programs as a strategy of counter-insurgency to maintain political stability for further investment and trade.

The low economic status of a high percentage of the Filipino population affected their nutritional status. The Philippine government and international development agencies did not ignore the problem of widespread malnutrition in the Philippines; instead, they were very active in developing programs to alleviate the problem. But, the nutrition programs of the Philippine government and international development agencies historically followed a mainly western, biomedical, primary health care model, which emphasized an individual, depoliticized, and project orientation, including medically treating malnourished individuals; educating their family members, primarily women; implementing immunization programs; introducing project-oriented attempts to facilitate family economic improvement, such as through gardening projects; improving sanitation; implementing infrastructure development programs; attempting to raise women's gender status; and introducing other individual, family, and community level programs. At the same time, changes in economic and social structures that could increase the quality of nutrition, economic, and general living status for the lower class of the Philippines did not occur. Nor have significant numbers of people acquired greater access to productive resources, as evidenced, in part, by the failures of the agrarian reform programs over past decades, though this may have been slowly improving in the late 1990s.

International development programs, such as those in Ifugao, which treat individuals who are malnourished at the individual, family, and community levels and which provide an image of development of societies, serve to support larger unequal social class and international economic relationships. These programs often work to deflect community disaffection and action geared toward fundamental social change. In part, this is achieved by promising substantial social and economic change through development projects and by localizing the cause of social and health problems, such as malnutrition, through development instructions provided to individuals (often women), families, and communities.

More specifically, the biomedical approach to malnutrition, designed to aid improperly and inadequately nourished individuals, has included an intense focus by international, national, and local health care personnel on identifying, monitoring, weighing, providing "food supplements," educating, and surveying deprived and inadequately nourished bodies. This approach transfers the cause of hunger and malnutrition away from social power relations (involving elite government officials, large landowners, and industrialized countries through IMF/World Bank lending institutions) and locates the causes instead within an ideology of individual and family responsibility, mainly "mother's" responsibility.

The concomitant attempts by national and international health and development organizations to involve women in development through essentially top-down development programs are also oriented toward the individual, family, and community. They are also reformist in nature. International and state funded development programs in Ifugao focused on women primarily as "mothers," who were portrayed as being mainly responsible—and often to blame—for their children's and their families' nutritional status. In Ifugao, the larger international development programs indirectly influenced Ifugao people to conform to existing social structures, while at the same time preparing them to accept a western, individualistic, capitalist mode of economic development. These social structures and economic models historically had been biased against women both economically and politically in the public realm and in the domestic sphere.

The major international health and development programs operating at the local level in the Philippines, such as those implemented through USAID, EC, UNICEF, the Japanese and German governments, were funded and directed by the same industrialized states that were simultaneously implementing IMF/World Bank development, loan, and structural adjustment programs.[5] Scholars have argued that structural adjustment programs have resulted in increased impoverishment and malnutrition in the Philippines (Lindio-McGovern 1977). Through these biomedically influenced and project-oriented approaches to malnutrition, national and international health and development agencies exerted a subtle form of control over poor, malnourished bodies, exhorting them, especially women, to look inward for the causes of malnutrition, rather than outward to the social and political powers, such as those delineated above, that played a significant role in generating and maintaining inequality, mass poverty, and malnutrition. In Ifugao, national and international development agents presented the concept of "poverty" to program participants as an ahistorical, inherently existing condition, which in one development meeting was said to be caused by their own culture and religion, thereby placing blame for poverty squarely on the Ifugao people themselves. Some lower class Ifugao people who could not understand why they were the ones who faced poverty, resigned themselves to the explanations that their poverty was due to fate or the will of God.

The biomedical and international development programs' structuring of hunger, malnutrition, and lack of access to food as a medical, educational, family income, and community problem, while neglecting to take action on the larger political and economic causes of malnutrition, aided in controlling the discontent of the Filipino people. This discontent was, nevertheless, expressed by thousands of Filipinos, including Ifugao people, over the last century through rebellions, revolutionary movements, wars, political protests, strikes, and other forms of resistance. Development programs, including health programs, were used historically as a strategy of counterinsurgency in the Philippines—and continued to be used in the early 1990s, as seen in the case of Ifugao.[6] The branding of NGO health organizations as communist, and threats and attacks by the military on the workers of these organizations, were examples of attempts made by the state to control a form of health care that sought to understand malnutrition and other illnesses as social problems rooted in historical, social, political, and economic processes. These processes themselves generated inequality and hunger in Ifugao.

As seen through the experiences of the Ifugao people, international development programs through the early 1990s were often based on a western, individualistic model. Further, international development programs in Ifugao neglected to analyze closely the social and cultural power relations, such as unequal gender relations, that operated at the micro-level. Instead, the project orientation of the programs resulted in the disregard of local unequal gender relations and social processes that significantly affected Ifugao people's lives in ways which contradicted the intended goals of their programs, including the raising of women's position and the alleviation of malnutrition. The local social processes negatively affecting women's social position and nutritional status included lower pay rates for culturally constructed female labor; women bearing primary responsibility for child care and nutrition within their families; few wage labor opportunities available for women outside of farming, which relatedly influenced their opportunities to enter positions of leadership and power in the community; and fundamentalist Christian organizations' blaming of the Ifugao religion for poverty and their instructing women to be submissive to their husbands and to the men in their communities. The national and international health and development agencies tended to implement projects that did not have much impact on unequal gender relations and that actually reinforced the prioritization of the mother role for women; the naturalization, as a biological imperative, of women being best suited for the responsibility of primary provider of health and child care; and the devaluation of women's labor through their policies of underpaying or not paying women for their labor in many development programs (i.e., child care and health care where women's full-time labor did not generate even a minimum wage).

The national and international health and development agencies also did not realize—or were not concerned with—the complexity of the various relations of power operating in Ifugao, including social class, gender, religious, and ethnic relations. For example, they did not question the ways their alliances with some fundamentalist Protestant organizations, which were perceived by the agencies to be modern, progressive, and pro-development, actually hindered the progress of some of their development goals. The fundamentalist Christian groups in Ifugao resisted raising Ifugao women's social position in areas in which their position was lower than that of men (i.e., economic, domestic, and political). The Christian groups also played a role in the breakdown of cultural institutions that historically had aided the poorest families nutritionally (such as by reducing the local Ifugao religion's practice of ritual sacrificing of animals and rice, and their being shared with community members). As noted above, the Christian groups also scapegoated the Ifugao religion as being the cause of "massive poverty," as Ifugao people often described their condition.

While poverty is not the sole cause of malnutrition, as was seen in the case of malnutrition in Ifugao wherein children of all social classes were found to be malnourished, poverty does exacerbate the severity of malnutrition. This was depicted in my sample of Ifugao children, among whom all of the third degree, or severely, malnourished children were of the lower economic class. Processes such as the development and modernization of Ifugao, which resulted in the introduction of inexpensive refined sugar and sugar laden food products, had a significantly negative impact on the nutritional status of children of all social classes. Also, women's heavy work load (including their culturally constructed responsibility to provide most of the general child and nutritional care for their children) and their lower gender position in important areas of their lives were observed to have an impact on the nutrition of children and women of all social classes.

Without the availability of adequate child care practices or services, children baby-sitting for younger children throughout the daytime continued and resulted in children not always receiving meals that provided them with adequate nutrients. Also, nutritional deficiencies, such as goiter and anemia, which primarily affected women, had only sporadically been treated through iron supplements and iodized salt, and, less frequently, through free surgical goiter removal for the lower class.

The use of the western, biomedical concepts of nutrition and malnutrition created difficulties of understanding for Ifugao adults, whose local conception of *na-ong-ong* did not really correspond to the concepts of first or second degree malnutrition, wherein children do not appear to be severely underweight and wasted. Nor did their local understanding of *na-ong-ong* include a conception of vitamins, proteins, carbohydrates, and other nutrients. Women felt blamed by biomedical providers for a problem the women could not remedy without either an increase in their family's resources or the lowering of food prices. Many lower class Ifugao women strongly held the view that their children's poor nutritional status was primarily a result of their family's lack of access to adequate food resources; a lack of access due to their small rice field size and seasonal restrictions on cultivating food, few employment opportunities, and their lack of money to purchase additional food in local markets. Lower class Ifugao people tried to compensate for their lack of adequate food resources through networks of assistance with relatives and friends, as well as through systems of loaning with interest from wealthier individuals in their communities and assistance provided by economic development programs.

International development programs had adverse effects on local cultures, knowledge, and practices, numerous people's physical well-being, and, in some cases, their sense of identity. International development projects, although usually implemented by well-intentioned local and foreign personnel, often restricted women's lives and perspectives rather than enhanced them—by molding women to conform to western standards of development, modernization, and womanhood, and by diffusing women's political action. Local political movements involving women, on the other hand, which are culturally and historically specific, could place women in a more favorable position from which to express and act upon their needs and desires as economic and political actors.

Considering again the ways in which international development programs have been operating, the negligible results they have achieved, and the adverse impacts they have had on local peoples (Hobart 1993; Bodley 1988), one must question whether it is worthwhile to involve or include women in these forms of western development programs as means to raise women's social position and to improve their and their children's nutritional status. It is not adequate to critique national and international development agencies for their lack of "gender sensitivity" in development programs or for their lack of inclusion of women in development programs, including those aimed toward alleviating malnutrition in non-industrialized countries. The very basis of the contemporary western development project itself must be questioned. The concept of a country's need to "develop," to become like industrialized nations, needs to be called into question as a western notion exported to non-industrialized countries.

There is lack of real engagement of western-based international development organizations with non-western cultures' gendered values and norms, religious, political, and economic processes and contestations—on both the macro-level and micro-level—all of which have inhibited substantial change in the nutritional, class, and gender (for women) positions of lower class people. This lack of engagement contributed to the fact that there had been very little substantial improvement in the economic, social, and health conditions of lower class Ifugao people, including women, as well as the poor of other non-industrialized societies over the last few decades.

Development programs that involve women in projects, but do nothing to deal seriously with gender power relations, ideology, and practices already operating in local communities that compromise women's position, are not likely to significantly enhance women's social position. Also, programs that seek to modernize non-western societies sometimes result in detrimental nutritional effects, such as the practice in Ifugao of feeding children sugar in place of more nutritious foods like vegetables or proteins.

An analysis of malnutrition in a country experiencing LIC must assess the complex relationships that exist between the conflict, the social constructions of the causes of malnutrition, the role development plays as a LIC strategy, and the resistance to state power imposing national ideologies and policies on ethnic groups in local communities. One aspect of the Philippine violence was that of opposing groups (e.g., the state, NPA, and Moro National Liberation Front) vying for political and economic power. By the late 1990s, despite recent factionalization of the NPA and attempted peace negotiations between the Aquino and Ramos governments and the NPA, the war between the Philippine state and the communist revolutionaries continued. Although the war remained a struggle for access to power, the struggle was initiated, in part, because of a lack of access to agricultural land, food, and other basic resources and services, as manifested by the poor nutritional status of poverty stricken Filipinos. While there were many other reasons for the resistance movement, the human right to adequate health, food, and nutrition were some of the fundamental goals of the struggle.

Class systems and systems of inequality are always dynamic and often involve struggle, if only at low levels. Nutritional needs will always be an integral aspect of these struggles as long as they are not being met. Lower class women have long been active in trying to provide health services and to meet the nutritional needs of lower class people in the Philippines. This took the form in one Ifugao community, and in other communities in the Philippines, of providing voluntary health services to poor people in the face of military threats of violence, abuse, or death, and the attempted repression by the state—represented by the military—of forms of health care which addressed larger social structural problems in the Philippines and critiqued state social policies. Resistance to state repression demonstrates that we must not view people in non-industrialized societies as passive recipients of outside pressures and influence; rather, they should be seen as subjects actively engaged in the construction of their daily lives and interpretations of their reality.

International development programs in the Philippines presented themselves as apolitical and offered reformist strategies to solving problems such as malnutrition, while maintaining the basic social structures existing in the country. The great majority of personnel working in both national and international health and development programs were highly dedicated to their work. They believed that their goals of providing the best health services possible to people of all social classes in the Philippines and alleviating the health problems of Filipino people, including malnutrition, could be achieved through their health care programs. While the forms of health care and development being provided may have benefitted some Filipino people in the short-term, in the long-term the lives of Filipino and other poverty stricken people will only be significantly improved if broad social structures of inequality—including international, social class, gender, and ethnic—are simultaneously transformed.

Shifts in conceptions of social change, progress, and equality continue to emerge through community-based social movements—including grassroots community, non-governmental, peoples, feminist, environmental, gay and lesbian, some religious, and others—within the Philippines and societies globally (Lindio-McGovern 1997; Escobar and Alvarez 1992). Members of these groups, local people, and scholars are redefining ideas about "development" on local, national, and international levels. The community-based social movements may provide the poor and the hungry with new avenues to pursue in their efforts to achieve equality, good nutrition, and overall well-being.

Notes

1. A 1997 UNICEF document reported that 30 percent of children under five years old were underweight in the Philippines (UNICEF 1997). This figure may only have included second and third degree malnutrition, while leaving first degree malnourished children unaccounted for. This figure also did not include other nutritional deficiencies experienced

by Filipino children and adults such as iodine, iron, vitamin A, B, and C deficiencies, or conditions such as stunting.

2. See Lindio-McGovern 1997; Dios and Rocamora 1992; Hildebrand 1991; Broad 1988; and Bello et al. 1982.

3. The daily minimum wage for Metro Manila was raised on December 16, 1993, to 135 pesos. Similar adjustments were made in other regions (HAIN 1994:7).

4. Racelis reported that 37 percent of Filipino children were employed nationally in 1997 (Racelis 1997).

5. The top investors in the Philippines from 1981 to 1991 were Japan, the United States, and European countries (IBON 1992b:6).

6. Examples can be found in 702nd Infantry (SOT) Brigade 1992a:5; Davis 1989:10-11; and Bello et al. 1982:25.

Glossary

The terms listed below are a compilation of Ifugao, Tagalog, and Ilocano words, all terms spoken by Ifugao people. The Ifugao terms are not derived from one Ifugao village, but rather from a number of different villages within Ifugao. The spellings are my own, since Ifugao is not a written language.

amat. A wild vegetable.
ampalaya. A vegetable.
ampti. A wild vegetable, similar to spinach.
aninito. Spirits living above the earth; also *anito.*
anito. Spirits living above the earth; also *aninito.*
aphong. House not built on stilts.
bacnang. The newly wealthy in Ifugao; also *bfwatnang.*
baddang. Provision of unpaid assistance, usually reciprocal.
bago-ong. Salty, fermented fish paste.
bagor. Ifugao ritual to introduce a newborn baby to spiritual beings; a form of *baki.*
baki. Local Ifugao religion and ritual; also *bfuni* and *kanyao (canao).*
baki di pagke. Ifugao ritual for rice agriculture.
Balitok. Ifugao son of *Bugan* and the god *Maingit,* who was among the first humans to learn *baki* from *Maingit.*
baond. Lunch, or food supply when travelling.
barangay. Barrio; village; a subdivision of a municipality.
barkada. Closely knit, usually single sex, social group.
bfwabfwa-ee. Female.
bfwaley. A wooden "native house," built on four stilts, with a thatched cogon or a galvanized iron roof.
bolo. Machete.
booris. Any form of diarrhea, or loose or watery stools.
botika. Health clinic and/or pharmacy.
Bugan. First Ifugao woman.
bulul. Carved, wooden rice gods, used in *baki di pagke* (ritual for rice agriculture) and in guarding rice.
bumayah. Ifugao ritual, only sponsored by the wealthy; a form of *baki.*
calamansi. A green citrus fruit.
camote. Sweet potato.
camoting kahoy. Edible root crop, or tuber.
campos. Small, wooden houses.
carabao. Water buffalo.
chinupchup. Ifugao healing ritual; a form of *baki*; also *dinupdup.*

Dalom. The underworld.
Daya. The western world.
dinupdup. Ifugao healing ritual; a form of *baki*; also *chinupchup.*
eebfwal-lo. Revenge.
fee-fee-o. Evil spirits living on the earth.
feter. Famine, a time when food is not available, or spirits who eat a family's rice.
gabi. Root crop, with edible root and leaves.
Gaddang. Filipino ethnic group.
gkufat. World War II.
hafar. Swidden agricultural field; also *kaingin* or *uma.*
hagoho. Ifugao healing ritual; a form of *baki.*
hapeed. Green leaf chewed with betel nut.
hardchang baki. Agricultural ritual.
herbalarium. A clinic which provides herbal treatment for illness.
hogop. Ifugao ritual to bless a newly built house; a form of *baki.*
honga. Unspecified Ifugao ritual.
hongan di pagke. Rituals for rice culture.
hongan di tagu. Rituals for humans.
hutlik. Ifugao healing ritual; a form of *baki.*
Ifugao. An ethnic group of people; also designates their language and province.
Iglesia ni Cristo. Church of Christ.
Igorots. Indigenous people of the Cordillera.
Ilocano. Philippine ethnic group and regional language.
ina. Mother.
inakum. Ifugao healing ritual; a form of *baki.*
inlawit. Ifugao ritual for extreme thinness; a form of *baki*; also *inlawitan* and *lawit.*
inlawitan. Ifugao ritual for extreme thinness; a form of *baki*; also *lawit.*
inyapoy. Ifugao healing ritual and ritual for agriculture; a form of *baki.*
jeepney. Public transportation jeep.
Kabunyan. Ifugao creator god; also called *Muntalug*; also refers to the world above.
kadangyan. The traditional wealthy in Ifugao.
Kiangan. Ifugao municipality.
kintib. Box of a *mumbaki*, containing ritual items.
Lagud. The eastern world.
lala-ee. Male.
lawit. Ifugao ritual for extreme thinness; a form of *baki*; also *inlawitan.*
linawa. The soul of all living things.
lugao. Rice gruel.
Luta. Earth.
Maingit. Ifugao god who impregnated *Bugan*, and taught *baki* to humans.
Maknongan. A set of male gods.
mama-o. Female spirit medium of the Ifugao religion.
manang. Elder sister or woman.
manong. Elder brother or man.
matabfwa. Stout, fat.
moma. Betel nut.
mongo. Mung beans.

mumbaki. Male "native priest" of the Ifugao religion.

munbfuni. Ifugao ritual; also *baki.*

munhakaang. Hunger or hungry.

munhapud. Ifugao divination ritual.

munhinaang. Hunger.

muniyak. An Ifugao curse ritual.

munlamhit. Having no appetite.

munpugyoh. Diarrhea; also *booris.*

Muntalug. Ifugao creator god; also called *Kabunian.*

na-akang-an. Hunger or hungry.

na-ina. An old woman spirit who can cause thinness (*na-ong-ong*).

na-ong-ong. Bodily thinness, which is usually extreme; also *napikot* and *nakotong.*

natumok. The traditional middle class in Ifugao.

nawotwot. The traditional poor, or lower class, in Ifugao.

orchay. Brown pea.

pahang. Ifugao healing ritual; a form of *baki.*

pancit. Noodles.

Partido Lakas Tao. People Power Party.

patis. Salted fish sauce.

pechay. Green leafy vegetable.

poblacion. Central area of municipalities.

pomelo. Citrus fruit, similar to a grapefruit.

pulong-pulong. In the Ifugao context, government military indoctrination seminars with civilians.

pumata. Murder or kill.

rattan fruit. Edible, sour fruit of the *rattan* palm tree.

Sangguniang Bayan. Municipal council.

Sangguniang Panlalawigan. Provincial board.

santol. A fruit.

sari-sari. Small store.

sayote. A vegetable, similar to summer squash, with edible green leaves.

sitio. A cluster of homes, a subdivision of a barrio.

Tagalog. Philippine ethnic group and national language.

tanig. Ifugao ritual for extreme thinness; a form of *baki.*

tikom. Leaves used during *baki.*

tomona. Founding family of a village.

torkay. Local, woven skirt; also *tapis.*

toyo. A small fish.

tuma-o. Afraid.

ubfu. Reciprocal, unpaid labor.

ucat. Fine paid to spouse's family to resolve a problem in marriage.

ugali. Tradition, custom.

ulun chi pamilya. Head of the family.

uma. Swidden agricultural field; also *kaingin* or *hafar.*

Unibersidad ng Pilipinas. University of the Philippines.

utang. Debt.

wanoh. Loin cloth.

Wigan. First Ifugao man.
wombok. A vegetable.

Acronyms

ABCSD. Area Based Child Survival and Development (UNICEF Program).
AFP. Armed Forces of the Philippines.
AIDS. Acquired immunodeficiency syndrome.
BEC. Basic Ecclesiastical Communities.
BHW. *Barangay* Health Worker.
BIDANI. *Barangay* Integrated Development Approach for Nutrition Improvement of the Rural Poor.
BNS. *Barangay* Nutrition Scholar.
BUNSO. *Balikatan at Ugnayang Naglalayong Sumagip sa Sanggol.*
CAFGU. Citizen Armed Force Geographical Unit.
CARL. Comprehensive Agrarian Reform Law.
CARP. Comprehensive Agrarian Reform Program.
CECAP. Central Cordillera Agricultural Programme.
CHDF. Civilian Home Defense Force.
CIA. Central Intelligence Agency.
CMC. Child Minding Centers.
COIN. Intensified Counterinsurgency Campaign.
CPA. Cordillera Peoples Alliance.
CPAR. Congress for a People's Agrarian Reform.
CPDF. Cordillera People's Democratic Front.
CPP. Communist Party of the Philippines.
CR. Comfort room.
CRS. Catholic Relief Services.
DAR. Department of Agrarian Reform.
DOH. Department of Health (Philippine Government).
EC. European Community.
EDSA. *Epifanio de los Santos* Avenue.
EFA. Education for All program.
EO. Executive Order.
FNRI. Food and Nutrition Research Institute.
FY. Fiscal Year.
GABRIELA. General Assembly Binding Women for Reform, Integrity, Equality, Leadership, and Action.
GI. Galvanized iron.
GNP. Gross National Product.
HAIN. Health Action Information Network.

310

Huks. Hukbo ng Bayan Laban sa Hapon (the Army of Resistance Against Japan) and
   Hukbong Magpapalaya ng Bayan (People's Liberation Army).
IBFAN. International Baby Food Action Network.
IBRD. International Bank for Reconstruction and Development.
IDA. International Development Association.
IMF. International Monetary Fund.
IRRI. International Rice Research Institute.
KALAYAAN. *Katipunan ng Kababaihan Para sa Kalayaan.*
KMP. *Kilusang Magbubukid ng Pilipinas* (Peasant Movement of the Philippines).
KMU. *Kilusang Mayo Uno* (May First Movement), a labor organization.
LGC. Local Government Code.
LIC. Low Intensity Conflict.
MAKIBAKA. *Malayang Kilusan ng Bagong Kababaihan,* a women's national liberation
   movement, and a member organization of the National Democratic Front.
MNLF. Moro National Liberation Front.
MSP. *Makabayang Samahang Pangkalusugan* (The Patriotic Health Association of the
   National Democratic Front).
M99. *Masagana 99.*
NCCFN. National Coordinating Council on Food and Nutrition.
NCP. Nutrition Center of the Philippines.
NDF. National Democratic Front.
NEDA. National Economic and Development Authority.
NGO. Non-governmental Organization.
NIC. Newly Industrialized Country.
NID. Nutrition in Development.
NIP. Nutrition Intervention Program.
NMCL. National Movement for Civil Liberties.
NPA. New People's Army.
ORT. Oral Rehydration Therapy.
PFNP. Philippine Food and Nutrition Program.
PPA. Program Plan of Action (UNICEF).
PTA. Parents-Teachers Association.
RA. Republic Order.
RAM. Reform the Armed Forces Movement.
RHU. Rural Health Unit.
SOT. Special Operations Team.
TNC. Transnational Corporation.
TUCP. Trade Union Congress of the Philippines.
UN. United Nations.
UNESCO. United Nations Educational, Scientific, and Cultural Organization.
UNICEF. United Nations Children's Fund.
UNIFEM. United Nations Development Fund for Women.
USAID. United States Agency for International Development.
WHO. World Health Organization.
WID. Women in Development.

Bibliography

Adiong, Yvette Jane. 1989. "Internal Refugees' Problems on the Rise." *Health Alert*, June, pp. 224-227.

Afshar, Haleh. 1987. *Women, State and Ideology: Studies from Africa and Asia*. Albany: State University of New York Press.

Agarwal, Bina, ed. 1988. *Structures of Patriarchy: State, Community and Household in Modernising Asia*. New Delhi: Kali for Women; London: Zed Books.

Agpalo, Remigio E. 1973. "Political Modernization in the Philippines: The Politics and the Political Elite of Occidental Mindoro," in Hans-Dieter Evers, ed., *Modernization in South-East Asia*. Pp. 36-62. New York and London: Oxford University Press.

Aguilar, Delia D. 1988. *The Feminist Challenge: Initial Working Principles Toward Reconceptualizing the Feminist Movement in the Philippines*. Manila: Asian Social Institute.

Aguillon, D. B., and C. U. Celestino. 1990. "Nutrition programs. FNRI Working Paper." Quoted in Melinda F. Lumanta, "Human Nutrition and Welfare Policy Issues: A Review and Synthesis," in Aida R. Librero and Agnes C. Rola, eds., *Agricultural Policy in the Philippines: An Analysis of Issues in the Eighties*. Pp. 229-251. Los Banos, Laguna: University of the Philippines at Los Banos, Philippine Council for Agriculture, Forestry and Natural Resources Research and Development, 1991.

AID (U.S. Agency for International Development). 1989. *A Report to Congress Planning for the Next Decade: A Perspective of Women in Development*. N.p.

Alampay, Roby. 1993. "Rice Price Increase Protested." *Philippine Daily Inquirer*, June 23, pp. 1, 6.

Alconaba, Nico. 1993. "Four Years After Digos Massacre Victims' Kin Still Await NDF Indemnification." *Philippine Daily Inquirer*, June 25, p. 10.

Alvarez, J. Benjamin C., and Patricia M. Alvarez. 1973. "The Family-Owned Business: A Matriarchal Model." *Philippine Studies* 20:547. Quoted in Delia D. Aguilar, *The Feminist Challenge. Initial Working Principles Toward Reconceptualizing the Feminist Movement in the Philippines*. Manila: Asian Social Institute, 1988.

Amnesty International. 1993. "Amnesty International Report 1993, Summary." *Annual Report Summaries 1993*. Embargoed for 0001 HRS GMT, Thursday July 8. AI Index: POL 10/03/93.

Anderson, Perry. 1976. "The Antinomies of Antonio Gramsci." *New Left Review* 100:5-78.

Andres, Tomas D. 1987. *Understanding Filipino Values on Sex, Love and Marriage*. Sta. Mesa, Manila: Our Lady of Manaoag Publishers.

Angeles, Leonora C. 1990. "Women's Roles and Status in the Philippines: A Historical Perspective," in Marjorie M. Evasco, Aurora Javate de Dios, and Flor Caagusan, eds., *Women's Springbook: Readings on Women and Society*. Pp. 15-24. Quezon City:

Women's Resource and Research Center and the *Katipunan ng Kababaihan Para sa Kalayaan.*
——— . 1989. "Feminism and Nationalism: The Discourse on the Woman Question and Politics of the Women's Movement in the Philippines." Master's Thesis, University of the Philippines, Diliman, Quezon City.

Aquino, Belinda A. 1987. *Politics of Plunder: The Philippines Under Marcos.* Quezon City: Great Books Trading in cooperation with the U.P. College of Public Administration.

Arao, Danilo Arana. 1992. "NGOs Gird for Local Governance." *Kabalikat, the Development Worker.* Pp. 1, 3-6. Manila: Council for People's Development.

Asiaweek. 1992. "Battle of the Bedroom," August 21, pp. 25-27.

Aspillera, Dahlia C. 1986. "An Educational Program on Indigenous Foods for Better Health and Better Economy for the Philippines." Ph.D. Diss., University of Massachusetts.

Atkinson, Jane Monnig, and Shelly Errington, eds. 1990. *Power and Difference: Gender in Island Southeast Asia.* Stanford, California: Stanford University Press.

Atwood, J. Brian. 1993. "Public Forum on U.S. Agency for International Development: J. Brian Atwood, Director." Lecture presented at San Francisco State University, San Francisco, October 18. Sponsored by the San Francisco Urban Institute.

Ayers, Denise. 1985. "Oral Rehydration Therapy." *World Health*, June, pp. 9-11.

Bader, Michael B. 1981. "Breast-Feeding: The Role of Multinational Corporations in Latin America," in Vicente Navarro, ed., *Imperialism, Health and Medicine.* Pp. 235-252. Farmingdale, New York: Baywood.

Baer, Hans, and Merrill Singer. 1995. *Critical Medical Anthropology.* Amityville, New York: Baywood.

Baer, Hans A., Merrill Singer, and John H. Johnsen. 1986. "Toward a Critical Medical Anthropology." *Social Science and Medicine* 23(2):95-98.

Baguio Cordillera Post. 1992. "Spirit Worship Hinders Cordillera Food Production Efforts: Unrelieved Poverty in the Highlands," January 19, p. 17.

Bailey. 1966. "Nutrition and Ascariasis in the Bayambang Applied Nutrition Project." N.p. WHO/WPRO.

Bairagi, Radheshyam. 1986. "Food Crisis, Nutrition, and Female Children in Rural Bangladesh." *Population and Development Review* 12(2):307-315.

Balderrama, Virginia Guzman, Sibilina Bibera, Herminigilda Lopez, Lina Somera, and Arturo Librea. 1976. "Patterns of Care, Illness, Nutrition, Growth and Development During the First Three Years of Life in a Rural Setting." *Journal of the Philippine Medical Association* 52(5 and 6):91-127.

Bango, Marina U. 1992. "BIG [Bio-intensive Gardening]: A Solution to Malnutrition." *Mountain Movers: A Monthly Publication of the Ifugao ABCSDP* 1(2):4, 8. UNICEF.

Barron, Bruce. 1987. *The Health and Wealth Gospel.* Downers Grove, Illinois: InterVarsity Press.

Barton, Roy Franklin. 1955. *The Mythology of the Ifugaos.* Vol. 46, Memoirs of the American Folklore Society. Philadelphia: American Folklore Society.

——— . 1938. *Philippine Pagans: The Autobiographies of Three Ifugaos.* London: George Routledge and Sons.

——— . 1930. *The Half-Way Sun: Life Among the Headhunters of the Philippines.* New York: Brewer and Warren.

——— . 1922 "Ifugao Economics." *American Archaeology and Ethnology* 15(5):385-446.

——— . 1919. *Ifugao Law.* Berkeley: University of California Press.

Barudy, Jorge. 1989. "A Programme of Mental Health for Political Refugees: Dealing With the Invisible Pain of Political Exile." *Social Science and Medicine* 28(7):715-728.

Batangantang, Honorio C., ed. 1989. *Agrarian Reform: Situations, Issues, & Initiatives.* Quezon City: Friedrich Ebert-Stiftung (FES), School of Labor and Industrial Relations (UP-SOLAIR), University of the Philippines.

Batliwala, Srilatha. 1987. "Women's Access to Food." *Indian Journal of Social Work* 48(3):255-271.

Bautista, Cesar. 1997. "Discussion for Panel: The Philippines: A 'Newly Industrialized Country?'" Discussion presented at the Focus on the Philippines Conference, May 7, in Los Angeles.

Bautista, Leticia M., A.I. Jimenez Alday, and T.O. and L.A. Raum. 1974. "Assessment of the Nutritional Status of Pre-schoolers of Bay Laguna." *Philippine Journal of Nutrition* 27(3):16-21.

Beale, David O. 1986. *In Pursuit of Purity: American Fundamentalism Since 1850.* Greenville, South Carolina: Unusual Publication.

Bellah, Robert N. 1964. "Religious Evolution." *American Sociological Review* 29(3):358-374.

Bello, Walden. 1992. "The Crisis of the Philippine Progressive Movement: A Preliminary Investigation." *Kasarinlan: A Philippine Quarterly of Third World Studies. Special Issue on the Philippine Left* 8(1):142-153. Diliman, Quezon City: Third World Studies Center, University of the Philippines.

———. 1987. "U.S.-Sponsored Low-Intensity Conflict in the Philippines." *Food First Development Report.* December. San Francisco: Institute for Food and Development Policy.

Bello, Walden, and Robin Broad. 1987. "20 Years of Intervention: The IMF in the Philippines," in Daniel B. Schirmer and Stephen Rosskamm Shalom, eds., *The Philippines Reader: A History of Colonialism, Neocolonialism, Dictatorship, and Resistance.* Pp. 261-267. Boston: South End Press. Originally published in *AMPO.* Tokyo, 1982. 14(3):28-31.

Bello, Walden, David Kinley, and Elaine Elinson. 1982. *Development Debacle: The World Bank in the Philippines.* San Francisco: Institute for Food and Development Policy.

Beneria, Lourdes, ed. 1982. *Women and Development: The Sexual Division of Labor in Rural Societies.* New York: Praeger.

Beneria, Lourdes, and Gita Sen. 1982. "Class and Gender Inequalities and Women's Role in Economic Development: Theoretical and Practical Implications." *Feminist Studies* 8(1):157-176.

Bhuiya, Abbas, Bogdan Wojtyniak, and Karim Rezaul. 1989. "Malnutrition and Child Mortality: Are Socioeconomic Factors Important?" *Journal of Bioscience* 21(3):357-364.

Biomedical Nutrition Division. 1992. *Weight-for-Height for Filipinos (25-65 Years).* Manila: Food and Nutrition Research Institute, Department of Science and Technology.

———. 1988. *Weight-for-Height Table at Given Weeks/Months of Pregnancy Chart.* May. Manila: Food and Nutrition Research Institute, Department of Science and Technology.

Birosel, Roger. 1993. "Trivializing the Tribes Is Racism." *Philippine Collegian,* June 15, p. 3. Diliman, Quezon City: University of the Philippines.

Black, R. E., K. H. Brown, and S. Becker. 1983. "Influence of Acute Diarrhea on the Growth Parameters of Children," in *Acute Diarrhea: Its Nutritional Consequences in Children.* Nestle Nutrition Workshop Series, 2:75-84. New York: Raven Press.

Blanc-Szanton, Cristina. 1990. "Collisions of Cultures: Historical Reformulations of Gender in the Lowland Visayas, Philippines," in Jane Monnig Atkinson and Shelly Errington, eds., *Power and Difference: Gender in Island Southeast Asia*. Pp. 345-384. Stanford, California: Stanford University Press.

———. 1982. "Women and Men in Iloilo, Philippines: 1903-1970," in Penny Van Esterik, ed., *Women of Southeast Asia*. Pp.124-153. Northern Illinois University Series on Southeast Asia, Occasional Paper, no. 9. De Kalb: Northern Illinois University, Center for Southeast Asian Studies; Detroit: The Cellar Book Shop.

Blau, David M. 1986. "Fertility, Child Nutrition, and Child Mortality in Nicaragua: An Economic Analysis of Interrelationships." *Journal of Developing Areas* 20(2):185-201.

Bodley, John H., ed. 1988. *Tribal Peoples & Development Issues: A Global Overview*. Mountain View, California: Mayfield Publishing Company.

Bongyo, Jennylyn. 1988. "Customs and Beliefs of the Mayoyao People on Health: Their Implications to Health Education." Master's Thesis, Baguio Central University, Baguio City, Philippines.

Boserup, Esther. 1970. *Women's Role in Economic Development*. New York: St. Martin's Press.

Bourque, Susan C., and Kay B. Warren. 1990. "Access is Not Enough: Gender Perspectives on Technology and Education," in Irene Tinker, ed., *Persistent Inequalities: Women and World Development*. Pp. 83-100. New York and London: Oxford University Press.

Boyce, James K., and Lyuba Zarsky. 1992. "Capital Flight from the Philippines, 1962-86," in Emmanuel S. Dios and Joel Rocamora, eds., *Of Bonds & Bondage: A Reader on Philippine Debt*. Pp. 25-44. Philippines: Transnational Institute, Philippine Center for Policy Studies, and Freedom from Debt Coalition.

Broad, Robin. 1988. *Unequal Alliance: The World Bank, the International Monetary Fund, and the Philippines*. Berkeley: University of California Press.

Broad, Robin, and John Cavanagh. 1991. *The Philippine Challenge: Sustainable and Equitable Development in the 1990s*. Quezon City: Philippine Center for Policy Studies.

Brown, Nancy Marie. 1987. "Child Rearing in the Philippines." *Childbirth Educator*, Summer, pp. 31-36.

Brown, Susan E. 1975. "Love Unites Them and Hunger Separates Them: Poor Women in the Dominican Republic," in Rayna R. Reiter, ed., *Toward an Anthropology of Women*. Pp. 322-332. New York and London: Monthly Review Press.

Browner, Carole H. 1989. "Women, Household, and Health in Latin America." *Social Science and Medicine* 28:461-473.

Brun, Suzanne de, and Ray H. Elling. 1987. "Cuba and the Philippines: Contrasting Cases in World System Analysis." *The International Journal of Health Services* 17(4):681-701.

Buenaventura, Cenon. 1992. "Contrasting Fortune." Vital Signs, *IBON Facts & Figures* 15(10):8. Manila: IBON Philippines Databank & Research Center.

BUNSO (Balikatan at Ugnayang Naglalayong Sumagip sa Sanggol). 1989. "Breastfeeding in the Philippines: A Report by BUNSO Prepared for IBFAN." *Health Alert* 2(97):93-100. Quezon City: Health Action Information Network.

Burridge, Kenelm. 1969. *New Heaven, New Earth: A Study of Millenarian Activities*. New York: Schocken Books.

Cadelina, Rowe V. 1985. "Social Networks: An Ecological Analysis of Social Transactions Within a Context of Crisis." *Philippine Sociological Review* 33(1-2):60-72.

Caldwell, John C. 1986. "Routes to Low Mortality in Poor Countries." *Population and Development Review* 12(2):171-220.

Callanta, Ruth S. 1988. *Poverty: The Philippine Scenario*. Manila: Bookmark.

Campbell, Carolyn E. 1984. "Nestle and Breast vs. Bottle Feeding: Mainstream and Marxist Perspectives." *The International Journal of Health Services* 14(4):547-568.

Capco, Bobby . 1992a. "Ramos Okays $4.8-B Foreign Debt Package." *Philippine Star*, July 8, p. 1.

—— . 1992b. "Herrera Proposes P25 Hike in Minimum Wage." *Philippine Star*, July 29, p. 5.

—— . 1992c. "Government Defends $4.8-B Debt Package Relief for RP." *Philippine Star*, July 22, p. 1.

Carling, Joan. 1996. "Same Face Different Mask." *Cordillera Currents* 8(2):1-4. Baguio City: Cordillera Resource Center.

Casambre, Athena Lydia, Gladys A. Cruz, Tala Aurora Salinas-Ramos, and Ricardo E. Torres, Jr. 1992. "A Preliminary Study on Women's Participation for Sustainable Development in the Cordillera." November. Baguio City, Philippines: Cordillera Studies Center, University of the Philippines College Baguio.

Cassidy, Claire Monod. 1987. "World-View Conflict and Toddler Malnutrition: Change Agent Dilemmas," in Nancy Scheper-Hughes, ed., *Child Survival*. Pp. 293-324. Boston: D. Reidel Publishing Company.

—— . 1982. "Protein-Energy Malnutrition as a Culture Bound Syndrome." *Culture, Medicine and Psychiatry* 6:325-345.

Castaneda, Catherine Quimpo. 1990. "The Kalinga Diet and Traditional Food Beliefs of Pregnant and Lactating Women: An Ethnography." Ph.D. Diss., University of the Philippines, Diliman, Quezon City.

Catholic Relief Services, United States Catholic Conference. 1993. *Annual Report 1992: Giving Hope to a World of Need*. Baltimore: Catholic Relief Services, United States Catholic Conference.

CECAP (Central Cordillera Agricultural Programme). 1992. "Average Income & Expenditure of 19 Farmers of...[an Ifugao barrio]." October. Ifugao: CECAP.

Center for Women's Resources Data Bank. 1993. "The Filipina Today." April. Quezon City: Center for Women's Resources.

Cerqueira, Maria Teresa., Lucrecia Monleon Cebollada, Pilar Torre Medina Mora, Adriana Ramos Beauregard, and Margarita Valverde Armendariz. 1985. "Infant Feeding Practices in Mexico," in *The Impact of Development and Modern Technologies in Third World Health*. Studies in Third World Societies 34:169-200. Williamsburg, Virginia: Department of Anthropology, College of William and Mary.

Chant, Sylvia, and Cathy McIlwaine. 1995. *Women of a Lesser Cost: Female Labour, Foreign Exchange and Philippine Development*. London and East Haven, Connecticut: Pluto Press.

Chen, Lincoln C., and Nevin S. Scrimshaw, eds. 1983. *Diarrhea and Malnutrition: Interactions, Mechanisms and Interventions*. New York: Plenum Publishing Corporation and United Nations University.

Chen, Lincoln C., Emdadul Huq, and Stanislaus D'Souza. 1981. "Sex Bias in the Family Allocation of Food and Health Care in Rural Bangladesh." *Population and Development Review* 7(1):55-70.

———. 1980. *A Study of Sex Biased Behavior in the Intra-Family Allocation of Food and the Utilization of Health Care Services in Rural Bangladesh.* September. International Centre for Diarrheal Disease Research, Bangladesh and Department of Population Sciences, Harvard School of Public Health.

Chipongian, Arleen C. 1992a. "RP Meets All Targets Under IMF-Sponsored Economic Program." *Philippine Daily Inquirer,* August 13, p. 17.

———. 1992b. "Economic Prosperity Not Expected With IMF-Imposed Plan." *Philippine Daily Inquirer,* March 16, p. 18.

———. 1992c. "RP Gets $1.7B in Loans, Grants." *Philippine Daily Inquirer,* March 14, p. 1.

———. 1992d. "IMF Plans to Enroll RP in Program for 'Poorest Developing Countries'." *Philippine Daily Inquirer,* March 2, p. 19.

Chossudovsky, Michael. 1983. "Underdevelopment and the Political Economy of Malnutrition and Ill Health." *International Journal of Health Services* 13(1):69-83.

Cliff, Julie, and Razak Noormahomed. 1993. "The Impact of War on Children's Health in Mozambique." *Social Science and Medicine* 36(7):843-848.

Clifford, James. 1986. "Introduction: Partial Truths," in James Clifford and George E. Marcus, eds. *Writing Culture: The Poetics and Politics of Ethnography.* Pp. 1-26. Berkeley: University of California Press.

Clymer, Kenton J. 1986. *Protestant Missionaries in the Philippines, 1898–1916: An Inquiry into the American Colonial Mentality.* Urbana: University of Illinois Press.

CODEPU. 1989. "The Effects of Torture and Political Repression in a Sample of Chilean Families." *Social Science and Medicine* 28(7):735-740.

Cohen, N., M. A. Jalil, H. Rahman, M. A. Matin, J. Sprague, J. Islam, J. Davison, E. Leemhuis de Regt, and M. Mitra. 1985. "Landholding, Wealth and Risk of Blinding Malnutrition in Rural Bangladesh Households." *Social Science and Medicine* 21(11):1269-1272.

Collins, Joseph. 1989. "The Philippines: A Nation of Children Under the Gun." *Food First Action Alert.* San Francisco: Institute for Food and Development Policy.

Colson, Elizabeth. 1982. *Planned Change: The Creation of a New Community.* Berkeley: Institute of International Studies.

Comaroff, Jean. 1985. *Body of Power, Spirit of Resistance: The Culture and History of a South African People.* Chicago: University of Chicago Press.

Comaroff, Jean, and John Comaroff. 1991. *Of Revelation and Revolution: Christianity, Colonialism, and Consciousness in South Africa,* Vol. 1. Chicago: University of Chicago Press.

Conklin, Harold C. 1980. *Ethnographic Atlas of Ifugao: A Study of Environment, Culture, and Society in Northern Luzon.* New Haven and London: Yale University Press.

Constantino, Renato. 1987. "The Miseducation of the Filipino: The Filipinos in the Philippines and Other Essays," in Daniel B. Schirmer and Stephen Rosskamm Shalom, eds., *The Philippines Reader: A History of Colonialism, Neocolonialism, Dictatorship, and Resistance.* Pp. 45-49. Boston: South End Press. Originally published by Quezon City: Malaya Books, 1966, pp. 39-65.

Constantino, Renato, and Letizia R. Constantino. 1988. *Distorted Priorities: The Politics of Food.* Quezon City: Foundation for Nationalist Studies.

Cordillera Human Rights Commission/Cordillera Peoples Alliance. 1996. "Securing the Mines." *Cordillera Currents* 8(2):5-6. Baguio City: Cordillera Resource Center.

Cordillera Peoples Alliance. 1993. "Petition Letter for Philippine President Fidel Ramos." *Nordis, Northern Dispatch* 5(28):14-16. Baguio City: Cordillera Resource Center.

Cordillera Resource Center. 1996. "Power and Development: One May Lead to the Other But the Social and Environmental Costs Are Incalculable." *Bantayan Environmental Alert,* December, pp. 1-3, 18-21. Baguio City: Cordillera Resource Center.

———. 1992. "Urgent Action. Case: Pinukpuk Killings." Human Rights Violations Document UA-92-KAP-003. Baguio City: Cordillera Resource Center.

———. 1990. "People Vote 'No' to Organic Act; Struggle for Autonomy Continues." *Cordillera Currents* 3(1):1-15. Baguio City: Cordillera Resource Center.

Cordillera Women's Education and Resource Center, Inc. 1991a. "How Will Women Survive This Crisis?" *CHANEG* 2(2).

———. 1991b. *TEBETA. From the Eyes of the Cordillera Women.* no. 1. Baguio City, Philippines: Cordillera Women's Education and Resource Center.

———. 1990a. "The Cordillera Women And Economic Crisis." *CHANEG* 1(2).

———. 1990b. *CHANEG* 1(3).

Coreil, Jeannine, and J. Dennis Mull. 1988. "Anthropological Studies of Diarrheal Illness." *Social Science and Medicine* 27(1):1-3.

Corporate Information Center. 1987. "The Republic of the Philippines: American Corporations, Martial Law, and Underdevelopment," in Daniel B. Schirmer and Stephen Rosskamm Shalom, eds., *The Philippines Reader: A History of Colonialism, Neocolonialism, Dictatorship, and Resistance.* Pp. 141-143. Boston: South End Press. Originally published in the *Corporate Examiner,* September, 1973, pp. 3B, 3D.

Danguilan, Marilen J. 1993. *Making Choices in Good Faith. A Challenge to the Catholic Church's Teachings on Sexuality and Contraception.* Quezon City: WomanHealth Philippines.

David, Rina Jimenez. 1992a. "What Filipinos Think About Family Planning." *Philippine Daily Inquirer,* August 17, p. 5.

———. 1992b. "Women and the Church." *Philippine Daily Inquirer,* April 16, p. 5.

Davis, Leonard. 1989. *Revolutionary Struggle in the Philippines.* Hampshire and London: MacMillan.

De Castro, Josue. 1952. *The Geography of Hunger.* Boston: Little, Brown and Company.

De Garine, Igor. 1984. "The Perception of Malnutrition in Traditional Societies." *Social Science Information* 23(4-5):731-754.

de la Torre, Edicio. 1986. *Theological and Political Reflections on the Philippine Struggle, Touching Ground, Taking Root.* Manila: Socio-Pastoral Institute.

DeJanvry, Alain. 1977. "Material Determinants of the World Food Crisis." *Berkeley Journal of Sociology* 21 (1976–1977):3-26.

Deles, Teresita Quintos. 1997. "Discussion for Panel: The Philippine Economy." Discussion presented at the Focus on the Philippines Conference, May 7, in Los Angeles.

Department of Health, Ifugao. 1989. "Report on Nutrition for Ifugao Province."

DeRaedt, C.I.C.M., Jules. 1964. "Religious Representations in Northern Luzon." *Research Series,* no. 4. Chicago: Philippine Studies Program, Department of Anthropology, University of Chicago. Reprinted from *Saint Louis Quarterly* 2(3) (1964).

Dettwyler, Katherine A. 1994. *Dancing Skeletons: Life and Death in West Africa.* Prospect Heights, Illinois: Waveland Press.

Dineros-Pineda, Josefina. 1992. "Beyond Nutrition: Empowerment in the Philippines." *International Social Work* 35(2):203-215.

Diokno, Ramon. 1987. "Roxas Violates the Constitution," in Daniel B. Schirmer and Stephen Rosskamm Shalom, eds., *The Philippines Reader: A History of Colonialism, Neocolonialism, Dictatorship, and Resistance.* Pp. 90-94. Boston: South End Press. Originally published in *Amerasia* 1946, 10(6):75-78.

Dios, Emmanuel S., and Joel Rocamora, eds. 1992. *Of Bonds & Bondage: A Reader on Philippine Debt.* Philippines: Transnational Institute, Philippine Center for Policy Studies, and Freedom from Debt Coalition.

Dizon, Alfred. 1995. "HR [Human Rights] Violations Down." *Nordis, Northern Dispatch,* September 29, 7(39):1. Baguio City: Cordillera Resource Center.

———. 1993a. "Members of 702 IB Charged for Sexual Opportunism." *Nordis, Northern Dispatch* 5(44):2-3. Baguio: Cordillera Resource Center.

———. 1993b. "Autonomy *Elalay*: Reclaiming Ruins Made in Search of 'Genuine Autonomy'." *Nordis, Northern Dispatch,* Fourth Anniversary Issue, September 26, pp. 1-3. Baguio: Cordillera Resource Center.

———. 1993c. "Banaue Rice Terraces to be 'CARPED'." *Nordis, Northern Dispatch,* 5(32):5-6. Baguio: Cordillera Resource Center.

Doronila, Amando. 1988. "Clash of Interests in Impasse of CARP." *Manila Chronicle,* June 2. Quoted in Yujiro Hayami, Ma. Agnes R. Quisumbing, and Lourdes S. Adriano, *Toward an Alternative Land Reform Paradigm: A Philippine Perspective.* Manila: Ateneo de Manila University Press, 1990.

Douglas, Mary. 1970. *Natural Symbol.* New York: Vintage Press.

———. 1966. "The Abominations of Leviticus," in *Purity and Danger.* Pp. 41-57. London: Routledge and Kegan Paul.

Doyal, Lesley, and Imogen Pennell. 1981. *The Political Economy of Health.* Boston: South End Press.

Draper, Patricia. 1975. "!Kung Women: Contrasts in Sexual Egalitarianism in Foraging and Sedentary Contexts," in Rayna R. Reiter, ed., *Toward an Anthropology of Women.* Pp. 77-109. New York: Monthly Review Press.

Driver, Edwin D., and Aloo E. Driver. 1983. "Social Class and Height and Weight in Metropolitan Madras." *Social Biology* 30(2):189-204.

Drucker, Charles. 1988. "Dam the Chico: Hydropower Development and Tribal Resistance," in John H. Bodley, ed., *Tribal Peoples & Development Issues. A Global Overview.* Pp. 151-165. Mountain View: Mayfield Publishing Company.

Druckman, Daniel, and Justin Green. 1995. "Playing Two Games: Internal Negotiations in the Philippines," in I. William Zartman, ed., *Elusive Peace: Negotiating an End to Civil Wars.* Pp. 299-331. Washington, D.C.: The Brookings Institute.

DuBois, Cora. 1944. *The People of Alor. A Social-Psychological Study of an East Indian Island.* Minneapolis: University of Minnesota Press.

———. 1941. "Food and Hunger in Alor," in L. Speir, A. I. Hallowell, and S. S. Newman, eds., *Language, Culture, and Personality: Essays in Memory of Edward Sapir.* Pp. 272-281. Menasha, Wisconsin: Sapir Memorial Publishing Fund.

Dulawan, Lourdes S. n.d. "Ifugao *Baki* (Rituals for Man and Rice Culture)." *Journal of Northern Luzon* 15(1-2).

Dumia, Mariano A. 1979. *The Ifugao World.* Quezon City: New Day Publishers.

Dumlao, Jr., Artemio. 1996a. "Possession of Medical Instruments Now a Crime?" *Nordis, Northern Dispatch* 8(28):3-4. Baguio City: Cordillera Resource Center.

───── . 1996b. "Human Rights Update: Nevertheless, More of the Same." *Cordillera Currents* 8(2):7-8. Baguio City: Cordillera Resource Center.

───── . 1993. "Rights Group Marks Oct. 30 as *Luksang Bayan* in Memory of Fallen Human Rights Advocates." *Northern Dispatch* 5(41):11.

Dumont, Jean-Paul. 1992. *Visayan Vignettes: Ethnographic Traces of a Philippine Island.* Chicago: University of Chicago Press.

Eide, W. B., and F. C. Steady. 1980. "Individual and Social Energy Flows: Bridging Nutritional and Anthropological Thinking About Women's Work in Rural Africa. Some Theoretical Considerations," in Norge W. Jerome et al., eds., *Nutritional Anthropology: Contemporary Approaches to Diet and Culture.* New York: Redgrave Publishing Company.

Ellis, Frank. 1988. *Peasant Economics: Farm Households and Agrarian Development.* Cambridge: Cambridge University Press.

Errington, Shelly. 1990. "Recasting Sex, Gender and Power," in Jane Monnig Atkinson and Shelly Errington, eds., *Power and Difference: Gender in Island Southeast Asia.* Pp. 1-58. Stanford, California: Stanford University Press.

Escobar, Arturo. 1995. *Encountering Development: The Making and Unmaking of the Third World.* Princeton: Princeton University Press.

───── . 1992. "Planning," in Wolfgang Sachs, ed., *The Development Dictionary: A Guide to Knowledge as Power.* Pp. 132-145. London and New Jersey: Zed Books.

───── . 1991. "Anthropology and the Development Encounter: The Making and Marketing of Development Anthropology." *American Ethnologist* 18(4):658-682.

───── . 1988. "Power and Visibility: Development and the Invention and Management of the Third World." *Cultural Anthropology* 3(4):428-443.

───── . 1987. "Power and Visibility: Development and the Invention and Management of the Third World." Ph.D. Diss., University of California, Berkeley.

Escobar, Arturo, and Sonia E. Alvarez, eds. 1992. *The Making of Social Movements in Latin America: Identity, Strategy, and Democracy.* Boulder, Colorado: Westview Press.

Esplanada, Jerry. 1993a. "Church-State War. Gov't Seeks Truce in Population Row." *Philippine Daily Inquirer,* July 30, pp. 1, 13.

───── . 1993b. "NUC [National Unification Commission] Submits Report, Seeks Total Amnesty." *Philippine Daily Inquirer,* July 2, pp. 1, 12.

───── . 1993c. "Ramos on Economy: $32-B Debt No Longer a Burden. "*Philippine Daily Inquirer,* June 22, p. 9.

───── . 1992. "Taiwan Offers to Contribute to RP Aid Plan." *Philippine Daily Inquirer,* August 18, p. 7.

Esterik, Penny van, ed. 1982. *Women of Southeast Asia.* Northern Illinois University Series on Southeast Asia, Occasional Paper, no. 9. De Kalb: Northern Illinois University, Center for Southeast Asian Studies; Detroit: Cellar Book Shop.

Esteva, Gustavo. 1992. "Development," in Wolfgang Sachs, ed., *The Development Dictionary: A Guide to Knowledge and Power.* Pp. 6-25. London and New Jersey: Zed Books.

Estrada-Claudio, Sylvia. 1988. "Health Dangers." *Solidaridad,* 2/July-December, pp. 21-23. Philippines.

Evans-Pritchard, E. E. 1940. *The Nuer.* New York and London: Oxford University Press.

───── . 1937. *Witchcraft, Oracles, and Magic among the Azande.* Oxford: Clarendon Press.

Evers, Hans-Dieter, ed. 1973a. *Modernization in South-East Asia.* New York and London: Oxford University Press.

———. 1973b. "Group Conflict and Class Formation in South-East Asia," in Hans-Dieter Evers, ed., *Modernization in South-East Asia.* Pp. 108-131. New York and London: Oxford University Press.

Eviota, Elizabeth U. 1986. "The Articulation of Gender and Class in the Philippines," in E. Leacock and H.I. Safa, eds., *Women's Work: Development and the Division of Labor by Gender.* South Hadley, Massachusetts: Bergin and Garvey.

Farhood, Laila, Huda Zarayk, Monique Chaya, Fadia Saadeh, Garbis Meshefedjian, and Thuraya Sidani. 1993. "The Impact of War on the Physical and Mental Health of the Family: The Lebanese Experience." *Social Science and Medicine* 36(12):1555-1567.

Feder, Ernest. 1981. "The Deterioration of the Food Situation in the Third World and the Capitalist System." *International Journal of Health Services* 11(2):247-262.

Fegan, Brian. 1993. "Entrepreneurs in Votes and Violence: Three Generations of a Peasant Political Family," in Alfred W. McCoy, ed., *An Anarchy of Families: State and Family in the Philippines.* Pp. 33-107. Madison: Center for Southeast Asian Studies, University of Wisconsin.

Feldman, Allen. 1991. *Formations of Violence: The Narrative of the Body and Political Terror in Northern Ireland.* Chicago: University of Chicago Press.

Felipe, Nicole, and Martina del Fuego. 1990. "Cherishing the People: NDF Defines Agricultural Development as the Main Thrust of Revolutionary Socio-economic Work." *Liberation,* November-December, 18(6):3-4, 6. Philippines: National Democratic Front of the Philippines.

Fiag-oy, Geraldine. 1988. "The Indigenous Women of the Cordillera Region, Northern Luzon: A Situationer." *Tribal Forum,* March-April, pp. 32-38.

Fishman, Claudia, Robin Evans, and Eloise Jenks. 1988. "Warm Bodies, Cool Milk: Conflicts in Post Partum Food Choice for Indochinese Women in California." *Social Science and Medicine* 26(11):1125-1132.

Florencio, Cecilia A. 1989. *Food And Freedom. Nutrition: A Springboard to Biosocial Uplift, a Test of a Nation's Resolve.* Quezon City: University of the Philippines Press.

Florentino, Rodolfo F., M.D., Ph.D., Perla Santos-Ocampo, M.D., Josefina A. Magbitang, M.S.P.H., Teresa S. Mendoza, M.S.P.H., Emilie G. Flores, M.D., M.P.H., and Bernadette J. Madrid, M.D. 1992. "FNRI-PPS Anthropometric Tables and Charts for Filipino Children." Manila: Food and Nutrition Research Institute, Department of Science and Technology, Philippine Pediatric Society, and Nestle Philippines, Inc.

Foucault, Michel. 1994. *The Birth of the Clinic: An Archaeology of Medical Perception.* 1973. Reprint, New York: Vintage Books.

———. 1990. *The History of Sexuality, Volume I: An Introduction.* Translated by Robert Hurley. 1978. Reprint, New York: Vintage Books.

———. 1981. *Power/Knowledge.* New York: Pantheon Books.

———. 1977. *Discipline and Punish: The Birth of the Prison.* New York: Vintage Books.

Fox, Robert. 1963. "Men and Women in the Philippines," in Barbara E. Ward, ed., *Women in the New Asia.* Netherlands: UNESCO. Quoted in Delia D. Aguilar, *The Feminist Challenge: Initial Working Principles Toward Reconceptualizing the Feminist Movement in the Philippines.* Manila: Asian Social Institute, 1988.

Frank, Andre Gunder. 1969. *Capitalism and Under-development in Latin America.* London: Monthly Review Press.

———. 1966. "The Development of Underdevelopment." *Monthly Review,* September 18, pp. 17-31.

Frankenberg, Ronald. 1980. "Medical Anthropology and Development: A Theoretical Perspective." *Social Science and Medicine* 14B:197-207.

Fry, Howard T. 1983. *A History of the Mountain Province.* Quezon City: New Day Publishers.

GABRIELA-National Women's Coalition. 1991. "The Culture of Foreign Domination: Women's Issues, Alternatives and Initiatives." *GABRIELA Women's Update* 7(3).

———. 1989. *An Introduction to Women's Health Issues in the Philippines. A Collection of Speeches and Essays of Women Leaders, Organizers, Activists and Grassroots Women.* Manila: The GABRIELA National Women's Coalition and the GABRIELA Women's Health and Reproductive Rights Commission.

Garfield, Richard M. 1989. "War-Related Changes in Health and Health Services in Nicaragua." *Social Science and Medicine* 28(7):669-676.

Gaspar, Karl M., CSsR. 1990. *A People's Option: To Struggle for Creation.* Quezon City: Claretian Publications.

Geertz, Clifford. 1973. "'Internal Conversion' in Contemporary Bali," in Clifford Geertz, ed., *The Interpretation of Cultures.* Pp. 170-189. New York: Basic Books.

George, Susan. 1977. *How the Other Half Dies: The Real Reasons for World Hunger.* Montclair, New Jersey: Allanheld, Osmun & Co.

Ghee, Lim Teck, ed. 1988. *Reflections on Development in Southeast Asia.* Singapore: Asean Economic Research Unit, Institute of Southeast Asian Studies.

Ghosh, Shanti. 1991. "Girl Child: A Lifetime of Deprivation and Discrimination." *Indian Journal of Social Work* 52(1):21-27.

Gladwin, Christina H. 1993. "Women and Structural Adjustment in a Global Economy," in Rita S. Gallin, Anne Ferguson, and Janice Harper, eds., *The Women and International Development Annual* 3:87-112. Boulder, Colorado: Westview Press.

Go, Marianne V. 1992. "P322.7-B Budget for 1993 Sought." *Philippine Star,* June 1, p. 17.

Goelz, Paul C. 1983. *The Economic System of Free Enterprise: Its Judeo-Christian Values and Philosophical Concepts.* San Antonio, Texas: St. Mary's University Press.

Gomez, Carla P. 1993. "Local Code Change Needed to Solve Funding Problems." *Philippine Daily Inquirer,* July 31, p. 25.

Gonzales, Stella O. 1992. "Bishops Get Tough on Bataan Nuke Plant, Birth Control, Death Penalty." *Philippine Daily Inquirer,* July 27, pp. 1, 7.

Grandin, Barbara E. 1988. *Wealth Ranking in Smallholder Communities: A Field Manual.* Rugby, England: Intermediate Technology Publications.

Green, Linda Buckley. 1989. "Consensus and Coercion: Primary Health Care and the Guatemalan State." *Medical Anthropology Quarterly* 3(3):246-257.

Group of 10. 1989. *Women, Development and Aid: Working Principles of the Group of 10.* Quezon City: Diwata Foundation.

Guthrie, George, Zenaida Masangkay, and Helen Guthrie. 1976. "Behavior, Malnutrition, and Mental Development." *Journal of Cross Cultural Psychology* 7(2):169-180.

Habito, Cielito. 1997. "Discussion for panel: The Philippine Economy." Discussion presented at the Focus on the Philippines Conference, May 7, in Los Angeles.

HAIN (Health Action Information Network). 1994. "Current National News: New Minimum Daily Wage." *Health Alert* 10 (January 1-5):7. Quezon City: Health Action Information Network.

——. 1992. "Justice for Kalinga Health Worker." *Health Alert* 134 (October):304. Quezon City: Health Action Information Network.

——. 1991. "Protests Continue Against Local Code." *Health Alert* 124 (December):359. Quezon City: Health Action Information Network.

——. 1989a. "The Advantages of Breastfeeding." *Health Alert* 2(98). Quezon City: Health Action Information Network.

——. 1989b. "CBHP's [Community Based Health Programs'] Statement on Medical Neutrality and the Total War Policy." *Health Alert* 5(97):127-128. Quezon City: Health Action Information Network.

——. 1989c. "Thousands Reconcentrated in Negros." *Health Alert* 5(94):250-251. Quezon City: Health Action Information Network.

Harris, Marvin. 1985. *Good to Eat: Riddles of Food and Culture*. New York: Simon and Schuster.

——. 1968. *The Rise of Anthropological Theory: A History of Theories of Culture*. New York: Thomas Y. Crowell.

Hartmann, Betsy, and James Boyce. 1979. *Needless Hunger: Voices from a Bangladesh Village*. San Francisco: Institute for Food and Development Policy.

Hayami, Yujiro, Ma. Agnes R. Quisumbing, and Lourdes S. Adriano. 1990. *Toward An Alternative Land Reform Paradigm: A Philippine Perspective*. Manila: Ateneo de Manila University Press.

Health NGO. 1990. Pamphlet. Philippines.

——. 1989. "A Manual on Community-Based Health Program (CBHP). Primary Health Care (PHC) Orientation Seminar-Workshop For Trainers." Philippines.

Hefner, Robert W., ed. 1993. *Conversion to Christianity. Historical and Anthropological Perspectives on a Great Transformation*. Berkeley: University of California Press.

Hernandez, Carolina G. 1997. "The Philippines in 1996. A House Finally in Order?" *Asian Survey* 37(2):204-211.

Hexham, Irving. 1982. "Some Aspects of Religion and Spiritual Healing in Cultsville, a Contemporary North American City," in W. J. Sheils, ed., *The Church and Healing*. Pp. 415-430. Oxford: Basil Blackwell.

Hildebrand, Dale. 1991. *To Pay Is to Die: The Philippine Foreign Debt Crisis*. Davao City, Philippines: Philippine International Forum.

Hill, Polly. 1986. *Development Economics on Trial: The Anthropological Case for a Prosecution*. Cambridge: Cambridge University Press.

Hobart, Mark, ed. 1993. *An Anthropological Critique of Development: The Growth of Ignorance*. London and New York: Routledge.

Hoben, A. 1982. "Anthropologists and Development." *Annual Review of Anthropology* 11:349-375.

——. 1980. "Agricultural Decision Making in Foreign Assistance: An Anthropological Analysis," in Peggy F. Bartlett, ed., *Agricultural Decision Making: Anthropological Contributions to Rural Development*. New York: Academic Press.

Holmberg, Alan R. 1950. *Nomads of the Long Bow: The Sirino of Eastern Bolivia*. Washington, D.C.: Government Printing Office.

Horsman, Reginald. 1981. *Race and Manifest Destiny: The Origins of American Racial Anglo-Saxonism*. Cambridge: Harvard University Press.

Horton, Susan. 1988. "Birth Order and Child Nutritional Status: Evidence from the Philippines." *Economic Development and Cultural Change* 36(2):341-354.

Hoskins, Janet, ed. 1996. *Headhunting and the Social Imagination in Southeast Asia.* Stanford, California: Stanford University Press.

Human Life Foundation. 1993. "Encyclical Letter Humanae Vitae Marks 25th Year: A Celebration of Conjugal Love." *Philippine Daily Inquirer,* July 25, p. 14.

Huston, Perdita. 1979. *Third World Women Speak Out.* New York: Praeger.

IBON. 1992a. "The Divided Unions." *IBON Facts and Figures* 15(10):6. Manila: IBON Philippines Databank & Research Center.

———. 1992b. "The Economy Under Aquino: Looking Back." *IBON Facts and Figures* 15(5):1-12. Manila: IBON Philippines Databank & Research Center.

———. 1992c. "Slice and Dice the 1992 Budget." *IBON Facts and Figures* 15(3):1-8. Manila: IBON Philippines Databank & Research Center.

———. 1991. "Poverty Situation, June 1991." Institute for Alternative Studies, Current Labor Statistics, in *Farm News & Views: A Bi-Monthly Publication of the Philippine Peasant Institute* 4(3):16.

Ifugao Provincial Nutrition Committee. 1991. "Masterlist of High Risk and at Risk Families, Province of Ifugao." Lagawe, Ifugao: Ifugao Provincial Health Office.

Ifugao Provincial Office. 1992. "Nutrition Statistics of...[an Ifugao barrio]."

Ifugao Rural Health Unit. 1992. "10 Leading Causes of Infant Mortality."

Ileto, Reynaldo Clemena. 1988. "Outlines of a Non-Linear Emplotment of Philippine History," in Lim Teck Ghee, ed., *Reflections on Development in Southeast Asia.* Pp. 130-159. Singapore: Asean Economic Research Unit, Institute of Southeast Asian Studies.

———. 1979. *Pasyon and Revolution. Popular Movements in the Philippines, 1840–1910.* Manila: Ateneo de Manila University Press.

Illo, Jeanne Frances I., and Cynthia C. Veneracion. 1988. *Women And Men in Rainfed Farming Systems: Case Studies of Households in the Bicol Region.* Quezon City: Institute of Philippine Culture, Ateneo de Manila University.

International Labour Office. 1987. "Sharing in Development: A Programme of Employment, Equity and Growth for the Philippines," in Daniel B. Schirmer and Stephen Rosskamm Shalom, eds., *The Philippines Reader: A History of Colonialism, Neocolonialism, Dictatorship, and Resistance.* Pp. 131-135. Boston: South End Press. Originally published by Geneva: ILO, 1974, pp. 3-13.

Israel-Sobritchea, Carolyn. 1992. "Sexism and Militarization in Philippine Society." *Lila: Asia Pacific Women's Studies Journal* 1:19-26. Manila: Institute of Women's Studies.

Jackson, Barbara, and Antonio Ugalde. 1985. "Health, Development and Technologies: An Appraisal," in *The Impact of Development and Modern Technologies in Third World Health.* Studies in Third World Societies 34:295-324. Williamsburg, Virginia: Department of Anthropology, College of William and Mary.

Jagan, Larry. 1988. "Social Volcano: The Philippines Revolution." *Class and Capital* 36-B:16-30.

Jayawardena, Kumari. 1986. *Feminism and Nationalism in the Third World.* London: Zed Books.

Jelliffe, Derrick B. and E. F. Patrice Jelliffe. 1988. *Child Nutrition in Developing Countries.* USAID/ McCardle Publishers.

Jenista, Frank Lawrence. 1987. *The White Apos: American Governors on the Cordillera Central.* Quezon City: New Day Publishers.

Jocano, F. Landa. 1973. "Ideology and Radical Movements in the Philippines: A Preliminary View," in Hans-Dieter Evers, ed., *Modernization in South-East Asia*. Pp. 199-222. New York and London: Oxford University Press.

Jonsson, Urban. 1981. "The Causes of Hunger." *Food and Nutrition Bulletin* 3(2):1-9.

Jordan, David K. 1993. "The Glyphomancy Factor: Observations on Chinese Conversion," in Robert W Hefner, ed., *Conversion to Christianity: Historical and Anthropological Perspectives on a Great Transformation*. Pp. 285-304. Berkeley: University of California Press.

Justice, Judith. 1986. *Policies, Plans, & People: Foreign Aid and Health Development*. Berkeley: University of California Press.

J. Y. G. 1992. "NDF Backs Church on Population." *Philippine Daily Inquirer*, 18 August, p. 19.

Kahn, Miriam. 1986. *Always Hungry, Never Greedy: Food and the Expression of Gender in a Melanesian Society*. Cambridge: Cambridge University Press.

Keesing, Felix M. 1937. *The Philippines: A Nation in the Making*. Shanghai: Kelly and Walsh. Quoted in Delia D. Aguilar, *The Feminist Challenge: Initial Working Principles Toward Reconceptualizing the Feminist Movement in the Philippines*. Manila: Asian Social Institute, 1988.

Kenyalang. 1990. "Are Not Religion and Politics the Same Thing?" *Bulletin of Concerned Asian Scholars* 22(4):60-66.

Kerkvliet, Benedict J. Tria. 1996. "Contemporary Philippine Leftist Politics in Historical Perspective," in Robert W. Hefner, ed., *The Revolution Falters: The Left in Philippine Politics After 1986*. Pp. 9-27. Ithaca: Southeast Asian Program Publications, Cornell University.

———. 1990. *Everyday Politics in the Philippines: Class and Status Relations in a Central Luzon Village*. Berkeley: University of California Press.

———. 1977. *The Huk Rebellion. A Study of Peasant Revolt in the Philippines*. Berkeley: University of California Press.

Kerkvliet, Benedict J. Tria, and Resil B. Mojares. 1991. "Themes in the Transition from Marcos to Aquino: An Introduction," in Benedict J. Kerkvliet and Resil B. Mojares, eds., *From Marcos to Aquino: Local Perspectives on Political Transition in the Philippines*. Pp. 1-12. Honolulu: University of Hawaii Press and Quezon City: Ateneo de Manila University Press.

Keyes, Charles F. 1993. "Why the Thai Are Not Christians: Buddhist and Christian Conversion in Thailand," in Robert W. Hefner, ed., *Conversion to Christianity. Historical and Anthropological Perspectives on a Great Transformation*. Pp. 259-284. Berkeley: University of California Press.

Kiefer, Christie W. 1992. "Militarism and World Health." *Social Science and Medicine* 34(7):719-724.

King, Jr., Martin Luther. 1967. *Where Do We Go From Here? Chaos or Community?* Boston: Beacon.

Kintanar, Thelma B., ed. and Jenny R. Llaguno, Associate. 1990. *Review of Women's Studies* 1(1). Diliman, Quezon City: University Center for Women's Studies, University of the Philippines, Diliman.

Kondo, Dorinne K. 1990. *Crafting Selves: Power, Gender, and Discourses of Identity in a Japanese Workplace*. Chicago: University of Chicago Press.

Kroeber, Alfred L. 1943. *Peoples of the Philippines.* 2d ed. New York: American Museum of Natural History.

Krohn-Hansen, Christian. 1994. "The Anthropology of Violent Interaction. *"Journal of Anthropological Research* 50:367-381.

Kulkarni, V. G., and Rodney Tasker. 1996. "Promises to Keep." *Far Eastern Economic Review,* February 29, pp. 22-23.

Kulkarni, V. G., Rodney Tasker, and Rigoberto Tiglao. 1996. "Bearer of the Torch." *Far Eastern Economic Review,* February 29, p. 24.

Kwiatkowski, Lynn. 1996. "Health Care as Political Weaponry: Healing Bodies in Political Conflict." *Urban Anthropology and Studies of Cultural Systems and World Economic Development* 25(4):385-417.

——. 1994. "Malnutrition, Gender, and Development in Ifugao, an Upland Community in the Philippines." Ph.D. Diss., University of California, Berkeley.

Lachica, Eduardo. 1971. *HUK: Philippine Agrarian Society in Revolt.* Manila: Solidaridad Publishing House.

Lacson, Liza. 1992. "Flavier Wants Meeting With Church Heads on Family Planning Program." *Philippine Star,* July 29, pp. 1, 11.

Laderman, Carol. 1987. "Destructive Heat and Cooling Prayer: Malay Humoralism in Pregnancy, Childbirth and the Post Partum Period." *Social Science and Medicine* 25(4):357-365.

——. 1983. *Wives and Midwives: Childbirth and Nutrition in Rural Malaysia.* Berkeley: University of California Press.

——. 1981. "Symbolic and Empirical Reality: A New Approach to the Analysis of Food Avoidances." *American Ethnologist* 8(3):468-493.

Lamperis, Ana Maria Turner. 1991. "Teaching Mothers to Read: Evidence from Columbia on the Key Role of Maternal Education in Preschool Child Nutritional Health." *Journal of Developing Areas* 26(1):25-52.

Lancaster, Roger. 1988. *Thanks to God and the Revolution.* New York: Columbia University Press.

Lappe, Frances Moore, and Joseph Collins. 1986. *World Hunger: Twelve Myths.* New York: Grove Press.

Leach, Edmund. 1964. "Anthropological Aspects of Language: Animal Categories and Verbal Abuse," in Eric H. Lenneberg, ed., *New Directions in the Study of Language.* Pp. 23-63. Cambridge: M. I. T. Press.

Lepowsky, Maria. 1987. "Food Taboos and Child Survival: A Case Study From the Coral Sea," in Nancy Scheper-Hughes, ed., *Child Survival.* Pp. 71-92. Boston: D. Reidel.

Levi-Strauss, Claude. 1966. *The Savage Mind.* Chicago: University of Chicago Press.

——. 1964. *The Raw and the Cooked: Introduction to a Science of Mythology: I.* Translated by John and Doreen Weightman. New York: Harper and Row.

Liberation. 1990. *The National Democratic Front of the Philippines* [NDF]. Philippines: National Democratic Front 18(6):2.

Librero, Aida R., and Agnes C. Rola, eds. 1991. *Agricultural Policy in the Philippines: An Analysis of Issues in the Eighties.* Los Banos, Laguna: University of the Philippines at Los Banos, Philippine Council for Agriculture, Forestry and Natural Resources Research and Development.

Lim, Linda Y. C. 1990. "Women's Work in Export Factories: The Politics of a Cause," in Irene Tinker, ed., *Persistent Inequalities: Women and World Development*. Pp. 101-122. New York and London: Oxford University Press.

Lindenbaum, Shirley. 1977. "The Last Course: Nutrition and Anthropology in Asia," in T. Fitzgerald, ed., *Nutrition and Anthropology in Action*. Pp. 141-155. Amsterdam: Assen van Gorcum.

Lindio-McGovern, Ligaya. 1997. *Filipino Peasant Women: Exploitation and Resistance*. Philadelphia: University of Pennsylvania Press.

Lock, Margaret, and Nancy Scheper-Hughes. 1990. "A Critical-Interpretive Approach in Medical Anthropology: Rituals and Routines of Discipline and Dissent," in Thomas M. Johnson and Carolyn F. Sargent, eds., *Medical Anthropology: Contemporary Theory and Method*. Pp. 47-72. New York: Praeger Publishers.

Lopez-Rodriguez, Luz. 1990. "Patriarchy and Women's Subordination in the Philippines." *Review of Women's Studies* 1(1):15-25.

Loste, Maureen. 1993. "Highlights of the World Conference on Human Rights." *Nordis, Northern Dispatch*, Fourth Anniversary Issue, September 26, pp. 8-10. Baguio: Cordillera Resource Center.

Lubis, Mochtar et al., eds. 1990. "Nongovernment Organizations in the '90s." *Solidarity, Current Affairs, Ideas and the Arts* no. 127 (July-September). Manila: Solidaridad Publishing House.

Lumanta, Melinda F. 1991. "Human Nutrition and Welfare Policy Issues: A Review and Synthesis," in Aida R. Librero and Agnes C. Rola, eds., 1991, in *Agricultural Policy in the Philippines: An Analysis of Issues in the Eighties*. Pp. 229-251. Los Banos, Laguna: University of the Philippines at Los Banos, Philippine Council for Agriculture, Forestry and Natural Resources Research and Development.

Luthra, Nirupama. 1983. "Socio-Economic Correlates of Child Growth." *Guru Nanak Journal of Sociology* 4(1):76-84.

Macaraig, Serafin, Socorro Espiritu, and Vitaliano Bernardino. 1954. "The Development and the Problems of the Filipino Family," in *Philippine Social Life*. Manila: Macaraig Publishing Co. Quoted in Delia D. Aguilar, *The Feminist Challenge: Initial Working Principles Toward Reconceptualizing the Feminist Movement in the Philippines*. Manila: Asian Social Institute, 1988.

Maderazo, Mario E. 1991. "More Farmers Are Sick." *Farm News & Views: A Bi-Monthly Publication of the Philippine Peasant Institute* 4(3):10-11.

Madew, Melinda. 1992. "The Historical and Cultural Context of Igorot Women's Struggle for Human Rights." *IGOROTA, The Alternative Women's Magazine in the Cordilleras* 6(3):4-6, 23. Baguio City: IGOROTA Foundation.

MAG (Medical Action Group). 1993. "Justice for Kalinga Health Worker." *Progress Notes: A Health and Human Rights Situationer* 7(3 and 4):6. Quezon City: Medical Action Group.

Magallanes, Josefino M. 1984. "Human Nutrition: The Impact of Family Size and Income on Dietary Intake." *Philippine Sociological Review* 32:1-4.

Makabayang Samahang Pangkalusugan (MSP). 1987. "A National Democratic Health Program. *Ilay Ang Kaalaman at Kasanayan sa Bayang Lumalaban*." Proceedings of the Second National Congress of the MSP. June. Philippines.

Malinowski, Bronislaw. 1939. *The Group and the Individual in Functional Analysis*. N.p.

Mananzan OSB, Sr. Mary John. 1991. *The Woman Question in the Philippines*. Pasay City, Philippines: Daughters of St. Paul.

Manila Chronicle. 1993. "25 years of 'Humanae Vitae'." July 26, p. 4.

Marchione, T. J. 1980. "Factors Associated with Malnutrition in the Children of Western Jamaica," in Norge W. Jerome, et al., eds., *Nutritional Anthropology: Contemporary Approaches to Diet and Culture*. Pp. 223-273. New York: Redgrave.

Mariano, Allen M. 1992. "The Cost of Internal War." *IBON Facts & Figures* 15(16). Manila: IBON Philippines Databank & Research Center.

Martin, Emily. 1994. *Flexible Bodies: The Role of Immunity in American Culture from the Days of Polio to the Age of AIDS*. Boston: Beacon Press.

———. 1987. *The Woman in the Body: A Cultural Analysis of Reproduction*. Boston: Beacon Press.

McAfee, Kathy. 1985. "The Philippines: A Harvest of Anger." *Oxfam America: Facts for Action*. October, no. 15. Boston: An Oxfam America Educational Publication.

McCoy, Alfred W. 1993. "Rent-Seeking Families and the Philippine State: A History of the Lopez Family," in Alfred W. McCoy, ed., *An Anarchy of Families: State and Family in the Philippines*. Pp. 429-536. Madison: Center for Southeast Asian Studies, University of Wisconsin.

McKenna, Thomas M. 1996. "Fighting for the Homeland: National Ideas and Rank-and-File Experience in the Muslim Separatist Movement in the Philippines." *Critique of Anthropology* 16(3):229-255.

Mead, Margaret. 1943. "The Problem of Changing Food Habits." Report of the Committee on Food Habits, 1941–1943. National Research Council, Bulletin no. 108. Washington, D.C.: National Academy of Sciences.

Medina, Belen T. G. 1991. *The Filipino Family. A Text with Selected Readings*. Diliman, Quezon City: University of the Philippines Press.

Melville, Bendley F. 1985. "A Research Note: The Roles of Community Health Aids and Economic Development in the Nutritional Status of Children in Western Jamaica, 1973–1984," in *The Impact of Development Technologies in Third World Health*. Studies in Third World Societies 34:225-231. Williamsburg, Virginia: Department of Anthropology, College of William and Mary.

Mendoza-Guazon, Maria Paz. 1951. *The Development and Progress of the Filipino Woman*. Manila: Kiko Printing Press. Quoted in Delia D. Aguilar, *The Feminist Challenge: Initial Working Principles Toward Reconceptualizing the Feminist Movement in the Philippines*. Manila: Asian Social Institute, 1988.

Merrill, William L. 1993. "Conversion and Colonialism in Northern Mexico: The Tarahumara Response to the Jesuit Mission Program 1601–1767," in Robert W. Hefner, ed., *Conversion to Christianity: Historical and Anthropological Perspectives on a Great Transformation*. Pp. 129-164. Berkeley: University of California Press.

Mikkelsen, Randall. 1992. "UN: Market Barriers Make Poor Countries Poorer." *Philippine Daily Inquirer*, April 24, p. 20.

Miller, Barbara D. 1987. "Female Infanticide and Child Neglect in Rural North India," in Nancy Scheper-Hughes, ed., *Child Survival*. Pp. 95-112. Boston: D. Reidel.

Mobile Register. 1998. "President Seeks Extra $48 Million for Peace Corps." January 4, p. 8A.

Mohanty, Chandra Talpade. 1991a. "Cartographies of Struggle: Third World Women and the Politics of Feminism," in Chandra Talpade Mohanty, Ann Russo, and Lourdes

Torres, eds., *Third World Women and the Politics of Feminism*. Pp. 1-47. Bloomington and Indianapolis: Indiana University Press.

———. 1991b. "Under Western Eyes: Feminist Scholarship and Colonial Discourses," in Chandra Talpade Mohanty, Ann Russo, and Lourdes Torres, eds., *Third World Women and the Politics of Feminism*. Pp. 51-80. Bloomington and Indianapolis: Indiana University Press.

Montes, Manuel F. 1992a. "The Effects of External Adjustment Efforts on the Population," in Emmanuel S. Dios and Joel Rocamora, eds., *Of Bonds & Bondage: A Reader on Philippine Debt*. Pp. 48-58. Philippines: Transnational Institute, Philippine Center for Policy Studies, and Freedom from Debt Coalition.

———. 1992b. "The World Debt Crisis: Consequences for the Philippines and Her People," in Emmanuel S. Dios and Joel Rocamora, eds., *Of Bonds & Bondage: A Reader on Philippine Debt*. Pp. 69-77. Philippines: Transnational Institute, Philippine Center for Policy Studies, and Freedom from Debt Coalition.

Montiel, Cristina, and Mary Racelis Hollnsteiner. 1976. *The Filipino Woman: Her Role and Status in Philippine Society*. Quezon City: Institute of Philippine Culture.

Morgan, Lynn M. 1987. "Dependency Theory in the Political Economy of Health: An Anthropological Critique." *Medical Anthropology Quarterly* 1(2):131-154.

Morrell, Jim. 1987. "Aid to the Philippines: Who Benefits?" in Daniel B. Schirmer and Stephen Rosskamm Shalom, eds., *The Philippines Reader: A History of Colonialism, Neocolonialism, Dictatorship, and Resistance*. Pp. 253-260. Boston: South End Press. Originally published in *International Policy Report* 1979, 5(2):1-9.

Morsy, Soheir A. 1990. "Political Economy in Medical Anthropology," in Thomas Johnson and Carolyn Sargent, eds., *Medical Anthropology: Contemporary Theory and Method*. Pp. 26-46. New York: Praeger.

———. 1988. "Islamic Clinics in Egypt: The Cultural Elaboration of Biomedical Hegemony." *Medical Anthropology Quarterly* 2(4):355-367.

———. 1979. "The Missing Link in Medical Anthropology: The Political Economy of Health." *Review in Anthropology* 6(3):349-363.

Moser, Caroline O. N. 1992. "Housing," in Lise Ostergaard, ed., *Gender and Development: A Practical Guide*. London and New York: Routledge.

Mountain Movers: A Monthly Publication of the Ifugao ABCSDP. Editorial. 1993. "Why Education." July, 1(8):2.

———. 1992. "Malnutrition: Famine Just Tip of the Iceberg." 1(2):5.

Mueller, Adele. 1986. "The Bureaucratization of Feminist Knowledge: The Case of Women in Development." *Resources for Feminist Research* 15(1):36-38.

Mukhopadhyay, Carol C., and Patricia J. Higgins. 1988. "Anthropological Studies of Women's Status Revisited: 1977–1987." *Annual Review of Anthropology* 17:461-495.

Mullings, Leith. 1984. *Therapy, Ideology, and Social Change: Mental Healing in Urban Ghana*. Berkeley: University of California Press.

Nanglihan, Jenny, and Paul Fianza. 1996. "San Roque Dam Opposition Heats Up." *Nordis, Northern Dispatch* 8(26-27):1-4. Baguio City: Cordillera Resource Center.

Nash, June, and Maria Patricia Fernandez-Kelly, eds. 1983. *Women, Men and the International Division of Labor*. Albany: State University of New York.

Nash, June, and Helen Safa. 1980. *Sex and Class in Latin America*. Hadley, Massachusetts: Bergin.

National Census and Statistics Office. 1980. "Census of Population and Housing, Ifugao Volume 1, Final Report." Manila: National Census and Statistics Office, NEDA (National Economic and Development Authority).

National Commission on the Role of Filipino Women. 1989. "Philippine Development Plan for Women 1989–1992." Manila: National Commission on the Role of Filipino Women.

———. 1985. "Filipino Women in Health Care and Welfare Services." Manila: National Commission on the Role of Filipino Women.

National Council of Churches in the Philippines. 1989. "Exploring the New Religious Movements in the Philippines." March. Quezon City: National Council of Churches in the Philippines.

National Economic Development Administration. 1986. "Health, Nutrition and Family Planning. Medium-Term Philippine Development Plan 1987–1992." Manila: The National Economic Development Administration.

National Nutrition Council, Republic of the Philippines. 1993. "Towards Nutritional Adequacy For All." A Country Paper of the Republic of the Philippines for the International Conference on Nutrition. Manila.

National Statistics Office, Republic of the Philippines. 1992a. "Highlights of the 1991 Family Income and Expenditures Survey Preliminary Results." Special Release, October, ISSN 0016 2640, Number 729. Manila: Office of the Administrator, National Statistics Office.

———. 1992b. "1990 Census of Population and Housing: Socio Economic and Demographic Characteristics, Ifugao." Report no. 3-39N. Manila: Republic of the Philippines National Statistics Office.

———. 1990. "Ifugao: Provincial Profile." December. Manila: Republic of the Philippines National Statistics Office.

———. 1970. "Ifugao 1970 Census of Population and Housing. Final Report, Volume 1." Manila: National Census and Statistics Office, NEDA.

Navarro, Vicente. 1986. *Crisis, Health and Medicine: A Social Critique.* New York and London: Tavistock Publications.

———. 1985. "U.S. Marxist Scholarship in the Analysis of Health and Medicine." *International Journal of Health Services* 15(4):525-544.

NDF (National Democratic Front of the Philippines) National Executive Committee. 1991. "Unite and Advance the National Democratic Alternative! Statement of the NDF on its 18th Anniversary." *Liberation* 14(2):3. Philippines: National Democratic Front of the Philippines.

Neher, Clark D. 1982. "Sex Roles in the Philippines: The Ambiguous Cebuana," in Penny Van Esterik, ed., *Women Of Southeast Asia.* Pp. 155-175. Northern Illinois University Series on Southeast Asia, Occasional Paper, no. 9. De Kalb: Northern Illinois University, Center for Southeast Asian Studies; Detroit: Cellar Book Shop.

Nieva, Antonio MA. 1993a. "Hacienda Luisita: Landmark Sellout." *Philippine Daily Inquirer*, June 13, p. 1.

———. 1993b. "DAR Bedevilled by 'Legal' and Illegal Land Conversions." *Philippine Daily Inquirer*, June 15, p. 1.

———. 1993c. "New Round of Violence Feared in RP." *Philippine Daily Inquirer*, June 16, p. 1.

NMCL Research Committee. 1992. "Woman Power." (Political poster.) Quezon City: Research Committee of the National Movement for Civil Liberties.

Nolasco, Cynthia. 1987. "The Woman Problem: Gender, Class and State Oppression," in Sr. Mary John Mananzan, OSE, ed., *Essays on Women. Women's Studies Series.* Metro Manila: St. Scholastica College, Women's Studies Program.

Nolledo, Jose N. 1987. *The Constitution of the Republic of the Philippines with Annotations.* 1977. Reprint, Manila: Rex Book Store.

Nordstrom, Carolyn, and JoAnn Martin, eds. 1992. *The Paths To Domination, Resistance, and Terror.* Berkeley: University of California Press.

Nourse, Jennifer W. 1996. "The Voice of the Winds Versus the Masters of Cure: Contested Notions of Spirit Possession Among the Lauje of Sulawesi." *Journal of the Royal Anthropological Institute* 2:425-442.

Nutrition Service, Republic of the Philippines. 1991. "Department of Health Comprehensive Nutrition Program 1992-1996." October. Manila.

Oculi, Okello. 1987. *Political Economy of Malnutrition.* Nigeria: Ahmadu Bello University Press.

Olivares, Ninez Cacho. 1993. "Government vs Church." *Philippine Daily Inquirer,* July 25, p. 4.

Omawale. 1984. "Nutribusiness: An Aspect of the Political Economy of Persistent Hunger." *International Journal of Health Services* 14(2):173-188.

Ong, Aihwa. 1990. "Japanese Factories, Malay Workers: Class and Sexual Metaphors in West Malaysia," in Jane Monnig Atkinson and Shelly Errington, eds., *Power and Difference: Gender in Island Southeast Asia.* Pp. 385-422. Stanford, California: Stanford University Press.

———. 1988. "Colonialism and Modernity: Feminist Re-presentations of Women in Non-Western Societies." *Inscriptions* 3/4:79-93.

———. 1987 *Spirits of Resistance and Capitalist Discipline: Factory Women in Malaysia.* Albany: State University of New York Press.

Ong, Aihwa, and Michael G. Peletz, eds. 1995. *Bewitching Women, Pious Men: Gender and Body Politics in Southeast Asia.* Berkeley: University of California Press.

Orozco, Wilhelmina S. 1983. *Philippine Women in the World of Work.* Manila: Wilhelmina Orozco.

Ostergaard, Lise. 1992a. "Health," in Lise Ostergaard, ed., *Gender and Development: A Practical Guide.* Pp. 110-134. London and New York: Routledge.

———. ed. 1992b. *Gender and Development: A Practical Guide.* London and New York: Routledge.

Owen, Norman G. 1987. "Measuring Mortality in the Nineteenth Century in the Philippines," in Norman G. Owen, ed., *Death and Disease in Southeast Asia: Explorations in Social, Medical and Demographic History.* New York and London: Oxford University Press.

Oyeneye, O. Y. 1991. "Family Health in Nigeria." *Journal of Sociology of the Family* 21(2):189-199.

Palpal-Latoc, Lucila. 1988. "Under Fire: Dedicated Doctors Are Under Attack." *Manila Chronicle,* in *Solidaridad* 2/July-December, 22. Manila.

Pelto, Gretel H. 1987. "Cultural Issues in Maternal and Child Health and Nutrition." *Social Science and Medicine* 25(6):553-559.

Perez, Angel. 1902. "*Igorrotes: Estudio geografio y etnografico sobre algunos Distritos del Norte de Luzon.*" Manila. Quoted in William Henry Scott, *The Discovery of the Igorots:*

Spanish Contacts with the Pagans of Northern Luzon. Rev. ed. Quezon City: New Day Publishers, 1974, p. 236.

Permanent Peoples' Tribunal Session on the Philippines. 1981. "Philippines: Repression and Resistance." *Komite ng Sambayanang, Pilipino* (KSP).

Pertierra, Raul. 1988. *Religion, Politics, and Rationality in a Philippine Community.* Manila: Ateneo de Manila University Press.

Philippine Daily Inquirer. 1993a. "FVR Launches Birth Control Program Today. State-Church Feud Expected to Worsen." August 2, pp. 1, 12.

———. 1993b. "Women Need Birth Control, Says Flavier." July 31, p. 6.

———. 1993c. "Church Girds for War Over Birth Control." July 23, pp. 1, 8.

———. 1993d. "922 Avail of Amnesty." July 15, p. 10.

———. 1993e. "Economic Outlook for RP Bleak." June 24, pp. 1, 12.

———. 1993f. "Rice Price Up by P1 Per Kilo." June 21, pp. 1, 6.

———. 1993g. "Farmers Hits (sic) Gov't Policy on Rice Production." June 19, p. 13.

———. 1992a. "Inflation Inches up to 8.7% in October." November 6, p. 17.

———. 1992b. "Radical Churchmen Attack Ramos." August 17, p. 6.

———. 1992c. "RP Economy Faces Tough Road to Recovery, Says Gov't Report." June 17, pp. 1, 12.

———. 1992d. "The Rich Get Richer, Says UN Report." April 24, pp. 1, 6.

———. 1992e. "Big Bank to Use Money for Family Planning." April 20, pp. 1, 10.

———. 1992f. "Mitra Vows to Solve Power Woes." April 20, p. 14.

———. 1992g. *Sablay.* Editorial, April 20, p. 4.

———. 1992h. "Industrialization Still an Elusive Dream." April 20, p. 22.

———. 1992i. "Economy Shrinks by 0.05% in '91." March 4, p. 15.

———. 1992j. "Borrowing Resumes: RP Gets IMF Approval." February 12, p. 1.

———. 1992k. "Gov't Overshoots 1991 Local Debt Ceiling." February 11, p. 17.

Philippine Family Planning Program. 1993. "More Than 60,000 Women and Children Will Die This Year Because of Unplanned Pregnancies and Birth Complications." *Philippine Daily Inquirer*, August 2, pp. 24-27.

Philippine National Economic Development Administration (NEDA). 1986. "Health, Nutrition and Family Planning. Medium-Term Philippine Development Plan 1987–1992." Manila: Philippine National Economic Development Administration.

Philippine Star. 1993. "Sin Calls on Faithful to Support Bishop's Stand on Birth Control." July 27, pp. 1-2.

———. 1992a. "US Envoy: RP Must Pursue Reforms to Boost Economy." July 1, p. 8.

———. 1992b. "WB to Take a Look at Military Spending in Future Loans to 3rd World Countries." May 12, p. 18.

———. 1992c. "Major Aid Donors to Review Economic Performance of Gov't." March 11, pp. 1-2.

Population Reference Bureau. 1984. "1984 World Population Data Sheet." Washington, D.C.

Prieto, Fray Juan. 1850. "Letter to Fr. Francisco Gainza, dated Mayoyao, October 1, 1850." APSR, MS, *Seccion "Cagayan," Cartas.* Quoted in William Henry Scott, *The Discovery of the Igorots: Spanish Contacts with the Pagans of Northern Luzon.* Rev. ed. Quezon City: New Day Publishers, 1974, pp. 286-287.

Puno, Jr., Ricardo. 1992. "Population Bomb or Dud?" *Philippine Star*, July 19, p. 11.

Putzel, James. 1992. *A Captive Land: The Politics of Agrarian Reform in the Philippines.* Manila: Ateneo de Manila University Press.

Quimpo-Espino, Margie. 1992a. "$450-M WB Loan Not Linked to P308-B Problem." *Philippine Daily Inquirer*, November 11, p. 17.

———. 1992b. "Due to Weak Consumer Demand Economy Forecast to Remain Stagnant." *Philippine Daily Inquirer*, October 12, p. 17.

———. 1992c. "ODA Availments up 40% in January-June." *Philippine Daily Inquirer*, August 13, p. 17.

Racelis, Mary. 1997. "Discussion for Panel: The Philippine Economy." Discussion presented at the Focus on the Philippines Conference, May 7, in Los Angeles.

Ramos, Fidel V. 1997. "Conference Opening Address." Address presented at the Focus on the Philippines Conference, May 6, in Los Angeles.

Ranger, Terence. 1993. "The Local and the Global in Southern African Religious History," in Robert W. Hefner, ed., *Conversion to Christianity: Historical and Anthropological Perspectives on a Great Transformation.* Pp. 65-98. Berkeley: University of California Press.

Raphael, Dana. 1988. "The Need for a Supportive Doula in an Increasingly Urban World," in Patricia Whelehan, ed., *Women and Health: Cross Cultural Perspectives.* Pp. 73-83. New York: Bergin and Garvey.

———. 1985. *Only Mothers Know: Patterns of Infant Feeding in Traditional Cultures.* Westport, Connecticut: Greenwood Press.

Republic of the Philippines. 1988. *The Comprehensive Agrarian Reform Law of 1988 (CARL) Republic Act No. 6657.* Quezon City: AFA Publications.

Republic of the Philippines National Statistics Office. 1990. "Ifugao Provincial Profile." Manila: National Statistics Office, Philippines.

Reyes, Ed Aurelio. 1993. "Try to Remember that Time of September." *Health Alert* Issue 146, 9 (October):343-345. Quezon City: Health Action Information Center.

Rhodes, Lorna Amarasingham. 1990. "Studying Biomedicine as a Cultural System," in Thomas M. Johnson and Carolyn F. Sargent, eds., *Medical Anthropology: Contemporary Theory and Method.* Pp. 174-186. New York: Praeger.

Richards, Audrey. 1948. *Hunger and Work in a Savage Tribe: A Functional Study of Nutrition Among the Southern Bantu.* 1932. Reprint, Westport, Connecticut: Greenwood Press.

———. 1939. *Land, Labour and Diet in Northern Rhodesia: An Economic Study of the Bemba Tribe.* New York and London: Oxford University Press.

Richter, Linda K. 1987. "The Status of Women in the Philippines," in Daniel B. Schirmer and Stephen Rosskamm Shalom, eds., 1987. *The Philippines Reader: A History of Colonialism, Neocolonialism, Dictatorship, and Resistance.* Pp. 135-139. Boston: South End Press.

Robertson, A. F. 1984. *People and the State.* Cambridge: Cambridge University Press.

Rocamora, Joel. 1994. *Breaking Through: The Struggle Within the Communist Party of the Philippines.* Pasig City, Philippines: Anvil Publishing.

———. 1992. "The NDF Program and the CPP Program for a People's Democratic Revolution: Umbilical Cord or Lifeline?" *Debate: Philippine Left Review* 5 (December):3-38.

Rola, A. C., D. D., Elazegui, C. A. Foronda, J. D. Lamanilao, F. P. L. Cruz, E. E. Dumayas, A. R. Chupungco, and M. F. Lumanta. 1991. "Overview and Summary of Findings," in

Aida R. Librero and Agnes C. Rola, eds., 1991, *Agricultural Policy in the Philippines: An Analysis of Issues in the Eighties.* Pp. 1-30. Los Banos, Laguna: University of the Philippines at Los Banos, Philippine Council for Agriculture, Forestry and Natural Resources Research and Development.

Rosaldo, Michelle. 1980. *Knowledge and Passion: Ilongot Notions of Self and Society.* New York: Cambridge University Press.

Rosaldo, Michelle Zimbalist, and Jane M. Atkinson. 1975. "Man the Hunter and Woman: Metaphors for the Sexes in Ilongot Magical Spells," in R. Willis, ed., *The Interpretation of Symbolism.* Pp. 43-75. London: Malaby Press.

Rosaldo, Renato. 1980. *Ilongot Headhunting 1883-1974: A Study in Society and History.* Stanford, California: Stanford University Press.

Rosenberg, Ellen. 1980. "Demographic Effects of Sex-Differential Nutrition," in Norge W. Jerome et al., eds., *Nutritional Anthropology: Contemporary Approaches to Diet and Culture.* New York: Redgrave.

Rossa, Alberto, CMF, ed. 1986. *The Theology of Liberation.* Diliman, Quezon City: Claretian Publications.

Rostow, W. W. 1960. *The Stages of Economic Growth: A Non-Communist Manifesto.* Cambridge: Cambridge University Press.

Rubbo, Anna. 1975. "The Spread of Capitalism in Rural Colombia: Effects on Poor Women," in Rayna R. Reiter, ed., *Toward an Anthropology of Women.* Pp. 333-357. New York and London: Monthly Review Press.

Rubenstein, Robert A., and Sandra D. Lane. 1990. "International Health and Development," in Thomas M. Johnson and Carolyn F. Sargent, eds., *Medical Anthropology: Contemporary Theory and Method.* Pp. 367-390. New York: Praeger.

Sabo, Lois E., and Joachim S. Kibirige. 1989. "Political Violence and Eritrean Health Care." *Social Science and Medicine* 28(7):677-684.

Sachs, Wolfgang. 1992. Introduction to Wolfgang Sachs, ed., *The Development Dictionary: A Guide to Knowledge and Power.* Pp. 1-6. London and New Jersey: Zed Books.

Sanchez, Rosena D., Lourdesita S. Sobrevega, and Maribeth D. Juarez, M.D. 1992. *An Analysis of Women's Health Situation in Six Selected Communities in Mindanao, Philippines.* Davao City, Philippines: Women Studies and Resource Center.

Sancho, Nelia, and Edith Espino, eds. 1989. *An Introduction to Women's Health Issues in the Philippines: A Collection of Speeches and Essays of Women Leaders, Organizers, Activists and Grassroots Women.* Quezon City: The GABRIELA National Women's Coalition and the GABRIELA Women's Health and Reproductive Rights Commission (GWHC).

Santos, Aida Fulleros, and Lynn F. Lee. 1989. *The Debt Crisis. A Treadmill of Poverty for Filipino Women.* Manila: *Katipunan ng Kababaihan Para sa Kalayaan.*

Sarmiento, Jr., J. V. 1992. "Aquino OKs Budget but Vetoes Debt Cap," *Philippine Daily Inquirer*, January 16, pp. 1, 10.

Scheper-Hughes, Nancy. 1992. *Death Without Weeping: The Violence of Everyday Life in Brazil.* Berkeley: University of California Press.

———. 1987. "Culture, Scarcity, and Maternal Thinking: Mother Love and Child Death in Northeast Brazil," in Nancy Scheper-Hughes, ed., *Child Survival.* Pp. 187-208. Washington, D.C.: American Anthropological Association.

———. 1984. "Infant Mortality and Infant Care: Cultural and Economic Constraints on Nurturing in Northeast Brazil." *Social Science and Medicine* 19(5):535-546.

Scheper-Hughes, Nancy, and Margaret Lock. 1987. "The Mindful Body: A Prolegomenon to Future Work in Medical Anthropology." *Medical Anthropology Quarterly* 1(1):6-41.
———. 1986. "Speaking 'Truth' to Illness: Metaphors, Reification, and a Pedagogy for Patients." *Medical Anthropology Quarterly* 17(5):137-140.
Schirmer, Daniel B. 1987. "The Conception and Gestation of a Neocolony," in Daniel B. Schirmer and Stephen Rosskamm Shalom, eds., *The Philippines Reader: A History of Colonialism, Neocolonialism, Dictatorship, and Resistance.* Pp. 38-44. Boston: South End Press. Originally published in *Journal of Contemporary Asia* 1975, 5(1).
Schirmer, Daniel B., and Stephen Rosskamm Shalom. 1987. *The Philippines Reader: A History of Colonialism, Neocolonialism, Dictatorship, and Resistance.* Boston: South End Press.
Schoepf, Brooke Grundfest. 1987. "Social Structure, Women's Status and Sex Differential Nutrition in the Zairian Copperbelt." *Urban Anthropology and Studies of Cultural Systems and World Economic Development* 16(1):73-102.
Schoepf, Brooke Grundfest, and Claude Schoepf. 1987. "Food Crisis and Agrarian Change in the Eastern Highlands of Zaire." *Urban Anthropology* 16(1):5-37.
Schramm Honculada, Jacquelyn. 1988. "The Bottle Feeding Scandal." *Health Alert* 2(83):209-217. Quezon City, Philippines: Health Action Information Network.
Schrijvers, Joke. 1988. "Blueprint for Undernourishment: The Mahaweli River Development Scheme in Sri Lanka," in Bina Agarwal, ed., *Structures of Patriarchy: State, Community and Household in Modernising Asia.* Pp. 29-51. New Delhi: Kali for Women; London: Zed Books.
Scott, James C. 1985. *Weapons of the Weak.* New Haven and London: Yale University Press.
Scott, William Henry. 1982. *Cracks in the Parchment Curtain and Other Essays in Philippine History.* Quezon City: New Day Publishers.
———. 1974. *The Discovery of the Igorots: Spanish Contacts with the Pagans of Northern Luzon.* Rev. Ed. Quezon City: New Day Publishers.
Senauer, Benjamin. 1990. "The Impact of the Value of Women's Time on Food and Nutrition," in Irine Tinker, ed., *Persistent Inequalities: Women and World Development.* Pp. 150-161. New York: Oxford University Press.
702nd Infantry (SOT) Brigade, 7th Infantry Division, Philippine Army. 1993a. "Top Ranking Ifugao Rebel Surrenders with Amazon Girlfriend." *Central Luzon Tribune, Defender of the People* 4(5):1, 2.
———. 1993b. "Another dental and medical civic action was recently conducted at the ISCAF compound in Nayon, Lamut, Ifugao by joint elements of the 702nd Infantry Brigade led by Captain Pedro Calabocal, Jr., seen here inspecting the teeth of Patricia Tayaban and local health practitioners led by Josephine Bokiangon, a registered nurse based in Lagawe town." (Photograph caption) *Central Luzon Tribune, Defender of the People* 4(5):2.
———. 1992a. "Killing Me Softly with a Song." *Central Luzon Tribune, Defender of the People* 3(7):5, 7.
———. 1992b. "COIN Campaign Intensified in Ifugao." *Central Luzon Tribune, Defender of the People* 3(7):1, 6.
———. 1992c. "Unity and Cooperation: Solution of Insurgency Problem Seen." *Central Luzon Tribune, Defender of the People* 4(5):1, 2, 4.

Shiva, Vandana. 1990. "Development as a New Project of Western Patriarchy," in Irene Diamond and Gloria Feman Orenstein, eds., *Reweaving the World: The Emergence of Ecofeminism.* San Francisco: Sierra Club Books.

———. 1988. *Staying Alive: Women, Ecology and Development.* London: Zed Press.

Sidel, John. 1993. "Walking in the Shadow of the Big Man: Justiniano Montano and Failed Dynasty Building in Cavite 1935–1972," in Alfred W. McCoy, ed., *An Anarchy of Families: State and Family in the Philippines.* Pp. 109-161. Madison: Center for Southeast Asian Studies, University of Wisconsin.

Singer, Merrill, Lani Davison, and Gina Gerdes. 1988. "Culture, Critical Theory, and Reproductive Illness Behavior in Haiti." *Medical Anthropology Quarterly* 2(4):370-385.

Sobo, Elaine Janine. 1993. *One Blood: The Jamaican Body.* Albany: State University of New York Press.

Solon, Florentino et al. 1979. "An Evaluation of Strategies to Control Vitamin A Deficiency in the Philippines." *American Journal of Clinical Nutrition* 32 (July):1445-1453.

St. Hilaire, Colette. 1992. "Canadian Aid, Women and Development: Re-baptizing the Filipina." Philippines Development Briefing 3 (December):2-15.

Stavrianos, L. 1981. *Global Rift: The Third World Comes of Age.* New York: William Morrow and Company.

Steedly, Mary Margaret. 1993. *Hanging Without a Rope: Narrative Experience in Colonial and Postcolonial Karoland.* Princeton, New Jersey: Princeton University Press.

Steinberg, David Joel. 1994. *The Philippines: A Singular and a Plural Place.* 3d ed. Boulder, Colorado: Westview Press.

Stocking, Jr., George W. 1968. *Race Culture and Evolution: Essays in the History of Anthropology.* Chicago: University of Chicago Press.

Strauss, John. 1987. "Households, Communities, and Preschool Children's Nutrition Outcomes: Evidence from the Rural Cote d'Ivoire." New Haven, Connecticut: Economics Department, Yale University.

Tabonares, Gina. 1992. "P20-P25 Wage Hike Sought by TUCP." *Philippine Star,* July 15, p. 13.

Tadiar, M. D., Florence M. 1993. "Gov't Workers and Family Planning." *Philippine Daily Inquirer,* August 1, p. 5.

Tallo, Veronica L., G. Eulalio, and Antonietta E. Zablan. 1979. "The Context: Population, Health, and Family Planning." *Studies in Family Planning* 10(6-7):188-194.

Tambiah, Stanley J. 1970. *Buddhism and the Spirit Cults in Northeast Thailand.* Cambridge: Cambridge University Press.

Tampus, Gemma. 1993. "Confrontation Over Birth Control Escalates." *Manila Chronicle,* July 26, pp. 1, 6.

Tan, Michael Lim. 1995. "Philippine Health Matters 1995." *Health Alert* Special Issue 182, 11 (May). Quezon City: Health Action Information Network.

———. 1992a. "Philippine Health Matters 1992. Women's Health in the Philippines: A Critical Analysis." *Health Alert* Special Issue 129-130 (May-June). Quezon City: Health Action Information Network.

———. 1992b. "Traditional Medical Practitioners in the Philippines." *Health Alert* Issue 134 (October):277-290. Quezon City: Health Action Information Network.

———. 1992c. "Bridging Medical Cultures in the Philippines." *Health Alert* Issue 128, 8 (April):132-136. Quezon City: Health Action Information Network.

——— . 1991. "Philippine Health Matters." *Health Alert* Special Issue 116-117, 7 (April/May). Quezon City: Health Action Information Network.

——— . 1987. *Usug, Kulam, Pasma*: Traditional Concepts of Health and Illness in the Philippines. Quezon City: AKAP

Tanada, Lorenzo M. 1987. "The Folklore of Colonialism," in Daniel B. Schirmer and Stephen Rosskamm Shalom, eds., *The Philippines Reader: A History of Colonialism, Neocolonialism, Dictatorship, and Resistance*. Pp. 154-157. Boston: South End Press. Originally published in Teodoro A. Agoncillo and Milagros C. Guerrero, eds., *History of the Filipino People*. Quezon City: R.P. Garcia Publishing Co., 1971, pp. 610-618.

Task Force Detainees of the Philippines, Baguio. 1993. "Human Rights Documents."

——— . 1992. "Human Rights Documents."

——— . 1991. "Human Rights Documents."

Taussig, Michael. 1987. *Shamanism, Colonialism, and the Wild Man: A Study in Terror and Healing*. Chicago: University of Chicago Press.

——— . 1980. "Reification and the Consciousness of the Patient." *Social Science and Medicine* 14:3-13.

——— . 1978. "Nutrition, Development, and Foreign Aid: A Case Study of U.S. Directed Health Care in a Colombian Plantation Zone." *International Journal of Health Services* 8(1):101-121.

Tefft, Sheila. 1991. "Filipino Catholics Debate Role. Roman Catholic Left and Right Are at Odds Over Enormous Problems Facing the Country." *Christian Science Monitor*, April 29, p. 6.

Thomas, G. C. 1981. "The Social Background of Childhood Nutrition in the Ciskei." *Social Science and Medicine* 15A(5):551-555.

Thompson, Mark R. 1995. *The Anti-Marcos Struggle: Personalistic Rule and Democratic Transition in the Philippines*. New Haven and London: Yale University Press.

Thorner, Daniel. 1987. "Peasant Economy as a Category in History," in Teodor Shanin, ed., *Peasants and Peasant Societies*, 2d ed. Pp. 62-68. 1971. Reprint, Oxford: Basil Blackwell.

Timonera, Bobby. 1993. "Kids Caught in Crossfire Top Cases of Child Abuse." *Philippine Daily Inquirer*, June 13, p. 11.

Tinker, Irene. 1990a. "A Context for the Field and for the Book," in Irene Tinker, ed., *Persistent Inequalities: Women and World Development*. Pp. 3-13. New York and London: Oxford University Press.

——— , ed. 1990b. *Persistent Inequalities: Women and World Development*. Oxford: Oxford University Press.

Torres, Amaryllis T. et al., eds. 1988. *An Anthology of Studies on the Filipino Woman*. Manila: UNESCO Regional Unit for Social and Human Sciences in Asia and the Pacific.

Tsing, Anna Lowenhaupt. 1993. *In the Realm of the Diamond Queen: Marginality in an Out-of-the-Way Place*. Princeton, New Jersey: Princeton University Press.

Turner, Bryan S. 1984. *The Body and Society: Explorations in Social Theory*. New York: Basil Blackwell.

Turner, Mark Macdonald. 1980. "Inequality in the Philippines: Old Bottlenecks and New Directions for Analysis." *Philippine Sociological Review* 30:23-32.

Turner, Paul R., and David Pitt, eds. 1989. *The Anthropology of War and Peace: Perspectives on the Nuclear Age*. South Hadley, Massachusetts: Bergin and Garvey.

Ugalde, Antonio. 1985. "Modernization, Agricultural Exports, Food Availability and Nutrition in Central America: 1960–1980," in *The Impact of Development and Modern Technologies in Third World Health.* Studies in Third World Societies 34:201-224. Williamsburg, Virginia: Department of Anthropology, College of William and Mary.

UNICEF (United Nations Children's Fund). 1997. *The Progress of Nations.* Available from www.unicef.org; INTERNET.

——. 1993. "UNICEF Report on the Women's Organizations Program Component of the Ifugao Area Based Child Survival and Development Programme" (Exact title unknown). Ifugao Province, Philippines: UNICEF.

——. 1992a. "IFUGAO Child Survival and Women Development Programme." (Pamphlet.) June. Manila, Philippines: UNICEF.

——. 1992b. "Ifugao Provincial Plan of Operations." Ifugao Province, Philippines: UNICEF.

——. 1991. "Masterlist of High Risk and at Risk Families: Province of Ifugao." Lagawe, Ifugao, Philippines: Ifugao Provincial Health Office.

——. 1990a. "IPUGO: Ifugao Child Survival and Women Development Program (ICSWDP). Midterm Review, May 21-25, 1990." Ifugao Province, Philippines: UNICEF.

——. 1990b. *Situation of Children and Women in the Philippines 1990.* August. Manila, Philippines: Government of the Republic of the Philippines and UNICEF.

——. 1987. *Situation of Children and Women in the Philippines.* Manila, Philippines: Government of the Republic of the Philippines and UNICEF.

UNICEF/Ifugao ABCSD (Area Based Child Survival and Development) Programme. 1990. "The Ifugao ABCSD Mid-Term Report." Ifugao Province, Philippines: UNICEF.

U.S. Department of State. 1987a. *Treaties and Other International Agreements of the United States of America, 1776–1949*, in Daniel B. Schirmer and Stephen Rosskamm Shalom, eds., *The Philippines Reader: A History of Colonialism, Neocolonialism, Dictatorship, and Resistance.* Pp. 88-90. Boston: South End Press. Originally published in *Department of State Publication 8728.* Compiled by Charles I. Bevins. Washington, D.C.: U.S. Government Printing Office, 1974, 11:7-18.

——. 1987b. "Bulletin," in Daniel B. Schirmer and Stephen Rosskamm Shalom, eds., *The Philippines Reader: A History of Colonialism, Neocolonialism, Dictatorship, and Resistance.* Pp. 95-96. Boston: South End Press. Originally published September 19, 1955, pp. 469-470.

Vaughan, Megan. 1987. *The Story of an African Famine: Gender and Famine in Twentieth Century Malawi.* New York: Cambridge University.

Villa, Rod L. 1993. "Speaker Backs Amnesty Plan." *Manila Bulletin*, July 3, pp. 1, 8.

Villaverde, Juan. 1879. *Informe sobre la reduccion de los infieles de Luzon, El Correo Sino-Annamita,* 13:1-107. Reprinted in *Memoria...Exposicion General de las Filipinas en Madrid 1887.* Pp. 101-125. Manila, 1887. Quoted in William Henry Scott, *The Discovery of the Igorots: Spanish Contacts with the Pagans of Northern Luzon* Rev. ed. Quezon City: New Day Publishers, 1974, pp. 323, 326.

Villavieja, G. M., T. E. Valero, E. R. Red, C. A. Nones, B. E. Raymundo, C. M. Cerdena, H. S. P. Abaya, and C. C. Tanchonco. 1989. "Trends in Philippine Nutrition Situation in Relation with Some Development Indicators." Paper presented at the Fifteenth Series of Seminars on Food and Nutrition Researches, FNRI, July 17-18, in the Philippines. Quoted in Melinda F. Lumanta, "Human Nutrition and Welfare Policy Issues: A Review and Synthesis," in Aida R. Librero and Agnes C. Rola, eds., *Agricultural Policy in the Philippines: An Analysis of Issues in the Eighties*. Los Banos, Laguna: University of the Philippines at Los Banos, Philippine Council for Agriculture, Forestry and Natural Resources Research and Development, 1991, pp. 229-251.

Vogt, Evon Z. 1976. *Tortillas for the Gods: A Symbolic Analysis of Zinacateco Rituals*. Cambridge: Harvard University Press.

Von der Mehden, Fred R. 1986. *Religion and Modernization in Southeast Asia*. Syracuse, New York: Syracuse University Press.

Waitzkin, Howard. 1986. "Micropolitics of Medicine: Theoretical Issues." *Medical Anthropology Quarterly* 17:134-136.

——. 1983. *The Second Sickness: Contradictions of Capitalist Health Care*. New York: Free Press.

——. 1981. "The Social Origins of Illness: A Neglected History." *International Journal of Health Services* 11:77-103.

Warren, Kay B., ed. 1993. *The Violence Within: Cultural and Political Opposition in Divided Nations*. Boulder, Colorado: Westview Press.

Warren, Kay B., and Susan C. Bourque. 1991. "Women, Technology, and International Development Ideologies: Analyzing Feminist Voices," in Micaela di Leonardo, ed., *Gender at the Crossroads of Knowledge: Feminist Anthropology in the Postmodern Era*. Pp. 278-311. Berkeley: University of California Press.

Watts, Michael. 1983. *Silent Violence: Food, Famine and Peasantry in Northern Nigeria*. Berkeley: University of California Press.

Weber, Max. 1956. *The Sociology of Religion*. 1922. Reprint, Boston: Beacon Press.

Weekley, Kathleen. 1996. "From Vanguard to Rearguard: The Theoretical Roots of the Crisis of the Communist Party of the Philippines," in *The Revolution Falters: The Left in Philippine Politics After 1986*. Pp. 28-59. Ithaca, New York: Southeast Asian Program Publications, Cornell University.

Weismantel, M. J. 1988. *Food, Gender, and Poverty in the Ecuadorian Andes*. Philadelphia: University of Pennsylvania Press.

Whitehead, Ann. 1991. "Food Production and the Food Crisis in Africa," in T. Wallace and C. March, eds., *Changing Perceptions: Writings on Gender and Development*. Oxford: Oxfam.

Whitehead, Ann, and Helen Bloom. 1992. "Agriculture," in Lise Ostergaard, ed., *Gender and Development: A Practical Guide*. Pp. 41-56. London and New York: Routledge.

Wolf, Eric. 1966. *Peasants*. Englewood Cliffs, New Jersey: Prentice-Hall.

Women Development and Technology, Inc. 1992. "A Gender in Development Framework for the UNICEF Assisted Third Country Programme for Children in the Philippines." March. Quezon City: Women Development and Technology, Inc., and the Department of Social Welfare and Development, Government of the Republic of the Philippines.

World Bank. 1993. *World Development Report 1993*. Oxford: Oxford University Press.

Yengoyan, Aram A. 1993. "Religion, Morality, and Prophetic Traditions: Conversion Among the Pitjantjatjara of Central Australia," in Robert w. Hefner, ed., *Conversion to Christianity: Historical and Anthropological Perspectives on a Great Transformation*. Pp. 233-258. Berkeley: University of California Press.

Young, Allan. 1982. "The Anthropologies of Illness and Sickness." *Annual Review of Anthropology* 11:257-285.

Young, Kate. 1992. "Household Resource Management," in Lise Ostergaard, ed., *Gender and Development: A Practical Guide.* London and New York: Routledge.

Young, Kate, R. McCullough, and C. Wolkowitz. 1981. *Of Marriage and the Market.* London: CSE Books.

Youngblood, Robert L. 1987. "Church Opposition to Martial Law in the Philippines," in Daniel B. Schirmer and Stephen Rosskamm Shalom, eds., *The Philippines Reader: A History of Colonialism, Neocolonialism, Dictatorship, and Resistance.* Pp. 210-218. Boston: South End Press. Originally published in *Asian Survey* 1978, 18(5):505-520.

Zaidi, S. Akbar. 1988. "Poverty and Disease: Need for Structural Change." *Social Science and Medicine* 27(2):119-127.

Zapata, Maricor. 1993. "Imports From the US Rising Again." *Manila Chronicle*, June 16, p. 11.

Index

Agrarian reform (*also* land reform), 34,
39-43, 51, 55, 58, 59 n. 1, 59 n. 9,
76-77, 101 n. 19, 129-130, 232, 234,
257, 259, 267, 295-298
Agribusiness, historical development,
35-47, 57-58, 297
Aguilar, Delia D., 91
Alternatives to international development,
303
  see also agrarian reform, autonomy,
    Cordillera Peoples Alliance, health
    care and NGO, health care and
    revolutionary NDF/NPA,
    international development and
    NGOs, LIC and health care
    volunteers, LIC and health NGOs,
    MAKIBAKA, National Democratic
    Front, New People's Army, NGOs,
    peasant resistance, women's
    movement, worker resistance
Anemia, 8, 192, 211-214, 233, 237, 301
Aquino, President Corazon, 43-46, 51, 53,
55-56, 59 n. 12, 112, 114, 132-133,
139, 222, 284, 286, 288, 302
Atkinson, Jane Monnig, 78, 96
Autonomy, Cordillera regional, 76, 101 n.
18, 222, 275
  see also Cordillera Peoples Alliance

Baddang, 80, 101 n. 23, 172, 244-246,
261 n. 4
Baer, Hans A., 2, 10
Baki, 179 n. 1
  agriculture, 5, 145-146, 149-151, 157-
158, 178, 179 n. 8, 273-274, 276
  Balitok, 146
  Bugan: descendant of original, 146;
    original, 146

and change, 146-147, 178, 267-270,
275-280
class, 72, 145-146, 157, 218-219, 276-
280
denigration of, 28, 146, 160, 162, 167,
171-172, 175, 214, 265-280, 289,
299, 300-301
food taboos, 151, 174, 185, 214, 266,
268
gender, 68, 149-151, 178, 179 n. 7
healing, 3, 27, 145-158, 171-172, 177,
263, 270-272, 276, 279: illness
causation as multi-causal, 27, 153,
173-174; illness causation, theories
of, 151-153, 177; illness prevention,
158; multiple healing practices, 27,
147, 153-157, 164, 173-174, 176,
270; social relations, 145-154, 157-
158, 178; understandings and
healing of thinness (*na-ong-ong*),
27, 145, 147-148, 151, 154-157,
178, 179 n. 5, 179 n. 10, 181, 214
218, 220, 226 n. 31, 301
LIC, 116, 123, 134, 140, 147
Maingit, 146
Maknongan, 148, 154, 270
mama-o, 149-154, 179 n. 7
mumbaki, 116, 124, 146-156, 167, 178,
179 n. 7, 265, 270-271, 276
Muntalug, 146, 148, 179 n. 2
myths as part of, 5, 151
prestige, 75, 145-146, 218-219, 278
resistance to, 163-164, 171-172, 175,
214, 264-280
ritual food sharing, 28, 75, 157-158,
164, 174, 184-188, 218-221, 254-
255, 278-280
symbolic meanings, 146

Wigan, 146
see also food sharing, Ifugao,
    international development
Barros, Maria Lorena, 130
Bello, Walden, 111
Biomedicine
    Cartesian dualism, 182
    as a cultural system, 181-184
    definitions, 29 n. 2, 181
    family planning program (also
        contraception), 280-288
    history of, 181-182
    in Ifugao, 2-3, 7, 28, 96, 98, 181-223,
        211, 276: and class, 199; costs,
        48-51, 53-54, 124-125, 134, 176,
        190-191, 199, 212, 220, 279, 291-
        293; Day Care Centers, 62, 208,
        242; history of, 107, 147, 214-215;
        interpretations of nutrition
        programs, 200-201, 215-217, 231,
        254-256; problems of, 181-183,
        254-256
    Philippine Department of Health
        (DOH), 1-2, 47-48, 53-54, 57, 59 n.
        13, 121, 132-134, 147, 283-288:
        Barangay Health Workers (BHWs),
        51, 60 n. 15, 175, 221, 258, 286,
        301; *Barangay* Nutrition Scholars
        (BNSs), 51, 60 n. 15, 156, 168, 200,
        203-204, 215-216, 221, 239, 255,
        286, 301; nutrition services and
        programs, 48-52, 58, 112, 183, 202-
        204, 211-217, 232-256, 291-293,
        298-301; RHUs, 24-25, 50-51, 116-
        117, 170, 194, 237
    power of, 21, 57-58, 182-183, 298
    private health services, 2, 7, 147, 164,
        166-171
    problems with provision of, 7, 47-54,
        60 n. 14, 124-125, 134-135, 147,
        176, 179 n. 3, 189-191, 212, 221,
        223, 237-238, 257, 272, 278-279,
        295
    and religion, 121, 145-146, 164-171,
        173, 214, 263-264, 288
    see also body, Christianity, food,
        vitamin, and mineral supplement

programs, health care, hunger,
    individualism, international
    development, LIC, malnutrition,
    motherhood, UNICEF, volunteer
    health workers
Body
    biomedical approaches to, 2, 21, 298
    and class, 72, 184-188
    and contraception, 287, 289
    Ifugao conceptions of, 177, 181, 184,
        215-216, 282: and eating, 181, 184-
        188, 205, 215-216, 278; and food,
        71-74, 89, 181, 184-188
    and malnutrition, 187, 298
    political conversion, site of, 107, 111,
        124-125, 142; AFP, 125-128, 132-
        133; NPA, 124-125, 128-134
    religious conversion, site of, 28, 146,
        164-165, 167-170, 275-280
    theory, 2
    see also Christianity
Boserup, Esther, 22
Bottle feeding, 217-218, 291-292
    and breast feeding, 48-49, 51-52, 97,
        189, 205, 215, 218, 233, 238
    debate, 11, 48-49, 52
Bourque, Susan C., 23
Brown, Susan E., 13

Cadelina, Rowe V., 221
Capitalist expansion, 16-21, 35-39, 147,
    159-163, 252
    see also international development
CECAP, 9, 77, 118, 167, 194, 231, 235-
    236, 241, 251, 257-260, 261 n. 5
    see also European Community,
        international development
Christianity
    and American colonialism, 36, 107,
        121, 147, 159-162, 164, 252-253,
        274-275
    class, 159, 162-164, 172, 263, 276-
        280, 290 n. 1, 299
    contraception, 266, 280-288
    conversion, 158, 160-165, 274-280,
        290 n. 2
    gender, 76, 163, 264

in Ifugao, 4, 27-28, 140, 145, 158-178,
180 n. 15, 193-197, 300:
Catholicism, 88, 145, 147, 158-170,
180 n. 21, 283-288: liberation
theology, 264, 288; and body, 177,
186; and food production, 176-177,
276; gender, 68, 79, 85, 88, 92,
252-253, 264, 280-288, 300;
healing, 3-4, 26-28, 145, 147, 164-
174, 178, 184: healing and social
relations, 173-174, 178; historical
development of, 163-164; illness
causation as multi-causal, 27, 172-
174, 178; illness causation, theories
of, 26-27, 171-174, 266-267;
multiple healing practices, 27, 165,
171, 174-176, 191; missionaries, 5,
35, 107, 111, 121, 124-125, 147,
159-165, 170-171, 174, 180 n. 15,
180 n. 20, 180 n. 21, 252, 274-276,
287; networks of assistance, 276,
279; Protestantism, 88, 145-147,
164-166, 180 n. 21, 286:
Evangelical clinic/hospital,
170-171, 180 n. 20; Methodist
church, 172-174, 276, 280-282,
287; Protestant fundamentalism,
172, 263-268, 271-272, 274, 278-
279, 287-289, 300; resistance to,
270-271, 279, 281-288;
understandings of malnutrition, 28,
166-170, 174, 176, 178, 214, 221,
268, 289
and international development, 1,
17-18, 28, 135-136, 158, 162-163,
234, 250-251, 261 n. 10, 264-270,
272, 274, 276, 282, 287-288, 300
modernization, 158-159, 162, 179 n.
14, 252-253, 264, 267, 269-270,
274, 277, 289
and NGOs, 259, 263, 280, 286, 288
in Philippines: contemporary, 280-289;
historical, 159, 161-163, 252-253
power relations, masking, 264,
267-268, 278-279, 288-289, 300
and prestige, 159, 162, 164, 274-275
Spanish colonial Catholicism, 35, 147,

159-164, 252-253, 274-275
see also biomedicine, body, food
vitamin, and mineral supplement
programs, hegemony,
individualism, LIC
Class, socioeconomic
and gender, 11-15, 60 n. 16, 69-75, 96
in Ifugao, 1, 69-75, 79, 81-82, 100 n. 5,
100 n. 12, 162-163, 184, 223, 225
n. 21, 274, 277-280
and international development, 23,
199, 236, 259, 268, 293-303
in Philippines, 33-34, 39-40, 56, 104,
130, 295, 298-299
use of, author's, 8
see also baki, biomedicine,
Christianity, malnutrition
Colonialism
in Ifugao: American, 5-7, 107-111,
136, 147, 199, 252-253; resistance
to, 105-107; Spanish, 5-7, 106-107,
147, 252-253
in Philippines, 3, 27, 33-37, 143 n. 3
see also Christianity
Comaroff, Jean and John, 29 n. 4, 138
Communism
and AFP, 51, 103, 125-127, 135-141,
299, 302
Communist Party of the Philippines
(CPP), 7, 37, 40, 55-57, 60 n. 18,
103, 111, 114, 128-134, 144 n. 17,
299
and international development, 17-20,
162
in Philippines historically, 19, 37-40,
136
see also LIC and New People's Army
(NPA)
Contraception, 14-15, 91-92, 221
and nutrition, 287, 289
see also biomedicine, body,
Christianity, malnutrition
Cordillera Peoples Alliance (CPA), 3, 59
n. 6, 76, 122-123, 132, 275
see also autonomy
Corruption, 56, 296
see also Ifugao

Critical-interpretive theory in medical
anthropology, 10

Debt, national, 21, 33, 45-47, 53, 56, 58,
294-295
DeRaedt, C.I.C.M., Jules, 146

EDSA "revolution" (People's Power),
45-46, 167, 284
Elites, 33-37, 39-44, 55, 59 n. 5, 136,
162-163
Errington, Shelly, 61, 70, 78, 91, 96
Escobar, Arturo, 2, 16-18, 22
Ethnocide, 123
Europe
European Community, 118, 121, 167,
194, 231, 236, 241, 251, 257-260
influence in Philippines, 33, 37, 167-
168, 294, 299
see also CECAP

Fieldwork, author's, 24-27, 31-32 n. 50,
137 n. 24, 137 n. 25, 195-196, 225 n.
19
Flavier, Juan, Secretary of Health,
132-133, 283
Food sharing
networks of assistance, through, 28,
109, 177, 218-221, 254-255, 290 n.
3
reduced, 28, 164-165, 219, 221, 263-
264, 267-268, 275-280, 289, 300
see also baki, Ifugao
Food, vitamin, and mineral supplement
programs
Catholic Relief Services (CRS),
166-170, 180 n. 21, 180 n. 22
concept of, 254
DOH, 211-214, 221, 232, 298-299, 301
parents' perceptions of, 168-170, 216-
218, 221, 254-256
UNICEF, 221, 254-256, 261 n. 7, 261
n. 8, 298-299
Foucault, Michel, 3, 16, 21-22, 61, 124,
139, 181-182
Frankenberg, Ronald, 10

Gender
inequality, 1, 11-16, 77-99, 104, 129,
150, 163, 222-223, 236-237, 300
see also baki, Christianity, class,
hunger, Ifugao, international
development, land ownership,
malnutrition, NGOs, pay rates,
UNICEF, women in development,
women's position or "status"
Goiter, 8, 130, 189, 192, 212-214, 224 n.
14, 233, 237, 301
Growth standards, 51, 183, 224 n. 11, 224
n. 12
Guthrie, George, 206
Guthrie, Helen, 206

Health care, ideologies of
biomedical, 112, 121, 255, 298-299,
301
NGO, 134-142, 256-260, 301
Philippine Government, 111, 125-126,
135-136, 138, 141, 298-299, 300
revolutionary, NDF/NPA, 129-132,
302
see also baki, Christianity,
international development, LIC
Hegemony, 3, 16, 21, 28, 29 n. 4, 134,
138, 159, 162
Hollnsteiner, Mary Racelis (*also* Mary
Racelis), 241, 294, 296-297
Huks, 39-40, 55, 111, 136
Human rights violations, Philippine state
(AFP/CAFGU), 41, 55-56, 122-124,
127-128, 135-136, 138-139, 143 n. 12,
143 n. 15, 223, 275, 303
see also LIC, political violence
Hunger
access to food, 27, 33-34, 47, 71, 98,
105-110, 112-115, 160, 176-177,
184-188, 193-195, 198-203, 205,
210-221, 231, 275-280, 295, 299,
301
anthropological studies of, 9-11
emic perceptions of, 11, 15, 199, 254-
256, 292: *feter*, 157; *munhinaang*,
157; *na-akang-an*, 157
and gender, studies of, 11-16

and war, 103-105, 108-110, 123, 127-
128, 141-142, 299
see also baki, biomedicine,
colonialism, Ifugao, malnutrition,
pre-Hispanic period

Ifugao
age: children, 7-8, 10-12, 22-23, 25,
28, 53-54, 61-70, 72-74, 77, 79-81,
87-93, 95-99, 108-110, 112, 115-
118, 122, 146, 148, 152-157, 162,
167-175, 177, 179 n. 7, 179 n. 21,
183, 186-223, 241-256, 270,
292-293, 299-302; elderly, 66, 81,
106-110, 155, 159, 164, 74-75, 117,
202, 211, 215, 226 n. 26, 291-293;
ranking, 75
child care, 61-67, 69, 74, 80, 87-89,
92-93, 95-96, 183, 198, 221
corruption, 88, 221-222, 267
domestic laborers ("helpers"), 62, 64-
65, 74, 100 n. 5, 198, 292
economy, 3-5, 7, 79, 86, 107, 188, 252,
263-264, 277, 289
environmental degradation, 123, 177,
188, 274
ethnicity, 28, 70, 75-77, 272-275, 300-
301
famine, 105, 108, 157
gender: feminism, 79, 222; ideologies,
61-99, 198, 202-204, 208-209, 212,
237-240, 250-254, 260, 264, 280-
282, 287, 289, 300-302; men, 3-7,
27-28, 61-99, 100 n. 4, 104-110,
113, 116, 118, 121, 138-140, 146,
152, 155-156, 159, 164, 171-174,
176, 185, 188, 192, 195-199, 202-
204, 206-207, 209, 211-212, 216-
217, 221-222, 225 n. 22, 237-242,
246-254, 264-292, 300; men's
resistance, 254; pregnant women,
54, 94-95, 97-98, 152-154, 168,
192, 211-212, 218, 236-237, 254;
roles, 27-28, 69, 79-96, 236, 273;
single women, 54, 67-69, 74, 88,
94-95, 188, 195, 202, 209-211, 225
n. 20, 291-293; women, 3-12,

14-15, 21-23, 25-28, 49, 53-54, 58-
59, 60 n. 16, 61-99, 99 n. 1, 100 n.
5, 100 n. 9, 101 n. 28, 104-105,
110-122, 131, 134-141, 146, 149-
156, 159, 163, 166-169, 172-173,
175, 177-178, 179 n. 7, 188-223,
225 n. 22, 226 n. 26, 226 n. 29, 226
n. 30, 226 n. 31, 226 n. 32, 232-
266, 268-269, 271-272, 274-276,
280-289, 291-293, 295, 298-303;
women's resistance, 92-93, 204,
216, 253-254, 282
indebtedness, 70, 72, 82-83, 100 n . 12,
106, 191, 201, 219-221, 276-279,
291, 301
inheritance, 70-72, 74, 184, 201
kinship, 3, 70-72, 78, 143 n. 7, 157-
158, 219-221, 244, 278-279,
292-293
labor, 4, 62-74, 79-91, 99 n. 1, 99-100
n. 2, 100 n. 4, 100 n. 5, 100 n. 9,
101 n. 26, 184-186, 237, 295:
migrant, 5, 55, 62-64, 69, 74, 76,
89-91, 101 n. 28, 187-188, 204,
221, 253, 272, 291-292; wage,
61-64, 68-69, 71-75, 85-88, 93,
185, 187-188, 195-199, 201, 207,
221, 253, 291-293, 295, 300
leadership, 6-7, 61, 72-73, 75, 82, 87-
96, 124, 127, 131, 133, 139-140,
155, 159-160, 162-164, 167, 178,
237, 249, 252, 264-265, 271, 274-
275, 279, 286-288, 300
local religion, 3, 5, 123, 145-158, 162,
167, 197: Ifugao origins myth, 146
networks of assistance, 68, 75, 106,
109, 177, 219-221, 301
power and prestige, 75-77, 158-159,
162, 164, 184, 235-237, 253-254
slavery, 106, 108, 143 n. 8
social change, 3, 5, 85, 86, 104, 133-
135, 171, 188, 199-200, 220-223,
252, 263-264, 268-270, 272-280,
288-289, 300-303
society, 3-7, 143 n. 6
see also baki, biomedicine, body,
Christianity, class, colonialism,

food sharing, health care, hunger,
income distribution, international
development, land ownership, LIC,
malnutrition, modernization,
mortality, motherhood, overseas
workers, pay rates, political
violence, pre-Hispanic period,
UNICEF, United States, women in
development, World War II
IMF, 21, 40-41, 286
  apex loans, 59 n. 11
  structural adjustment, 27, 33, 44-47,
    50-57, 59 n. 11, 201, 233, 293-299
Income distribution
  in Ifugao, 7, 71-75: poverty level, 29 n.
    6, 100 n. 16, 101 n. 17
  in Philippines, 8, 34, 40-41, 57, 59 n.
    2, 289, 294
  see also class
Independence, Philippine, 38
Individualism, ideologies of
  biomedical, 2, 254-256
  Christian, 163, 169, 219, 263-264, 276-
    280
  international development programs,
    21-22, 221, 254-255, 298-300
International development
  and *baki*, 264-270, 273-274
  bilateral aid, 19, 31 n. 42, 58
  and capitalist expansion, 16-21, 36-39,
    123
  critiques of, 16, 19-24, 28, 288, 301-
    303
  development, author's use of, 21,
    28-29 n. 1
  failures of, 134, 191, 217, 223, 231-
    233, 249-254, 259-260, 293-303
  gender, 22-24, 53-55, 222, 232-254,
    256-260, 263-264, 280, 282-289,
    300-302: constructions of women,
    253, 301
  history of, 16-24, 235, 298
  in Ifugao, 1-4, 7-9, 12, 14-16, 21-23,
    25, 27-28, 71, 76, 79, 99, 179 n. 14,
    180 n. 16, 194, 199, 201, 206-208,
    213, 221-223, 232-260, 260 n. 1,
    261 n. 3, 261 n. 5, 261 n. 6, 261 n.

7, 261 n. 8, 261 n. 9, 261 n. 10,
    298-303
  perceptions of, 200, 232-233, 244-248,
    251-252, 259-260, 261 n. 9
  and martial law, 40-41
  multilateral aid, 19, 31 n. 42, 40, 58
  neglecting social and cultural relations,
    2-3, 27, 33-34, 99, 121-123, 221,
    231-248, 252-256, 259-260, 267,
    297-303
  and NGOs, 136, 141, 263
  paradigm, western cultural, 2-3, 16-24,
    28, 231-232, 235, 241, 257-258,
    263-264, 269-270, 301-302
  pay rates, 251-254, 260, 300: CECAP,
    240-241, 251; UNICEF, 241-243,
    254
  in Philippines, 1-3, 19, 27, 33-34, 38-
    58, 59 n. 7, 59 n. 10, 60 n. 14, 159,
    172, 293-303, 304 n. 5
  power of, 3, 15-24, 243, 263-264, 299,
    302
  as a reform strategy, 58, 121-124, 132,
    142, 143 n. 14, 259-260, 297-299,
    302
  resistance to, 3, 123, 134, 242-248,
    253-256, 302
  and social evolutionism, 2-3, 17-18,
    272-273
  volunteer labor, 63, 244-248, 252-254,
    300
  see also baki, biomedicine, CECAP,
    Christianity, class, communism,
    debt, European Community, health
    care, hegemony, IMF,
    individualism, LIC, malnutrition,
    motherhood, UNICEF, United
    States, women in development,
    World Bank, World War II
Israel-Sobritchea, Carolyn, 82

Japan
  early traders in Philippines, 5
  postwar period, 33, 40, 294, 299
  World War II, 38-39, 108-111
Johnsen, John H., 2, 10

Kerkvliet, Benedict J. Tria, 136

Land ownership
    in Ifugao, 70-74, 76-77, 86, 93, 98, 101
        n. 19, 123, 143 n. 5, 184, 196-197,
        201-202, 222, 275, 296, 301
    in Philippines, 59 n. 8, 295-296, 302:
        history of, 33-39
    significance to cultural identity, 123
    see also agrarian reform, malnutrition
Lock, Margaret, 2, 10
Low intensity conflict (LIC)
    AFP (Armed Forces of the
        Philippines), 27, 41, 51, 55-56, 75,
        104-105, 111-128, 131-142
    CAFGU (Citizen Armed Force
        Geographical Unit), 104-105, 116-
        117, 123, 140, 143 n. 2
    control over food, 104-113, 123, 127-
        128, 141-142
    definition of, 111
    development and health care as
        strategy of, 27, 111, 121-134, 142,
        297-299, 302
    feeding soldiers, 113-115, 142
    food relief, 113
    and health, 104, 108, 115, 117-118,
        121-125, 127, 134, 147, 302
    and health care volunteers, 104-105,
        112, 117, 127-128, 134-141, 259-
        260, 299
    and health NGOs, 117, 121, 123, 127-
        128, 134-141, 144 n. 16, 259-260,
        299
    in Ifugao, 7, 27, 103-143, 147
    and international development, 118,
        121-123, 136, 144, 234, 297-298,
        302
    Live-in-Seminars, 125-126
    MAKIBAKA, 130-131, 286
    and missionary health, 107, 111, 121,
        124, 147
    National Democratic Front (NDF), 40,
        56-57, 59 n. 6, 59 n. 12, 128-131,
        133-134, 142, 286, 288
    New People's Army (NPA), 7, 27, 40,
        55-58, 59 n. 6, 59 n. 12, 60 n. 19,

        75, 103-104, 111-118, 122, 124-
        134, 136, 140-142, 167, 222, 299,
        302
    peace talks, 112, 302
    in Philippines, 7, 55-58, 302
    Special Operations Teams (SOT),
        125-127
    "total war" policy, 27, 51, 59 n. 12,
        123, 125, 144 n. 17, 260
    U.S. government, 111, 121, 128, 130,
        136
    see also baki, body, colonialism,
        communism, human rights
        violations, hunger, political
        violence

Malnutrition
    adult, 211-214
    biomedical: approaches to alleviating,
        28, 181-183, 231-235, 238-240,
        252-256, 298, 300-301;
        constructions of, 2, 28, 181-182,
        188-189, 214-215, 223, 224 n. 13,
        231, 299
    blaming women for, 14, 16, 202-204,
        206, 208, 223, 232, 238-240, 250,
        298, 300
    and child care, 198, 202-204, 208,
        221-222, 238-240, 241-243, 252-
        254, 260-261 n. 2, 291-293, 300-
        301: child babysitters, 207, 217,
        221, 301
    chronic (protein) protein energy, 8,
        188-190, 224 n. 10
    and class, 181, 189-191, 193-197, 201,
        211, 216-223, 289, 298, 300-303:
        and gender, 197-200, 202-210, 212-
        214, 300-303
    deconstructing the concept of, 181-184
    and diarrhea, 143 n. 11, 189-190, 199-
        200, 215
    effects of, mind/body, 189-191
    and ethnicity, 222-223
    family size, 211
    and gender, 77, 99, 182, 198, 200, 202-
        204, 206, 208, 236, 240, 249, 287,
        293, 300

in Ifugao, 7-9, 25-28, 93, 188-223, 225
n. 15, 225 n. 16, 225 n. 17, 225 n.
18, 225 n. 19, 225 n. 24, 225 n. 25,
231-260, 260 n. 1, 260-261 n. 2,
291-293, 299-301
and illness, 156-157, 176, 189-191,
211, 215-217, 220
and international development,
298-300: constructions of, 231-235,
238, 252, 298; resulting in
widespread, 33, 142, 199, 221, 299,
302
intrahousehold eating practices,
208-209
iodine deficiency, *see* goiter
iron deficiency, *see* anemia
knowledge of nutrition concepts, 188,
199-201, 204-207, 215-218, 298,
301
and land ownership, 201-202
men's role in, 14-15, 31 n. 36, 93,
202-208, 217, 237-240, 242, 260-
261 n. 1, 291-293
perceptions of, Ifugao people's,
186-188, 200-201, 254-256
in Philippines, 7-9, 27, 34-59, 104,
130, 187, 209, 295, 297-299, 302-
303, 303-304 n. 1
responses to, Ifugao people's, 28,
104-105, 134-142, 181, 218-223,
291-293, 301-303
and sanitation, 199-200, 231, 238, 249,
266-267, 298
sugar and junk foods, 193, 198-199,
204-207, 211, 292, 301-302
Vitamins, 191, 211, 215-218, 301:
Vitamin A deficiency, 8, 130, 191;
Vitamin B deficiency, 8; Vitamin C
deficiency, 8, 226 n. 27
women's, 212-214
women's experience and
understandings of, 28, 86-87, 96-
99, 197-223, 226 n. 29, 254-256,
300-303
women's role n, 14, 24, 93, 99, 198,
202-208, 231-260, 300: single

women, 209-211, 291-293
see also baki, body, Christianity,
colonialism, contraception, food
sharing, hunger, LIC,
modernization, UNICEF, women in
development
Marcos, President Ferdinand, 31 n. 44, 40-
49, 55-56, 59 n. 5, 59 n. 6, 79, 96, 111,
117, 124, 132-133, 167, 215, 288
Masangkay, Zenaida, 206
Modernization
in Ifugao, 3-7, 20, 79, 179 n. 14, 199,
206-207, 211-212, 272-273, 300-
302
theory, and W. W. Rostow, 18-19
see also Christianity
Montiel, Cristina, 241
Morbidity, leading causes in Ifugao,
189-190
Morsy, Soheir A., 10
Mortality
in Ifugao: infant, 8-9; leading causes,
8-9, 189; maternal, 236-237, 285
in Philippines, 8, 29 n. 7: infant, 9
Motherhood, conceptions of
biomedical and international
development programs, 11, 13-14,
22, 168, 202-204, 206, 208, 223,
231-233, 236, 240, 242, 248-250,
252, 260, 298-300
Ifugao, 22, 61, 63-69, 79-82, 87, 90,
92-93, 95-99, 223, 237, 243

Neocolonialism, 1, 3, 18, 21, 27, 33, 38,
56, 162
NGOs (non-government organizations),
health, 9, 25, 28, 52, 58, 194, 256-260,
280, 286, 289, 303
gender, 79, 222, 251-252
Volunteer Health Workers, 25, 60 n.
15, 221-222, 251-252, 256-260,
286-287, 301, 303
see also Christianity, health care,
international development, LIC

Overseas workers, 54-55, 63-64, 73, 253

Pay rates (also wage), 295, 297
    gendered, 12-13, 31 n. 46, 54-55, 62,
        83-91, 96, 101 n. 24, 201, 208, 222,
        237, 242-243, 251-254, 280, 295,
        300
    health care, 53-54, 246-248, 254, 300
    Philippines, 45, 46-47, 51, 53
    regional, 83, 242, 257, 295
    see also international development
Peasant
    resistance, 37-41, 43, 55-58, 123,
        128-133, 140-141, 169, 299, 302-
        303
    use of, author's, 30 n. 30
    see also autonomy, Christianity,
        colonialism, communism, EDSA
        "revolution," Ifugao, international
        development, LIC
Pertierra, Raul, 267-268, 277-278
Political economy
    of hunger in Philippines, 33-58
    in medical anthropology, 10
Political violence, in Ifugao, 1, 5-7, 27, 75,
    79, 302
    see also colonialism, human rights
        violations, LIC
Power, author's use of, 29 n. 3
    see also biomedicine, Christianity,
        colonialism, Ifugao, international
        development, LIC
Pre-Hispanic period
    Ifugao, 5, 105
    Philippines, 34-35

Ramos, President Fidel, 46-47, 51, 56, 59
    n. 12, 111-112, 114, 123, 132-133, 144
    n. 17, 222, 234, 283, 296-297, 302
Religion
    struggles, 263-289, 299-300
    syncretism, 158, 174-175, 178, 279,
        289
    see also baki, body, Christianity,
        contraception, food, vitamin, and
        mineral supplement programs,
        individualism, LIC
Robertson, A. F., 18-19
Rosenberg, Ellen, 13

Scheper-Hughes, Nancy, 2, 15, 190, 255
Schoepf, Brooke Grundfest, 11-13, 77
Schoepf, Claude, 13
Schrijvers, Joke, 12-13
Senauer, Benjamin, 12, 77
Sex-differential nutrition practices
    in Ifugao, 209
    studies of, 13
Sin, Archbishop Jaime Cardinal, 284
Singer, Merrill, 2, 10
Social Welfare, Department of, 113, 200
St. Hilaire, Colette, 22
Stavrianos, L., 17

Tan, Michael Lim, 51, 183
Taussig, Michael, 231

UNICEF
    "High Risk Families," 206, 238-239,
        260 n. 1
    malnutrition, 8-9, 231-252
    perceptions of, Ifugao people's, 201,
        231, 233-234, 240, 242-243, 246-
        248, 252-256, 258-260
    programs: in Philippines, 121, 294,
        299; in Ifugao, 121, 124, 162, 201,
        206, 208, 213, 231-260, 261 n. 1,
        261 n. 3, 261 n. 6, 261 n. 7, 272-
        273, 293: child minding centers
        (CMCs), 233, 242-243, 254, 258,
        261 n. 3, 300
    women's organizations, 248-252
    women's "status," 77, 235-237, 240,
        248-249
    see also food vitamin, and mineral
        supplement programs, international
        development, LIC, malnutrition,
        women in development
United States
    business, 33, 36-39
    criticisms of, 128, 130
    influence in Ifugao, 73, 110, 167-170
    influence in Philippines, 31 n. 44, 33,
        41, 55, 58, 59 n. 4, 121, 128, 162,
        167
    USAID, 20, 22, 48, 121, 283, 294, 299

see also Christianity, colonialism, LIC, World War II

Violence, author's use of, 143 n. 1
   see also colonialism, LIC, political violence

Warren, Kay B., 23
Weighing surveys, child, 21, 51, 53-54, 98, 183, 195, 204-205, 215-217, 224 n. 11, 224 n. 12, 224 n. 13, 225 n. 15, 225 n. 16, 225 n. 17, 225 n. 18, 225 n. 24, 225 n. 25, 226 n. 26, 232, 237, 255, 298
Women in development (WID) programs
   critiques of, 13-14, 22-24, 260, 293, 298-303
   history of, 22-23, 236, 298-299
   in Ifugao, 9, 28, 61, 235-260, 183-185
   as a reform strategy, 298
   reinforcing gender inequality, 1, 28, 99, 204, 235-243, 246, 248, 252-253, 260, 300-302
   research on, 22-24, 31 n. 46, 236
   social management of women, 22, 299, 301
   women and children's nutrition, 13-15, 77, 232, 235-243, 249, 252, 260, 293
   women's "status" or position, attempts to improve, 1, 9, 14-15, 27-28, 77, 99, 235-237, 239, 240-242, 248-252, 260, 287, 293, 298, 300-302
   see also international development, malnutrition, UNICEF
Women and technology, approaches to research on, 23
Women's movement, Philippines, 59 n. 6, 75-77, 79, 173-174
Women's position or "status"
   Filipino, 77-79, 99, 264
   Ifugao, 27, 72-99, 139-140, 151, 208, 223, 235-237, 251, 264, 300-301
   Southeast Asian, 78
   see also gender inequality, UNICEF, women in development
Worker resistance, 37
World Bank, 19, 21, 31 n. 43, 33, 40-41, 43-47, 51, 53, 55, 57-58, 59 n. 7, 59 n. 10, 233, 286, 293-295, 299
World Health Organization (WHO) 51, 121, 294
World War II
   and Ifugao, 7, 73, 105, 108-111, 164
   and international development, 17-20
   and Philippines, 38-39, 136